The Actor-Managers

The
Actor-Managers

Frances Donaldson

Henry Regnery Company . Chicago

Library of Congress Catalog Card No: 73–124399

First published in England by
Weidenfeld and Nicolson

First published in the United States of America by
Henry Regnery Company,
114 West Illinois Street,
Chicago, Illinois 60610

Printed in Great Britain by
Willmer Brothers Limited, Birkenhead

Contents

Illustrations

Except where otherwise stated, all photographs were provided by the Raymond Mander and Joe Mitchenson Theatre Collection.

Acknowledgements

I would like to acknowledge the sources listed below for granting me permission to reproduce quotations from the books mentioned after their names.

Ernest Benn Ltd (*A Player Under Three Reigns*, Sir Johnston Forbes-Robertson); The Bodley Head (*Ellen Terry and Bernard Shaw: A Correspondence*, ed. Christopher St John); Curtis Brown Ltd (*Gerald, A Portrait*, Daphne du Maurier and *Henry Beerbohm Tree, Some Memories of Him and of His Art*, ed. Max Beerbohm); Granada Publishing (*Around Theatres*, Max Beerbohm); Laurence Irving (*Henry Irving: The Actor and His World*); Macmillan & Co (*The Bancrofts On and Off the Stage, By Themselves*); John Murray Ltd (*The Bancrofts*, Squire and Marie Bancroft); Gilbert Samuel & Co (*Ellen Terry's Memoirs* and *Ellen Terry*, Roger Manvell); Society of Authors (*Ellen Terry and Bernard Shaw, A Correspondence*, ed. Christopher St John and *Our Theatres in the Nineties*, Bernard Shaw); A. P. Watt & Son (*Beerbohm Tree: His Life and Laughter*, Hesketh Pearson).

Throughout I have made great use of *Our Theatres in the Nineties* by George Bernard Shaw, and *Around Theatres*, by Max Beerbohm. There is a short bibliography of the other books from which I have quoted or which I have found particularly valuable at the end of the book.

The BBC kindly granted me permission to quote a passage from the transcript of the television programme *Omnibus*, and the Raymond Mander and Joe Mitchenson Theatre Collection gave me valuable advice and help with the illustrations.

Frances Donaldson

Introduction

The great years of the actor-managers were from 1865 to 1914, although the climate remained sufficiently favourable to them into the 1920s. Actors have a natural desire to form their own companies and impose their own style on productions, and the actor as manager was not unknown before this time and will probably always occasionally appear. Earlier, however, the area of opportunity was exceedingly small, and latterly the management of a theatre has become a financial undertaking of such magnitude that it is not easily performed as an occupation secondary to that of a particularly demanding art. But, in any case, the actor in management today is merely a man who combines, usually for a comparatively short period, two normally separate functions. In the late nineteenth and early twentieth centuries he was a power in the land and a social phenomenon of unusual interest and charm.

The pride and the place of the actor-manager were comparable then to those of men born to a great hereditary position; the companies of actors were like small courts to the heads of the profession and the public their willing slaves. When Irving died the streets were lined with people who silently watched his last journey to Westminister Abbey. Nowadays bravura is sadly out of fashion, but men were not believed equal then, stars shone without impropriety on their fellows, and acting was expected of the actor, both on and off the stage.

Because the position of the actor-manager was so exalted, it was heavily guarded. As a result, young actors with unusual gifts had often little choice between chancing their own arm in management – with all the attendant risks but with all the

additions to personality that success in the role would bring –
or restricting their performances to a few lines spoken in the
shade of some existing luminary. The play was not the thing.

That is the key to an understanding of the period. By the
middle of the nineteenth century no literary figure of distinction was writing for the theatre. Such new plays as were put on
were mostly melodrama, adaptations from the French, or
farce, knocked together by literary hacks. Two things
followed. Plays were seldom put on for a 'run'; instead the
extensive bills were frequently changed, and, secondly, play-
goers went to the theatre, not so much to see a new play, as
to see a new actor in an old play. Actors were expected to
make their mark in the roles of their predecessors, and play-
goers went regularly to the theatre to see them perform not
merely such roles as Hamlet or Sir Peter Teazle but others such
as Claude Melnotte in *The Lady of Lyons, Robert Macaire,* or
Kean's old role of Sir Giles Overreach in *A New Way to Pay
Old Debts.*

Many of these plays seem today meretricious and silly, and
it is difficult to understand how audiences could sit through
them again and again unless one realises that the audiences of
the mid-nineteenth century were no more disturbed by the conventions of the old-fashioned drama than are the audiences of
today by the conventions of opera and ballet. The comparison
is valid in more ways than one. The opera-goer of today does
not refuse to go to *La Traviata* because he has seen it before or
to *Figaro* because the characters recognise each other or fail to
recognise each other when dressed to resemble some other
character to suit the convenience of the plot. On the contrary
he is more willing to hear a new singer in an old role than to
hear a new work; and often he takes pleasure in a new production just to see how these absurd old situations have been
treated. This comparison falls to the ground when we stop to
remember that the really vital element in opera is the genius of
the composer, but it nevertheless remains true that we can
better understand the Victorian theatre if we bear it in mind.

In a situation of this sort the actor is everything, and he is
conscious that it is he who draws the crowds into the theatre
and is concerned to find roles that will allow him to show him-

self off at his best. He chooses a play because it is a vehicle for the art of acting not because it is art itself.

It has sometimes been said that the lives of actors are not of interest after they are dead because their art dies with them. If this were true it would be a rather curious exception to the general rule that the lives of human beings, particularly exceptional human beings or those that lived in an earlier age, are always of interest to their fellows. But the question of quality arises. If we are to involve ourselves, even for a short while and purely for entertainment, with the life of some man long dead, we want to know that he was worth our attention. If he was an actor and his life is presented to us because he was an actor we want to be sure he was a good one. It is precisely here that, before the invention of the moving pictures, assurance was hard to find. Desmond MacCarthy wrote 'The triumphs of dead actors live for us only in pictures, in half-obliterated tradition, and in the pages of the few dramatic critics who happen to be still readable on account of their style.'

Of these three, 'half-obliterated tradition' plays the greatest part. One actor passes his method on to another actor and in this way the body of technique is built up. But 'half-obliterated tradition' is no more available to the historian or biographer than the art of the actor himself. For a lively impression we have to depend on 'pictures . . . and . . . the pages of the few dramatic critics who happen to be still readable on account of their style.'

Max Beerbohm complained that the biographies of actors are too often undertaken by 'some hack-journalist who knew the deceased slightly, or . . . some pious understrapper who knew him too well, in too special relationship to have the faintest notion of what roundly he was like', and although in recent years several excellent biographies of Victorian actors have appeared, to recapture the quality of their acting we still depend on contemporary accounts. Fortunately in the heyday of the actor-managers several writers of great distinction were interesting themselves in the theatre.

Since the earlier history of the theatre had great influence on that of the nineteenth century some knowledge of it is necessary to an understanding of the latter. The Puritans attempted to suppress the drama altogether and when, at the Restoration, Charles II renewed the right to put on plays he did so by granting a licence to two of his courtiers to form companies of actors and present plays. These licences were handed on from one man to another and in the course of time were sold, but they came to be vested in the two theatres at Covent Garden and Drury Lane, and only in these two great patent houses could drama be legally performed.

This was a situation which made it practically certain that the bad would drive out the good. The drama could thrive only when one or both the houses were well and successfully managed, while the standards of each could be dragged by the standards of the other towards the popular taste. Success at one house often meant a policy of circuses at the other, and this in its turn forced circuses on the first. The policy of the patent houses was dictated by the people of London.

Inevitably the licensing laws were not kept, and it was largely in the breaking of them that, in the eighteenth and early nineteenth centuries, traditions developed to which the actor-managers succeeded. New methods to evade the law were continually invented. Plays were performed between two halves of a concert and, because musical plays could be performed without licence, a play could be put on at any theatre providing there were five songs to each act. Shakespeare was often performed with musical interpolations and sometimes the law was acknowledged by no more than a chord struck at regular intervals. At the same time the patents, originally given to revive the drama, became no more than a commercial monopoly of the right to put it on, and although the managers of the two patent houses bitterly opposed any attempt to alter the law they could no more afford to disregard the public demand for music and spectacle than could the managers of the little theatres which by now were springing up all over London.

In the provinces the law was not so severely enforced and patent houses were established at many of the main towns during the eighteenth century. A system developed called the 'Circuit' system whereby companies of actors adopted certain towns in their district, eventually building small theatres in them. At these theatres the resident company, called the 'stock' company, was ready to play the parts in a whole repertory of plays, while the leading parts were played by visitors, in summer by great stars from London. In the stock companies each actor undertook a particular type of role. In addition to a Leading Man, a Juvenile Lead and a Leading Lady, every company included such types as a Low Comedian, a Heavy Father, a Chamber Maid, later to be known as a Soubrette, Walking Ladies and Gentlemen, later to be known as Supernumeraries or Supers, all terms that have passed into the English language.

These stock companies were the only schools for young actors and here they learned, not how to interpret the ideas of the playwright in terms of human character, but how to present the 'stock' figure. Bernard Shaw said that the playgoers in their towns grew so desperately tired of the actors in a stock company, and so unable to imagine them to be anything but their too-familiar selves that 'they performed in an atmosphere of hatred and derision which few of their members had talent or charm enough to conciliate'.

Both in London and in the country actors were excessively badly paid and often starving. They received part of their salary through the 'benefit' system, by which the profits of the theatre were given on a particular night to one, sometimes two, of the actors. These actors were allowed to choose the play in which they would appear and were supported by their fellows. Obviously the 'benefit' of a leading and popular actor would be very much more profitable than that of a struggling small-part player, and it was a vicious system which caused much humiliation and hardship.

At last in 1843 an Act for Regulating the Theatres made an end of the patent system and for the first time, if certain conditions were observed, plays might legally be performed all over England. But by now the theatre had fallen very low and the twenty years that followed have been described as 'the winter solstice' of the British drama. In terms of a serious art, there were no playwrights, no school of acting, above all no audience. The middle and upper classes no longer went to the theatre except to hear Italian opera, and the managers of the theatres had learned that to entice people in they had continually to change the bill and must compete with acrobats, performing animals, hippodramas, panoramas, spectacle of every kind. The theatregoers of the time insisted on bills of inordinate length and there were curtain-raisers and epilogues, burlesques and burlettas, while even Shakespeare's plays were put on with at least two other entertainments in the bill. Conditions in the theatre were such that contemporary writers complained it was merely an ancillary to the brothels.

Thus was the scene set when the Bancrofts appeared upon it.

Sir Squire and Lady Bancroft
1841-1926 & 1839-1921

In the years immediately following the First World War a married couple of great distinction and extreme age were sometimes to be seen in the foyers of London theatres or the dining room of one of the leading hotels in Folkestone – he with a truly leonine shock of completely white hair, a white moustache and an eyeglass, she a small pouter pigeon surviving from the reign of Queen Victoria. To an onlooker it might have been apparent that this couple were treated with a deference exceeding that to which their age alone entitled them, but if so he would not have been able to account for this by associating them with some public role. This was not because there had never been a public role but because it had been performed so long ago that only the initiated would now know Sir Squire and Lady Bancroft, and remember that in their day they had been responsible for a small revolution in the English theatre.

We have learned a great deal of what is known about this couple from themselves, because in their old age they told their own story at such length and with so much detail that little was left for anyone else to say. There is plenty of corroboration for the claims they make, however, and, combined with a rather absurd pomposity, there is an essential modesty, a straightforward honesty in the manner of the telling.

Place aux dames. Lady Bancroft begins her part of the joint biography with these words and it is a fact that the first of our actor-managers was a woman. However, this is only one of several ways in which this management was untypical of the heroic age of the Victorian theatre. The Bancrofts are taken first because they were first in time and also because their innovations provided the groundwork for a whole edifice, but they do not completely illustrate either the characteristic actor-manager of the time or the description of him in the introductory chapter to this book.

Marie Wilton was born in 1839, not to one of the old theatre families but to parents who had, nevertheless, both been disastrously connected with the stage. Her father, a gentleman from Gloucestershire, had been intended for the church but in early life he was stage-struck, and in spite of the many obstacles put in his way, became in the end an actor and, in the words of his daughter, 'an exile from home, family, friends and general respectability'. On the stage he found neither fame nor fortune to compensate for the loss of these things, but he met and married a Miss Faulkner, the daughter of a scholar and a gentleman who had lost all his money by investing it in the York Theatre Circuit. Miss Faulkner eloped with Mr Wilton and they lived in poverty and anxiety for the rest of their lives.

Not so their daughter. Lady Bancroft tells in her autobiography of the time when as a baby she cried and moaned inconsolably all night. In the morning it was discovered that her body was completely covered with finger-and-thumb marks as though it had been pinched. That day, as her mother, unable to quiet her cries, despairingly rocked her in her arms, an old peasant woman entered their garden to sell her wares. When, in response to questions, the mother showed her baby's body with the pinch-marks on it, the old woman declared the child had been bewitched. She predicted that at sunset the marks would disappear and the child would grow to be the luckiest in the world. 'She'll tell of things before they come to pass and bring good to them she wishes to and woe to them as wrongs her.'

In her last years Lady Bancroft used still to tell this story, and it was clear that, followed by good fortune all her life, she much more than half believed in the pinch-marks and the interpretation put upon them by the gypsy, just as she believed in the powers of the black cats which had so often crossed her path on her way to the theatre.

But if she had more than her share of good luck Marie Wilton had to work for it from the earliest age. One of the favourite turns in the long bills demanded by the public in those days was that of the child actor, and Marie Wilton was set to earn her living on the stage before she could even speak properly. Among the recitations with which the little girl was taught to edify her public were the trial scene from *The Merchant of Venice*, the balcony scene from *Romeo and Juliet*, and the sleep-walking scene from *Macbeth*.

Her family depended on her earnings and, like the children who worked in the factories, she was dragged from her bed to go to the theatre and returned to it, weary in temper and limb, long after most children were sound asleep. When not actually performing she was endlessly coached by her parents. She tells us that her father and mother stood one in each wing during her performances, her father prompting her with the line she should speak, her mother assuming the expression she should wear upon her face. Although her father had no talent for acting, her mother had great gifts as a teacher. Marie profited from the teaching, but she possessed the talent her father lacked and it is clear that she was a born comedienne.

As she grew older she abandoned her recitations and took part in the performance of plays. Once she played Fleance to Macready's Macbeth, and once she played Prince Arthur in *King John* while Charles Kemble sat watching in a box. Both these great actors sent for her at the close of the performance and both gave her a piece of advice. Macready, upon asking her what part she hoped to play when she had grown to be a great actress, received the reply: 'Lady Macbeth.'

'Do not,' he said to her, 'play Lady Macbeth too soon; begin slowly or you may end quickly!'

And when Charles Kemble sent for her he advised her:

'Climb not the ladder too quickly, or you may come suddenly to the ground again.'

Sir John Gielgud has said he believes it takes fifteen years to make an actor. Marie Wilton had no difficulty in following the advice of these great practitioners because, born with a talent for acting and a capacity for hard work, she had been fifteen years on the stage at an age when most young actresses have hardly started their careers. When she was still a child she and her mother left her father in Bristol and travelled to London so that she might take up an engagement at the Lyceum. From this time onwards she had one engagement after another on the London stage.

She seems only twice in her life to have been seriously thwarted. The first time was when, still a child, she was cast again and again in the role of Cupid until she feared she was going to spend the whole of her professional life appearing through trapdoors from unexpected and impossible places. The second time was when as a young woman she seemed to be doomed to play boys in burlesque for the rest of her life.

The burlesque is a dramatic form with a distinguished history. The first and most famous burlesque was *The Rehearsal* (1671) written by the Duke of Buckingham in parody of the pseudo-heroic plays in rhyming verse of which Dryden was the master. Buckingham parodied playwrights, actors and critics and he personally coached the actor who played the part of Bayes, the author, to mimic Dryden's rather eccentric speech and gestures. Dryden accepted the hit in silence at the time but later he returned it in full in *Absalom and Achitophel*. *The Rehearsal* became a theatrical sensation for the second time when the young David Garrick discarded the traditional imitation of Dryden and parodied instead the style of each of the leading actors of the day. Burlesque became a recognised dramatic form of which other famous examples are Gay's *The Beggar's Opera, Tom Thumb* by Henry Fielding and Sheridan's *The Critic*, but by the nineteenth century the satiric impulse had been lost and it had degenerated into light musical entertainment. Usually it was still related to the plot of some popular play, but male and female impersonators had become part of the comic tradition and by the time Marie Wilton grew up, burlesque was little more than a vehicle for the execrable puns so much relished by Victorian audiences. Many of the most popular burlesques of the day were by H. J. Byron, and a good idea of the spirit of the thing can be gained merely from the programme of *Lucia di Lammermoor; or the Laird, the Lady and the Lover*, which he wrote for the Prince of Wales's Theatre company:

HENRY ASHTON (an *ash-tonishingly* revengeful party, who in depth and bitterness acts up to his character as a Bass-o-profundo)
Mr. F. Dewar.

DR. RAYMOND (his guide, philosopher and friend, tutor to Lucy, physician to the family, accustomed to dog Henry and dog-Latin)

Mr. H. W. Montgomery.

EDGAR OF RAVENSWOOD (an interesting young operatic hero of the regular conventional type whom Henry attempts to make a butt of, but only succeeds in making a little pale)

Miss Marie Wilton.

NORMAN (Head Huntsman to Henry)

Mr. Harry Cox.

ARTHUR BUCKLAW (a great swell in his way, and also in Edgar's)

Miss Fanny Josephs.

LUCY of LAMMERMOOR (Henry's only sister, a simple dove-like creature given by her own admission to melancholy and by her brother to Bucklaw)

Mr. J. Clarke.

ALICE (her confidential maid, who, like all confidential people speaks her mind pretty freely to everybody)

Miss Hughes.

As a young girl Marie Wilton joined Miss Swanborough's company at the Strand Theatre, which was largely given over to burlesque. Here she played boys for so long that on being given the part of Pippo in *The Maid and the Magpie* she wrote to Miss Swanborough to ask if some change could be made in the cast. When Miss Swanborough saw her to discuss the matter she was accompanied by H. J. Byron, the author of the piece, then only a young man. He begged her to play Pippo, saying: 'I am only a beginner, you know, and this burlesque may make or mar me.'

Miss Wilton was unable to refuse a request so persuasively put, and the play proved a great success for both her and its author. At this time in her career we have a description of her written by Charles Dickens.

I really wish you would go to see *The Maid and the Magpie* burlesque. . . . There is the strangest thing in it that ever I have seen on the stage – the boy Pippo, by Miss Wilton. While it is astonishingly impudent (must be, or it couldn't be done at all), it is so stupendously like a boy, and unlike a woman, that it is perfectly free from offence. I never have seen such a thing. She does an imitation of the dancing of the Christy Minstrels – wonderfully clever – which, in the audacity of its thorough-going, is surprising.

A thing that you *cannot* imagine a woman doing at all; and yet the manner, the appearance, the levity, impulse and spirits of it are so exactly like a boy, that you cannot think of anything like her sex in association with it. I never have seen such a curious thing, and the girl's talent is unchallengeable. I call her the cleverest girl I have ever seen on the stage in my time, and the most singularly original.

Nevertheless Miss Wilton remained totally dissatisfied. She had her heart set not merely on achieving the right to assert her sex but on leaving burlesque behind her and playing comedy. There were very few theatres at which comedy was played, and when she applied to the managers of these she found them enthusiastic to engage her – but to play boys in burlesque.

In despair she called one day on a married sister and her husband, Mr and Mrs Francis Drake. When she explained to them her position – not for the first time – Mr Drake said: 'I see no chance for you but management. How would it be if you had a theatre of your own?'

Marie Wilton replied confusedly that she could not take a theatre without money, but her brother-in-law told her to return the next day to discuss the matter again. At this second interview he offered to lend her £1,000 if she could find a theatre to let, and he said to her: 'Should you succeed you will return the money, if you fail I will lose it.'

It was a large sum to risk on the young actress, who was at this time twenty-six, but it must be remembered that Marie Wilton had been providing for her sisters since she could first walk on a stage, while her brother-in-law had presumably already had some opportunity to observe the courage, judgment and originality she was later to show in management.

Her first action, once she had decided to take up her brother-in-law's offer, was to ask H. J. Byron, now a very popular writer, to go into partnership with her, giving her his exclusive services as an author. Byron agreed, with the qualification that as he was not in a position to put up any money he should be indemnified against loss. Then a theatre had to be found. In Tottenham Street off the Tottenham Court Road there was a little theatre called the Queen's, at which in former days many an illustrious actor and actress had appeared. But now it had become a minor theatre in a bad part of the town, frequented by a low kind of audience and nicknamed the Dusthole. It was not to let but the lessee Mr James was willing to come to some arrangement. Marie Wilton, against much advice since there was considerable doubt that the kind of audience she wished to attract could be induced to come to this theatre, proceeded to make an arrangement with him. She took possession of the theatre one month before she opened it, and during this time it was not merely cleaned and re-decorated but given new seats and new furniture. By the opening night the curtains and carpets and the new stalls were all pale blue, the latter covered with white anti-macassars.

Here are some details of the purchasing power of money at the time. After the complete transformation of the theatre £150 was left of the original £1,000. Marie Wilton had come to an arrangement by which she rented the theatre from Mr James and at the same time hired his services as acting-manager for £20 a week. She and Byron had agreed each to draw £10 a week as salary while she was to draw a further £10 a week as interest on her capital. This she paid to her brother-in-law. After these charges had been met the profits were to be shared equally between the two partners. When the theatre, re-named The Prince of Wales's Theatre, was first opened the price of a stall was 6s. Later it rose to 7s and still later to 10s. After two years Byron retired from the partnership, his place being filled by a young actor named Sidney Bancroft. Twenty years from the opening date Mr and Mrs Bancroft retired with a fortune of £180,000.

Marie Wilton and H. J. Byron were great favourites with the public but Miss Wilton was advised that while her aim in going into management was to finish with burlesque she could not afford to do this until she had established herself in the theatre. Her first programme therefore consisted of a comedietta called *The Winning Hazard*, followed by a burlesque of Mr Byron's, *La! Sonnambula! or the Supper, the Sleeper and the Merry Swiss Boy* (Miss Wilton played the Merry Swiss Boy), and a farce called *Vandyke Brown*.

The portents were, as usual with Miss Wilton, favourable. On the day that she opened, her mother, unable to stand the strain of remaining in London, went for a country drive to Willesden, accompanied by another of her daughters.

'What would I not give,' she said to her daughter, 'to know the end of this undertaking!' And, raising her eyes, she saw written on a signpost, 'Mary's Place, Fortune Gate'.

Sure enough the words were prophetic. Miss Wilton tells us that she never borrowed a further shilling in connection with this enterprise. 'I was successful in a modest way from the very first gradually but surely my lucky star led me on to fortune.'

All this time two young men were approaching the point when they would join Marie Wilton in a configuration happy for themselves and for the future of the British theatre.

In *Around Theatres* Max Beerbohm has an essay entitled 'The Invariable Badness of Amateur Acting' in which he asks why, since much may be said for the amateur in other arts, no one has ever beheld an amateur mime whose performance seemed comparable with even the worst professional performance. And he replies that there are no good amateur actors because acting is essentially a public art.

The fact that his work does not endure beyond the moment of its performance makes it essential for him [the actor] to be heard at large. . . . The man who has any real impulse for acting will not be satisfied with private or semi-private triumphs . . . will crave for a wider field. Consequently, he becomes a professional actor as soon as ever he can. And thus the amateur stage is always automatically deprived of such persons as might, if they tarried on it, become its ornaments.

Can this be true? one wonders. Does everyone with a talent for acting take to the professional stage? Is it so common for actors to discover this talent in amateur societies and then, depriving the amateur stage of all its ornaments, to give up all thought of another career?

At the time that Beerbohm was writing the stage had been given a measure of distinction and respectability, mainly by the actors and actresses whose lives are considered here, but this was new. For centuries the members of this profession had been regarded, if not as rogues and vagabonds, at least as low, licentious persons totally unfit to mix with the rest of the world. The fact that every great artist from Garrick to Irving was welcomed into London society should not mislead us as to the status of the ordinary member of the profession. No member of the middle or upper classes could contemplate with equanimity the prospect of a son or daughter joining the depraved company of the players, and any young man who wished to do so had to be willing to face, as Marie Wilton's father had, the prospect of being ostracised by his family. In addition actors were so badly paid that even men of talent had to be willing to struggle for years in poverty and wretchedness before they made their mark. 'Can you starve, cocky?' Edmund Kean is said to have asked a young man who came to ask his advice as to what he needed to do to become an actor, and not until the late nineteenth century did conditions begin to change for the better.

In consequence, it became a common thing for young men with talent for this outlawed art to honour their parents' wishes by sitting on an office stool all day, but to temper the ardour of their private longings by performing in the evening in one of the amateur companies which were a feature of Victorian society. When we read the lives of the great actors and actresses of that time we find that, while many of them came from old theatrical families and learned, like Marie Wilton, to act when they could barely walk, almost as many began as amateurs and only later succumbed to their craving for a wider field.

Sidney ('Squire') Bancroft did neither of these things. Born in 1841, two years later than the girl who was to become his wife and in the same year as King Edward VII and the magazine *Punch*, he was the son of a gentleman who died when he was a child, leaving his widow with very little money. As a result, he had to forego the education at public school and university for which he had been intended, although he seems to have been reasonably well educated, partly in England but also in France. As a child he was stage-struck and his toys were little theatres; as a youth, in spite of his mother's poverty, he seems to have been well enough endowed to go regularly to the play. He saw most of the leading actors of the day and, in addition, a child called Marie Wilton who made his mother and himself cry by her pathetic acting in *Belphegor* with Charles Dillon at the Lyceum.

When Bancroft was a young man, his mother died, and alone

in the world with no parent's heart to break or gladden, he determined to become an actor. He merely wrote to the lessees of all the leading provincial theatres and waited until one of them expressed a wish to see him. Then in 1861, with the smoothness which was to characterise his whole career, he was offered and accepted an engagement at twenty-one shillings a week from Mr Mercer Simpson at the Theatre Royal, Birmingham.

During his first season as an actor Squire Bancroft played thirty-six different parts, many of them in 'blood-and-thunder' plays. Towards the end of the season a visiting star, T. C. King, offered him an engagement in Cork for the Birmingham vacation and here he played forty fresh characters. Back in Birmingham again he played sixty-four parts in the next season, some of them with Phelps and some with G. V. Brooke. From here he went to Devonport and from there to Dublin, learning his profession as he travelled about the countryside, playing such parts as came his way. In Devonport he achieved a small amount of fame by an imitation of Edward Sothern, a famous actor of the day, as Lord Dundreary in *Our American Cousin*. Lord Dundreary was the first example of the caricature stage Englishman and one of the classics of its time. Squire Bancroft's youthful attendance at the theatre now paid him well because the manager of the theatre at Devonport, after watching him imitate Sothern for the benefit of his friends one night, prevailed upon him to repeat the performance publicly. Bancroft succeeded in filling a previously half-empty theatre. Then in Dublin he was praised by Charles Kean, who told him that were he still the lessee of a London theatre, 'it would be your own fault if you were not a member of my company'.

So he went on for several years learning his job in provincial companies in England and Ireland. During an engagement in Liverpool he met the celebrated burlesque company from the Strand theatre, which included Marie Wilton and a young actor called John Hare. Later Marie Wilton came to Liverpool again to play a short starring engagement before opening the Prince of Wales's with Mr Byron. She acted with Bancroft then for the first time and, as a spectator, watched her future husband play several parts. When she left Liverpool she and Byron offered Squire Bancroft an engagement in London. Writing of this time,

Squire Bancroft remarks that since he had refused several offers to appear in London, including one proposal to join Charles Fechter at the Lyceum, his decision to play burlesque in a speculative venture at a little, obscure theatre can be explained only by love at first sight. This may well be, but Bancroft was to find much besides love at this little theatre and it is not for his gifts as an actor that he is remembered today.

Miss Wilton had followed her successful opening bill with a comedy by H. J. Byron called *War to the Knife*, with which she again had a distinct success. In her second season her company was joined by John Hare[1] and her opening programme included a burlesque of *Lucia di Lammermoor*. Then Byron asked her to read a comedy by a friend of his called Tom Robertson. He told her quite frankly that the play had been turned down by numerous managements, partly because of a scene in a London pub called The Owl's Roost, in which the author had undisguisedly based his characters on journalists and critics of the day. London managers were nervous that this scene might give offence.

Miss Wilton, aged twenty-seven, with less than a full year in management, and very little money behind her, showed her courage and judgment by putting into rehearsal the play which so many established managements had turned down, coolly remarking that danger was better than dullness. On 11 November, 1865, *Society*, an original comedy by T. W. Robertson, opened at the Prince of Wales's Theatre, introducing a new theatrical style.

T. W. Robertson was born in 1829 and at the age of five became the fourth generation of his family to appear on the stage. His father was the manager of the Lincoln circuit and his mother an actress in that company. This couple had a very large family and it was said of them that they always had a juvenile stock company ready for any emergency. Their youngest child, Madge, who as Mrs Kendal was later to be famous on the London stage, made her first appearance in a play called *The Stranger* when she was four years old.

---

[1] Hare, Sir John, 1844–1921. Actor-manager. In management at the Court Theatre and afterwards in partnership with Mr and Mrs Kendal at the St James's. Knighted in 1907.

In his starveling youth Tom Robertson's life differed from that of dozens of other children born to theatre families only because he was immensely studious. He went to school as long as his family could afford to send him there, acting only in the holidays. But by the time he was fifteen business on the Lincoln circuit had become so bad that he returned home to write plays (he dramatised Christmas stories, among them those of Charles Dickens), for a cast composed of his brothers and sisters, paint scenery, manage, prompt and act in his father's company. As a young man he went to Utrecht in the position of English-speaking usher to a school, but this did no more for him than to suggest later the character of Krux in *School*. He returned to the stage, this time in London, and for many years he divided his time between acting and writing, making from neither of these occupations enough money to live in anything approaching comfort. As an actor he played everything from Shakespeare to farce, and as a writer he adapted plays in quantity from the French, selling these to Thomas Lacy, a theatrical publisher, the predecessor of Samuel French.

Not until he was thirty-six did he have any success with a new play and then it was only a version from the French, the theme of the play being one that had been used again and again and described by Théophile Gautier as 'the everlasting story of Garrick, Talma or Kean curing some foolish girl of a passion for them as actors by exhibiting themselves in private life under the most repulsive conditions'. In Robertson's version it is Garrick who, meeting from the stage the gaze of a young girl leaning out of a box at Drury Lane, is convinced that the love he instantaneously feels is reciprocated. Later he is asked by her father to use the art that has won her to disgust her so much as to kill her unsuitable passion. In the next act Garrick goes to dinner to meet the young lady and there plays the drunken scene which made the part so attractive to generations of leading actors. In Robertson's version the young lady, broken-hearted in this act, discovers in the next that although the drunkenness of the actor was an expression of the nobility of his character, the young man she has now dutifully consented to marry is really a drunkard. She then takes refuge with Garrick. The play ends with the future of the romantic couple in some doubt, left to the imagination of the audience. In a preface to a novel on the same theme Robertson asserts that, although the incidents that occur in the book are not in accordance with biographical fact, they are not certainly untrue. They might have happened. That may be, but if to the taste of today it seems that the play might have been more effective if the leading character had been based on an imaginary rather than an actual figure, it is a fact that this story brought success to numberless writers, not least of them T. W. Robertson. David Garrick was played by Edward Sothern at the Haymarket Theatre and he continued to play the part to crowded audiences in London and the provinces for the rest of his acting career. Afterwards the role was taken over by Charles Wyndham, who played it not merely in England but also in Berlin, Moscow and St Petersburg.

Elated by the success of this play, Robertson immediately wrote for Sothern the part of Sydney Daryl in *Society*. But Buckstone, the manager of the Haymarket, declared that the piece was rubbish and refused to put it on. *Society* was then offered to most of the managements of London and finally, as we have seen, to Marie Wilton.

It was an immediate and great success. The pressure to get seats became so great that an extra row of stalls had to be added, and shortly after its opening the Prince of Wales paid the first of many visits to the theatre that had been named after him. *Society* was followed by another success, an original play by H. J. Byron called *A Hundred Thousand Pounds*, and this was followed by Robertson's second comedy for Miss Wilton's management, *Ours*.

In the year 1867 Byron, who had become involved in the management of the theatres in Liverpool, resigned from his partnership with Miss Wilton and in the same year she married Squire Bancroft.

The Bancrofts produced altogether six plays written by T. W. Robertson: *Society*, which ran originally for 150 nights, at that time an extraordinary run; *Ours*, which also ran for 150 nights; *Caste*, which ran 156 nights and was withdrawn while still playing to big houses because the Bancrofts were by now concerned to build up a repertory of plays that could be produced again and again *Play*, 106 nights; *School*, which was withdrawn after 380 performances still playing to full houses, and *M.P.*, which ran for about 160 nights and was succeeded by a revival of *Ours*. Throughout the course of the Bancrofts' management, both at the Prince of Wales's and later at the Haymarket, the Robertson comedies were revived again and again.

Robertson was in no sense of the word a great playwright. Henry James described his plays as 'infantile' and today the word seems not entirely inappropriate. It is, however, the fate of all but great plays to become increasingly childish as they grow older, and in this respect Robertson's plays do not seem more aged than many of fifteen, twenty or thirty years ago. It is significant that St Aldegonde, one of the most sophisticated young men in the whole of fiction, went 'in the most immoral manner' to see *School*, of which he had read in *Galignani*, on the first evening of his return from his travels, although Lothair was so displeased with this unfeeling conduct that he declined to accompany him.[2]

Robertson wrote small, neat plays, just as the Bancrofts were small, neat artists. The very attributes that make them unimportant today made them most striking in their time. In an age used to declamation, melodrama, spectacle, large theatres and romantic acting, Robertson wrote light comedies and the Bancrofts cast them with actors and actresses capable of giving comedy performances. Squire Bancroft quotes Garrick as saying to a young actor: 'You may humbug the town as a tragedian, but comedy is a serious thing, my boy, so don't try that just yet.'

As a result of his appearance in Robertson's plays Squire Bancroft became associated with a certain type of part – that of the well-dressed, drawling man about town – but there is every indication that he was a very good actor with a far wider range than his success in management gave him the chance to display. After his retirement from management he appeared at the Lyceum with Sir Henry Irving in a play called *The Dead Heart*.

'What a big name you might have made for yourself,' the great man remarked to him one night as they walked off stage, 'had you never come across those Robertson plays! What a

² The Earl of Beaconsfield (Benjamin Disraeli), *Lothair*, Hughenden Edition, p. 432.

pity, for your own sake; for no actor can be remembered long who does not appear in the classical drama.'

But Irving was wrong. Without Robertson Bancroft might have been one more great actor of classical drama; with him he is remembered not merely for his part in a revolution in theatrical productions but also for a revolution in theatrical customs.

The thing that most excites one's admiration for the Bancrofts is that in almost everything they did they ran counter to the spirit of the time. At a time when actor-managers chose plays for their value as a vehicle for their own talents and cast only minor actors in support of the main role, the Bancrofts chose and commissioned plays with a wide range of parts and cast them with the best actors they could find, often playing minor roles themselves. At a time when declamation was the order of the day, they introduced light comedy. At a time when actors and actresses were underpaid and harshly treated, they were known for their wise and benevolent management and for the introduction of a number of long-overdue reforms.

In speaking of the rehearsals of *Society* Marie Wilton says: 'My views of acting so entirely agreed with Mr Robertson's that we encountered no difficulties whatever, and everything went smoothly and merrily.' This is a remarkable fact, for Robertson's views on acting were very strong and completely original, while his views on production as carried out by the Bancrofts resulted in the introduction of modern scenic effects. Twenty years earlier Madame Vestris had used scenic cloths, carpets and elaborate furnishings, but it was left to the Bancrofts to employ these so successfully that they became an accepted part of theatrical productions. They put real rugs on the floor, real furniture on the sets, the rooms in which their performances took place had real ceilings and, which caused at the time the greatest sensation of all, real knobs on the door-handles. Their style became known as the 'cup-and-saucer' comedy because of the realistic effects in the kitchen scene in *Caste*. Before this time it was customary in a conversation scene merely to bring down two or three chairs to the middle of the stage for the actors to sit on while talking and afterwards to take them away. The Bancrofts earned theatrical fame for all these innovations but Tom Robertson had an equal responsibility.

W. S. Gilbert said that he 'invented' stage management and acknowledged that he had learned a great deal from him. George Rowell says in *The Victorian Theatre* that the appearance of the artistic director who was neither actor nor prompter marked a definite stage in the evolution of the modern producer or director, and that the dramatist-director was an influential factor in the late Victorian theatre, the succession passing from Robertson to Gilbert, to Pinero and ultimately to Shaw. And he points out that, although Robertson's own ideas were largely superficial, he did suggest how more forceful ideas could be given dramatic form.

Robertson more or less successfully killed the 'stock' character. Here are two of his stage directions:

The author requests this part may be played with a slight French accent. He is not to pronounce the words absurdly or duck his head towards his stomach like the conventional stage Frenchman.

And:

The actor playing Dunscombe is requested not to make too much of this situation. All that is required is a momentary memory of childhood – succeeded by the external phlegm of the man of the world. No tragedy, no tears, no pocket-handkerchief.

As actors, both Bancroft and John Hare paid tributes to Robertson, Hare saying that he had a gift peculiar to himself of 'conveying by some rapid and almost electrical suggestion to the actor an insight into the character assigned to him'.

Hare carried the Robertson style to the Court Theatre where he worked with Ellen Terry, and to the St James's where he was in partnership with the Kendals. Later actors such as Wyndham and Alexander developed Robertson's ideas, and so they passed into the tradition of acting. Writing to Squire Bancroft on the death of Lady Bancroft, Sir Arthur Pinero said:

The work of a writer for the stage should be judged in relation to the period which produced it, and, so judged, Robertson was a man of vision and courage. There is no dramatist now writing, 'advanced' or otherwise, who is not in a measure indebted to Robertson.

Without the Bancrofts Robertson might have made no mark of

any sort. His plays for other theatres showed none of the originality of the series of plays he wrote for them and are rather feeble in the sensational manner of the time. The Bancrofts were also responsible for many innovations in theatrical management. The little Prince of Wales's Theatre, with its carpeted auditorium and blue and white stalls, provided something new in London – an evening's entertainment suitable for the families of the middle and upper classes. Thus they laid the foundations for the change in status of the theatre which was to take place over the next twenty years.

At first they conformed to custom by including two or more items in their bills but, as they became certain of their audience and this came to consist more of the classes who dined late and preferred a shorter evening in the theatre, they gradually reduced the bill to the presentation of a single piece.

As early as 1867, they sent one of the first touring companies to travel the provinces in *Caste*. The railways now made it possible to transport scenery and properties, and gradually touring companies replaced the old resident 'stock' companies.

Another innovation for which they were partly responsible was the matinée. The Bancrofts first gave a morning performance of *School* but this was not successful and for five or six years they did not try it again. Then they gave a morning performance of *Sweethearts*, a play written by W. S. Gilbert, so that Sothern might see it. On this occasion the theatre was crowded and, thus encouraged, they gave several afternoon performances of *Peril* in the following year. Then in 1878 they gave regular matinées of *Diplomacy*.

Bancroft combined the sure instinct of the born moneymaker with the genuine humanity of the reformer. He never feared to invest money in order to make it and he was lavish for those days, not only in the dressing of his plays, but in the treatment of his company. He disliked the old 'benefit' system by which actors were forced to chance their arm for a proportion of their salary, and from the first he paid a living wage, increasing salaries as soon as success made this possible. As examples of the changes during twenty years' management, he tells us that an actor named George Honey was paid £60 a week to play a part in a revival of *Caste* for which four years before he had received £18 a week, while when Mrs Stirling played

B

in the final revival of that comedy, she got eight times the salary paid to the actress who first played her part.

As a young man Bancroft had been very much mortified by the system by which actors were paid. Everyone in the theatre, from cleaners and dressers to the principal actors, had to assemble on Saturday mornings outside the treasury to receive their pay. His first act when he came into management was to institute the custom by which the salary of an actor was delivered to him in his dressing room.

He tells us that he thinks the most valuable quality in the management of a theatre is courage, and he adds that he is speaking chiefly in respect of the strength of will necessary to withdraw a play while it is still remunerative, so that it becomes part of the repertory of the theatre and may be revived when the time is ripe or used as a stop-gap in the event of the failure of some other play. It was largely this policy that accounted for the financial success of the Bancroft management. On the few occasions when one of their productions was a failure it was withdrawn immediately and when they were at a loss for a new production they used one of the Robertson comedies as a stop-gap.

The dramatic critics seemed to feel then, as many do now, that managements had a moral duty to find new plays by English writers even at some cost to themselves, and although the Bancrofts did not share this feeling, they, like other managements, would have welcomed the opportunity to put on a new play by a writer of talent. It was a sign of the times that after Robertson's early death in 1871 and after 'long and well-weighed consideration', they decided that the first successor to the Robertson comedies should be Lord Lytton's *Money*. 'They looked about them for an "original" English comedy, and it is certainly not their fault if they found nothing fresher nor weightier than this poor artificial *Money*, covered with the dust of a hundred prompters' boxes, and faded with the glare of a thousand footlights.'[3]

Money, to the modern reader more 'infantile' than any of Robertson's plays, gave the Bancrofts their most successful season, with the one exception of the year they prdouced

[3] Henry James, *The Scenic Art*, p. 149. In fact James wrote this about the later production of *Money* at the Haymarket.

School. During the next thirteen years of their management they occasionally produced a new English play, notably *Man and Wife* by Wilkie Collins and *Sweethearts* by W. S. Gilbert, but apart from the constantly revived Robertson comedies they were dependent in the main on new productions of old plays or adaptations from the French.

Of the revivals the two most notable at the Prince of Wales's Theatre were *The School for Scandal* (1874) and *The Merchant of Venice* (1875). In the production of these plays the Bancrofts reached the high point of their particular style. The staging and dressing of the former involved many visits to the British Museum and also to Knole House, 'there to choose such types of rooms as, from their wealth of pictures and old furniture, might serve the purpose best'. In Lady Sneerwell's drawing-room amber curtains were drawn back from quilted panels of gold satin, and Lady Sneerwell in powder and brocade sat in a high marquetry chair drinking tea out of real china. At Sir Peter Teazle's a real chandelier suspended by a crimson silken cord lit tapestries on the semi-circular walls. In Charles Surface's room the genuine Turkish carpet was of thick pile, the bookcases were of oak and the books bound in russia leather. Lady Teazle in powder, satin and diamonds was followed at Lady Sneerwell's by a page who was a real Negro and who lived in Mrs Bancroft's house during the run of the piece. The minuet was danced at Lady Sneerwell's reception for the first time, although it has since been so often repeated as to be believed part of the original work.

The Merchant of Venice was one of the most famous failures in theatrical history. During the preparations for its production Mrs Bancroft paid a call on a young actress named Ellen Terry who, known to the public as a child, had then disappeared into seclusion with her lover E. W. Godwin the architect, but had recently returned to London bringing with her the two illegitimate children who were to become known as Edward Gordon Craig and Edith Craig. Mrs Bancroft asked Ellen Terry to play Portia in the coming production, and she added that she and her husband hoped also to employ Godwin in the capacity of archaeological supervisor of the production design. 'My work,' Ellen Terry wrote to the Bancrofts, 'will, I feel certain, be *joyful* work, and joyful work *should* turn out *good* work.'

The Bancrofts travelled to Venice with their principal scene painter and his assistant, where drawings were made from which the scenery and drop curtains were designed. Neither trouble nor money was spared, but, in spite of the beauty and authenticity of the costumes, the production was a failure, although a memorable one. Squire Bancroft wrote:

It all looked so unlike a theatre and so much more like old Italian pictures than anything that had previously been shown upon the stage. Some of the dresses seemed to puzzle many among the audience, notably those worn by Bassanio and the Venetian nobles, who accompanied him to Belmont in their velvet robes of state, the gorgeous attendants on the Prince of Morocco; and the Spaniards who accompanied the Prince of Aragon. It may be that it all came a little before the proper time, and that we saw things too far in advance. . . . I account it a failure to be proud of.

But probably the real reason for the failure was Charles Coghlan's performance as Shylock. Bancroft said that the extent of his failure was a mystery and that he was so undecided how to play the part that on the night of the first performance he lingered on the staircase and then went back to his dressing-room and tore off his wig and make-up. And Ellen Terry said: 'Coghlan's Shylock was not even bad. It was *nothing*.'

However, the audiences, if small, were distinguished. Ellen Terry wrote that 'a poetic and artistic atmosphere pervaded the front of the house as well as the stage itself', while a member of the audience wrote of her: 'Imagine never having seen Ellen Terry, expecting nothing, and having her sprung upon you in the heyday of her youth and beauty and exquisite art!'

The paucity of English dramatists forced the Bancrofts to do as the rest of London did, after Robertson's death, and produce adapatations from the French. Victorien Sardou was the most popular playwright of his time and wrote many plays for Sarah Bernhardt. He had great dramatic power and was a brilliant craftsman, excelling in what is known as the 'well-made' play. His characters, it has been said, lack only life. At this time a school of writers was arising who regarded the 'well-made' play with contempt and Shaw spoke of 'Sardoodledum'. Yet, except where genius is present, a more successful formula is seldom found. The music of Puccini has preserved for us an example of

Sardou's work and, now that the bloom of the contemporary is off, the well-contrived melodrama of *Tosca* seems to many people to wear better than the pseudo-philosophic verbiage of most of Shaw's plays. Squire Bancroft had suffered on more than one occasion from playwrights who delivered two excellent acts and then a weak third, and he did not despite the well-made play. After the failure of a new play by H. J. Byron, he commissioned an adaptation of Sardou's *Nos Intimes* from a writer named B. C. Stephenson, who wrote under the name of Bolton Rowe, Clement Scott, the dramatic critic, was brought into collaboration with Stephenson, taking for the purpose the name of Saville Rowe. *Nos Intimes* was done at the Prince of Wales's in 1876 as *Peril* and, with the Kendals in the company, was extremely successful. Following this Bancroft went to Paris to see Sardou's new play *Dora* and, after the scene for three men, for which *Dora* became famous, he bought the English rights without waiting for the end. *Dora*, in adaptation again by Bolton and Saville Rowe and re-named *Diplomacy*, became one of the most successful of all the Bancroft plays and indeed of the plays of this period. It was revived as late as 1913 by Gerald du Maurier with Gladys Cooper, in 1924 by Gladys Cooper and in 1932 by du Maurier once more. Later at the Haymarket Bancroft gave the first London production to *Fedora*, another of Sardou's plays to become part of the English repertory, a famous production of it being given by Beerbohm Tree with Mrs Patrick Campbell.

When we come to consider the enormous fortune that Squire Bancroft made it is interesting to speculate how much of it would have gone to his authors had there been a royalty system. Tom Robertson was simply on the salary list of the Prince of Wales's Theatre, while the English rights in *Diplomacy* were acquired for the initial purchase price of £1,500 – at that time by far the largest sum ever paid for a foreign play.

Many famous actors and actresses played with the Bancrofts at the Prince of Wales's Theatre. Those that are remembered today include Johnston Forbes-Robertson, William Terriss, Albert Chevalier, Ellen and Marion Terry. But the actor who contributed most to the success of the Bancroft company and

the Robertson comedies was John Hare, who joined the Prince
of Wales's company almost at the beginning, and who played
in all six Robertson comedies and Sir Peter Teazle in *The School
for Scandal*. His gift for comedy was so great that he made his
own name, while contributing to the success of *Society*, merely
by going to sleep.

Hare was a close friend of the Bancrofts and their good
relationship was maintained although he became a rival. After
playing in *The School for Scandal* Hare left the Prince of
Wales's Theatre and went into management himself at the
Court. For several years the companies at these two small
theatres presented London with a choice of comedy, because
Hare took with him the acting style and the scenic innovations
developed in the productions of the Robertson comedies. Squire
Bancroft, believing there was room for two comedy theatres,
did not fear the rivalry of his friend and indeed went out of his
way to help him.

Then in 1879 Bancroft was offered the lease of the St James's
Theatre which had lately been bought by Lord Kilmorey. He
refused the offer, partly because he felt no particular need to
leave the Prince of Wales's at that time and partly because the
Haymarket Theatre, the London theatre most beloved of actors,
had lately been through a period of bad luck and he believed it
might become available. A week or two later he heard that
John Hare had acquired the lease of the St James's in partnership with the Kendals. 'The amicable rivalry of our old friend
Hare [Bancroft writes] at another small outlying theatre, as the
Court was, had mattered little – indeed, was often good for both
of us – but this news mattered much. So powerful a trio as
himself with the Kendals, in a new and better-placed house,
rendered handsome and up-to-date, "gave me pause". It was a
supreme moment to search for the possibility of saying
"check"! '

Less than twenty-four hours after he heard the news Bancroft
was shown into the office of J. S. Clarke, the lessee of the Haymarket Theatre, a man he had never met. 'I am going to put
my cards at once on the table,' he said. 'I want the Haymarket
Theatre: what do you want for it?'

Bancroft's sense of an opportunity was not mistaken, and a
few days later the remainder of Clarke's lease was assigned to

him together with a new lease for a further period of ten years
– the period he already believed should be long enough to make
his fortune.

Bancroft acquired the Haymarket for an annual figure which
did not exceed £5,000 including rates and insurance, but
he pledged himself to spend £10,000 on it. In fact, he spent
£17,000 before the curtain rose on his first production and a
total of £20,000 altogether. The whole of the auditorium of
the famous theatre was pulled down and re-built, and in the
new auditorium the pit was abolished. Originally the pit had
occupied the entire ground floor of London theatres, the richer
classes being seated in the dress circle and private boxes.
Gradually the modern stall was introduced and, row by row, in
Bancroft's words, the cushioned chairs encroached upon the
narrow benches, until at last in many theatres all that was left
of the old-fashioned pit was a low ceilinged cavern hidden
away under the dress circle. Bancroft was the first to do away
with the pit altogether and to put the cheaper seats entirely
in the upper parts of the house. The pit remained in many
London theatres well into the twentieth century.

On the night when the curtain rose for the first time on the
new Haymarket theatre it did so to howls and hooting and
angry cries of 'Where's the pit?' which, with the OP riots
graven deep in theatrical memory, must have been a singularly
terrifying circumstance. And indeed when Bancroft walked on
to the stage it was twenty minutes before peace was restored.
But the disapproval of the audience on this occasion was only
partial, since the occupants of the stalls applauded violently as
long as the cheaper parts kept the uproar going, and the popularity of the manager and his wife was so great and the desire
of the whole audience to see the play so urgent that, once the
demonstration had been made, the protest died and the abolition
of the pit became an accepted fact.

Here is a description of the new Haymarket by Henry James;

Mr. Bancroft has transformed the Haymarket—which was an
antiquated and uncomfortable house with honourable traditions,
which had latterly declined – into the perfection of a place of
entertainment. Brilliant, luxuriant, softly cushioned and perfectly
aired, it is almost entertainment enough to sit there and admire
the excellent device by which the old-fashioned and awkward

proscenium has been suppressed and the stage set all around in an immense gilded frame, like that of some magnificent picture. Within this frame the stage, with everything that is upon it, glows with a radiance that seems the very atmosphere of comedy.[4]

James could not, however, refrain from some gloomy head-shaking over the prospects of the venture.

The Haymarket has gained by being taken by Mr. and Mrs. Bancroft, but we are not sure that this humorous couple have bettered themselves with the public by leaving the diminutive playhouse to which they taught the public the road. The Prince of Wales's is a little theatre and the pieces produced there dealt mainly in little things – presupposing a great many chairs and tables, carpets, curtains, and knicknacks, and an audience placed close to the stage. They might, for the most part, have been written by a cleverish visitor at a country-house, and acted in the drawing-room by his fellow inmates. The comedies of the late Mr. Robertson were of this number, and these are certainly among the most diminutive experiments ever attempted in the drama. It is among the habits formed upon Mr. Robertson's pieces that the company of the Prince of Wales's have grown up, and it is possible that they may not have all the success they desire in accommodating them-selves to a larger theatre.

The success of the Bancroft management at the Haymarket has no parallel in theatrical history. Irving said later: ' "B" is the only actor since Garrick who made a fortune purely by management of his own theatre – I mean without the aid of provincial tours or visits to America.'

Opening with a revival of *Money*, which to his surprise quite quickly made a profit of £5,000, Bancroft followed with a revival of the 'diminutive' *School*, which made £10,000 in the same season. He learned from this that in the larger theatre big money could be made during the early part of the run of a piece when the house was sold out. He adopted a policy of short runs mainly of revivals of the repertory he had built up at the Prince of Wales's Theatre. He put on *Money*, *Masks and Faces*, *The School for Scandal*, *Diplomacy*, and the Robertson comedies *School*, *Ours*, *Society* and *Caste*.

[4] Since praise from this critic was so hardly won it is worth recording that in a different context he wrote: 'The company at the Prince of Wales's play with a finish, a sense of detail, what the French call *ensemble*, and a general good grace, which deserve explicit recognition.'

The policy of revivals was more or less forced upon him. He continually sought new plays but he found very few. During his years at the Haymarket he put on a new play by Arthur Pinero, *Lords and Commons*, and two adaptations from the French of Victorien Sardou, *Odette* and *Fedora*.

As time went on Bancroft had more and more difficulty in casting plays because of competition from the ever increasing rival managements. One notable addition to his company came to him unsought. He received one day a visit from Mrs Labouchere, the wife of the Liberal politician and journalist, who acted under her professional name of Henrietta Hodson. She told him that Mrs Langtry, the Jersey Lily, had determined to go upon the stage and was to make her debut at an afternoon performance for the Royal General Theatrical Fund as Miss Hardcastle in *She Stoops to Conquer*. Mrs Labouchere had come to ask if she might have the use of the Haymarket Theatre for this purpose. Reflecting that the history of Mrs Langtry's extraordinary career disposed of any fear that she might fail through the ordeal of 'facing the public', and knowing that if he refused her his theatre she would not have far to seek another, Bancroft agreed immediately. It is well known that Mrs Langtry had a long and successful career on the stage. Her first professional part, following the success of her matinée, was Blanche Hay in a revival of *Ours*.

In general, however, the casting of plays became an ever-increasing worry and one cannot help wondering whether Bancroft, having in so short a time so thoroughly put all the old comedies to work, did not also begin to ask himself how long he could go on using *Society* or *School* or *Caste* as a stop-gap for new plays that failed to materialise. Neither of these things might have weighed very strongly with him, however, but for a third and totally unexpected development. He had confidently assumed that it would be possible to make a fortune at the Haymarket in ten years or so. After four years had passed he found he had already done this.

He began to look about him for some means of easing the burden of management and achieving some leisure to enjoy the riches that were his. At first he considered taking a partner and he boldly suggested to Hare that he should give up the St

James's Theatre and, bringing the Kendals with him, join his wife and himself at the Haymarket.

Roughly the proposition was that he and they should give up that theatre and join forces with us – as partners – at the Haymarket, my idea being that the combined strength of our five names would be unassailable; that the theatre, like the Comédie Française, should rarely be closed; that three of the names at the least should always be in the programme, and the whole five of them for a considerable part of the year.

But here he met with a refusal.

The project did not proceed far enough with Hare for me to go into figures; and those dreadful things, very likely, seemed to him an insurmountable objection. The large profits made by us at the Haymarket were, I think, as little suspected as known; and, naturally enough, at the first glance it may have seemed impossible that they could have borne such division as I proposed. Or it may be that what was really strength looked like weakness. At any rate, our old friend decided against my proposal.

So, having failed to divide the work of managing the theatre, Bancroft, aged forty-four, his wife two years older, calmly decided to give it up altogether. In 1885, twenty years after Marie Wilton opened at the Prince of Wales's Theatre, Mr and Mrs Bancroft retired with a fortune. They owed a great deal of their phenomenal success to a willingness to risk money in order to make money; much, too, to their excellent judgment of plays and willingness to cut the loss on any mistake they made (at the Haymarket they made none, although on more than one occasion they decided against plays they had intended to produce after hearing them read). How extraordinarily shrewd was their general conduct in management is revealed by the fact that it was possible for John Hare, at the St James's Theatre round the corner, following the same policies, with the Kendals in his company, not to 'suspect' the profits that were being made at the Haymarket.

Marie Bancroft lived to be 82, Squire Bancroft to be 85. Ellen Terry was to write of them:

The brilliant story of the Bancroft management of the Old Prince of Wales's Theatre used to be more familiar twenty years back

than it is now. I think that few of the present generation of play-
goers who point out on the first night of important productions a
remarkably striking figure of a man with erect carriage, white
hair, and flashing, dark eyes – a man whose eyeglass, manners and
clothes all suggest Thackeray and Major Pendennis, in spite of
his success in keeping abreast of everything modern—few play-
goers, I say, who point this man out as Sir Squire Bancroft could
give any account of what he and his wife did for the English
theatre. Nor do the public who see an elegant little lady starting
for a drive from a certain house in Berkeley Square realise that
this is Marie Wilton, afterwards Mrs. Bancroft, now Lady Bancroft,
the comedian who created the heroines of Tom Robertson.

And she added:

I have never, even in Paris, seen anything more admirable than
the *ensemble* of the Bancroft productions. Every part in the domestic comedies the presentation of which they made their policy,
was played with such point and finish that the more rough, uneven,
and emotional acting of the present day has not produced anything
so good in the same line.

And fifteen years after this was written, Frederick Lonsdale
(who in some respects might be regarded as in the direct succession from Tom Robertson) could still describe Lady Bancroft as
an 'inimitable' raconteur, while she could still cast spells on
his children by telling them stories of her youth and the
repeated omens of her good fortune.

During all the long years of their retirement the Bancrofts
re-appeared seldom on the stage. In 1893 they acted together in
a revival by John Hare of *Diplomacy* at the Garrick Theatre in a
cast which included Forbes-Robertson and Olga Nethersole,
and in the following year Lady Bancroft appeared as Lady
Franklin under the same management in *Money*. In 1895 at the
Haymarket Theatre she appeared with Herbert Beerbohm Tree
and Mrs Patrick Campbell in a revival of *Fedora*. These seem
to have been her only professional appearances during the
whole period with the exception of single performances. In
1889 Bancroft made a notable appearance at the Lyceum
Theatre with Sir Henry Irving in a play called *The Dead Heart*.
In this play there is a duel between the characters played by
Bancroft and Irving. Both men were short-sighted and at all rehearsals Irving wore his pince-nez and Bancroft his eyeglass,

but on the first night these were necessarily abandoned. Here is Bancroft's account of it.

From all I have heard said of it the fight must have been very well done – real, brief and determined. It was a grim business, in the sombre moonlit room, and certainly gave the impression that one of the two combatants would not leave it alive. The scene remains in the memory, and I often still hear from many old play-goers that it was the best thing of the kind they ever saw.

And Bancroft adds in a book written after Irving's death, that he refrained from asking Irving, as William Terriss had done when rehearsing a similar scene in *The Corsican Brothers*, whether some of the moonlight might fall on him, as 'nature is impartial'.[5]

Bancroft had another characteristic in common with Irving – the zest with which he played the part of actor-manager. Although he is known for his wise and benevolent management and for the innovations for which he was responsible rather than for the exceptional quality of his talents, it must not be thought that he neglected his opportunities to pay tribute in his personal behaviour to the profession in which he stood so high. Marguerite Steen has given us the following description of the two men. 'Irving swaggered about the town with long hair, a "wide-awake", and a fur collared overcoat; Bancroft swaggered about with a top-hat, an eyeglass and a cane. Neither of them ever ceased acting, on the stage or off. In days before "publicity" was commercialised, each was his own best publicity agent.'

For nearly forty years Squire Bancroft and his wife lived the life of the rich and leisured classes. They liked travel and they had a taste for pictures and furniture. They had one son, George, who wrote *The Ware Case* and a new adaptation of *Diplomacy* for Gerald du Maurier's production of 1913. Bancroft raised many thousands of pounds for hospitals when he emerged from his retirement to travel round England giving readings of *A Christmas Carol*. In 1897 he was knighted for the services rendered to the theatre by himself and his wife.

[5] Terriss, William, 1847–97. One of the few actors who was openly unafraid of Henry Irving. He was assassinated on his way into the Adelphi Theatre in 1897.

Sir Henry Irving
1838-1905

Henry Irving once said that Edmund Kean's reputation was a posthumous one. 'If you read the newspapers of the time you will find that during his acting days he was terribly mauled.' And he added that Garrick's impersonations were not much written about in his lifetime.

The point he wished to emphasise was that he himself might expect a 'posthumous reputation'. He found it necessary to do this because at no time in his career was there general agreement about the quality of his acting. William Archer[1] said of him:

There has probably never been an actor of equal prominence whose talent, nay whose mere competence has been so much contested. He is the idol of a select circle of devotees but even it is small, and its fervour is apt to be tempered with apology. . . . In no single part has general consent pronounced him ideal; in many it has emphatically pronounced him quite the reverse, though the Lyceum was nonetheless crowded on that account.

And Henry James said the same thing in a different way.

Mr Irving's critics may, I suppose, be divided into three categories: those who justify him in whatever he attempts, and consider him an artist of unprecedented brilliancy: those who hold that he did very well in melodrama, but that he flies too high when he attempts Shakespeare; and those who, in vulgar parlance, can see nothing in him at all.

[1] Archer, William, 1856–1924. One of the leading dramatic critics of the late nineteenth century. Wrote in *Figaro*, the *World*, the *Tribunal* and the *Nation*. Translated Ibsen's plays and edited his collected works. Author of many books on the theatre and a play called *The Green Goddess*. In 1877, as a young man in Edinburgh, he was joint author

Today we must still attempt to reach a decision on the matter in spite of the conflicting evidence, because Henry Irving's claim on our attention is that he was one of the greatest actors in our history. The Bancrofts' pretensions were of a much smaller kind. Honest perfectionists, modestly intent on fame and fortune, they happened to launch a revolution in theatrical style and customs. Irving gave his whole life to his art and he would not wish to be remembered except by the quality of his contribution to it.

It is not of course true that his circle was small or apologetic. As to the first, Archer contradicts himself immediately in the sentence 'the Lyceum was nonetheless crowded on that account', and anyone who has read Edward Gordon Craig on Irving, or Joseph Hatton, or Ellen Terry, or any of a dozen others, will know that it was not apologetic. Gordon Craig opens his book *Henry Irving* by saying: 'Let me state at once, in clearest unmistakable terms, that I have never known of, or seen, or heard, a greater actor than was Irving.' Yet in order to understand the extent and vigour of the controversy one has only to turn again to Henry James.

That an actor so handicapped, as they say in London, by nature and culture should have enjoyed such prosperity is a striking proof of the absence of a standard, of the chaotic condition of taste. Mr Irving's Macbeth, which I saw more than a year ago and view under the mitigations of time, was not pronounced one of his great successes; but it was acted, nevertheless, for many months, and it does not appear to have injured his reputation. Passing through London, and curious to make the acquaintance of the great English actor of the day, I went with alacrity to see it; but my alacrity was more than equalled by the vivacity of my disappointment. I sat through the performance in a sort of melancholy amazement. There are barren failures and there are interesting failures, and this performance seemed to me to deserve the less complimentary of these classifications. It inspired me, however, with no ill-will toward the artist, for it must be said of Mr. Irving

---

with Robert Lowe and George Halkett of a pamphlet called *The Fashionable Tragedian* which deplored Irving's popularity, claiming that his diction was execrable, his mannerisms grotesque and his scholarship a pretence. Later Archer developed a greater admiration for Irving and attempted an impartial analysis of his acting in *Henry Irving, Actor and Manager: A Critical Study*, from which the quotations in the following pages are taken.

that his aberrations are not of a vulgar quality, and that one likes him, somehow, in spite of them. But one's liking takes the form of making one wish that really he had selected some other profession than the histrionic. Nature has done very little to make an actor of him. His face is not dramatic; it is the face of a sedentary man, a clergyman, a lawyer, an author, an amiable gentleman – of anything other than a possible Hamlet or Othello. His figure is of the same cast, and his voice completes the want of illusion. His voice is apparently wholly unavailable for purposes of declamation. To say that he speaks badly is to go too far; to my sense he simply does not speak at all—in any way that, in an actor, can be called speaking. He does not pretend to declaim or dream of declaiming. Shakespeare's finest lines pass from his lips without his paying the scantiest tribute to their quality. Of what the French call *diction* – of the art of delivery – he has apparently not a suspicion. This forms three-fourths of an actor's obligations and in Mr. Irving's acting these three-fourths are simply cancelled. What is left to him with the remaining fourth is to be 'picturesque'; and this even his partisans admit he has made his speciality. This concession darkens Mr. Irving's prospects as a Shakespearean actor. You can play hopscotch on one foot, but you cannot cut with one blade of a pair of scissors, and you cannot play Shakespeare by being simply picturesque.

Henry James means more to us today than Gordon Craig, and the tendency would be to identify ourselves with him except for one thing – he goes too far. In the first place he condemns the taste of a whole generation of playgoers as well as Henry Irving and, secondly, he would have us believe that this actor had the face of 'a sedentary man', an amiable gentleman'. The first charge is so extreme it arouses curiosity, the second comes into conflict with one of the few pieces of evidence we have by which we may judge for ourselves. We know from photographs what Irving looked like and may decide for ourselves whether he had the face of an amiable, sedentary man.

One of the most famous of all descriptions of acting is Gordon Craig's description of Irving in *The Bells*. He begins by telling us that one of the characters on the stage has just mentioned the night, many years ago, when the Polish Jew was murdered. Then he goes on :

Irving was buckling his second shoe, seated, and leaning over it with his two long hands stretched down over the buckles. We suddenly saw these fingers stop their work; the crown of the head suddenly seemed to glitter and become frozen – and then, at the pace of the slowest and most terrified snail, the two hands, still motionless and dead, were seen to be coming up the side of the leg. . . . the whole torso of the man, also seeming frozen, was gradually, and by an almost imperceptible movement, seen to be drawing up and back, as it would straighten a little and to lean a little against the back of the chair on which he was seated.

Once in that position – motionless – eyes fixed ahead of him and fixed on us all – there he sat for the space of ten to twelve seconds, which I can assure you seemed to us all like a lifetime, and then said – and said in a voice deep and overwhelmingly beautiful 'Oh, you were talking of that – were you?' And as the last syllable was uttered, there came afar off the regular throbbing sound of the sledge-bells. . . .

He moves his head slowly from us – the eyes still somehow with us – and moves it to the right – taking as long as a long journey to discover a truth takes. He looks to the faces on the right – nothing. Slowly the head revolves back again, down, and along the tunnels of thought and sorrow, and at the end the face and eyes are bent upon those to the left of him . . . utter stillness . . . nothing there either. . . .

The difficulty however with detailed descriptions of acting is that they tell us what was done but not how it was done and this kind of thing – 'taking as long as a long journey to discover a truth takes' – requires a preliminary faith if we are to be sure of anything more than that Irving's method was a slow one. Here, for instance, is Shaw's description of Irving in *A Story of Waterloo* to put beside it.

A squeak is heard behind the scenes : it is the childish treble that once rang like a trumpet on the powder-waggon at Waterloo, Enter Mr. Irving, in a dirty white wig, toothless, blear-eyed, palsied, shaky at the knees, stooping at the shoulders, incredibly aged and very poor, but respectable. He makes his way to his chair, and can only sit down, so stiff are his aged limbs, very slowly and creakily. . . . The corporal cannot recognise his grandniece at first, when he does, he asks her questions about children – children who have long gone to their graves at ripe ages. She prepares his tea, he sups it noisily and ineptly, like an infant. . . . He gets a bronchial attack and gasps for paregoric. . . . He rises more creakily than before, but with his faithful grandniece's arm fondly supporting him. He dodders across the stage, expressing a hope that the flies will not be too 'owdacius', and sits down on another chair with his joints crying more loudly than ever for some of the oil of youth. We feel that we could watch him sitting down for ever.

It is clear that in this second passage Shaw is guying Irving, but he does also show how meaningless is any direct attempt to reveal an actor's art by a narrative description of it. In both these passages the miming might be of the highest quality or that of an old ham in a Victorian melodrama; it might hold us entranced or reduce us to giggles.

One of the strangest aspects of the accounts of Irving is that even where they relate to matters of fact an extremity of state-ment on one side does nothing to prohibit an equal extremity on the other. Gordon Craig, for instance, tells us that Irving could 'bring the house down.'

I think it has not been your fortune to hear what is called 'the house coming down'. Even in the epoch of Irving it was seldom that anyone else 'brought the house down' – but Irving 'brought it down'.

A terrific sweep of applause is not 'bringing the house down'. 'Bringing the house down' is when everybody simultaneously calls out and applauds simultaneously and electrically. . . . You have been to the Russian Ballet perhaps on one of its great nights, or you have heard Chaliapine's reception at Covent Garden. Well, that is not what I mean either. Those are ovations, but mild ovations. The thing I mean had three times the capacity.

Music-lovers will find this a very extreme statement but it does nothing to prevent the following. 'The crowded audiences at the Lyceum as a rule applaud but feebly and the attendants in the front of the house are not above contributing to the rapturous ovation. . . . The true explanation is that the majority of the audience are intellectually interested not emotionally excited.' In the second of these sentences William Archer con-tradicts almost every other account of Irving's acting. Irving gave much thought to his interpretations of the major roles and particularly in Shakespeare often forsook the traditional read-ings, but his contemporaries speak again and again of his almost mesmeric hold over the emotions of his audiences, of his power to inspire fear and communicate his own excessive guilt.

It is clearly impossible to arrive at an opinion of the quality of Irving's acting by the method of balancing one man's words against another's, and we must look for some more positive means to judge it. Two things must prejudice us heavily towards the view that Irving is to be ranked among the great actors of all time. The first concerns the composition of the 'select' circle which Archer says 'idolised' Irving. In this circle, apparently uninterested in the controversy and the criticisms, certainly not tempering fervour with apology, was the whole of the acting profession.

Irving arrived in London in 1867, an almost unknown actor from the provinces. Four or five years later he was the acknowledged head of his profession, a position he retained until his death in 1905. This supremacy was awarded him without strife. Actors idolised him and fell in behind him with unreserved loyalty and devotion. It is difficult to find a theatrical biography of the time in which Irving's quality is questioned or his right to the position of leader challenged, either by the subject or the author of the book. Squire Bancroft was in management for six years before Irving took over the Lyceum, but, when he speaks of Irving, he does so with an assumption that it was natural to pay him homage, telling little stories that have no point other than that Irving called on his wife and himself late one evening, or spoke kind words to their son. The list of actors who regarded him as the 'Chief' or the 'Guvnor' includes the most famous of the day in spite of the fact that the Lyceum productions were designed round himself and Ellen Terry and that he gave no quarter to young and aspiring performers. The list of books in which he is spoken of in that peculiarly Victorian tone of reverent sentimentality usually reserved for the Queen is as long as the list of actors. From Ellen Terry herself and her son Edward Gordon Craig, who, if not a remarkable actor was an innovator and a man of great talent, through William Terriss, Sir Arthur Pinero, Sir Johnston Forbes-Robertson and Sir George Alexander to Sir John Martin Harvey, his devoted personal circle included the leading names of the day, while outside the Lyceum Company he was accorded the same measure of respect as within it.

Irving might have been regarded by the actors of today as the old, ham actor who played in Victorian melodrama, but he is not. No intervening generation has queried his unique talent.

'Do as the great Irving did,' Gerald du Maurier remarked, instructing a young actor on some particular point. And as witness for our own day we have the greatest of them all. In a recent series of televised interviews with actors, Kenneth Tynan asked Sir Laurence Olivier about his performance of Richard 11 and Sir Laurence replied: 'First of all I had heard imitations of old actors imitating Henry Irving; and so I did, right away, an imitation of these old actors imitating Henry Irving's voice – that's why I took a rather narrow kind of vocal address.' And in the same series of interviews Sir John Gielgud talking about his first performance of Hamlet said: 'Of course, Irving was my god, although I'd never seen him; I'd just read about him being Ellen Terry's partner. But the whole idea of this magnetic, strange man, whom I knew I could never be anything like, somehow appealed to me more than any past actor that I'd ever read about. I didn't try to copy, I only took note of all the things he'd done and looked at the pictures of him and so on.'

Why, then, if in the theatre itself recognition of the greatness of Henry Irving is implicit in everything that is said of him, did so great a controversy wage outside it? Sir Laurence Olivier supplies the clue.

As an actor Sir Henry Irving had great faults. First of all there was this narrow, almost nasal kind of vocal address Sir Laurence speaks of, secondly there was his strange manner of pronouncing the English language, and thirdly there was, according to some accounts, an almost grotesque method of moving about the stage. Sir Henry, we are told, said 'Gud' for 'God', 'Cut-thrut dug', 'Tak the rup frum mey nek', 'Ritz' for 'rich', 'seyt' for 'sight', 'stod' for 'stood', 'hond' or 'hend' for 'hand', while for 'To trammel up the consequence', he said 'tram-mele up-p the cunsequence'. And, while so hideously distorting the language, he moved about the stage with depressed head, and protruding shoulders, making with his legs sidelong and backward skirmishes.

In Irving's day there were no schools of acting, no repertory theatres. There were the provincial theatres and the old stock companies where a young man might learn from the old stock actors how to play stock characters and for the rest might teach himself. As Irving painfully acquired a technique with which to express his natural talent, he could neither see nor hear himself. Faults that today would be corrected during his early training became a part of his personality. 'Do I say Gud when I say Gud?' he once asked.[2]

How, then was it possible for Gordon Craig to say: 'I have never known of, or seen, or heard a greater actor than was Irving'? The answer, of course, is that to be great is not to be faultless but to be great. It speaks for Irving's superb quality that it could transcend his absurd diction and his grotesque walk. The crime that those who write critically for money are always in danger of committing is not to fail in the detection of faults but to fail to recognise genius when it appears unheralded.

In Irving's case the trouble was not that his great talents went unsung but that they were so trumpeted that anyone, hurrying to experience for the first time the impact of his acting and confronted with a thinnish voice, a strange diction and some odd mannerisms, was apt to be so engrossed and repelled by these as to be incapable of perceiving his merits. To take a further example from opera, it sometimes happens that a singer has one or two notes that are so ugly that people who know her only by reputation are on first acquaintance shocked out of critical judgment and musical appreciation.

'Is that what all the fuss is about?' they ask, and only on closer acquaintance fall victim to the general artistry of a whole performance. Archer says of Irving:

The taste for his art must be acquired, and the mere commencement of the process is so irksome that they [his critics] never get beyond the first sip, as it were, but make a wry face and refuse to repeat the dose. Familiarity with Mr. Irving's art, so far from lessening respect, may almost be called a necessary condition of the merest tolerance.

And:

At first I did not like it at all, but little by little, I found my nerves adjust themselves to the inevitable. My attention was no

[2] In an earlier generation Leigh Hunt complains bitterly of John Philip Kemble's pronunciation, of which he gives the following examples: aitches=aches; bird=beard; churful=cheerful; conshince=conscience; airth=earth; air=err; farwell=farewell; furful=fearful. And in our own day we have a leading politician who adopts the airth= earth vowel sound.

longer absorbed in making the phonetic changes necessary to transmute Mr. Irving's speech into English, or wondering where his limbs were going to carry him next.

Then an anonymous critic in *The Evening Transcript* writing of Irving's performance in *Hamlet* said:

He delivers long speeches in a curious monotone as to pitch; he cuts up sentences into disjointed bits with apparently little reference to the meaning, taking breath, as one would say of a singer, in most adventurous places. Yet, with these indubitably grave faults, he manages by some magic to get the full meaning out of almost every sentence, and the emphasis falls upon the right word; one finds little or nothing of that over-valuing adjectives and the smaller parts of speech at the expense of nouns and verbs. . . . With all his peculiarities of speech, the ear is never wounded by a common, cheap or vulgar inflexion. . . . Mr. Irving may have many ungainly idiosyncrasies of pose and gesture, yet, such is the innate dignity of the man, that we never find them ludicrous; never was a man more gracefully awkward.

That passage, apart from what it tells us about Irving, is valuable as an illustration of the second reason for believing in his greatness as an actor. There is so much difficulty in re-creating the splendours of art that when two talents fuse to accomplish it – as when a talented writer speaks of a talented actor – the result is convincing. It requires no particular ability to detect and condemn faults of taste and execution but it requires truth and skill to communicate what is remarkable in a performance. Irving's acting was written about by some of the great literary talents of his day, and, in spite of Henry James, there are passages that cannot be set aside. One may discard entirely the views of his henchmen and quote only from those who were regarded as critical of him, or those of that happily cynical nature which inspires later generations with confidence, and we can find more than enough to support the claim that Irving, like Kean, was worthy of his posthumous reputation. Bernard Shaw said of him:

Those who understood the art of the theatre and knew his limitations could challenge him on every point except one; and that was his eminence. Even to call him eminent belittles his achievement: he was pre-eminent. He was not pre-eminent in or for this, that or the other talent or faculty: his pre-eminence was

abstract and positive: a quality in itself and in himself so powerful that it carried him to Westminster Abbey.

And elsewhere:

He was utterly unlike anyone else: he could give importance
and a noble melancholy to any sort of drivel that was put into his
mouth; and it was this melancholy, bound up with an impish
humour, which forced the spectator to single him out as a leading
figure with an inevitability that I never saw again in any other
actor until it rose from Irving's grave in the person of a nameless
cinema actor who afterwards became famous as Charlie Chaplin.

William Archer said of Irving that he possessed in quite
abnormal measure that 'magnetic personality' whose power is
'irresistible and indefinable' and that when he walked on the
stage at his first entrance no special stage-management, no
reception, no reference to the play-bill was needed to assure
even the least initiated spectator that he was the most remarkable man on the stage. He thought there might be better stage
faces than Irving's but few more remarkable.

The high forehead, the marked overhanging but flexible eye-
brows, the dark eyes which can by turns be so penetrating, so
dreamy so sinister and so melancholy, the thin straight nose, the
narrow almost lipless sensitive mouth, the hollow cheeks and
marvellously mobile jaw, combine to form an incomparable
vehicle for the expression of a certain range of emotion.

One of the most illuminating comments was made by Ellen
Terry, who said that she admired Irving for what she termed a
'bizarrerie' in his acting which invited derision and mocking
imitation but which lifted his performance above common
realism. And Max Beerbohm seems to be describing something
of the same quality when he says: 'He had, in acting, a keen
sense of humour – of sardonic, grotesque, fantastic humour. He
had an incomparable power for eeriness – for stirring a dim
sense of mystery; and not less masterly was he in evoking a
sharp sense of horror.' And Beerbohm leaves us in no doubt of
Irving's quality in a passage in which he says that one of the
regrets of his life is that he did not see Irving play Hamlet.

I can imagine the gentleness (with a faint strain of cruelty), the
aloofness, the grace and force of intellect, in virtue of which that

performance must have been a very masterpiece of interpretation.
I can imagine, too, the mystery with which Irving must have
involved, rightly, the figure of Hamlet, making it loom through
the mist mightily, as a world-type, not as a mere individual –
making it loom as it loomed in the soul of Shakespeare himself –
not merely causing it to strut agreeably, littly, as in the average
production.

Irving carried the star system as far as it can be carried.
Gordon Craig says that he actually preferred plays that had no
real merit because when the playwright has done his work too
well the actor is not required to put out his full powers. It was
when the play was about to crumble that Irving was at his
most prodigious.

Today the theatre has been democratised and the economic
circumstances ensure that in the theatre our leading actors play
only to a small section of the public whose intellectual appreciation is the highest that has ever been known. The Victorian
theatre must not be judged by these standards. It was a theatre
of personality, of actors who were expected to fill the theatre
almost unaided by their colleagues, or by playwrights, or by
any great refinement of taste among their audiences. In an
actors' theatre audiences must be held by emotional force.

John Henry Brodribb was born in 1838 in a Somerset village
called Keinton Mandeville. He was the son of Samuel Brodribb,
himself a travelling salesman but the descendant of several
generations of farmers, and his wife Mary Behenna, a Cornish
girl and a devout Methodist. In 1842, when the child was four
years old, the times being exceedingly bad in Somerset, Samuel
and Mary Brodribb moved to Bristol to find more lucrative
employment; but Mary, who feared in their straitened circumstances to bring up her child in a town, sent him to Cornwall
to her sister, Sarah, married to Isaac Penberthy, in the confidence that there he would enjoy at least the benefits of simple
food and fresh air. Johnnie Brodribb lived with his aunt and
two cousins until he was ten years old, when, on the death of
Isaac Penberthy, his aunt could no longer afford to keep him
and he was returned to his parents. Mary Brodribb had sent
him away in a spirit of self-sacrifice and it seems to have
been accepted by all biographers that her decision was wise.

No-one writing about Irving seems ever to have related this separation from his parents at so early an age to his known characteristics as an actor.

In Cornwall the child, who was sweet-tempered and cheerful, gave cause for worry only by a tendency to play-act. At that time a company of actors travelled from village to village performing in a tent and although, if the young Brodribb visited these, it was in defiance of the Methodist rules of his upbringing, it seems to be established that before the age of ten he had announced his ambition to become an actor, could recite passage after passage from Shakespeare and practise the art of ventriloquism. He took revenge for the children of the whole village on an old woman who had persecuted them with threats of hell-fire by appearing at her bedside, wearing a mask, horns and a tail. However, shortly after his tenth birthday, he somewhat allayed anxiety by falling into an ecstasy during a service and professing his conversion to the religion of his fathers.

As a child John Brodribb suffered from a stammer. When he was returned to his parents, who by now were living in London, he attended the City Commercial School and he was lucky in that the headmaster, Dr Pinches, attached much importance to elocution and took this class himself. Here, for the first time, he was encouraged in his passion for recitation and he worked hard to eradicate his stammer. On one occasion at the end of prize-giving at this school, he was congratulated on his performance by an actor named William Creswick, who was at the time playing Hamlet at the Surrey Theatre, and, taking advantage of the fact of his gentleman's presence on so respectable an occasion, he managed to persuade his mother to allow him to be taken to the theatre. As a result, shortly before his twelfth birthday he went with his father to Sadler's Wells to see Phelps play Hamlet, and here he underwent a second conversion described by his biographer as 'as intense and heartfelt as the first'. Laurence Irving writes: 'The close succession of one emotional crisis upon the other may have imbued his self-dedication to the art of acting with the almost religious idealism which was to govern his attitude towards the principle and practice of his profession.'

In all these circumstances it is not surprising to find John Henry Brodribb, on leaving school at the age of thirteen, sitting on a clerk's stool by day but joining by night in the popular pastime of amateur acting and visiting with other stage-struck clerks a school of elocution run by a Mr Henry Thomas. Mr Thomas was an admirer and friend of Charles J. Matthews, a famous comedian of the time, and Laurence Irving suggests that by encouraging his pupils to adopt, when acting comedy, the jaunty, jerky stride successfully employed by Matthews, he was responsible for Irving's peculiar gait, later to be so much criticised.

Mary Brodribb could not compromise her own stern faith to meet her son's passionate longings because she fervently believed that to become a play-actor was to invite hell-fire. At this time she used to beg the friends her son brought home to do all in their power to dissuade him from going on the stage. She received little help from them but she did receive some backing for her views from an unexpected quarter. John Brodribb had made friends during the course of his many visits to Sadler's Wells with a leading actor in Phelps's company named William Hoskins, and for some time he used to go at eight o'clock every morning to Hoskins's house to receive private tuition in elocution and pantomime. When, in the course of time, Hoskins decided to leave Sadler's Wells and try his luck in Australia, he asked his pupil to accompany him. Brodribb hesitated to adopt so extreme a course, and Hoskins then offered, before leaving, to introduce him to the great Phelps himself. 'Sir,' Samuel Phelps said to him then, 'do not go on the stage; it is an ill-requited profession.'

Finding, however, that the young man could not be put off, he offered him two pounds a week to join his company. This Brodribb refused because he had already considered the matter and believed that he must go through the hard school of the provincial stock companies. Hoskins then gave him a letter of recommendation to a provincial manager named Davis, saying: 'You will go on the stage. When you want an engagement present that letter and you will get one.'

At this time actors were expected to find their own properties, and a young man wishing to go on the stage had somehow to provide himself with wigs, swords, buckles, lace, sham jewellery and so on. When John Brodibb received from an uncle a gift of £100, the moment he had awaited seemed to him to have arrived. He made a large investment in stage properties, including among them three swords – symbols of the romance of life that lay ahead. Then he spent some of his remaining capital in a trial of skill. In response to the great vogue for amateur acting the managers of some small theatres allowed amateurs to pay for the privilege of giving a single performance, the importance of the role being graded according to the size of the fee. For the sum of three guineas Brodribb played Romeo at the Soho Theatre. It was for this performance that he first took the name Irving, at this time signing himself J. H. B. Irving but, since for stage purposes he preferred the name Henry, he soon dropped John altogether.

When Hoskins's letter of recommendation to Davis produced the offer of an engagement in the stock company of the new Royal Lyceum theatre at Sunderland, Brodribb had, before becoming Irving, to break the news to his parents. At the age of eighteen he was again and this time permanently separated from his mother, who, having left him at the age of four in pursuit of what she believed to be her duty, now saw him depart without her approval or forgiveness, his dedication to his art being matched by her faith in her religion.

Henry Irving's time as a provincial actor in stock companies lasted for ten lean and terrible years. He learned at first hand why Phelps had said: 'It is an ill-requited profession,' and even why Kean had asked: 'Can you starve, cocky?' His life had none of the charmed ease of Bancroft's, who followed the same road at about the same time. Bancroft seems always to have had a large measure of control over a lesser talent, but Irving had to strive for a technical equipment adequate to carry the force of genius. Shaw says: 'When Nature intends anyone to be a highly cultivated artist, she generally forces them on by condemning them to fiendishness or loutishness until they fulfill her intention.' Irving was not a lout but he lacked style, polish and control over the means of expression.

Bancroft says of him, describing a chance meeting when he himself was already in management at the Prince of Wales's Theatre and Irving still a struggling provincial actor:

Irving was a born leader . . . and certainly in his later years would have graced, in manner and aspect, any position in life.

This personal attribute came to him gradually when, as it were, he recreated himself. Truth to tell, in the early part of his career he had none of it. In those distant days there was a strong smack of the country actor in his appearance and a suggestion of a type immortalised by Dickens in Mr. Lenville and Mr. Folair.

During his provincial years Irving became a changed personality. Gordon Craig, and following him Laurence Irving, make much of the metamorphosis of Brodribb into Irving, a pictorial and rather simplified concept, but one which for the ordinary reader adequately emphasises the great changes that occurred as the dedicated, intense youth with the slight impediment to his speech and a sweetness of nature that won him many friends became, over the course of his provincial years, the mysterious, magnetic, slightly bohemian, powerful and secret man who dominated the London theatre. The validity of the Brodribb–Irving dissociation is strengthened by the extent to which, as he built up the equipment through which he at last expressed himself, he also perfected the romantic portrait of the actor-manager.

As he steeled himself against poverty and near-starvation he had certain traumatic experiences. The first of these occurred in Sunderland soon after his first appearance on the professional stage. Having survived performances of *Richelieu*, *The Enchanted Lake* and *The Lady of Lyons*, in which he had only a line or two to speak, he dried up while playing the part of Cleomenes in *The Winter's Tale*, no words coming from his lips when he received his cue. He was forced to rush off the stage to the hisses of the audience. Laurence Irving believes that he did not dry up as a result of stage-fright but because momentarily he could not control the only half-conquered impediment to his speech. In any case he was lucky in that his manager stood by him and two old actors, Sam Johnson and Tom Mead, restored some of his confidence with firm and practical advice. It was then he made the promise later punctiliously kept: 'If ever I rise I shall not forget this.'

But his humiliation was, nevertheless, complete and when he got an offer of an engagement at Edinburgh, he gladly left the scene of his disaster.

In Edinburgh the stock company under the management of the Wyndhams had a high reputation and Irving stayed here

for two and a half years, during which time he played over
four hundred parts – making a name for himself, among other
things, as a low comedian. At the end of this time he received
from Augustus Harris Sr the offer of a London engagement
which, delighted, he accepted. Before leaving the Wyndhams he
performed the part of Claude Melnotte in *The Lady of Lyons* for
his benefit performance and then, as his grandson puts it,
packing in his hamper 'the scrappy components of four hundred
and twenty-eight characters', he left for London, in the
reasonable belief that his novitiate had come to an end.

Irving left Edinburgh a well-established juvenile lead, ready
for the London stage. By one of those unexplained and inconsequent acts which abound in the history of the theatre,
Augustus Harris gave him a part of half a dozen lines in a play
called *Ivy Hall*, which was an undistinguished failure, and
followed this by casting him as Osric to the Hamlet of a very
indifferent provincial actor who was advised by the London
press to return to the melodrama from whence he sprang.
Disappointed and humiliated, Irving asked and received his
release from his contract and arranged to return to the provincial stage. Before doing this he made what his biographer
has called 'a demonstration of force to cover his retreat'. In
those days public readings of plays or poetry at cheap prices
attracted large audiences from among those who would not
in the ordinary way enter the theatre. At the Crosby Hall in the
City of London Irving gave reading of *The Lady of Lyons* and a
second one of Sheridan Knowles' *Virginius*, and attracted
recognition of his unusual talent. The critics were in attendance
and were generally approving, the audience sobbed at the end
of *The Lady of Lyons* and one critic wrote of the 'finer and
indefinite something which proved incontestably and instantaneously that the fire of genius is present in the artist'.

Fortified by these opinions, Irving travelled to Dublin, little
knowing that there a trap was laid for him in which he was to
suffer an experience which, as much as any other single thing,
has been held accountable for his development. Henry Webb,
the manager of the Queen's Theatre, Dublin, had recently dismissed his juvenile lead, George Vincent, for insubordination.
Vincent recruited a gang of hooligans to revenge himself on his
manager and indirectly on his successor. Irving made his first

appearance in a role Vincent had never played and all passed smoothly, but two nights later his entrance on the stage was the signal for an outburst of savage and derisive yelling and whistling sufficient to bring the play to a standstill. For three weeks this was repeated every time Irving appeared in a part that had previously been played by Vincent.

On almost all the famous occasions in theatrical history that an actor has been given 'the bird' it has been because of a gang organised to protest on the part of someone else rather than the result of a spontaneous outburst of disapproval directed at himself. The fact that the booing and screaming are not inspired by the personality or art of the man who suffers them seems not to diminish the appalling shock that is received or the bitterness which such treatment inspires. In later life Irving held himself apart from audiences, treating them if not with contempt at least with indifference, and this has been regarded as a consequence not only of the years he had to wait for recognition of his talent but also of his experience in Dublin. Gordon Craig writing of this time says:

As later on in life he never accepted the applause he received, so we may suppose that he refused to accept this disapproval. How often have I and those who were in his theatre seen him standing while the applause rained down like a cataract, and he obviously there – bowing so *slightly* to show that he was not only there, but aware: yet *never* accepting the applause – enduring it.

However, Gordon Craig grew up in the shadow of Irving and his attitude to him is always solemn, sometimes idolatrous. There are suggestions that Irving possessed two qualities his biographers occasionally lack – a sense of proportion about himself and a sense of humour. His method of taking calls may have been in consequence of his early experiences; or he may have considered that this gravely aloof treatment of an audience he had previously raised to the heights of emotion was effective.

In 1865, the year Marie Wilton opened at the Prince of Wales's Theatre, Irving terminated an engagement at the Theatre Royal, Manchester, after falling out with the management on a matter of principle. He had now been nine years on the stage and he was probably near the height of his powers.

Yet he was penniless, for weeks at a time unemployed and in debt to his friends. When he found employment it was often with wretched companies and for short periods. He drifted from Manchester to Edinburgh and back, to Bury, from there to Oxford, to Birmingham and from there to Liverpool, where he was left stranded when his company was disbanded, and was forced to travel to the Isle of Man for a three-night engagement with an amateur company. Often nearly starving, his frustration was complete.

Then one day in the summer of 1866 he called at the stage-door of the Prince of Wales's Theatre in Liverpool hoping to hear of work. As he turned away empty-handed, forlorn and despairing, the stage-door-keeper ran after him with a letter he had overlooked. It was from Dion Boucicault[3] and it offered Irving a part in a new play to be produced in Manchester. His long and hard apprenticeship was over.

As Rawdon Scudamore, an unscrupulous villain in *The Two Lives of Mary Leigh*, Irving made the play such an overwhelming success in Manchester that, in spite of a far-fetched plot and poor dialogue, offers were made for it by two London managements.[4] Boucicault closed with Miss Herbert at the St James's Theatre, making a condition, immediately accepted, that Irving should play Rawdon Scudamore.

There is often a particular moment in the lives of great singers and actors when – through a peculiar identification with some particular part or through sympathetic and masterly direction – they miraculously raise their performance on to a new plane. It is doubtful if anything of this sort happened to Irving. He knew in advance that in Rawdon Scudamore he had a part in which he could force recognition of his technical skill and exceptional talent as he could have done at any time in the previous year or so given an opportunity. In any case, although he had still to wait four years before his performance in *The Bells* would carry him to the head of his profession, his reputation and his livelihood were from this time no longer in doubt, and among the distinguished audience who witnessed

<hr/>

[3] Boucicault, Dionysius Lardner, 1822–90. Actor and dramatist. His plays include *The Corsican Brothers*, *Louis XI*, *The Shaughraun* and *The Colleen Bawn*. It is possible that he was the first playwright to receive a royalty. His son Dionsysius (Dot) Boucicault, 1859–1929, was also an actor and dramatist.

[4] In London the title was changed to *Hunted Down*.

his first night in London, there were those who already
recognised the full extent of his genius.

During the next four years he played sometimes in London,
sometimes on tour, once with Sothern in *Our American Cousin*
in Paris, when he saw for the first time the technical accomplishment of the actors at the Comédie Française. In 1868 he was
engaged by Alfred Wigan to play at the Queen's Theatre in a
company which included a young actress named Ellen Terry.
They played the leading parts in a new play by Charles Reade
which was a failure, a stop-gap revival of *Still Waters Run
Deep*, and in *Katherine and Petruchio*, Garrick's version of *The
Taming of the Shrew*. Irving found little to admire in Ellen
Terry – at that time between her marriage with G. F. Watts
and her life with Edward Godwin – who seemed to him
frivolous. She in return found him frightening in his fierce
application and earnestness of purpose. On Friday nights,
always in a hurry to leave the theatre, she accepted the place
he politely offered her in the queue waiting for salaries. Years
later, talking to Sir Mortimer Menpes, she was to say: 'How
conceited he was in those days. Why, he could hardly speak at
that time for conceit. But in later years what a difference.'

In 1870 Irving was playing at the Vaudeville Theatre when
he received an invitation to meet James Albery. Albery had
written a new play *Two Roses* and he had merely sketched in
the chief part of Digby Grant in the hope that Irving would
play it and help at rehearsal to develop it. *Two Roses*, Albery's
only entirely successful play, was in the comedy style of T. W.
Robertson, and the part of Digby Grant (who, believing himself
to have inherited a title and fortune, snubs his former friends
to find his claim rejected in favour of one of them) was a part
which Irving again recognised as completely suitable for him
and one in which he could this time demonstrate his talent for
light comedy.

The play was enormously successful and Digby Grant
entered the repertory of classical Victorian parts. The first run
of the piece was memorable for an event which opened the last
lap of Irving's long journey to eminence. On the two hundred
and ninety-first night of the run of the piece he took his benefit
and, at the close of the comedy, appearing in evening dress, he
announced that he would recite Hood's poem *The Dream of*

Eugene Aram. Then for the first time, without scenery or properties, he revealed to a London audience the intensity, the almost hypnotic magnetism and the power to convey terror and guilt which in a few years' time would make him the greatest drawing power in the theatre of his day.

In the audience witnessing the performance and the ovation sat Hezekiah Bateman, an American theatre manager, who, having at different times had three daughters on the stage, had now taken a lease of the Lyceum Theatre, where he proposed to launch his fourth daughter, Isabel. He immediately offered Irving an engagement at the Lyceum in the following autumn.

Bateman, like so many managers before him, failed at first to make any use of Irving. His ambitions were centred on his daughter and, having engaged Irving because he had witnessed his great powers as a tragedian, he cast him in support of Isabel Bateman, first as a lovesick peasant in an adaptation from the French and secondly as Alfred Jingle in a version by Albery of *The Pickwick Papers.* When both these plays failed – in spite of Irving's success as Alfred Jingle – Irving reminded Bateman of his promise to put on a play called *The Bells,* an adaptation from a French play, *Le Juif Polonais,* by Erckmann and Chatrian.

The Bells is part of the history of the theatre. It is not of a quality to remain in the repertory of acted plays but it aroused a fervour of enthusiasm in its time which ensured it a place in the annals of dramatic events. For the rest of Irving's life it would be so often performed that it is hardly possible to recall his name without recalling *The Bells.* Writing of later performances Gordon Craig says: 'At his entrance the applause was so instantaneous that it became part of the play. . . . In *The Bells,* the hurricane of applause at Irving's entrance was no interruption . . . it was something that can only be described as part and parcel of the whole, as right as rain. It was a torrent while it lasted. Power responded to power.'

The story of the play is of a respected burgomaster who fifteen years before, the poverty-stricken and despairing father of a starving family, had on a foul night given shelter to a Polish Jew and, on a sudden impulse after his guest's departure, had taken a short cut to a point on his route and there murdered him for the money he carried. Now, unsuspected and respected,

Sir Squire and Lady Bancroft

1 Marie Wilton (Bancroft) as
Pippo in *The Maid and the Magpie*,
the burlesque by J. J. Byron in
which Charles Dickens so much
admired her. Strand Theatre, 1858.

2 Marie Bancroft as Polly Eccles
and John Hare as Sam Gerridge
in *Caste* by T. W. Robertson, the
play in which the use of real
china inspired the term 'cup-and-
saucer comedy'. Prince of Wales's
Theatre, 1867.

3 Squire Bancroft in the early nineties.

4 *Diplomacy*. John Hare's production at the Garrick Theatre in 1893 when the Bancrofts returned to the stage to play in it. From left to right: standing, Arthur Cecil, Lady Monckton, Sir Squire Bancroft, John Hare, Johnston Forbes-Robertson. Sitting: Olga Nethersole, Gilbert Hare, Lady Bancroft, Kate Rorke.

5   Irving as Matthias in *The Bells*,
Act 2. Counting out the money
for his daughter's dowry, Matthias
recognises one of the coins that
had belonged to the Polish Jew.
Lyceum Theatre, 1871.

6   Cartoon of Irving by Max
Beerbohm in the possession of the
Garrick Club.

7   Irving as the Vicar and Ellen Terry as Olivia in the Lyceum production of *Olivia*, 1885. Between 1880 and 1890 Irving refused to allow any photographs to be taken of himself other than portrait photographs and a few with Ellen Terry in *Olivia*. This is the only one of the two together and is described as 'the only authorized photograph' of Irving as the Vicar and Ellen Terry as Olivia.

8   Ellen Terry in the costume designed by E. W. Godwin for *The Cup* by Alfred Tennyson. Lyceum Theatre, 1881.

Sir Johnston Forbes-Robertson

10, 11, 12 Three Hamlets. *below* At the Lyceum in 1897, *opposite top* his last at his farewell production at Drury Lane in 1913; he wore a similar costume for both productions. *opposite bottom* The film made from this production by Cecil Hepworth, also in 1913. The castle for the ghost scene was built at Lulworth Cove at a cost, then considered very high, of £400.

13 *Caesar and Cleopatra*. Forbes-Robertson as Caesar, the role originally written for him by Bernard Shaw, with his wife Gertrude Elliot in the first London production at the Savoy Theatre in 1907.

14 *The Passing of the Third Floor Back*, by Jerome K. Jerome. Left to right: Agnes Thomas as Mrs Sharpe, Forbes-Robertson as the Third Floor Back and Gertrude Elliot as Stasia. St James's Theatre, 1908.

the burgomaster is inwardly haunted by the sound of the bells on his victim's sledge. In the last act of the play, virtually a monologue, the burgomaster dreams of a trial and dies from self-induced terror – a scene which was perfectly conceived for this actor in whom intensity and guilt seemed natural characteristics.

As an actor-producer Irving was pre-eminent and with *The Bells* he for the first time rehearsed the production so that everything contributed to his own performance. His contemporaries speak again and again of his almost mesmeric powers and thus raise again and again the question whether he was a great actor or merely a great personality. It is a matter of considerable interest, therefore, that on its first night *The Bells* was followed by *Pickwick*, and Irving showed his versatility by playing Matthias and Alfred Jingle on the same evening.

Irving owed Bateman his opportunity to impress his genius on a London audience. He owed to him, too, his first meeting with William Gorman Wills. Wills was an Irishman, a poet and painter, who was introduced to Bateman by Herman Vezin[5] for whom he had written two plays, neither of them very successful. Bateman, nevertheless, took to Wills and commissioned him to write an adaptation of *Medea* for his eldest daughter, Kate, and at his supper table his two protégés met. There began then a partnership which caused Shaw later to describe Wills as the resident playwright at the Lyceum. During the run of *The Bells* Wills prepared a play entitled *Charles I*, a romantic domestic tragedy which owed little to history and much to Irving's noble appearance and his portrayal of the scene in which the King is betrayed by the Earl of Moray and that in which he says farewell to his Queen – played by Isabel Bateman – and his children. Following this Wills made a play of the poem *Eugene Aram*, with which Irving had first startled London. In both these plays Irving increased his hold on the public, and in *Eugene Aram* he bowled out Clement Scott who ended a rapturous notice with the words: 'The task of the play is herculean for any actor; and once more Mr Irving has triumphed.'

Then in *Richelieu*, which Lytton wrote for Macready, Irving

[5] Vezin, Herman, 1829–1910. English actor born in USA but came to England 1850. Played Macbeth, Othello and Iago. Acted with both Irving and Tree.

C

began his challenge to the old masters of his art, on this occasion not entirely successfully, as for the first time the critics were divided in their opinions. Over the years, however, *Richelieu* came to be regarded as one of his greatest parts. In 1879 Jules Claretie – a future administrator of the Comédie Française, with whose company Henry James believed nothing in London could be compared – wrote of him: '*Richelieu* was the first play in which I saw Mr Irving in London. Here he is superb. His performance amounts to a resurrection. . . . And what an artist the tragedian is.'

After *Richelieu* he played Hamlet. It had almost invariably been the case that, when a great new actor has appeared to entrapture theatregoers, much of the excitement and astonishment has been because of the *naturalness* of his acting. Whether it was little Garrick who came 'bounding on to the stage', or Macklin who inspired Pope to the couplet 'This is the Jew that Shakespeare drew', or Kean wearing a plain black wig and making his first appearance as Shylock, they all captured their audiences by a convincing representation of the character they played. As the influence of the great actor died, the less talented body of the profession returned to conventional declamation and gesticulation, interpretations of an essentially dramatic kind. This on the whole is easier and is an art that can be learned, and although there have been very good actors who cultivated a beautiful voice and practised a formal declamatory style – as for instance, the Kembles – they have always had to give way to the genius of an actor who could convince an audience that he *was* the character he played.[6]

Irving stood against the 'new school', represented by Shaw and Ibsen and developed at the Court Theatre by Granville Barker, and today he is thought of as a romantic actor of the old school; but when he first played Hamlet he departed from tradition and risked disaster by playing him as a human being. Laurence Irving says:

Irving's unusual appearance gave the audience their first shock of bewilderment. Gone were Hamlet's funereal plumes and trappings of woe and the air of pompous melancholy. Irving was, indeed, dressed in black, relieved only by the gold chain which he

[6] Henry James was much influenced by Fanny Kemble, in whose company he used to visit the theatre, but according to Laurence Irving when acting she spoke of 'Ham-a-lette'.

wore round his neck, and the cold sparkle of his silver sword hilt
and sword belt. But his loose fitting tunic, deeply skirted and
heavily collared with beaver, was such as a young man of action
might have ordered to his own design. . . . His bearing and manner
were those of a young aristocrat in whom grace and self-assurance
were modestly combined. There was nothing to distract the
attention from the pale face framed in his own raven curls; there
was little in the expression of his features to deflect the message
of the troubled eyes in whose gaze there lurked the hint of sorrow,
dejection and suspicion.

For the whole of the first act the success of Irving's Hamlet
hung in the balance. Clement Scott writing the next day said:

So subtle is the actor's art, so intense is his application, and so
daring his disregard of conventionality, that the first act ends with
comparative disappointment. Those who have seen other Hamlets
are aghast. Mr. Irving is missing his points, he is neglecting his
opportunities . . . but over all, disputants or enthusiasts, has already
been thrown an indescribable spell. None can explain it; but all are
now spellbound. The Hamlet is 'thinking aloud', as Hazlitt wished.
He is as much of the gentleman and scholar as possible and 'as
little of the actor'.

Hamlet ran for two hundred nights at the Lyceum – a run
equalled by the Bancrofts with modern comedies but never
before achieved with Shakespeare. Irving's position at the head
of his profession was from now on undisputed.

Hamlet was produced at the Lyceum in October 1874. Four
months later Bateman died and Mrs Bateman took over the
management. During the next two years under her management Irving appeared as Macbeth and later as Othello. Neither
of these parts did much for his reputation, although the production of Macbeth ran for eighty nights and that of Othello for
forty-nine – at that time a record. In both parts Irving gave an
unconventional interpretation – playing Macbeth as a craven
who shrinks from the crimes to which his murderous ambition
has driven him, and Othello with a bronze complexion and in
the clothes and armour, designed by Sir John Tenniel, of a serving Venetian general instead of with the dark complexion and
in the turbans of tradition. In both parts Irving's powers at this
time were inadequate to his conception and: 'For nature,' one
critic wrote, 'we got exaggeration; for elocution, scolding; for

affection, melancholy; and for deportment, tricks.' In spite of which, Henry James, who could never reconcile himself to the idea that Irving was a great tragic actor and who wrote of his performance of Macbeth in the same tone of baffled disbelief he invariably used when speaking of him, had on this occasion one or two good things to say.

He has been much criticized for his conception of his part – for making Macbeth so spiritless a plotter before his crime, and so arrant a coward afterward. But in the text, as he seeks to emphasize it, there is fair warrant for the line he follows. Mr. Irving has great skill in the representation of terror, and it is quite open to him to have thrown into relief this side of the part. His best moment is his rendering of the scene with the bloody daggers – though it must be confessed that this stupendous scene always does much toward acting itself. Mr. Irving, however, is here altogether admirable, and his representation of a nature trembling and quaking to its inner-most spiritual recesses really excites the imagination. Only a trifle less powerful is his scene with Banquo's ghost at the feast, and the movement with which, exhausted with vain bravado, he muffles his head in his mantle and collapses beside the throne.

The season of 1876, although it ended with a successful revival of *Hamlet*, marked a decline in the fortunes of the Lyceum and of Henry Irving. All his life Irving took successful productions on tour in the provinces and thereby built up a nation-wide audience who would restore his fortunes and his confidence when London was adverse. In the autumn of this year he took out the production of *Hamlet*, *Charles I* and *The Bells*. 'My success,' he wrote to a friend, 'has been far beyond my expectation – surprising. But *Hamlet* is *the* thing and swamps all else – which makes my work very hard.' Of the seventy-eight performances which the tour entailed, fifty-six were of *Hamlet*.

This tour was important not merely for its phenomenal success but because in Dublin Irving met Bram Stoker. Stoker was a civil servant who also wrote dramatic criticism for the *Dublin Mail*. He impressed Irving originally by the understanding he showed in his articles and indelibly by bursting into hysterics after a private recital of *Eugene Aram*. Bram Stoker became Irving's business and acting manager, served him all his life and after his death wrote his biography. During this tour Irving also engaged H. J. Loveday as stage manager for the Lyceum. Loveday's father had been musical director at Drury Lane when Edmund Kean was acting there, and both he and his wife are described by Laurence Irving as 'trusted and perceptive witnesses' who could describe to Irving Kean's performances 'with every nuance of gesture and inflection'. Thus it is possible that in Sir Laurence Olivier's Richard we saw something of Edmund Kean.

Richard III was produced at the Lyceum Theatre on 29 January 1877. Irving, very conscious of the partial failure of *Macbeth* and *Othello*, had given great thought to the production. Since 1700, when Colley Cibber[7] re-wrote Shakespeare's play, all Irving's predecessors from Garrick to Macready had used his version. Irving's *Richard III* is memorable not merely because the part was so admirably suited to his talents but also because for the first time in nearly two hundred years he restored Shakespeare's Richard to the stage.

By the end of the evening Irving had won back his position as the greatest living actor of Shakespeare, and it was now that the esteem in which he was hereafter to be held by the members of his own profession began to be demonstrated. After the performance he was presented with a sword which Edmund Kean had used as Richard and with David Garrick's ring in which was mounted a miniature of Shakespeare.

In 1878 Irving wrote to Mrs Bateman asking her permission to engage a leading lady of his own choice who would give him stronger support than Isabel Bateman was able to do and who would bring with her a personal following. Mrs Bateman, who seems to have been aware that her leading man had over the last few years developed a strength which must finally burst the bonds of their business relationship, replied that she could not for Isabel's sake accept his suggestion but offered to allow him to take the Lyceum Theatre off her hands. By August of that year she announced the transfer of the lease of the Lyceum to Irving and her own intention to move with Isabel to Sadler's Wells. Thus by her generosity she solved easily a situation that would have had to be solved in some way; but

[7] Cibber, Colley, 1671–1757. Actor, playwright and theatre manager. Part of the 'Triumvirate' that managed Drury Lane. He re-wrote *Richard III* interpolating scenes from *Henry V* and *Henry VI: Part III*, freely embellishing the text.

Irving felt always a little uneasy towards the Batemans until late in life Isabel wrote to him expressly forgiving him for anything there might have been to forgive.

Before opening at the Lyceum as manager he was committed to a provincial tour. He paid one visit to the theatre before he left London to see Ellen Terry at the Court. Then he invited her to become his leading lady when he returned.

In 1863, while playing in Manchester, Irving, still a poor and unknown provincial actor, had met and fallen in love with a young actress named Nellie Moore. Nellie Moore, who is described as having a round and intelligent face, wide-set eyes, a fair complexion and a mass of golden hair, was very talented and already successful, and had come to play in Manchester between two London engagements. Too poor and as yet occupying too humble a position in her own profession to think of proposing marriage to her, Irving nevertheless became her constant companion while she remained in Manchester and wrote to her constantly when she returned to London. Then in 1866, when he achieved success in London in the part of Rawdon Scudamore, he resumed his relationship with her on more equal terms.

At this time in his life Irving began, because of his great success, to be asked about in London society. One evening he was on his way to a party given by Clement Scott, the dramatic critic of the *Daily Telegraph*, when there occurred one of those strange long shots, which, more credible in the smaller society of that day, make one wonder whether the coincidences of Victorian novels are really so improbable as they seem. When Irving arrived at what he believed to be his destination, he entered the wrong house. As the maid was explaining to him his error the daughter of the house, Miss Florence O'Callaghan, came into the hall bound, like himself, for Clement Scott's party. Miss O'Callaghan was an ardent playgoer; she immediately recognised Irving and during the evening became infatuated with him. From now on she made it her business to keep in touch with him, although he, still in love with Nellie Moore, was not seriously responsive.

There came a time, however, when his relationship with Nellie Moore was, for reasons that are not known, broken.

Laurence Irving suggests that some imagined slight may have come between them but it seems possible that, in spite of the fact that they loved each other, the difference between them was not imagined but inevitable to two proud and sensitive natures, ambitious in the same profession. In any case, whatever the reason of their parting, the fact of it was soon known to Miss O'Callaghan, who now made more open and more successful advances to Irving. He, no doubt sore at losing Nellie Moore, was in a mood to respond and the fact that her parents were initially against the attachment seems only to have strengthened it. From the beginning, however, the characters and the lives of these young people made them unsuited to each other. During Irving's engagement with Alfred Wigan at the Queen's Theatre, Nellie Moore joined the company, provoking a letter from Florence to Irving expressing anxiety at this renewed association and criticism of the actress. Irving's reply is notable both as an example of the strength and nobility which are often attributed to him and for the asperity with which he treated a rather natural jealousy.

I received both letters today. Although somewhat prepared for the contents of the first, I was, perhaps, a little astonished. It is painful to murmur any fault of those whom we regard and to conceal the wherefore. Say of her to me, Flo, what you will – I willingly accept it, but sayings or opinions of others keep back – especially expressions of condescension. These I cannot endure. They tingle through my veins and cause my blood to circulate at a rate to a phlegmatic man – objectionable.
The end all is that our position is as before. I will do all I can to trust in you. . . .

Then in 1869 Nellie Moore died. While leaving the house in which she died Irving was met by a friend, Miss Friswell, who attempted to sympathise with him. He replied: 'It is not always a misfortune to die young.' Laurence Irving writes:

His remark was not a careless one; death, he suspected, had spared Nellie Moore much unhappiness. Before she died he had discovered that a supposed friend had come between them and, although he had no conclusive evidence, he had good cause to believe she had suffered grave injury at his hands.
Later, in cold anger, he confronted this man and made it clear to him that although evidence of his guilt had been buried with his

victim, suspicion would rest upon him as long as his accuser lived.
Toole, fearful for Irving's self-control, was near at hand and never
forgot the faces of the two men when they came from the room
in which they had faced one another alone. The wound in
Brodribb's heart never healed; the armour of Irving was tempered
further by this cold shock of personal tragedy.

This is a curious passage, written in terms so like those of
Irving's own melodramas that one cannot help suspecting that
it was inspired by the account of some 'henchman'. It seems
beyond doubt that we are meant to understand from 'a grave
injury . . . buried with her' that Nellie Moore died of a pregnancy, or, since death from an early pregnancy is unusual, from
an abortion, but, as even the name of this actress is now
unknown to us except in this connection, there seems no reason
not to say so. In the same way there is a lack of conviction in
this talk of 'cold anger' and 'cold shock', which is of a piece
with the further information that when Irving died a photograph of Nellie Moore was found in his pocket book pasted to
the back of one of himself.

Irving was undoubtedly a normal heterosexual male and,
although the facts are wrapped in mystery, there seem to have
been only short periods of his life when he had no attachment
to any woman. Nevertheless, he was a man with a vocation
and only one true love – the stage. Shaw said that 'Irving
would not have left the stage for a night to spend it with
Helen of Troy' and Gordon Craig wrote: 'So devoted was Irving
to our stage, that he really was innocently selfish. My mother
often used to say, with a lovely twinkle in her eyes, "Yes, yes –
were I to be run over by a steamroller tomorrow, Henry would
be deeply grieved: would say quietly 'What a pity!' and would
add, after two moments' reflection: 'Who is there – er – to go
on for her tonight?' " '

Men whose lives are dedicated to their profession often find
a woman who is prepared to devote herself entirely to them.
Irving failed to find anyone of this kind until possibly when
late in life he met Mrs Aria. Before that he was driven to leave
the women who loved him, including his mother, in circumstances connected with his profession. He lived in a romantic
age and had an unusually romantic temperament. It is not
surprising that it pleased him to believe that the love of his

life died young – even though she died separated from him and pregnant by another man – but it is curious that the notion should be so unquestionably accepted by other people.

When Florence O'Callaghan's parents withdrew their opposition, she and Irving were married. From the first there seemed little chance of happiness. Florence was vain, bad-tempered, snobbish and unloving. A few days before their marriage Irving wrote to her:

I hope my dearest with all my soul that when the day is past an end will be put to all reproaches from you or misunderstandings by me.

On Sunday night your manner I thought was unsurmountably cold. It was but thought I hope. Nothing I think could so soon dull affection in man or woman as indifference.

You at first lavished on me such love that if I became spoiled – the fault is all your own. But you still love me as you did – don't you my darling? *Answer this.*

Irving was married to Florence O'Callaghan in July 1869. By 1870 she was pregnant and he studying the part of Digby Grant in *Two Roses*. All his life he enjoyed the company of actors and one of the pleasures he had hoped for in a home of his own was to bring them back to supper after the evening's work. His wife could already not disguise her dislike of his friends and of these supper parties, and thus early in his married life the atmosphere of nagging disapproval in his home drove him to hire a cheap lodging in which to study his part in peace. Irving was an affectionate and proud father and the birth of his first child brought the couple together again. But not for long. It is not too much to say that Florence seems almost to have hated him. When he was at home she nagged him, when he was on tour she wrote reproving him for spending money on a reasonably comfortable room. Later in 1870 they parted but early in the following year Florence came to Irving and begged him to return to her. He at once agreed to her request and soon after wrote to her: 'At once disabuse your mind, dear, of any desire of mine to delay our union. I am more than anxious to be with you and our child.'

After their reunion Florence conceived their second child and Irving joined Bateman at the Lyceum. In the autumn of the following year he appeared in *The Bells*.

When Kean made his first success in *The Merchant of Venice* he spoke to no one at the theatre but went straight home to his wife. 'Mary,' he is supposed to have said to her, 'Charles shall go to Eton and you shall ride in your carriage and pair.' After the enormous success of *The Bells* and following a supper party at which Irving received the ecstatic praise and congratulations of everyone around him – a scene of excitement and jubilation from which his wife held curiously aloof – he drove home with her in a brougham. As they were crossing Hyde Park Corner he laid his hand on her arm and said: 'Well my dear, we too shall soon have our carriage and pair.' This innocent and modest reference to his own success was too much for his wife's jealous hostility. 'Are you going on making a fool of yourself like this all your life?' she asked.

Irving stopped the driver of the brougham, got down and, in one of the most dramatic partings in history, walked away. He never returned to his wife and he never spoke to her again. He left with her his two sons, one as yet unborn.

Ellen Terry, like Marie Wilton and Madge Robertson, was born to a theatre family and her parents, like the Robertsons, could find a juvenile stock company from among their offspring. Ellen made her first appearance at the age of nine in Charles Kean's company, playing the child Mamillius in *The Winter's Tale*. From this time onwards she lived the hard life of the professional actor, rehearsing by day and playing by night, dropping to sleep in the Green Room when she was released from the stage. She was taught her professional technique by Mrs Kean, of whom she later wrote: 'No one ever had a sharper tongue or a kinder heart than Mrs Kean. Beginning with her I have always loved women with a somewhat hard manner. I have never believed in their hardness, and have proved them tender and generous to the extreme.'

Mrs Kean's heart may have been particularly soft towards this graceful child, who could walk naturally with a blanket pinned round her waist and trailing several inches on the ground. The critic Dutton Cook said of Kate and Ellen Terry that their talents went far beyond the usual charm of well-trained child players. 'A peculiar dramatic sensitiveness and susceptibility characterized the sisters Terry; their nervous organization, their

mental impressibility and vivaciousness not less than their
personal charms and attractions, may be said to have ordained
and determined their success upon the stage.'

In 1862, when Ellen Terry was fifteen, these two impressionable and talented girls were sent to visit the painter, G. F.
Watts, Kate to sit for him and Ellen to chaperone her while she
did so. Watts was weak, indolent, idealistic, melancholic and
hypochondriacal and he was dominated all his life by a series
of patronesses. Yet in addition to his artistic talents he must
have had immense charm because, until very late in his life
when he married a woman much younger than himself, he was
passed from the family of one woman prepared to devote herself to his interests to that of another. At this time he was living
at Little Holland House in London with Mr and Mrs Thoby
Prinsep.

The two girls were sent to him by the playwright, Tom
Taylor, because Watts had seen Kate on the stage and had
wished to paint her. At Little Holland House Ellen saw spacious
rooms and beautiful things for the first time in her life, and
she fell in love with it, with Watts's paintings and a little with
Watts himself. Watts at this time had the idea that he needed a
wife and he believed himself in love with Ellen. One day he
kissed her. Years later she wrote to Shaw: 'I told no one for a
fortnight, but when I was alone with Mother one day she looked
so pretty and sad and kind, I told her – what do you think I
told the poor darling? I told her I *must* be married to him *now*
because I was going to have a baby ! ! ! ! *and she* believed me.
Oh, I tell you I thought I knew everything then, but I was
nearly 16 years old then – and I was *sure* that kiss meant giving
me a baby.'

Mrs Prinsep was prepared to do anything to meet the artistic
needs of the 'Signor', as Watts was known to this household
and she is believed to have thought that, if Watts wished to
marry, this unformed young girl would make a suitably malle-
able wife. So before Ellen was seventeen, she left the stage to
marry Watts, who was then forty-seven.

Ellen Terry spent much of her married life in Watts's studio,
where she posed continuously. He afterwards destroyed many
of the sketches he made of her but among the portraits that
can be seen today in public galleries are 'Ellen Terry' in the

National Portrait Gallery and 'Ophelia' in the Watts Gallery, while 'Choosing' and 'The Sisters' are in private collections. This was generally a very productive period of Watts's life and if, as is seldom questioned, this was the only consummation of the marriage, it is also true that her association with Watts permanently benefited Ellen Terry. Graham Robertson says of her: 'Her charm held everyone, but I think pre-eminently those who loved pictures. She was *par excellence* the Painter's Actress and appealed to the eye before the ear; her gesture and pose were eloquence itself.' Mrs Prinsep, however, was not well satisfied. She found the high-spirited and talented girl infinitely less manageable than she had hoped and she persuaded Watts that his young wife was a disruptive influence in his life. Then Ellen committed an indiscretion which gave Mrs Prinsep her opportunity, and to her indignation and shame she was sent home to her parents. Five weeks later a deed of separation was signed in which the cause of separation was set down as 'incompatibility of temper' and Watts agreed to pay his wife £300 a year 'so long as she shall lead a chaste life'.

Ellen was completely bewildered and very unhappy. During her married life she had had, she later asserted, 'not one single pang of regret for the theatre'. 'I wondered at the new life and worshipped it because of its beauty,' she said, while the marriage, 'was in many ways very happy indeed'. I was miserable, indignant, unable to understand that there could be any justice in what had happened.'

Ellen did not need to work because she had £6 a week from Watts, but after a while she was 'practically *driven*' back to the stage by her parents and by Tom Taylor. It was during this period that she appeared in *Katherine and Petruchio*, Garrick's shortened version of *The Taming of the Shrew*, opposite a serious young actor called Henry Irving.

Then in the spring of 1868 she left the stage for the second time without word or warning to her family, and disappeared into the country to set up house with the architect E. W. Godwin. Ellen Terry had two children by Godwin who later became known to the world as Edith Craig and Edward Gordon Craig. She lived with him for six years at Harpenden and she loved him very much. At first their love was a great happiness to both but they were short of money and Godwin had to work in London. There was no telephone and, as time went on and he became busy, he had no means of letting her know whether or not he was coming home. There are sad tales of Ellen's harnessing the pony and driving to the station at night, only to drive home again alone; and others, almost equally sad, of how when he did come he discovered that his talented, beautiful but unpractical love had failed to provide any food for his supper. Above all, they had too little money and in the end the bailiffs tramped up the garden path. Then there occurred the famous meeting with Charles Reade.

Charles Reade, the novelist, was also the author of a number of plays, among the most famous of which were *The Courier of Lyons*, revived by Irving as *The Lyons Mail*, *It's Never Too Late to Mend* and, in collaboration with Tom Taylor, the Peg Woffington play, *Masks and Faces*. Both he and Tom Taylor were devoted to the Terry sisters, whom they had known as children, Tom Taylor's favourite being perhaps Kate, while Charles Reade adored Ellen.

In the winter of 1873–4 Charles Reade, in full pink, went out hunting in the Harpenden area. Jumping a hedge into a lane, he came across a young woman struggling with a pony trap, the wheel of which had come off. He went up to her to offer assistance and recognised Ellen Terry.

'Good God,' he cried, 'it's Nelly. Where have you been all these years?'

When she said she had been having a very happy time, he replied: 'Well, you've had it long enough,' and commanded her to come back to the stage in a play called *The Wandering Heir* which he was about to put on. Ellen, remembering the children and the bailiffs, replied that she would do so for £40 a week, and, in the words of Roger Manvell, 'England's greatest actress since Sarah Siddons returned to the stage, very unwillingly, and through a chance meeting with an old friend in a country lane'.

Charles Reade, who was responsible for teaching her a great deal at this time, has left a famous description of her. 'Ellen Terry is an enigma. Her eyes are pale, her nose rather long, her mouth nothing particular. Complexion a delicate brick-dust, her hair rather like tow. Yet somehow she is *beautiful*. Her expression *kills* any pretty face you see beside her. Her figure is lean and boney; her hand masculine in size and form. Yet she is a pattern of fawn-like grace. Whether in movement or repose, grace pervades the hussy.' He also said of her: 'A young lady highly gifted with what Voltaire calls *le grand art de plaire*.'

When Ellen Terry first came back to London Godwin took and furnished for her a house in Taviton Street. Godwin was interested in theatre design and had lately written a series of articles entitled 'The Architecture and Costume of Shakespeare's Plays'. At Taviton Street he covered the floor of the drawing room with straw-coloured matting and hung cretonne with a Japanese pattern in delicate grey-blue on the white walls. The furniture was of wickerwork and in the centre of the room he placed a full-sized caste of the Venus de Milo. Presently, however, the bailiffs appeared again, so that on the historic occasion when Mrs Bancroft called on Ellen Terry, apart from the young actress herself, she found nothing in the room but the Venus de Milo. Looking at this, she put her hand to her eyes in her best farcical manner and murmured 'Dear me!' Then she asked Ellen Terry if she would come to the Prince of Wales's Theatre to play Portia in *The Merchant of Venice*. She added that Mr Godwin would be asked to take over the archaeological supervision of the production design.

In spite of the failure of *The Merchant of Venice*, Squire Bancroft claimed that Ellen Terry's performance was the foundation stone of her brilliant career. Writing about it herself, she said:

I had had some success in other parts, and had tasted the delights of knowing that audiences liked me, and had liked them back again. But never until I appeared as Portia at the Prince of Wales's had I experienced that awe-struck feeling which comes, I suppose, to no actress more than once in a lifetime – the feeling of the conqueror. In homely parlance I knew that I had 'got them' at the moment when I spoke the speech beginning, 'You see me, Lord Bassanio, where I stand.'

After this she appeared for the Bancrofts in Lytton's comedy *Money*, and, for one night only, as Pauline in *The Lady of Lyons*; she played a supporting role to Mrs Bancroft in Reade and Taylor's *Masks and Faces*, and finally Blanche Haye in Robertson's comedy *Ours*. It is said that by now her success was not altogether to the taste of Mrs Bancroft, and indeed it would have been very remarkable if it had been. In the autumn of the year 1876, she went to the Court Theatre under the management of John Hare.

He commissioned W. G. Wills (Irving's resident playwright) to adapt *The Vicar of Wakefield* for the stage and, re-named *Olivia*, this play became a valuable property for Ellen Terry for almost as long as she remained on the stage. At the time of its first performance it caused a fashion, Olivia hats and kerchiefs and Ellen Terry photographs being on sale everywhere.

By now Godwin had left her and in January 1876 he married his student, Beatrice Phillips. Gordon Craig writing of his parents' separation said: 'Then by mutual disagreement they parted. Sad: but there was no unkindness, no dissension – they were neither of them desertable people.' By this he meant that his mother was not a desertable person. Godwin left her and she never made any secret of her love for him or of her unhappiness when their relationship, which had been frayed by poverty, came to an end.

In March 1877 Watts instituted proceedings for divorce and in November of that year Ellen Terry married Charles Wardell, who acted in the company at the Court Theatre in the name of Charles Kelly. Edy, Ellen Terry's daughter, was to say of her: 'All through her life the man of brains competed for her affections with the man of brawn.' Wardell was rather the man of brawn and Ellen Terry appears to have married him mainly to give her children a name. The strange conventions of the society of her time were satisfied by this gesture and her parents, from whom she had been separated since her elopement with Godwin, were gladly reconciled to her and to their two small grandchildren. These now became overnight Edith and Edward Wardell. The Wardell family moved into 33 Longridge Road, Earls Court and it was here that Henry Irving called on Ellen Terry to invite her to become his leading lady.

The partnership between Henry Irving and Ellen Terry lasted for twenty years and was the most memorable in the history of the theatre. Henry Irving's qualities as an actor have already been discussed. Ellen Terry's consisted primarily in a radiance of personality and all-conquering charm, but she had also a mastery of technique which enabled her to deploy a very considerable talent. Apart from her extraordinary power to please, the quality for which she was most famous was her naturalness. Graham Robertson, an ardent playgoer who knew her well, has left these memories of her most famous roles.

As Portia I think she must have realised almost everyone's ideal – she *was* Portia; as Beatrice she realised something so far above *my* ideal that I could hardly recognise the character, for I have the bad taste not to admire Beatrice.

For the (in my eyes) noisy, pushing, unmannerly, Messinine minx Ellen Terry contrived to substitute a wholly delightful creature whose bubbling and infectious high spirits were never allowed to hide her gentle kindliness and well-bred grace of manner.

From what she evolved her I have never made out; I cannot find her in the play, even with the aid of the crib supplied by Miss Terry, but I hope that my blindness is at fault and that Shakespeare really wrote the part as she played it.

Her Cordelia, he says, captured all hearts; 'Lovely and gracious, she was Cordelia as she had been Portia, though I regret to say that, when studying the character, she wrote "FOOL" in large letters against the young lady's refusal to admit her love for her old father.' It was as Imogen, the last great Shakespearean part she played at the Lyceum, that she outdid all former achievements. 'Her scene of joy, on receiving the false letter, a joy so great that sorrow must needs be close behind, was absolutely overwhelming; it moved to tears.'

Ellen Terry never played Rosalind because there is no part in *As You Like It* which suited Henry Irving, but this was so much lamented and the felicities she might have brought to the role so often imagined that the absence of her Rosalind made almost as much mark on the annals of the play as the greatest performances of it.

Throughout Henry Irving's life there would always be those who could not appreciate the qualities which won from others so much ardent admiration. Ellen Terry pleased everyone save Henry James. He complained that she lacked the polish and finish of the actresses of the Comédie Française and he could not find compensation in the qualities peculiarly her own. He wrote:

By many intelligent persons she is regarded as an actress of exquisite genius, and is supposed to impart an extraordinary interest to everything that she touches. This is not, in our opinion, the truth, and yet to gainsay the assertion too broadly is to fall into an extreme of injustice. The difficulty is that Miss Terry has charm – remarkable charm; and this beguiles people into thinking her an accomplished actress. There is a natural quality about her that is extremely pleasing – something wholesome and English and womanly which often touches easily where art, to touch, has to be finer than we often see it.

Yet a great deal of technique – in Ellen Terry's case learned from the time when as a child she played for Mrs Charles Kean – goes into an appearance of naturalness on the stage. Ellen Terry invariably gave a lively intelligence and a great deal of hard work to the parts she played and people who saw her annotated texts or with whom she discussed the professional aspects of her life were often amazed.

It is true, however, that the quality which made her the idol of London in her youth and a legend in her old age and which, in her written words, is still compelling, was charm. Her charm consisted in a splendid generosity of spirit and a great joy in life as well as physical and mental attributes which defy analysis. One of her physical attractions was her voice, about which Bernard Shaw said: 'Her slightly veiled voice reached the remotest listener in the theatre without apparent effort, though the nervous athleticism behind it was of championship quality.' And Henry James, having said that her countenance was happily adapted to the expression of pathetic emotion, went on: 'To this last effect her voice also contributes: it has a sort of monotonous husky thickness which is extremely touching, although it gravely interferes with the modulation of many of her speeches.'

Tributes to Ellen Terry abound in the memoirs of the day but George Bernard Shaw, who loved her, wrote of her unforgettably. He said 'Ellen Terry is the most beautiful name in the world; it rings like a chime through the last quarter of the nineteenth century.' And: 'Every famous man of the last quarter of the nineteenth century, providing he were a theatre-goer, had been in love with Ellen Terry.' And in a comparison with Irving:

They both had beautiful and interesting faces, but faces like Irving's have looked at the world for hundreds of years past from portraits of churchmen, statesmen, princes and saints, while Ellen Terry's face had never been seen in the world before. The much-abused word 'unique' is literally true of Ellen Terry. If Shakespeare had met Irving in the street, he would have recognised a distinguished but familiar type. Had he met Ellen Terry, he would have stared at a new and irresistibly attractive species of womankind.

And, speaking of a chance meeting with her when she was growing old, he wrote:

She was astonishingly beautiful. She had passed through that middle phase, so trying to handsome women, of matronly amplitude, and was again tall and slender, with a new delicacy and intensity in her saddened expression. . . . She asked me why I did not give her some work in the theatre. 'I do not expect leading parts,' she said: 'I am too old. I am quite willing to play a charwoman. I should like to play a charwoman.' 'What would become of the play?' I said. 'Imagine a play in which the part of a canal barge was played by a battleship! What would happen to my play, or to anyone else's, if whenever the charwoman appeared the audience forgot the hero and heroine, and could think of nothing but the wonderful things that charwoman was going to say and do?' It was unanswerable; and we both, I think, felt rather inclined to cry.

But when Ellen Terry joined Irving at the Lyceum she was not old. She was thirty-one.

The productions at the Lyceum were an advance on anything previously seen in the theatre and were notable for their taste and quality and for a lavish expenditure of money, time and trouble. Hawes Craven, who was in charge of the scene-painting, was a master craftsman and the design of the sets was often undertaken by the famous artists of the day. Edward Burne-Jones designed the sets for Tennyson's *King Arthur* and Alma-Tadema those for *Henry VIII, Coriolanus* and *Cymbeline;* while Edward Godwin, at Ellen Terry's request, advised on the scenes and dresses for *The Cup,* also by Tennyson, and Sir Arthur Sullivan was responsible for the incidental music of the productions of *Olivia, Macbeth* and *King Arthur.*

Irving was a great stage-manager and we are told that he

personally superintended every detail of the productions – setting, lighting, even music. William Archer said of him: 'Mr Irving has the art of inspiring to the verge of genius his scenic artists and machinists.... There rises to the mind a whole gallery of scenic pictures, each as worthy of minute study as any canvas of the most learned archaeological painter.' And Ellen Terry tells of the effort that went to the achievement of these results: 'When there was a question of his playing Napoleon his room in Grafton Street was filled with Napoleonic literature. Busts of Napoleon, pictures of Napoleon, relics of Napoleon were everywhere.... It was not Napoleon that interested Henry Irving, but *Napoleon for his purpose* – two very different things.'

It was sometimes suggested that Ellen Terry herself was responsible for the beauty and quality of the Lyceum productions. But her son Gordon Craig denies this. She had, he says, a woman's taste for lovely things and was responsive to music, painting, sculpture and architecture, 'but creative as a stage producer, no'.

She was, nevertheless, influential, and particularly so over the costumes. Many of her own were designed by her friend Alice Comyns Carr and in later days by her daughter, Edy. Materials were often more gorgeous than those of today, but they were less various, and stage effects were sometimes contrived by curious means. The dress worn by Ellen Terry in *Macbeth*, in which Sargent painted her, was made of a yarn crocheted in green silk and blue tinsel which gave the effects of scales; it was sewn all over with real green beetle wings and had a narrow border in Celtic designs worked out in rubies and diamonds. To this was originally added a cloak of velvet in heather tones upon which great griffins were worked in flame-coloured tinsel – but Irving, seeing this cloak at rehearsal, appropriated it for himself.

Irving's method at rehearsal was to begin by reading the whole play aloud to his company, acting every part including his own. From the very start he imposed on the actors his interpretation of their roles, which were in all cases, except that of Ellen Terry, merely in support of his own. Gordon Craig said that at the Lyceum 'an important part was like the leg of a table – not much to look at', and that 'a good actor was one who could do the bit he was given to do and do it as he was told to do it.' Irving was often criticised for surrounding himself with mediocre actors, although most of the famous actors of the day passed at one time or another through the Lyceum school — but his method allowed no place for greatness except in himself. There was an absolute integrity about his egotism. He saw the picture as a whole and in the middle of the picture he saw himself. His loyalty was entirely to the picture and it would have been quite impossible for him to compose it in any way except to enhance and set off the central figure. Therefore he sought good supporting players and he drilled and drilled them until 'the skin grew tight over his face' and 'he became livid with fatigue yet still beautiful', but they became strong and reliable as table legs.

Bernard Shaw complained that the taste and judgment which allowed Irving to achieve so much visual beauty did not extend to literature and, speaking of Irving's performance as King Arthur in the play by J. Comyns Carr, he said: 'While the voice, the gesture, the emotion expressed are those of a hero-king, the talk is the talk of an angry and jealous coster-monger . . .'

Max Beerbohm also had something to say about Irving's taste in literature. In a review of a book called *Impressions of Henry Irving*, he said:

If I had been, like Mr. Pollock, constantly in touch with Irving, and charged thoroughly with his magnetism . . . then perhaps . . . I should, like Mr. Pollock, not dare to breathe on the legend that Irving was, in addition to his genius for acting, a great scholar and a man of exceedingly fine taste in literature. Mr. Pollock must know, none better, how absolute a legend this is; but he will not breathe on it. In 'Much Ado About Nothing' Irving 'fell upon employing an entirely modern phrase' as an 'aside' in one of the dialogues with Beatrice. Some weeks later Mr. Pollock saw the play again, and the offending 'aside' was still in use. Then he spoke to Irving who was grateful for the hint. For 'by an oversight' read 'because he did not know any better.' Left to act for himself, Mr. Pollock was always bold enough to help Irving in matters of litera-ture. But he was, on occasion at any rate, easily deflected by 'a light, meaning touch' on his arm from 'one of the trusted and con-fidential marshals' who guarded Irving's majesty. One evening 'Irving was sympathetically and generously enthusiastic over

Tennyson's work, and, referring to the beautiful lines beginning "There was a little fair-hair'd Norman maid" – a speech which he always delivered as one rapt in it – he expressed a strong doubt if there was anything in Shakespeare to be preferred to it.' Mr. Pollock, 'startled' – but was he really startled? – 'by such a delivery from such a source,' was about to protest. when he felt the afore-said touch on the arm, and said nothing. I wonder if it was Mr. Loveday, that faithful henchman, who administered the touch. Irving was trying various sets of sledge-bells for 'The Bells.' He 'began to eliminate them one by one until one set was left for final consideration. Then he listened more carefully than ever to that set, and then he turned to Mr. Loveday, a very accomplished musician, and said: "Now isn't that the right set?" – a question which pro-voked an emphatic "Not a doubt about it" ' – an answer which Mr. Pollock offers as a proof of Irving's omniscience, and not having the slightest element of comedy in it.

The voice of the henchman can also be heard in the following passage from Laurence Irving on Irving as musician. Having explained that Sir Arthur Sullivan had written a piece of music for certain alarums and trumpets, he says:

The result was dismissed by Irving as wholly inappropriate – 'as music it's very fine – but for our purpose it's no good at all'. Sullivan asked Irving to try and explain what he had in mind. The actor, thereupon, with a combination of rhythmic pantomime and sug-gestive hummings, strove to convey his idea of what was needed. Sullivan grasped his meaning which he translated rapidly into musical phrases; when these were rehearsed, he and Irving agreed that they were musically and dramatically right.

Nevertheless, the zeal of the henchman must not be allowed to diminish appreciation of Irving's total commitment or the splendour of many of his productions. Ellen Terry was to write: 'When I am asked what I remember about the first ten years at the Lyceum, I can answer in one word: *Work*. I was hardly ever out of the theatre. What with acting, rehearsing, and studying – twenty-five reference books were a simple "coming-in" for one part – I sometimes thought I should go blind and mad.' And:

The men were as much like him when they tried to carry out his instructions as brass is like gold; but he never grew weary of 'coaching' them, down to the most minute detail. Once during the

rehearsals of 'Hamlet' I saw him growing more and more fatigued
with his efforts to get the actors who opened the play to perceive
his meaning. He wanted the first voice to ring out like a pistol shot.

'Who's there?'

'Do give it up,' I said, 'it's no better!'

'Yes, it's a little better,' he answered quietly, 'and so it's worth
doing.'

His ruthless conduct of rehearsals often resulted in his being
at his worst on first nights. When dead tired in body and mind
he assumed his place in the centre of the picture, the weak-
nesses of his voice and physique often prevented him from
doing himself justice. By the third or fourth night his performance was often transformed.

Shakespearean productions at the Lyceum included
Coriolanus, *Cymbeline*, *Hamlet*, *King Lear*, *Macbeth*, *The
Merchant of Venice*, *Much Ado About Nothing*, *Othello*,
Richard III, *Romeo and Juliet* and *Twelfth Night*. Irving failed
as Othello and as King Lear because his voice could not sustain
the great moments of these roles and he fell to raving and
ranting. He was not much praised as Romeo, although his
production was very successful with the public and ran for
over 100 nights, partly because he was too old when he played
the part and partly because as an actor he never seemed young.
But he was as memorable as Shylock, Hamlet and Richard *III*,
and Ellen Terry equally so as Portia, Ophelia, Beatrice and
Imogen. Sir John Gielgud, writing in 1963 of the Lyceum production of *Much Ado About Nothing*, said:

An outstandingly successful production of a classical play can
kill that play's popularity for many years afterwards. So it happened in Engand with *Much Ado About Nothing*.

Henry Irving produced the play at the Lyceum Theatre in 1882,
with himself as Benedick and Ellen Terry as Beatrice, and afterwards revived it several times during his twenty years of management in London, besides touring it in the English provinces and in
America. Ellen Terry presented it again under her own management
in 1901, with Matheson Lang and later Harcourt Williams, as
Benedick. But subsequent revivals, during the succeeding forty
years or so were not greatly successful, and playgoers and critics
too young to remember Ellen Terry seemed to find the play ill-
balanced and even tedious and unconvincing.

As an actor-manager Irving was chiefly criticised because, when not playing Shakespeare, he stuck to the old melodramas or to new plays in the old romantic tradition. Twenty years earlier this criticism might not have occurred to anyone and behind it lay the real charges that he refused to play Ibsen and (largely put forward by Shaw) that he refused to play Shaw.

Irving came at the end of a long tradition of romantic actors and he was never more old-fashioned than his public or than nine out of ten contemporary writers for the stage. He was always looking for new plays and he produced as many as he believed had a reasonable chance of financial success, numbering Tennyson among his dramatists. However, he had a great theatre to fill: the day would come when Ibsen and Shaw could fill a theatre, but it had not come yet. Pioneers acted the plays of both writers for one or two performances at a financial loss. Neither writer could with any certainty have paid the bill for Irving's stage hands alone.

Looking back over almost 100 years we are no longer concerned with the old or new fashion of the Lyceum productions, but with their quality. The truth is that Henry Irving was in the same predicament as almost all theatre managers throughout history. Actors of genius greatly outnumber playwrights of genius, good actors abound, good playwrights are far to seek. The best actors of every generation have been forced to lean heavily on the classics and on rivals of recent successes.

There is no doubt, however, that Irving actually enjoyed fustian and, whereas Ellen Terry was never happy in such parts as Pauline in *The Lady of Lyons*, he delighed in Claud Melnotte. But audiences, too, revelled in this incredible old play and the Lyceum repertory of melodrama and romantic drama drew, not merely the ordinary public, but also the intelligentsia of London. Irving cannot be criticised, as a poet or painter might be, for not being in advance of his time, because it is the nature of the actor's interpretative art that it cannot exist without the active participation of the public. Not for him the uncertain consolations of posterity. Small experimental theatres with low costs may hope to keep open while they educate their audiences, but the big theatres with big productions depend on giving the public what it will pay to see. Ellen Terry writing to Shaw expressed the dilemma: 'Now all the colour and warmth we get into Shakespeare plays would never, never (at this particular time) be (oh, I can't express what I mean), never be *made up for* to our audiences by substituting the tremendously powerful *bare* hardness of Ibsen's Borkman. As far as the Lyceum goes, it's much too big a theatre to play delicately any of Ibsen's modern plays.'

We should be careful before we are too scornful of melodrama. *Macbeth* and *Othello* are both melodrama although of exceptional quality. When we visit the theatre we accept in advance certain conventions. It is these conventions which vary from one generation to the other rather than the intellectual or artistic level. Many of the melodramas that Irving played were played for years after him by such actors as Sir John Martin Harvey and many had genuine power. Thus when Max Beerbohm saw *The Corsican Brothers* by Alexandre Dumas for the first time in 1908, although he wrote teasingly of the conventions of the play, he added: 'The solid fact remains that *"The Corsican Brothers"* really thrilled me, even moved me.'

When Ellen Terry joined the Lyceum company for the rehearsals of *Hamlet* she was surprised and disconcerted by the fact that Irving rehearsed every detail of the play except the scenes with Ophelia. As the first night drew near she went to him and begged him to rehearse her scenes.

'We shall be all right,' he replied, 'but we are not going to run the risk of being bottled up by a gasman or a fiddler.'

Irving had a real and lively admiration for her. Her pathos, he said, was 'nature helped by genius'. But on her first appearance at the Lyceum as Ophelia she felt that she had failed and she left the theatre as soon as she had finished her part, without waiting for the curtain calls. She drove up and down the Embankment in a cab for a long time until she felt the strength to go to her home in Longridge Road. Later that evening, so she told Marguerite Steen years afterwards, Irving, having missed her at the theatre, followed her to her house. There then began 'an attachment that lasted twenty years'.

Both Laurence Irving and Roger Manvell have been at great pains to establish the view, also held by members of the Terry family, that the love between Henry Irving and Ellen Terry was never consummated. This involves setting aside the evidence of Marguerite Steen, who reports the following conversation with Ellen Terry in her old age. 'The conversation had turned on some troublesome affair of my own, and led to my asking Ellen point-blank whether she had ever been Irving's mistress. She answered without hesitation: "Of course, I was. We were terribly in love for a while. Then, later on, when it didn't matter so much to me, he wanted us to go on, and so I did, because I was very, very fond of him and he said he needed me." ' Roger Manvell, quoting this conversation, says that he is inclined to think that 'she meant no more than that Irving and she were "lovers", and much together, but *not* that she had at any period actually *consummated* the relationship', a view which in its turn involves the belief that in her advanced age Ellen Terry was not aware of the precise meaning usually given to the word 'mistress'. She was at this time attempting to persuade Marguerite Steen to write about herself and the other Terrys.

The anxiety of the two biographers that their view of the matter should prevail may be because very few letters between the couple remain – suggesting that they regularly destroyed their correspondence and indicating a wish that their privacy might be respected. Nevertheless, a desire to preserve a secret that might be dangerous at the time does not completely establish a desire to keep the truth from posterity, while the very destruction of the letters – they both kept hundreds from other people – implies some special reason for it.

Possibly Irving's descendants have an inherited tendency to defend him against his wife. To other people it may seem natural and sympathetic that he should have had one complete relationship in his life. In all the thousands of words that have been written about him Irving so seldom emerges as a credible human being and, although this is partly because he deliberately built up a pontifical manner as a barrier between himself and the rest of the world, it is also because his personality has been obscured by the reverential manner with which writers have so often treated him. Yet there is evidence that he loved Ellen Terry and was prepared to risk a great deal for her. Laurence Irving says:

He believed, no doubt sincerely, that he loved her, and was prepared to sacrifice his jealously guarded independence for her sake. There was a time when he had hoped she might marry him – indeed he pressed her to do so. . . . Irving could not marry her unless his wife would agree to divorce him. If, in a moment of reckless passion, Irving had declared his readiness to suffer the indignity of a divorce case in which he would be the guilty party, she had been level-headed enough to count the cost, financially and artistic-ally, of such a scandal – a scandal such as had ruined Edmund Kean. . . . He owed much to her intuitive wisdom.

There is also evidence to suggest a very intimate day-to-day relationship between the two. A slight but charming glimpse of her everyday life is given by D. S. MacColl, who lived oppo-site Ellen Terry in Longridge Road, and who with a single refer-ence to Irving evokes a small, private world. He and his family were ignorant of the theatre and its stars, and, not recognising the actress, they dubbed her 'The Greek Lady'. He begins with a description of her departure for the theatre each day:

She raised and kissed two little tots who were to be known as Edith and Gordon Craig. She greeted the next-door neighbours, family of a Rabbinical scholar, who had promptly become slaves of her apparition and stood ready on the pavement. Her cushions were brought out, placed and patted in the open carriage; herself installed; the air became tender and gay with wavings and blown kisses: the wheels revolved and greyness descended once more on Longridge Road.

The MacColl family, he then says, felt that the figure of Charles Kelly 'the manly bulldog sort of man', did not fit in with this 'Phantom of Delight' – he presented a false concord. 'When a year had passed that too substantial figure disappeared, and a new figure was seen in Longridge Road, spare and grim-jaunty, in close-fitting jacket, and tilted wide-a-wake; Henry Irving.'

And Gordon Craig, reciting a whimsical catalogue of Ellen Terry's doings during the week, ends: 'Saturday was always a half-holiday, spent in promising her advisers that she would be good next week – and on Sunday she generally drove away to Hampton Court with Irving, waving her lily white hand.' Then Laurence Irving says in a phrase which again suggests an intimate relationship: 'One Sunday evening Irving came to supper with Walter Pollock and his wife. Usually he brought Ellen Terry with him, but this time he came alone.' Most revealing of all, in Roger Manvell's biography we are given a few letters from Irving to Ellen Terry – of which with its splendid sense of ardour and urgency, the most attractive is:

Soon – Soon!
I shall be near you on Sunday.
God bless you my only thought.
Your own till Death.

And the most explicit: 'I am anxious to see Ted and hear of you. You gave me a lovely letter to take away with me on Monday. – My own dear wife as long as I live.' While in the only surviving letter she wrote him, she said: 'Dear – I'm better now and hope to come back to work tomorrow – I was dreadfully ill – but I struggled hard before I broke down – Thank you for *missing* me and for your loving letter. Your Nell.'

Behind the scenes at the Lyceum Theatre was the Old Beefsteak Club Room, built by Samuel Arnold, the composer, for the Sublime Society of Beefsteaks, of which Sheridan was a member. When Irving took over the management of the theatre he restored this room and the kitchen behind it. Here he entertained at supper after the theatre, finding at last an outlet for his hospitable nature and for his desire to relax over food and conversation after the strain of his performances. The Beefsteak Room served also as an ante-room when on special occasions, marking, for instance, the long run of a piece or a first night, Irving gave large parties on the specially decorated stage.

First nights were invariably treated as an occasion for hospitality, the large part of the audience consisting of Irving's invited guests. Among these, occupying the stage box, were always to be seen two boys with their mother – Irving's wife and sons. Florence Irving never relaxed the hatred and malice she felt for her husband, and she brought his sons up to regard their father with ridicule and contempt and Ellen Terry as the final insult to herself. They referred to their father as 'the Antique' and to his leading lady as 'the Wench'. But, in spite of her unrelenting spite, Mrs Irving never failed to appear at first nights in the place of honour as her husband's wife, and Laurence Irving suggests that to her hostile presence might be attributed the fact that Irving was then so often at his worst. Certainly he cannot have found much encouragement in the near presence of someone who on her return home on one occasion commented in her diary: 'First night of *Romeo and Juliet* at Lyceum – jolly failure – Irving awfully funny.'

Irving was a naturally hospitable man and the entertainments at the Lyceum were his greatest interest apart from his work. There are many descriptions of the parties in the Beefsteak Room but he himself moves through these a shadowy and lifeless figure. Few people penetrated the mystery of his personality when he was alive, none has left a vivid picture of him. His speeches were often written for him by other people and give no clue to his personality and, although Ellen Terry, at least, succeeds in conveying his personal appearance and physical charm, his recorded utterances, so often prefaced by the old actor's 'me boy', are mainly suggestive of the 'stock' character he himself did so much to outdate. Here once again Max Beerbohm, who scarcely knew him, has left a picture of him which has a natural authenticity.

He was always courteous and gracious. and everybody was fascinated by him; but I think there were few who did not also fear him. Always in the company of his friends and acquaintances —doubtless, not in that of his most intimate friends—there was an air of sardonic reserve behind his cordiality. He seemed always to be watching, and watching from a slight altitude. As when, on the first or last night of a play he made his speech before the curtain, and concluded by calling himself the public's 'respectful— devoted—loving—servant', with special emphasis on the word 'servant', he seemed always so like to some mighty cardinal stooping to wash the feet of pilgrims at the altar steps, so, when in private life people had the honour of meeting Irving, his exquisite manner of welcome stirred fear as well as love in their hearts. Irving, I think, wished to be feared as well as loved. He was 'a good fellow'; but he was also a man of genius, who had achieved pre-eminence in his art, and, thereby, eminence in the national life; and, naturally, he was not going to let the 'good fellow' in him rob him of the respect that was his due. Also, I think, the process of making himself feared appealed to something elfish in his nature. Remember, he was a comedian, as well as a tragedian. . . . He enjoyed the dignity of his position, but enjoyed even more, I conjecture, the fun of it.

Sir Mortimer Menpes also succeeds in a small but authentic
glimpse of the actor, who sat to him for his portrait. One felt,
he says, immediately one saw him, the 'generous soul of the
man' – a remark that is saved from banality by the ring of
truth. Irving had, no doubt, a nobility which was a part of his
hold over audiences, and this was not diminished by a sardonic
and slightly malicious humour of which Menpes gives an
example. While he painted, Irving talked continuously, telling
anecdotes and walking about illustrating them with mimicry.
Once he described going in the company of Coquelin to see
Tree play Falstaff.[8] Coquelin, he said, had been in constant fear
that Tree would float right out of the theatre. 'Will he rise
now?' he continually asked. 'Do you think he is going to rise?'

Irving had, in addition to a love of hospitality, a motive for
the grand entertainments at the Lyceum to which he asked, as
well as actors, writers and artists, the high society of London.
He was concerned to raise the status of his profession and by
acting as host to all the most influential people of the day he
pursued an ambition only less important to him than his
ambition as an actor.

In 1895, when Irving was fifty-seven and had been at the
head of his profession for fifteen years or more, he gave a
lecture at the Royal Institution of Great Britain. He began
with a formal claim to have acting classified *officially* among
the fine arts. He said : 'Official recognition of anything worthy
is a good, or at least a useful thing. It is a part, and an important part, of the economy of the State : if it is not, of what
use are titles and distinctions, names, badges, offices, in fact all
the titular and sumptuary ways of distinction?'

Bernard Shaw, writing soon afterwards, said :

Here the 'formal claim' is put as precisely as Mr. Irving himself
feels he can decorously put it. I, who am not an actor, and am therefore not hampered by any personal interest in the claim, can put it
much more definitely. What Mr. Irving means us to answer is this
question : 'The artist who composed the music for King Arthur
is Sir Arthur Sullivan; the artist who composed the poem which
made King Arthur known to this generation died Lord Tennyson;
the artist who designed the suit of armour worn by King Arthur is

[8] Coquelin, Constant-Benoit, 1841–1909. Famous French actor and director, the
original of Rostand's Cyrano de Bergerac.

Sir Edward Burne-Jones: why should the artist who plays King
Arthur be only Mister Henry Irving?'

Henry Irving was indeed asking that, as leader of the
theatrical profession, he should receive the same recognition
as the leaders of other professions. It says a great deal for the
integrity and single-mindedness of his purpose that no one at
any time seems to have been astonished at this explicit and
public claim to a knighthood or to have confused his motives
with those of personal ambition. 'We owe him,' Bernard Shaw
said, 'an unhesitating assumption that his jealousy is for the
dignity of his art and not of himself, and that it would never
have been advanced if the friend of Sir Joshua Reynolds had
been Sir David Garrick, and if every successive P.R.A. had had
for his officially recognised peer the leading actor of his day.'

On 24 May 1895, a few weeks after he made this speech,
Irving received two letters. The first, from Lord Rosebery, told
him that the Queen had conferred on him the honour of a
knighthood, and the second brought him the congratulations
of the Prince of Wales. Thus for the first time in history acting
was officially recognised as an art.

We owe to the occasion on which he received his knighthood, and once more to Max Beerbohm, one of the most
charming of all the rare peeps behind his pontifical manner.
Crossing the road opposite Marble Arch Beerbohm saw Irving
in a brougham on his way to Paddington to take the train to
Windsor Castle.

Irving [he says] in his most prelatical mood, had always a touch
– a trace here and there – of the old Bohemian. But as I caught
sight of him on this occasion . . . he was the old Bohemian and
nothing else. His hat was tilted at more than its usual angle, and
his long cigar seemed longer than ever: and on his face was a look
of such ruminant, sly fun as I have never seen equalled. I had but a
moment's glimpse of him; but that was enough to show me the
soul of a comedian revelling in the part he was about to play – of
a comedic philosopher revelling in a foolish world. I was sure that
when he alighted on the platform of Paddington station his bearing
would be more than ever grave and stately, with even the usual
touch of Bohemianism obliterated now in honour of the honour
that was to befall him.

Irving made his first tour in America in 1883. It had been customary for many years for English and American actors to cross the Atlantic and appear in London or New York, as the case might be, as visiting stars. Because of the dearth of playwrights in the English language both countries relied heavily on the classics and the French for their plays, so that visitors to either had to stand comparison with the greatest actors of the past in roles that were equally well-known to both. Irving, however, took with him not merely the whole Lyceum company but the Lyceum productions and he introduced to the United States an entirely new conception of theatrical production.

He was accompanied throughout the tour by Joseph Hatton, who was there to write a record of it. In *Henry Irving's Impressions of America* Hatton has left a charming account of the arrival in New York harbour of the *Britannic* carrying Irving, Ellen Terry and the rest of the company. Although the ship arrived in the early hours of the morning it was met by two yachts – one carrying the impresario who had arranged the tour and thirty serenading Italian musicians, the other carrying the famous actors Lawrence Barrett and William Florence. Irving and Ellen Terry were immediately transferred to the yacht *Blackbird*, where they encountered for the first time that typically American phenomenon, the 'interviewer'. At four o'clock in the morning a party of journalists had left New York to meet the *Britannic* and put Irving and Ellen Terry through the customary and much advertised 'grilling' – an ordeal the couple had awaited with some fear since leaving England's shores. The ease with which Irving talked to these journalists did a great deal to assure the success of his visit.

'Now gentlemen,' he said, in the prolonged silence which greeted his arrival among them, 'time flies. . . . I have a dread of you. Don't ask me how I like America at present – I shall, I am sure; and I think the bay superb. There, I place myself at your mercy. Don't spare me.'

And when asked what he did for exercise, he replied: 'I act.'

In New York, although well treated by the newspapers and royally entertained he was made very nervous before his first night by the activity of the ticket speculators. In New York speculators in theatre tickets are protected by the law and managers are obliged to sell to them. These dealers, if they can

persuade the public to pay, can double or treble the price of
the tickets, making as much out of a great success as the
management of the theatre and, as Irving feared, putting the
holders of tickets into a highly critical mood. On the advice of
William Winter, a New York critic, Irving had decided to open
with *The Bells*. Winter had said that Irving and his audience
would be in a mood of great excitement on the first night
and that it would be best to take advantage of this agitation to
play the exacting part in which he had made his name, which
would also allow him to avoid comparison with any established
favourite. It had the disadvantage, however, of having no part
for Ellen Terry.

From the moment Irving, dressed as Matthias, appeared on
the stage with the cry: 'It is I!' the success of the Lyceum
tour was assured. James Hatton tells us that, interviewed in his
dressing room at the end of the play, he was asked whether he
felt he had been judged on his merits, whether there was any
trace of independence in the manner of the audience.

'Yes, yes, – there was certainly,' said the actor, rising and pacing
the room. 'It is not presumption in me to say that I am sure I was
judged solely on my merits, and that the audience went away
pleased with me. There were times tonight when I could feel the
sympathy of my hearers – actually feel it.'

And asked later: 'Do you look upon your reception tonight
as a success?' he replied:

'In every way. One of your greatest actors told me that American
audiences are proverbially cold on first nights. He was trying to
save me from a possible disappointment. In addition to this "The
Bells" is not a play for applause, but for earnest, sympathetic
silence. Need I say that the demonstrations which burst forth on
every occasion that good taste would allow, are the best evidence
that to-night I have won an artistic triumph.'

The following morning the New York newspapers confirmed
the impressions of the actor, and on the following night, as
Henrietta Maria in *Charles I*, Ellen Terry made an almost equal
success.

In New York Irving presented in addition *Louis* xi, *The
Merchant of Venice*, *The Lyons Mail* and *The Belle's Stratagem*,
reserving *Hamlet* for the more intellectual audience of

Philadelphia and *Much Ado About Nothing* for Chicago, and playing both on a return visit to New York. At the end of his first tour of Boston, Baltimore, Chicago, St Louis, Cincinnati, Columbus, Washington and the larger towns of New England a little over 400,000 dollars had been paid direct to the theatres to see him, of which he received a half share. His profit on the whole enterprise was £11,700.

Irving and the Lyceum company returned to America in the following autumn of 1885 and, starting in Quebec, toured in North America for seven months. George Alexander was in this company, having taken the place of William Terriss, and also John Martin Harvey. In view of the success of the first tour Irving had decided to arrange and manage the second one himself. As a result he this time cleared a profit of £15,000 out of takings of £80,000. Laurence Irving remarks that this was a great thing for Irving, who 'could foresee that by touring periodically in the provinces of England and the United States he could endow the Lyceum so handsomely that he could maintain his ever-increasing establishment and be free to experiment as he chose without undue risk.' This was a slightly optimistic view of the ultimate requirements of the Lyceum, but it did not over-estimate the importance for the rest of his life of Irving's popularity in America.

In 1892 Edmund Yates, the editor of a fashionable weekly called *The World*, gave his musical critic a letter he had received from Ellen Terry asking his advice on a young 'composer-singer friend of mine'. As a result there began a correspondence which is among the most famous and extraordinary ever written. It is extraordinary because for years Bernard Shaw and Ellen Terry never met and, when they did, saw each other only occasionally on business. It was a love affair on paper and, if one examines the other relationships of this pair with the opposite sex, one cannot help feeling it was ideally suited to both – engaging their desire to love and be loved and their talents for letter-writing, while excluding the need to evade greater demands. The correspondence did not completely come to an end until late in Ellen Terry's life, but it was in the 1890s that it was at its height. In 1896 the couple wrote to each other on average every four days and in 1897 every three.

D

Their correspondence is relevant here only where it touches the life of Henry Irving. Roger Manvell says that the love between Irving and Ellen Terry began to cool in the middle nineties and, although this process may have begun before the correspondence with Bernard Shaw, there is no doubt that Irving was hurt and bewildered by his leading lady's friendship with one of his leading critics. Shaw railed incessantly at Irving in the press, because – he was later to say – having marked Irving when young as the actor for the new theatre in which he was interested and Ellen Terry as the actress, he could never forgive him for wasting his own and Ellen Terry's talents in old-fashioned melodramas and what he described as 'costly Bardicide'. In fact Shaw was completely cold to Irving's romantic school of acting, although he wasted a great deal of energy in an attempt to persuade Irving to put on one of his own plays, but he adored Ellen Terry. This was bad enough when criticism of the actor-manager combined with praise of his leading lady were merely a regular feature of notices of the Lyceum productions, but it must have seemed incredible to Irving that Ellen Terry should condone the process Bernard Shaw afterwards described in the following terms: 'I destroyed her belief in him and gave shape and consciousness to her sense of having her possibilities sterilized by him.'

In an analysis of the character of Desdemona Ellen Terry, having remarked that she is 'genially expressive', wrote: 'The pertinacity with which she begs Othello to reinstate Cassio does not strike me as evidence that she is a rather foolish woman. . . . Her purity of heart and her charity (charity "thinketh no evil") are sufficient explanation of her being slow to grasp the situation.'

This might be a description of Ellen Terry herself. She was not a stupid woman but she badgered Irving about Shaw – begging him to put on *The Man of Destiny*, quoting Shaw's views, working to bring about a meeting between the two and so on – and in the accounts of these conversations written to Shaw there is no suggestion that she felt any compunction, anything except an honourable sense of doing her duty towards Irving.

We know very little of Irving's side of this matter but we do know that he referred to Shaw as Mr Pshaw and he told his son Laurence that he would 'cheerfully have paid Shaw's funeral expenses at any time.'

That in fact Ellen Terry's deep feeling for Irving was never weakened by her flirtatious relationship with Shaw is proved in a letter written to Shaw in 1897. 'If you worry (or try to worry) Henry I must end our long and close friendship. He is ill, and what would I not do to better him?'

However, Bernard Shaw apart, Irving and Ellen Terry were by now beginning to turn away from each other for the satisfaction of their emotional needs. Their biographers once more are inclined to pass over this period of their lives, and in everything written about them there is only a sentence or two that breaks an otherwise complete silence on the subject. If these sentences seem here to be seized upon, it is not only because of their rarity but also because of their meaning, which, while it attaches to trivial things, is nevertheless unequivocal. The first occurs in Laurence Irving and concerns the year 1896.'Tongues', he says, 'had begun to wag over Ellen Terry's undisguised partially for Frank Cooper.'[9] The second sentence occurs in one of Ellen Terry's letters to Bernard Shaw, dated 18 January 1898. 'Henry,' she says, 'is so nice to me lately that I'm convinced he has a new "flame" (he is always nicer then, which I think is to his credit).' Henry had, in fact, met someone whose importance to him was to be much greater than that of a new 'flame', and a month later Ellen Terry, again writing to Bernard Shaw, asked: 'But who is Mrs Aria? I only know she is "a journalist" and "a friend" of H.I.s. I never set eyes on her and she has no idea I know of her. (This is fun, and would be better fun, if I knew something about her.) If you know her personally don't "give away" that I know of her existence.'

In answer to the question: 'Who is Mrs Aria?' Bernard Shaw replied that as far as he could judge she was 'a good sort'. Years later Marguerite Steen brought a book of Mrs Aria's to

[9] Frank Cooper was an actor who played Laertes at the Lyceum and now returned to play Modred in *King Arthur*. On 11 June 1897 Bernard Shaw wrote to Ellen Terry: 'Cooper is quite a pretty, amiable-looking, chubby fellow off the stage, with a complexion as charming as wig paste. Perhaps it *is* wig paste. Why can't he be taught to act? Has he NO intelligence?' But in October of the same year Ellen Terry wrote to a friend: 'No – I fear I can't snap up Frank Cooper (!) and marry him, for he happens to have a wife – and she's nice too – so he can't "cut her throat with a bar of soap" – She is a jealous little lady too, but *not* of me – and I'm fond of her. They marry me to every man I act with.'

Ellen Terry because it contained a study of Henry Irving. She writes:

Ellen Terry glanced at the title and the name of the author and laid the book quietly aside.

'Thank you, my dear. . . . Henry left me for Mrs. Aria.'

And Marguerite Steen adds: 'After twenty years that wound still ached.'

Mrs Aria was, in fact, the solace of Henry Irving's last years and she describes her friendship with him in a book entitled *My Sentimental Self*. She is described by Laurence Irving as 'educated by the conversation of Labby, Wilde, George Moore and their satellites', and as 'the Récamier of Regent's Park – rarely leaving a chaise-longue round which literary tigers like Courtney, Wells, Arnold Bennett and George Moore purred in happy competition.' But she is unskilled with the pen and in her memoirs assumes a degree of piety towards Irving which today is distasteful. The witch, Ellen Terry, possessed of all the talents, has no difficulty in retaining our sympathies over the years. That she was at this time in need of them is suggested in the remark by which Roger Manvell introduces sentences from her private diary, reflecting on Irving as a man and an actor. 'This splendid analysis,' he says, 'is warm, yet accurate, and most courageous in the face of what Ellen realised she must be losing as his affections moved elsewhere.'

As Irving's sons grew up they gradually established a relationship with him. This was delayed by the hatred they had been brought up to feel for Ellen Terry, whom they still referred to as the Wench, and by the desire of both to go on the stage, which he opposed. They had been encouraged by their mother, in a purely amateur way, in careers as child actors and they seem in their youth to have suffered from the idea, often held by children of the very talented, that the world which their father had made available to himself was in part available to them. They resented the fact that even when he consented to their theatrical ambitions he would not immediately help them to leading parts. They resented to the presence of Edward Gordon Craig in the Lyceum company. In 1891 Laurence wrote to his brother as follows: 'I cannot say I was astonished at Irving being at Malvern with Terry. I might have been had he been there without Terry. We are cutting ourselves adrift from the old hulk and very soon we shall not need to fear his hatred or win his love. That he could not take us into his company was true whilst he is stuffing the goose with bastards of the fell Terry breed.' And soon after: 'Irving was very dull. He was so icy and obnoxious. I was glad to leave him to himself.'

In the end it was Ellen Terry's genuine admiration for Laurence as a playwright and her interest in his career in the theatre as much as anything else which finally brought him, and following him Harry, into a real relationship with their father. By 1898 after the production by his father of his play *Peter the Great*, Laurence is writing to him: 'I can't tell you how full my heart was and is of admiration and gratitude.... Your exquisite judgment has guided the play safely into harbour so far and I can rely on it implicitly. Best Love. "My father is great. I am proud to be his son." ' And when Harry discovered that his mother's family had used the occasion of his marriage to work themselves into a frenzy of conjecture as to whether Ellen Terry would accompany Irving to the wedding, he wrote to Dorothea Baird:

I am sorry all this E.T. business is cropping up again in South Kensington. How wretched it is! I had hoped they would have spared you all unpleasantness. Whatever the whole business means my father is now at an age when the matter may surely be set at rest, and the family linen not washed to every newcomer. Heaven knows it is distressing enough to Laurence and myself to be planted in the midst of all this scandal and we have done our best to steer some sort of course between it. And why all this excitement? I don't anticipate any trouble from E.T. She is not so blind or foolish as yet.

You will have to meet her as I met her and be rather bored by her, but she will not want to come to the wedding or to our house or do anything that might be inconvenient.

In the end Irving himself refused to go to the wedding but he joined his son and his bride at Bamburgh during their honeymoon. From this time both sons were more or less fully reconciled to their father, Laurence eventually becoming a member of the Lyceum company.

Irving had a splendid unconcern with money and, like so many people who do not care for it, he needed a great deal in order to do as he wished in the realm of the things he did care for. The productions at the Lyceum were never stinted of anything needed to complete the beauty or authenticity of the effects aimed at. They continued to draw the public and this lavishness might not have been fatal if the henchmen, so devoted in many ways, had included among them a good business manager. But the discipline which was so notable a feature of the artistic sphere at the Lyceum did not extend to the financial departments. The number of camp followers grew and abuse of Irving's generosity infected almost every part of the theatre. Money was wasted and misappropriated.

In December 1896, after the first night of a revival of *Richard III*, Irving slipped on the narrow stairs of his flat and ruptured the ligatures of his knee. Ellen Terry was away in Germany and the Lyceum had to be closed for a week. *Cymbeline* was revived with Julia Arthur as Imogen and later with Ellen Terry herself. The play covered only about 25 per cent of the costs. *Olivia* was then tried and ran at only a small loss to the end of the season. It was then discovered that £10,000 had been lost and it became clear on how narrow a margin the Lyceum company operated. Handsome profits on the autumn tour enabled Irving to forget the situation for a while.

Then in February of the following year a disaster occurred. Over the past twenty years a great store of scenery and properties had been acquired, much of it the work of the greatest scenic artists of the day. This was Irving's capital, and the basis on which he had operated a policy to withdraw plays before their attraction was exhausted so that these successful productions might, in London, but more especially in the provinces and America, take care of his declining years. All this property was under-insured – quite recently the insurance had been reduced in an effort towards economy – and when the buildings in which it was stored were burned down and with them 260 scenes – the settings for forty-four plays – £6,000 was all that remained of the accumulation of a lifetime.

Irving is said to have taken this disaster with great philosophy and courage, and once more he took to the provinces to restore some of his fallen fortunes. On his way to a train one night he got his feet wet before a journey in an unheated carriage. By the end of the week he was suffering from pneumonia and pleurisy and again it was demonstrated that the star system requires the star. By the end of a tour in which the profit was only £500, Bram Stoker, his business manager, was forced to let the Lyceum and arrange a further provincial tour for the company.

Irving's finances were by now so reduced that in order to tide himself over his illness he was forced to sell most of his collection of theatrical books and prints and, for the first time since he had ceased to be a provincial actor, to borrow from friends. In the circumstances the step he now took was more or less forced upon him, although the arrangements made should have been more favourable to him. For certain immediate financial considerations and against the advice of his own staff he engaged himself to a company to be called the Lyceum Theatre Company, on terms which made it possible for it to make a profit at the same time as he made a loss. At the end of the first season he had lost £4,000 while making a large profit for the company. He had never recovered from the effects of pneumonia, which left him with a chronic inflammation of the throat, but he now undertook an extensive tour of the provinces followed by a long tour through Canada and America. The takings of this tour were £111,000 and although this was no greater than the takings of previous tours, the Lyceum Company on this occasion justified itself by taking out of it four times as much profit, on which Irving's share was £24,000.

During this tour he and Ellen Terry discussed for the first time the possibility of her ceasing to play with him. She was by now fifty-two and the range of parts in Irving's repertoire suitable to a woman of that age was naturally becoming narrow. This difficulty might somehow have been overcome but for the fact that their relationship had become one in which it was possible for them to contemplate parting. Laurence Irving says of Irving at this time: 'The last two years had had their effect upon his outward bearing; a shield of cynicism concealed his bruised pride; an affection of republicanism, the refuge of the dethroned autocrat, tempered his austerity. He evaded a difficult decision and was more tolerant of the incompetence of others. In short, he was a sick man.'

In the same year Ellen Terry wrote to Bernard Shaw: 'Ah, I feel so certain Henry just hates me! I can only *guess* at it, for

he is exactly the same sweet-mannered person he was when
"I felt so certain" Henry loved me! We have not met for
years now, except before other people, where my conduct
exactly matches his of course. All my own fault. It is *I* am
changed, not he. It's all right, but it has squeezed me up
dreadfully.' But she was also rebellious of Irving's management
and contemplating leaving him. Before the American tour she
had written to Shaw:

When I come back I shall probably *be quite* a year younger, and
if H.I. gives me only half a fairly good part, I shall play it, but if a
part is offered me like the kind of thing I did (or didn't) in *Peter
the Great*, *Medicine Man* or *Robespierre* I shall 'refuse to act' (for
the first time in my life) and give it all up and come and settle
quietly in a place like this and perhaps act sometimes, on occasions
when I could fit in better than another. I should never say good-bye.
Just leave off.

However, neither Irving nor Ellen Terry was ultimately yet
prepared to make the break. Laurence Irving says that Irving
'would not scruple to use every subtle inducement to keep her
at his side', while Ellen Terry could still write to Shaw: 'I
appear to be of strange *use* to H., and I have always thought
to be useful, really useful, to any one person *is* rather fine and
satisfactory.'

Between 1894 and 1900 Ellen Terry made notes in a diary
'About H.I.' In 1895 she wrote the following description of him.

A splendid figure. and his face very noble. A superb brow: rather
small dark eyes which can at moments become immense, and hang
like a bowl of dark liquid, with light shining through; a most
refined curving Roman nose, strong and delicate in line. and *cut
clean* (as all his features); a smallish mouth, and full of the most
wonderful teeth, even at 55; lips most delicate and refined – firm,
firm, firm – and with a rare smile of the most exquisite beauty, and
quite-not-to-be described kind. (He seems almost ashamed of his
smile, even in very private life, and will withdraw it at once in
public.) His chin, and the line from ear to chin is firm, extremely
delicate, and very strong and clean defined. He has an ugly ear!
Large, flabby, ill-cut, and pasty-looking, pale and lumpy. His hair
is superb: beautiful in 1867, when I first met him, when it was
blue-black like a raven's wing, it is even more splendid now (1895)
when it is liberally streaked with white. . . . Never have I seen such

hands, 'in form and moving how *express* and admirable'. He always makes them up for the stage very brown.

In 1896 she wrote:

H.I. is much handsomer now than when I first knew him in 1867. Handsomer, but somehow more furtive looking. . . . If it could be possible for him to take infinite pains for another, he would be a perfect being, but self-concentration spoils the porridge.
Indifference is personified in H.I.

In 1897 she wrote:

Very odd. He is not improving with age.

And in 1898:

For years he has accepted favours, obligations to, etc., *through* Bram Stoker! Never will he acknowledge them himself, either by business-like receipt or by any word or sign.

In 1899 she wrote an account of a visit she paid him in Bournemouth where he was recovering from a serious illness. After remarking that 'poor old King H.' was at his 'downest' she goes on to say that she is amazed at the few in number of his useful friends. 'He wanted to tell me that not only was he broken in health but he was what is called "ruined". At which words I refused to shed tears, for, I said: "As long as you and I have health, we have means of wealth. We can pack a bag, each of us and trot round the Provinces. Yes, and go to America, Australia, India, Japan." ' To her astonishment Irving replied that the reason he had asked her to come to see him was to tell her that he was already arranging a tour of the English provinces with a small company playing *The Bells*, *Louis XI* and *A Story of Waterloo* – all plays in which there was no part for her.

'*What* plays?' she asked, and 'Where do I come in?' and she says that Irving looked exceedingly silly when he replied that as there was no chance of acting at the Lyceum 'you can, of course, er, *do as you like*'.

'I felt,' she writes, 'a good many feelings. At the top of all came amusement to save the situation. Then,' said I, 'I have in plain terms what Ted would call "the dirty kick out"?'

But, if it was the 'dirty kick out', it was at this time only temporary. In the following year, as has been seen, she was back and touring in the provinces and in America with him.

Nevertheless, the glorious days were over and in front only the steady decline. When Irving returned from America he was informed that the London County Council, which had embarked on a policy of enforcement of safety regulations against fire, required alterations to the Lyceum Theatre which would cost £20,000. This ultimatum caused the company, an 'over-capitalised concern built on the quivering sands of theatrical speculation' to close the theatre and call in the Receiver. This was a very bitter blow to Irving.

At the end of the Lyceum season of 1902, both this great theatre, so long a feature of the London scene, and the most famous partnership in theatrical history came to an end when Irving led Ellen Terry forward to acknowledge the applause after a performance of *The Merchant of Venice*. They played together once more at an all-star matinée in aid of the Actors' Benevolent Fund, and they did not formally part until she refused to accompany him to America in an absurd play about Dante by Sardou, on which he had already lost a great deal of money at the Theatre Royal, Drury Lane. Irving then left for America without her.

They were to meet only once more. Irving's popularity was so great both in Britain and America that it was true, as she had told him at Bournemouth, that as long as he had health he could have continued to earn money touring with a few old plays. But his health was rapidly failing. In 1905 he was so ill at Wolverhampton that his company had to be disbanded in the middle of a tour. Ellen Terry then travelled at once to see him.

I found him sitting up in bed, drinking his coffee. He looked like some beautiful grey tree that I have seen in Savannah. His old dressing-gown hung about his frail yet majestic figure like some mysterious grey drapery. We were both very much moved, and said little. 'I'm glad you've come. Two Queens have been kind to me this morning. Queen Alexandra telegraphed to say how sorry she was I was ill, and now you – '.

Irving never recovered his health. He continued to tour but it became more and more obvious that he was a sick man struggling to carry on. In Bradford in the same year, 1905, he appeared in *Becket* in which the last lines he spoke were: 'Into thy hands, O Lord, into thy hands!' He left the theatre alone with his valet and died in the hall of his hotel.

Like so many actors before him, he died penniless. His pictures, theatrical relics, clothes and properties were sold to provide for his only dependant, his widow. He was buried in Westminster Abbey under a pall of laurel leaves and he entered immediately into his posthumous reputation.

Sir George Alexander
1858-1918

George Alexander secured a place in the annals of the theatre by what at first sight seems to be an extraordinary instinct for the historical occasion.

He was born on 19 June 1858 at Reading and named George Alexander Gibb Samson. His father had an agency in the dry-goods trade and he received most of his education at the High School of Stirling. He left school at the age of fifteen to become a clerk in a London office and at this time he took part at least once a year in amateur dramatic performances. Then in 1879, at the expense of a total, although, as it turned out, only temporary breach with his father, he dropped the last two of his four names and joined a stock company at the Theatre Royal, Nottingham. His rise was very rapid and two years later he was engaged by Henry Irving to play Caleb Deecie in a revival of Albery's comedy *The Two Roses* at the Lyceum. Following this he had an engagement with Hare and Kendal at the St James's Theatre and then he returned to the Lyceum Company where he remained for six years.

Alexander was a very good-looking man with a good figure and excellent legs – a dandy and the original matinée idol. In a belittling and rather too much quoted sentence, Henry Irving is supposed to have said to him at rehearsal one day: 'Now Alexander, not quite so much Piccadilly.' However, in spite of a natural propensity for 'too much Piccadilly' he was a very good actor who during his six years at the Lyceum learned his trade the hard way. He is quoted as saying: 'When I was at the Lyceum, after five or six hours of rehearsal by Irving I would go home almost crying. I would tell my wife that I was afraid

I had made a dreadful mistake in going on the stage. And I made up my mind that if I ever had a company of my own, I would let them down pretty easy.'

Alexander went to America with the Lyceum company and in Boston, where Irving developed a painful swelling of the leg, he had to go on as Benedick at a few hours notice and with an imperfect knowledge of the lines. In London he took William Terriss's place in the company, his most notable role being that of Faust.

In 1889, there being no part for him in the Lyceum production of *The Amber Heart*, he accepted an engagement at the Adelphi with the Gattis. During this period he took a short lease of the Avenue Theatre and put on a play called *Dr Bill*. Because the Gattis would not release him to act in it, he engaged Fred Terry to play the part he might have played himself.[1] Then in 1890, against the advice of Henry Irving, who told him that he could return to the Lyceum after six months if he wished to, he signed a lease for the St James's Theatre, installed electric light there, re-upholstered the seats and started his long career as an actor-manager.

Alexander, like Bancroft, was a naturally shrewd administrator and much of his success at the St James's can be attributed to the efficiency of his management of the theatre. A large part of it was due, however, to his policy of promoting the work of British playwrights. He was the first to recognise that in the new prosperity and status of the theatre writers of the highest quality might be persuaded to work in it. He suggested to men who had never thought of writing a play that they might consider doing so, and he invited them to bring ideas to him so that the dramatic possibilities might be discussed in advance. He had chosen his moment correctly and his policy brought him success: he produced sixty-two full length plays and nineteen one-act plays in twenty-seven years of management, and only eight of these were of foreign origin.

It was this policy rather than some uncanny flair that made his period at the St James's memorable in the history of the theatre.

---

[1] Terry, Fred, 1863–1933. Ellen Terry's brother. In the Bancroft company and played Sebastian to Ellen Terry's Viola at the Lyceum. Chiefly remembered as Sir Percy Blakeney in *The Scarlet Pimpernel*.

On 20 February 1892, just over a year after he had opened in management at the St James's, Alexander put on the first of the plays for which he is remembered. This was *Lady Windermere's Fan*, for which he had paid an advance of royalties of £100 before a line or even a scenario was written. When he first read the play he offered to buy it for £1,000, but Wilde replied: 'I have so much confidence in your excellent judgment, my dear Aleck, that I cannot but refuse your generous offer.' And in fact Wilde made £7,000 out of royalties from the original run.

Lady Windermere's Fan conforms to the stage conventions of the time and is distinguishable from dozens of other comedies only because of the talent, wit and wisdom of the dialogue. As an actor-manager Alexander gave far more consideration to the views of his playwrights and the casting of supporting roles than did, for instance, Irving, but he was master of his own theatre and well aware of his own importance to any play produced in it. It was not to be expected that he and Wilde would reach the first performance of this play without some differences of opinion, but all the evidence suggests that most of Alexander's proposed alterations were finally accepted by the author because they were genuine improvements on the original text.

One of these alterations was merely the interpolation of two lines at the end of Act 2. Mrs Erlynne, before rushing off to find her daughter, instructs Lord Augustus Lorton to take Lord Windermere to his club and keep him there as long as possible. Originally the Act-drop followed immediately on the following speech:

Mrs Erlynne:Don't let Windermere out of your sight tonight. If you do I will never forgive you. I will never speak to you again. I'll have nothing to do with you. Remember you are to keep Windermere at your club, and don't let him come back to-night.

Alexander wanted a different ending and suggested to Wilde that two lines should be added.

Lord Augustus: Well, really, I might be her husband already. Positively I might. (*Follows her in a bewildered manner.*)

A second alteration was of greater importance. Originally

the secret that Mrs Erlynne is Lady Windermere's mother was kept until the last act. Alexander felt, in the words of his biographer, 'that to allow the audiences to remain unaware of the reason for Lord Windermere's submission to the demands of Mrs Erlynne for the greater part of the play and then with a sharp twist to let them into the secret, would introduce a trickiness quite alien from and probably fatal to the success of the play. *Lady Windermere's Fan* would become a riddle long drawn out, instead of a play of real emotion and suspense.'

The request for these alterations produced a letter from Wilde in which he complained that the first of the two had been made in his absence 'through illness caused by the worry and anxiety I have gone through at the theatre', but said that, although the new ending came as a shock of surprise, he did not in any degree object to it. And he added plaintively: 'To reproach me on Wednesday for not having written a speech for a situation on which I was not consulted and of which I was quite unaware was, of course, a wrong thing to do.'

He was much more upset by the suggestion for the second alteration, and wrote:

With regard to your other suggestion about the disclosure of the secret of the play in the second act, had I intended to let out the secret, which is the element of suspense and curiosity, a quality so essentially dramatic, I would have written the play on entirely different lines. I would have made Mrs Erlynne a vulgar, horrid woman and struck out the incident of the fan. The audience must not know till the last act that the woman Lady Windermere proposed to strike with her fan was her own mother. The note would be too harsh, too horrible.

Writing of this incident, A. E. W. Mason says: 'Wilde gave way in the end, which suggests that he gave way to pressure from Alexander. But the play seems to have had its first performance with the sequence unchanged and six days afterwards Wilde wrote to the editor of the St James's Gazette asking permission to correct a statement put forward 'in your issue of this evening' to the effect that he had made the alteration in consequence of the newspaper criticisms.

The facts are as follows. On last Saturday night, after the play was over, and the author, cigarette in hand, had delivered a delightful and immortal speech, I had the pleasure of entertaining at supper a small number of personal friends: and, as none of them was older than myself, I naturally listened to their artistic views with attention and pleasure. The opinions of the old on matters of Art are, of course, of no value whatsoever. The artistic instincts of the young are invariably fascinating.

He goes on to say that the opinion of his friends was that the psychological interest of the second act of the play would be greatly increased by the disclosure of the actual relationship existing between Lady Windermere and Mrs Erlynne, 'an opinion I may add, that had previous been strongly held and urged by Mr Alexander'. 'This determination, however, was entered into long before I had the opportunity of studying the culture, courtesy and critical faculty displayed by such papers as the *Referee*, *Reynolds*, and the *Sunday Sun*.'

On 27 May 1893 Alexander produced *The Second Mrs Tanqueray* by Arthur W. Pinero. In the course of time Pinero has come to be regarded as a good craftsman but not a great artist, a playwright with a strong dramatic sense but one whose characters speak a stilted, rather pretentious dialogue and are moved in improbable situations by artificial emotions.[2] But the first night of *The Second Mrs Tanqueray* was a great theatrical occasion. Mrs Tanqueray is a woman with a 'past' – by which in this case is meant that she has had physical intercourse with men in return for money – who, as the second wife of a country gentleman, is attempting to forget it. During the course of the play it is discovered that her step-daughter's fiancé has formerly been her lover and in the last act she commits suicide. The novelty and the daring of presenting such a woman on the stage was confused, as daring so often is, with truth and naturalness. William Archer wrote:

It is not merely or mainly superior gifts, then, but superior strength of character, which has given this victory to Mr Pinero rather than to Mr Oscar Wilde, Mr Henry Arthur Jones, Mr Grundy or Mr Carton. Any difference of endowment between him and them is not sufficient to account for the immense difference between

[2] Pinero's virtues, particularly as a writer of farce, should not be underrated, however. *The Second Mrs Tanqueray*, *Trelawny of the Wells* and *The Magistrate* have all been revived in the 1960s and welcomed by the critics – the last named being thought to stand comparison with Feydeau's farces.

The Second Mrs Tanqueray and the very best work of any of these writers. It is the attitude of mind in which he approached his task, the artistic ideal he proposed to himself, and his unflinching devotion to that ideal, that have enabled him to produce the one play of what may be called European merit which the modern English stage can as yet boast.

The first night of *The Second Mrs Tanqueray* is famous not only for the emergence of a new dramatist who seemed of 'European' quality but of the young actress who played Paula Tanqueray. There had been difficulty in casting the part. Olga Nethersole, Janet Achurch and Winifred Emery had all been suggested and Elizabeth Robins actually engaged, but when after some reluctance the Gatti brothers agreed to release Mrs Patrick Campbell from her contract with them, Miss Robins resigned in favour of the younger woman. Mrs Patrick Campbell's success in the play is part of theatrical history. So, too, are her quarrels with Alexander. She became notorious for the havoc she caused in the theatre through a mixture of caprice and moodiness, a liking for practical joking and a sharp tongue. Hesketh Pearson wrote of her that she ruined Alexander's natural good temper and was the occasion of hysteria and heat, bawling and disputing in his normally beautifully run theatre. She herself says that once she and Alexander rehearsed 'only addressing each other in the words of our parts'. And on another occasion:

Mr Alexander in this play by Mr Jones had to look into my face and tell me I was beautiful and that he adored me, or some such words. And one night he said it with such a look in his eyes, as though he would willingly have wrung my neck, that I burst out laughing. When the curtain fell, his stage-manager came with pompous dignity to the door of my dressing-room and said, 'Mr Alexander's compliments and will you please not laugh at him on the stage.' I replied, 'My compliments to Mr Alexander, and please tell him I never laugh at him until I get home.'

The Second Mrs Tanqueray ran for nearly a year and was followed by *The Masqueraders*, an almost equally successful play by Henry Arthur Jones. During the run of *The Second Mrs Tanqueray* Henry James had completed *Guy Domville*, which he had agreed to write for Alexander, and it caused him

much pain when he had to wait for the whole of the long run
of Henry Arthur Jones's play before his own could be produced.

James's attitude to the theatre was ambivalent. He had for
long been drawn to the dramatic form but he had a very low
opinion of the theatre in London. His unrestrained, even vicious
criticism of the work of other people and his sensitive, almost
craven concern for his own show him, unusually, in an
unsympathetic light. Elizabeth Robins, who sometimes accompanied him to the theatre, wrote: 'One never grew wholly
acclimatised to the nipping airs that now and then would blow
about the startled stalls. Mr James's all too audible remarks,
conveyed in terms always "chosen", often singularly
picturesque, sometimes diabolic, as though he revelled in
mercilessness – would send cold shivers down his companion's
spine.' And his biographer says:

He was attracted to the theatre and at the same time was repelled
by it. He wanted its successes and rewards and yet was afraid to
chance its pitfalls. . . . When a magazine rejected a story – this
was a private matter between editor and writer. But when a play
was announced, publicized, promised to the public, and then not
produced, or failed in production, the author was, in the process,
publicly rejected. This was what Henry James feared more than
anything else.

In 1888, after the unappreciative reception of *The Bostonians*
and, following that, of *The Princess Casamassima*, James
received an invitation from Edward Compton, a young actor-
manager whose company toured the provinces, to dramatise
The American. James said sometimes that he was influenced
by the comparatively large income made by playwrights such as
Pinero and Wilde and at other times he confessed to an almost
lifelong temptation to write for the theatre. He accepted the
invitation. 'Don't be hard on me,' he wrote to Robert Louis
Stevenson, 'simplifying and chastening necessity has laid its
brutal hand on me and I have had to try and make somehow or
other the money I don't make by literature.' And speaking of a
rehearsal he is about to attend as 'a base theatrical errand', he
also wrote: 'My zeal in the affair is only matched by my
indifference.' But at the same time he was writing to his brother
William: 'I feel at last as if I had found my *real* form, which

I am capable of carrying far, and for which the pale little art of fiction, as I have practised it, has been, for me, but a limited and restricted substitute.'

The American, after playing successfully in the provincial towns, was brought to London, where it ran sufficiently well for James to be able to write: 'Honour is saved, but I grieve to say nothing else, for the piece made no money.'

Soon after this he saw Alexander's production of *The Second Mrs Tanqueray* and he felt that he had 'at last found a manager for whom he could do a serious play'. He discussed three different ideas with Alexander but finally sent him the first act and the scenario for two more acts of the play which became known as *Guy Domville*. Alexander offered him royalties of £5 a performance with a ceiling of £2,000, after which the full rights to go to the actor-manager, and James replied: 'I should be obliged to you if you can put the case to me more dazzlingly another way.' It is not known what terms were decided between them.

Leon Edel says of Alexander that, although he was not a man of large imagination, he compensated for this by a kind of furious energy. He surrounded himself with good actors and showed discrimination in his choice of plays. In the winter of 1894 James wrote to his brother that his play would be 'exquisitely mounted, dressed &c. and as well acted as London can act'. Later he wrote asking him to 'unite in family prayer for me on Saturday, January 5 at 8.30,' and to a friend that 'the dew of agony is already on my brow....' On 3 January he wrote: 'I have changed my policy. I recognise that the only way for me to arrive at 10 o'clock with any patience is to *do* something active or at least positive; so I have had the luminous idea of going to see some other play.' And he added: 'I am more or less already under chloroform.'

On 5 January in this rather indecent state of fear he went to the Haymarket to see *An Ideal Husband*. He did not enjoy Wilde's play: he found it crude, clumsy, feeble and vulgar. How could his play, he asked himself, possibly succeed with a public who enjoyed this one.

Meanwhile one of the most brilliant first-night audiences that have ever assembled sat in the stalls of the St James's Theatre. It included Sir Edward Burne-Jones, Sir Frederick

Leighton, G. F. Watts, George du Maurier and John Singer Sargent. Graham Robertson was there, and Mrs Humphry Ward, Edmund Gosse and Thomas Anstey Guthrie (F. Anstey); Elizabeth Robins and Kate and Florence Terry; Bernard Shaw (in the first week of his life as a dramatic critic), H. G. Wells and Arnold Bennett.

The curtain rose on an elaborate and realistic representation of a garden, and in this setting, Leon Edel tells us, 'the actors caught and sustained the romantic mood', while 'the graceful and rhythmic dialogue. . . delighted the audience'. The first act was as well received as the playwright could have wished and at the fall of the curtain the audience, genuinely moved, felt itself in the presence of an exceptional dramatic talent. 'Whatever may have been hoped for from the author of such a first act [Leon Edel writes] was not the act that followed.'

In the second act Guy Domville, a devout and noble churchman, destined in the first act for the ministry, falls at a reckless speed for the rather crude temptations that are placed in his way. He is seen as a swaggering dandy, embroiled in a theatrical intrigue; and on the first night he was required to take part in a scene, afterwards cut, in which two characters, both shamming drunkenness, attempted to make the other drunk. Leon Edel writes: 'James had yielded to the clap-trap of artificial drama, to the *ficelle* structure of Sardou and the other dramatists he had studied with such assiduity at the Théâtre Français. . . .'

The trouble was that in the realm of artificial drama James had none of Sardou's natural talent. One critic wrote, after seeing *The American*: 'We are as anxious as the critics of the newest school to hail the advent on our stage of literary men, but it is on condition that they bring their literature with them.'

In the third act James returned to the scene and to the mood of the first act. But it was by now too late. Coughing and fidgeting in the audience had created a tension which made the work of the nervous, first-night cast impossible. There had been tittering and interruptions in the second act and when in the third Alexander spoke the line, 'I'm the last, my lord, of the Domvilles', a voice from the gallery replied, 'It's a bloody good thing you are.'

When Henry James arrived at the St James's Theatre at the

end of the play no one told him that it had been badly received. The curtain came down at first to applause. Calls were taken and Alexander received his accustomed ovation. It is difficult to understand why a manager of his experience did not at this point ring down the curtain, turn up the lights and thank his stars to have reached the end of this uneasy first night without worse mishap. But in reply to a few calls of 'Author' from the stalls Alexander led Henry James on to the stage and at that moement pandemonium broke loose. In Henry James's words: 'All the forces of civilisation in the house waged a battle of the most gallant, prolonged and sustained applause with the hoots and jeers and catcalls of the roughs (like those of a cage of beasts at some infernal zoo). . . .' And Leon Edel tells us that it seemed like hours that James and Alexander stood on the stage listening to the 'sound of public scorn'.

He [James] stood there thunderstruck. The dark beard framed a half-open mouth, set off the pallor of the cheeks, the shocked stare. . . . Then James, in those seconds that seemed like hours, standing there white and tense, made a deprecatory gesture, a movement of the arms, a shrug of the shoulders. Alexander shifted nervously from one position to another. The novelist turned suddenly and fled, with Alexander close behind him.

On the following day the critics showed a great and almost unanimous desire to sustain and support Henry James. Bernard Shaw, writing one of his first dramatic criticisms, summed up with his usual spontaneous vigour the feelings of the more educated minority.

When some unmannerly playgoer . . . chooses to send a derisive howl from the gallery at such a situation, we are sorrowfully to admit, if you please, that Mr. James is no dramatist, on the general ground that 'the drama's laws the drama's patrons give.' Pray, which of its patrons? the cultivated majority who, like myself and all the ablest of my colleagues, applauded Mr. James on Saturday, or the handful of rowdies who brawled at him? It is the business of the dramatic critic to educate these dunces, not to echo them.

In an analysis of the qualities and faults of *Guy Domville*, he put first among the qualities a rare charm of speech. 'Line after line comes with such a delicate turn and fall that I unhesitatingly challenge any of our popular dramatists to write a scene in verse with half the beauty of Mr James's prose.' Second, he said, *Guy Domville* is a story, not a mere situation hung out on the gallows of a plot, and third, it relies on the performers not for the brute force of their personalities but for their finest accomplishments in grace of manner, delicacy of diction and dignity of style. But of the second act he said that little of it can be remembered with pleasure and that it had better 'have been left out'.

James received more letters from sympathisers and well-wishers than in all his years as a writer, and on subsequent nights *Guy Domville* was courteously received. At the end of a run of four weeks James wrote that 'what appears largely to have enabled *Guy Domville* to go even a month is the fact that almost everyone who has been to see it at all appears to have been three or four times.' But in spite of so much genuine sympathy and praise he wrote to Elizabeth Robins: 'It has been a great relief to feel that one of the most detestable incidents of my life has closed.'

With the failure of *Guy Domville* Alexander had to find a play to take its place. In the summer of 1894 Oscar Wilde had been considering writing a farcical comedy and he had written Alexander the following letter.

The real charm of the play, if it is to have a charm, must be in the dialogue. The plot is slight, but I think, adequate. . . . Well, I think an amusing thing with lots of fun and wit might be made. If you think so too, and care to have the refusal of it, do let me know and send me £150. If when the play is finished, you think it too slight – not serious enough – of course you can have the £150 back. I want to go away and write it, and it could be ready in October, as I have nothing else to do. . . . In the meanwhile, my dear Aleck, I am so pressed for money that I don't know what to do. Of course I am extravagant. You have always been a good wise friend to me, so think what you can do.

In August 1894 Wilde sent Alexander the scenario of a different play, one that was eventually written up by Frank Harris as *Mr and Mrs Daventry*, but later in the year he returned to his first idea and wrote to Alexander:

As you wished to see my somewhat farcical comedy, I send you the first copy of it. It is called *Lady Lancing* on the cover: but the real title is *The Importance of Being Earnest*. When you read the play you will see the punning title's meaning. Of course, the play is not suitable to you at all: you are a romantic actor: the people it wants are people like Wyndham or Hawtrey. Also, I would be sorry if you altered the definite artistic line of progress you have always followed at the St. James's. But, of course, read it, and let me know what you think of it. I have very good offers from America for it.

Wilde may have been seriously in doubt as to Alexander's suitability for the play, because after writing these letters he gave it to Charles Wyndham. But with the failure of *Guy Domville*, Alexander was in a hurry to find a play and he asked Wyndham, who was not in any immediate hurry, to let him have it.

Alexander engaged Allan Aynesworth to play Algernon Moncreiffe, Rose Leclercq for Lady Bracknell, Irene Vanbrugh and Evelyn Millard for the two girls, and among the small-part players were Franklin Dyall and Kinsey Peile. In spite of this excellent cast, rehearsals did not at first run smoothly. Wilde interrupted continually and made it impossible for the actors to get through the play. Finally Alexander took him aside and said that they now understood everything he wanted. 'If you'll leave us alone to get on with the rehearsals we shall try our best to give it to you. But if you don't we shall never be ready. So I'll send you a box for the first night and see you again after the performance.' Wilde was at first rather taken aback but, in dramatic mood, he asked Alexander and Aynesworth to dinner for the purpose of confiding to them, 'You are neither of you my favourite actor'. Yet he stayed away from the theatre. On the first performance, 14 February 1895, he spent most of the evening behind the scene standing in the wings. After the play's phenomenal success, he went to see Alexander who asked him what he had thought of it. 'My dear Aleck [he replied] it was charming, quite charming. And do you know, from time to time I was reminded of a play I once wrote myself called *The Importance of Being Earnest*.'

Earlier he had written to Franklin Dyall: 'I don't think I shall take a call tonight. You see, I took one only last month at the Haymarket, and one feels so much like a *German band*.' Today it is well known that the reason Wilde spent his evening

behind the scenes and refused to take a call was because he
knew that Lord Queensberry intended to create a disturbance.
George Alexander, warned of this possibility, had cancelled
the seat booked in his name. When Lord Queensberry arrived
with his bouquet of carrots and turnips he was prevented from
entering the front door of the theatre, and after trying every
other door, including the stage door, he finally went away.

In March, two nights before the libel suit, Wilde dined with
his wife and Lord Alfred Douglas and the three of them went
to a box at the St James's Theatre to watch his play. Lord Alfred
Douglas has told us that Constance Wilde was very much
agitated and at the end of the evening had tears in her eyes.
(She saw him only once again, visiting him in prison after his
mother died.) In spite of this Oscar paid a call on George
Alexander between the acts in an airy mood.

'I don't think you ought to have come to the theatre at such
a time' – Alexander said – 'people will consider it in bad taste.'

'Are you going to accuse everyone in the theatre of bad taste
for seeing my play at such a time?' Wilde asked – 'I would
consider it in bad taste if they went to anyone else's play.'

'Do be serious.'

'Then you mustn't be funny.'

In April, after Wilde had been arrested and taken to Hollo-
way Goal, Alexander omitted his name from the posters
and the programmes of *The Importance of Being Earnest*. Mason
enters the defence for him that, aware of Wilde's financial
difficulties, he believed he was doing the best thing for the
author as well as for himself in thus attempting to suppress his
connection with the play. When Wilde was made bankrupt
Alexander bought outright and for very little the acting rights
of *Lady Windermere's Fan* and *The Importance of Being
Earnest*.

He was to meet Wilde, according to Mason once more, but
in fact twice more. On 27 December 1898, in a letter to Robert
Ross from the Hôtel des Bains, Napoule, Wilde wrote: 'Yester-
day I was beside the sea and suddenly George Alexander
appeared on a bicycle. He gave me a crooked, sickly smile, and
hurried on without stopping. How absurd and mean of him!'
Before the publication of this letter Frank Harris had told the
story of this meeting, with some embellishments, in his life of

Wilde; Mason, quoting from him, does his best to dispose of it altogether. 'If there were any basis for the story at all, it might be that either Wilde mistook his bicycler or Alexander did not see Wilde. But it may well have been manufactured. Frank Harris was not very scrupulous whether the blow was fair, so long as the blow was dealt.'

However, Hesketh Pearson, writing much later, and with the evidence of the letter to Robert Ross, says that long afterwards George Alexander told Ross that he had been ashamed of his behaviour at Napoule and that, because of it, on seeing Wilde walking in Paris one day, he had got out of his cab to speak to him. Alexander had made a very good bargain in buying the rights of Wilde's two plays and how he generously agreed to send Wilde £20 every month. After Wilde's death he paid royalties to his estate on revivals of the plays, although he need not have done so, and on his death he left the rights to Wilde's son. Thus he made honourable amends for an involuntary failure in friendship.

Following the failure of *Guy Domville* and the withdrawal of *The Importance of Being Earnest* Alexander put on a play by Henry Arthur Jones with the title *The Triumph of the Philistines*.

At the end of 1906 when Alexander was forty-eight, his biographer tells us, his thoughts and ambition were taking a new direction. 'At one time he had it in mind to put some other actor into the St James's Theatre as its protagonist and to confine himself to running it as a business. At another he thought of letting it. His own hopes were beginning to be set on public service.'

In 1907 he stood at the LCC elections as candidate for South St Pancras, representing the Moderate Party, and won the seat. He continued to act eight times a week but he gave great enthusiasm and care to the LCC, serving on many committees and becoming chairman in 1909 of the Parks and Open Spaces Committee. He began also to develop a greater political ambition and would have liked to stand for Westminster. He had difficulty in finding a seat, however, and by the time one seemed in prospect he was known to be suffering from a serious disease. In 1911 he was knighted for his services to the theatre but by 1912 he was forced to give up his work on the LCC. He was suffering from diabetes for which at that time there was no cure. In spite of this he continued for some time to act and to manage his theatre. When the war came the system of actor-management, which had been so successful since the Bancroft's early days at the Prince of Wales's Theatre, was no longer able to meet the demands of the distracted public, who cared only for musical plays, revues or spy plays that ended in serious defeat for the Germans. Alexander produced five plays between the autumn of 1914 and the summer of 1915 and acted in them all, but all of them lost money. Later with a comedy of Pinero's called *The Big Drum* and a play called *The Aristocrat* he brought his reign to a successful end. He died of consumption in 1918.

Among the plays of note that Alexander produced during his twenty-seven years in addition to those already mentioned were *The Prisoner of Zenda* and *Rupert of Hentzau* by Anthony Hope, *The Witness for the Defence* by his biographer A. E. W. Mason and *His House in Order* by Sir Arthur Pinero. A play called *Bella Donna* by the best-selling novelist Robert Hichens in collaboration with James Fagan deserves to be mentioned because after *His House in Order* it was the most financially successful play he ever put on.

Alexander was a very talented if not a great actor. He was an excellent administrator and an excellent judge of a play. These qualities combined to make his long period at the St James's memorable in the history of the theatre.

Sir Johnston Forbes-Robertson
1853-1937

In July 1951 the BBC Third Programme broadcast a programme called 'Actors Speaking of Hamlet', in which many different actors spoke one of the famous speeches from that play. Several of these voices, including those of Johnston Forbes-Robertson and of Herbert Beerbohm Tree, were from the past, whilst others were those of contemporary actors. Forbes-Robertson spoke the advice of the players, and with the disadvantages of a comparitively early recording and of belonging to an age in which the acting conventions were not only very pronounced but very different from those of today, his performance seemed to be surpassed only by that of Sir John Gielgud. He was a very fine actor and a man of exceptional taste and talent. If in the constellation of stars his light shines with less than the illumination of the very brightest, the reasons for this will appear. One is that he was simply less flashy than many of his fellows. A man of intellect and education as well as of great beauty, he was the forerunner of the school of acting of our own day.

Forbes-Robertson was the child of a romantic union. His father saw his mother walking in the street and fell so deeply in love that he wrote to her asking her to marry him. This couple were of the upper middle classes, secure and cultivated, and Johnston Forbes-Robertson's childhood was very different from that of most of the actors who were his contemporaries. His growing pains were of a kind possible only in a sheltered and civilised society, safe from poverty and free from fear.

But the world in which Forbes-Robertson grew up had more

and rarer things to offer than those which result from security, education and leisure. His father was an art critic who for years wrote on the *Sunday Times* under the name of 'Artis Amator' and whose book *Great Painters of Christendom* was a review of artists from Cimabue to Turner. His mother was so gifted as a painter that her son believed, had she been given opportunities to study, she would have made a name for herself. These two belonged to a small world inhabited by many of the most talented people in England. When as a schoolboy their eldest son began to display an interest in acting and presented to them a performance of *Hamlet* in which his sister, Ida, doubled the parts of Ophelia and the grave-digger, the audience included Ford Madox Brown and his wife, Alma-Tadema, Richard Garnett, Dante Gabriel Rossetti and, 'lying on the floor in front of them all, close to "the floats", Swinburne, who disconcerted me somewhat by lowly chanting the lines in his melodious voice in unison with mine.'

On different evenings this child heard Swinburne declaim the whole of Webster's *Vittoria Corombona* (*The White Devil*) and much of *The Duchess of Malfi* and once heard him give a reading of *Atalanta in Calydon*, just before its publication, all in a 'sort of chant'. Once, when he himself had delivered a reading of some scenes from *King Lear*, one of his mother's guests taught him an exercise for the voice. Striking a note on the piano he instructed him not to sing but to speak a line of six or seven words on that note, afterwards repeating it from note to note until he was as high as it was possible for him to speak. Thus even as a child he learned to extend his speaking register and to acquire flexibility and variety of tone, and he tells us he carried on the practice for years, finding it 'of great help, especially in long sustained passages'.

In the houses of his parents' friends the world of painting was made as free to him as that of literature. (When Rossetti painted the picture of *Dante's Dream* in which Mrs William Morris sat as Beatrice, he borrowed the young Johnston Forbes-Robertson to sit for the head of Eros.) And every summer he spent his holidays in France in the company of a celebrated priest named Victor Godfroi who taught him the French language and an appreciation of Gothic architecture.

Thus he grew up saturated with all the arts of the civilised world and with an inherited taste that was developed and refined from birth. One day Rossetti, visiting his father's house, saw some of the boy's work in oil-colour and advised that he should study painting. As a result at the age of sixteen he was sent to 'Heatherley's in Newman Street, to draw from the Antique, to the end that I might compete for a studentship at the Royal Academy.' At Heatherley's he made friends with a young man who was anxious to become a student at the Academy but who failed again and again to pass into it. One day this friend gave him a small book he had written which had just been published. The student's name was Samuel Butler and the book was *Erewhon*. A photograph of Johnston Forbes-Robertson dressed in a suit of armour was taken by Samuel Butler at this time.

Unlike his friend, Forbes-Robertson passed easily into the Royal Academy and while he was there came in contact with Landseer, Millais and Leighton. At the end of the period W. G. Wills, the dramatist (whom Shaw had called 'the resident dramatist' at the Lyceum), having seen him act as a child, came to his parents' house with a proposal that he should take a part in his play, *Mary Queen o' Scots*, then running at the Princesse's Theatre in Oxford Street. 'Though I had a great love of the theatre [Forbes-Robertson wrote later], it was no wish of mine to become an actor, but I was the eldest of a large family, and it was time for me to get out of the nest and make my own living.' With these few casual words Forbes-Robertson dismisses his whole career as a painter, for which he had spent four years in preparation, and describes his entry into the theatre where he was soon to make his name. We may wonder in vain why his parents so easily allowed him to abandon a career in art for which he had proved that he had considerable talent, and why without hesitation they allowed him to join a profession which was so little respected and, except in the case of the very few, so poorly paid. All we know is that the next day this youth found himself reciting to Mrs Rousby, the actress who played Mary Queen of Scots, that he was approved and that within three or four days he made his first appearance on the professional stage. Nor, after this fortuitous introduction to the dramatic art, did he apparently ever consider taking up any other career. His youthful beauty and natural ability

were so considerable, however, that it is not surprising that
Wills, looking for a juvenile, should have thought of him.

Mary Queen o' Scots was not a great success and was soon
withdrawn. The young Forbes-Robertson was immediately
re-engaged, this time by Charles Reade to play in *The Wandering Heir*, the play for which, after meeting her struggling with
a pony cart in a lane, Reade had brought Ellen Terry back to
London. Reade suggested to him that it would be a good thing
if he called and introduced himself to Miss Terry and he made
the journey to Taviton Street where, like so many others, he
was impressed by the straw-coloured matting, the grey-blue of
the Japanese patterns on the hangings and the life-size Venus
de Milo, and where, again like so many others, he fell in love
with the young actress. Later he was to write of this first
meeting: 'Presently the door opened, and in floated a vision of
loveliness! In a blue kimono and with that wonderful golden
hair, she seemed to melt into the surroundings and appeared
almost intangible.... I was undergoing a sort of inspection,
but her manner was so gracious that it soon cleared away my
embarrassment.' While Miss Terry wrote of him: 'Everyone
knows how good-looking he is now, but as a boy he was
wonderful – a dreamy, poetic-looking creature in a blue smock,
far more of an artist than an actor – he promised to paint quite
beautifully – and full of aspirations and ideals.' Nevertheless,
Miss Terry did not at this time think much of Forbes-Robertson's
potentialities as an actor and she advised him to give up the
theatre and stick to painting.

He bore a charmed life and his passage to the forefront of
the profession he had chosen was assured. Immediately after
playing in *The Wandering Heir* he was engaged by Charles
Calvert, of the Prince's Theatre, Manchester. In those days Manchester was a considerable artistic centre. Charles Hallé was
conducting his orchestra and Calvert's productions were
celebrated all over the country. Forbes-Robertson writes:

Calvert had been reviving some of Shakespeare's plays with great
intelligence and taste. . . . All to do with the stage was designed by
the best artists of the time, and it is doubtful if ever before Shakespeare had been put upon the stage so correctly, from an archaeological point of view. Macready, Charles Kean and Phelps had paved
the way in a measure, but between their time and Calvert's the

arts had developed in every direction, and many books on costume became available, notably those of Planché, Racinet, and Viollet-le-Duc.

But great as was his good fortune in playing with this company, so suited to develop his own tastes and talents, these years were even more notable for his meeting with Samuel Phelps. The time came when Calvert's stock company was called upon to support the veteran actor in revivals of *A Midsummer Night's Dream* and *Henry IV Part II*. In the latter play Phelps doubled the parts of Henry IV and Justice Shallow and Forbes-Robertson played Prince Hal. During the first rehearsal of the scene between the King and Prince, Phelps suddenly spoke: 'Young man,' he said, 'you know nothing about this part; come to my dressing-room tonight at seven o'clock.' From that day there developed between the old actor and the young a special relationship in which Phelps not merely coached Forbes-Robertson but seldom again played an engagement without him. Later Forbes-Robertson wrote: 'He [Phelps] had been Macready's favourite actor. Macready had played with Mrs Siddons, and she had played with Garrick.' Thus the voice that was heard on the BBC sound programme in 1951 belonged to an actor in the direct line from Garrick.

A few months before Phelps died Forbes-Robertson painted his portrait dressed as Wolsey, the last part he ever played, and this was bought by the members of the Garrick Club where it hangs today.

Since they were always on the look-out for gifted young actors, it was inevitable that sooner or later Johnston Forbes-Robertson should join the Bancrofts at the Prince of Wales's Theatre. This he did in 1878, when he had been three years on the stage, taking over the part of Orloff in *Diplomacy* from Bancroft himself. In 1879 he played again with the Bancrofts' company in *Duty*, an adaptation by James Albery of a play by Sardou, and in *Ours*. He was much impressed by the consideration and courtesy shown the company by this management, particularly in the matter of the payment of salaries. He had so bitterly resented the usual custom by which actors waited in a queue on Saturday morning that on one occasion he had gone without his salary for three weeks rather than submit to it.

In the summer of 1880 Forbes-Robertson met Modjeska, the Polish actress who was regarded, with Duse and Bernhardt, as among the greatest of the nineteenth century. She made her reputation in America and played only for a short time in London, afterwards retiring from the stage and living with her husband in California. Forbes-Robertson first played Romeo to her Juliet at a charity performance in a rectory garden in Cornwall, but later he played it in London at the Court Theatre. Sir George Arthur tells us that she tried a good many leading men but 'there is reason to think that the one who approached most nearly to her ideal was Johnston Forbes-Robertson, her Maurice de Saxe and her Romeo.'

In October 1882 Forbes-Robertson played for the first time with Irving at the Lyceum. He played Claudio in *Much Ado About Nothing* and very much surprised Miss Terry, who ten years before had advised him to give up acting and stick to painting. He was quite exceptional among young actors in the Lyceum company in that he had a constitutional incapacity to 'play a table leg'. Bernard Shaw, speaking of the qualities required of a juvenile under the star system, said: 'His great secret is to keep quiet, look serious, and, above all, not act. To this day you see Mr Lewis Waller and Mr George Alexander struggling, even in the freedom of management, with the habits of the days when they were expected to supply this particular style of article, and to live under the unwritten law: "Be a nonentity, or you will get cast for villains." ' But he added: 'Only for certain attractive individual peculiarities which have enabled Mr Forbes-Robertson to place himself above this law occasionally as a personal privilege, our stage heroes would be as little distinguishable from one another as bricks in a wall.'

As soon as Forbes-Robertson began to get parts in plays that settled down for a run he used the leisure from rehearsals to give time to his first love, painting. He came under the influence of Millais who encouraged him in this work and got him several commissions to paint portraits. Now, at the Lyceum, Henry Irving commissioned him to paint the church scene in *Much Ado About Nothing* where the marriage between Claudio and Hero is suddenly interrupted. This picture, which includes the figures of himself, William Terriss and Evelyn Millard as well

15 *top Lady Windermere's Fan.*
Left to right: Ben Webster, A.
Vane Tempest, Nutcombe Gould,
H. M. Vincent, George Alexander.
St James's Theatre, 1892.

16 *bottom* Alexander as Guy
Domville in the second act of
Guy Domville, the occasion of
Henry James's theatrical disaster.
St James's Theatre, 1895.

17 Alexander and Mrs Patrick
Campbell in *The Second Mrs
Tanqueray*. St James's Theatre,
1893.

18 A cartoon of Tree by Max
Beerbohm.

19   Malvolio. Remarking that Tree was 'a richly creative comedian', Max Beerbohm said, 'His Svengali and his Malvolio abide in my mind as two of his especial triumphs.' His Majesty's Theatre, 1901.

20   Fagin in *Oliver Twist*, a stage adaptation by J. Comyns Carr. One of Tree's greatest roles. His Majesty's Theatre, 1905.

21   Tree as Svengali in *Trilby*, the play by Paul Potter adapted from the novel by George du Maurier. This play made a fortune and enabled Tree to build Her Majesty's Theatre. Haymarket Theatre, 1895.

22 Tree as Macbeth.
His Majesty's Theatre, 1911.

24 Tree as Beethoven in the play of that name adapted by L. N. Parker from the play by René Fauchois. This play was a failure but memorable for Tree's extraordinary transformation for the name part. 1909.

Shylock in *The Merchant of
Venice*. His Majesty's Theatre,
'8.

25 *top* Du Maurier as the
original Dodor in Tree's production
of *Trilby*, with Herbert Ross as
Fouzou. Haymarket Theatre, 1895.

26 *bottom* As Raffles in the
play of that name with Laurence
Irving (the second son of Sir Henry
Irving) as Crawshay. Comedy
Theatre, 1906.

27 *top*: *Diplomacy*: the 1913 production with du Maurier as Henry Beauclerc – the part once played by Squire Bancroft – Gladys Cooper as Dora and Annie Schletter as the Marquise de Rio-Zares. Wyndham's Theatre, 1913.

28 *bottom*: *The Last of Mrs Cheyney*. Gerald du Maurier as Lord Dilling overhears the conversation between Ronald Squire as Charles, the butler, and Gladys Gray as Lady Joan, during which he recognises Charles as a crook. St. James's Theatre, 1925.

29   Du Maurier as Sir John Marley
in *Interference* by Ronald Pertwee
and Harold Dearden. St James's
Theatre, 1927.

as those of Ellen Terry and Henry Irving, now hangs in the Players' Club in New York.

In November 1883 Forbes-Robertson joined the Bancroft company, by now at the Haymarket, for the third time, and on this occasion remained with them for nearly two years until their retirement in 1885. Then he crossed the Atlantic, for the first of many times, to become Mary Anderson's leading man for an extensive tour of America. Mary Anderson was so great a beauty that when she played at the Lyceum audiences were attracted merely to see her much-famed face. She was ranked by Sir George Arthur with Mrs Rousby – with whom Forbes-Robertson had played his first part in *Mary Queen o' Scots* – Adelaide Neilson, Mrs Langtry and Gladys Cooper, as among the greatest beauties of the stage. The impressionable Forbes-Robertson once more fell deeply in love. At first this feeling seems to have been returned and the two became engaged; but on her return to England Miss Anderson met a Mr de Navarro, a rich man who like herself was a Roman Catholic, and she broke her engagement to marry him. According to the account of his niece, Beatrice, Forbes-Robertson felt deeply unhappy.

He seems to have had no great desire to become an actor-manager: on his return to England he drifted from one theatre to another for a while, and then joined John Hare with whom he remained for six years. During this time he was several times released, once to go again to New York and twice to join Irving at the Lyceum. The first of his Lyceum engagements was to play Buckingham in *Henry VIII*, the second, to play Launcelot in Comyns Carr's *King Arthur*. Then in 1895, when he was 38, he began to feel that it was necessary to his career for him to go into management for himself. He says:

I would gladly have remained an actor pure and simple, to be called off the ranks, so to speak, by anyone who wished to engage me. For over twenty-one years I had great good fortune in not only being in continual engagement, but in having been associated with the best managements. Calvert, Hollingshead, Neville, the Bancrofts, Miss Mary Anderson, Clayton, Hare and Irving. I had acted with all the leading people of that time and, though at periods being very hard worked, I had comparatively no anxieties. The very speculative and gambling nature of theatrical management was distasteful to me, and I knew that my own personal efforts as

E

an actor would be considerably handicapped by all the extra labour and anxiety which management entails. On the other hand, several actors, younger than I, had taken up management very much earlier in their careers, and there was nothing for it but to take a theatre if I was to maintain my place. Though it is true that an ideal theatre would be that in which the manager did not act, the fact remains that all the ambitious work, all the higher standards of the Drama have been maintained by the much-abused actor-manager from the days of Shakespeare down to our own time.

In the autumn of 1895 Irving left London for a long tour of America and Forbes-Robertson took over the Lyceum during his absence. He engaged Mrs Patrick Campbell as his leading lady and opened with *Romeo and Juliet*. Alan Dent says: 'The noble actor was by this time "getting on" and he really ought to have given the world his Hamlet, his masterpiece, before he was forty-four years of age [1897]. There is implanted in the family [Forbes-Robertson's family] a strong conviction that he would have done so in the first Lyceum season, beginning 1895, if Mrs Campbell had not prevailed on him to play Romeo instead.'

During this first season in management Forbes-Robertson also put on a play by Henry Arthur Jones called *Michael and His Lost Angels* – chiefly remembered for the quarrels between the author and Mrs Patrick Campbell, who resigned her part with the maximum possible sensation shortly before the first night, an adaptation of François Coppée's *Pour La Couronne*; Louis N. Parker's adaptation of Sudermann's *Heimat* under the name of *Magda*, and *The School for Scandal*. It was not an immensely successful season; both Henry Arthur Jones's play and *Magda* – later to be one of Mrs Patrick Campbell's most famous roles – had to be quickly replaced because business was bad. His production of *Romeo and Juliet* was much admired, although Bernard Shaw said of him that 'his sense of colour is essentially and Britannically an imaginative and moral one: that is, he associates low tones ("quiet colours" they call them in Marshall & Snellgrove's) with dignity and decency, and white linen with cleanliness and respectability.' But he compared the results with a recent production of Augustin Daly's and said: 'Mr Daly's scene-painters copied bad work, and Mr

Forbes-Robertson's have copied good. That makes all the difference.'

Forbes-Robertson's performance seems generally to have been regarded as in rather 'low tone'. There is at least a suggestion that the reason for this lay not with his imaginative and moral sense but with the temperament of his leading lady. He says of his opening production as an actor-manager only this: 'The first performance was given under trying circumstances, for Mrs Campbell was very ill and in great pain, Coghlan was paralysed with nervousness at his reappearance in London after many years of absence, and Nutcombe Gould, who played the Friar, had one arm in a sling! . . . I remember my own performance was tame, lacking in fire and the buoyance of youth.' Mrs Patrick Campbell's biographer comments on this: 'Our Stella, being "very ill and in great pain" managed to keep this fact between herself and her new actor-manager, her Romeo. It emerges from none of the astonishingly diverse critical notices.'

Probably the greatest success of the season was *The School for Scandal*, of which Bernard Shaw wrote: 'Mr Forbes-Robertson is an excellent Joseph Surface. He gets at the centre of the part by catching its heartlessness and insincerity, from which his good looks acquire a subtle ghastliness, his grace a taint of artifice, and all the pictorial qualities which make him so admirable as a saint or medieval hero an ironical play which has the most delicate hypocritical effect.'

In July 1897, when Irving was preparing for his second tour to America, Forbes-Robertson had neither the money nor apparently a great inclination to take the theatre again. More important still, he had no play. He was about to abandon the idea of a second season altogether when Horatio Bottomley offered to back him. At the same time Irving suggested a play, offering to lend him the scenery and properties for *Hamlet*.

At his first performance of *Hamlet* at the Lyceum Forbes-Robertson was everywhere acclaimed the greatest Hamlet of his day. He took over that night the mantle from Henry Irving and wore it until he passed it in turn to Sir John Gielgud. The critics were unanimous in their praise and dozens of accounts testify to the particular felicities of this Hamlet whose voice was as beautiful as his face. Once more Bernard Shaw's account

F*

is the most illuminating. Having remarked that at this performance the story of the play was perfectly intelligible and
quite at times took the attention of the audience off the
principal actor, he went on: 'What is the Lyceum coming to?
Is it for this that Sir Henry Irving has invented a whole series
of original romantic dramas, and given the credit of them without a murmur to the immortal bard? . . . He no sooner turns
his back for a moment on London than Mr Forbes-Robertson
competes with him on the boards of his own theatre by actually
playing off against him the authentic Swan of Avon.' He says
then that Forbes-Robertson is essentially a classical actor, the
only one, with the exception of George Alexander, established
in London management, 'What I mean by classical is that he
can present a dramatic hero whose passions are those which
have produced the philosophy, the poetry, the art, and the
stagecraft of the world, and not merely those which have
produced its weddings, coroners' inquests and executions.'

In the following passage Shaw explains the importance of
Forbes-Robertson's contribution to the theatre. Carrying on the
tradition of the best Shakespearian acting from Phelps, he can
also be seen to have been a forerunner of the greatest actors of
our own day.

Mr Forbes-Robertson's own performance has a continuous
charm, interest, and variety which are the result not only of his
well-known grace and accomplishment as an actor, but of a genuine
delight—the rarest thing on our stage—in Shakespeare's art, and a
natural familiarity with the plane of his imagination. He does not
superstitiously worship William: he enjoys him and understands
his methods of expression. Instead of cutting every line that can
possibly be spared, he retains every gem, in his own part or anyone
else's, that he can make time for in a spiritedly brisk performance
lasting three hours and a half with very short intervals. He does
not utter half a line; then stop to act; then go on with another half
line; and then stop to act again, with the clock running away with
Shakespeare's chances all the time. He plays as Shakespeare should
be played, on the line and to the line, with the utterance and acting
simultaneous, inseparable and in fact identical. Not for a moment
is he solemnly conscious of Shakespeare's reputation or of Hamlet's
momentousness in literary history: on the contrary, he delivers
us from all these boredoms instead of heaping them on us. . . . How

completely Mr Forbes-Robertson has bowled them all out by being clever enough to be simple.

On 4 September Ellen Terry wrote to Bernard Shaw:

I only saw the last two scenes of the last act of Hamlet. . . . I could not gather much . . . about the acting. I went in the dark and heard whisperings that the people liked Johnston, and didn't like anything else, and I saw a very good Norse-like picture of Hamlet's death, heard Johnston's voice, and saw his poor dear face, worn to tatters, but now and again very beautiful.

And on 7 September she wrote again: 'I came back early from the country and (passing his door) went in and pulled the new Hamlet out of bed. Poor fellow. Hamlet's mother and young sisters and I cheered him up a bit. He looks sadly old for a young man. His poor long face.'

These pitying words, written about someone who had so recently reached the height of every great actor's ambition, are difficult to understand. But Bernard Shaw would have required no explanation of them, because it was widely known that Johnston Forbes-Robertson, who had once loved Ellen Terry, was now in thrall to a fury.

Mrs Patrick Campbell was one of the finest actresses of her time, and her natural beauty of face and figure were much enhanced by a physical coordination which gave every movement she made on the stage significance as well as grace. Her speaking voice was one of her natural charms and she had intelligence and wit. She was entrancingly attractive but she may fairly be said to have been possessed of a devil. In the long run she received even less mercy from this fiend than she felt for other people, and the day would come when, no manager daring to allow her inside a theatre, she 'toured and toured with unrewarding parts in unremarkable plays, a respected living legend but none the less an actress-mis-manageress', and later still when she would live out her life in idleness and poverty. But when she was young and at the height of her powers she ruthlessly provoked those who, like Alexander, were not under her spell, and those who loved her she savaged.

She rewarded the loves of Forbes-Robertson and (later) the young Gerald du Maurier by systematic torture. She outraged those who played with her because she was not serious in the theatre: when she was in a bad mood she would turn her back on the audience and stand pulling faces at her fellow actors. When Ellen Terry came to see her play Ophelia, she changed from a dark wig to a fair in the middle of the performance because she wished to know which Miss Terry thought suited her better.[1] During the rehearsals for *Hamlet*, Ian Forbes-Robertson, who was stage manager, said to her: 'You know Mrs Campbell, you are killing my brother.'

Forbes-Robertson was of an intense, passionate and sensitive nature. His grand-daughter says, speaking of Stella Campbell: He reacted to her flippancies with violence and suffering.' In the end he became physically ill and was forced to leave the stage and go abroad to recover his health. But this was not for four years and during this time she remained his leading lady.

Hamlet was played every night for a record run of over 100 performances. Forbes-Robertson found this exhausting. No actor, he said, should play any classic role more than three or four times a week. Then in February 1898 he took his company on tour in Germany and Holland, playing *Hamlet*, *Macbeth* and (for Mrs Campbell) *The Second Mrs Tanqueray* in Berlin, Hanover, Hamburg and Amsterdam.

Mrs Patrick Campbell's presence in his company influenced his choice of plays. For her sake, and rather against his own judgment, on his return to London he put on Maeterlinck's play *Pelleas and Melisande*. Forbes-Robertson played Golaud and cast Martin Harvey as Pelleas. 'Why do you want to make such a damned fool of Forbes?' Ian Forbes-Robertson asked her at the rehearsals of this play. Today *Pelleas and Melisande* is not often performed except as Debussy's opera but it has the fragile distinction of a myth and a place in the accumulation of the world's literature. Forbes-Robertson's Macbeth to Mrs Campbell's Lady Macbeth was not regarded as a great success for either.

In 1899, after a disastrous failure in joint management with a play called *The Moonlight Blossom*, by C. B. Fernald, the two parted and Forbes-Robertson, advised by his doctor and his friends to take a long rest, went abroad. When towards the end

---

[1] Mrs Patrick Campbell was not generally very much admired as Ophelia and in her book she says: 'The real truth was that Miss Terry had given such a lovely Ophelia to the world – still fresh in everyone's memory – that there was no room for mine'.

of this holiday Ian Forbes-Robertson began to engage a company for his brother to return to, he sent him a list of possible leading ladies. On the list was the name of a young American actress, Gertrude Elliott, the sister of the more famous Maxine.

Miss Elliott was not Forbes-Robertson's first choice because he wanted a leading lady with experience of playing Shakespeare and he sent a different name to his brother. Three days later he telegraphed: 'If not too late engage Miss Elliott.' Leon Quartermain was also engaged for this tour and two new productions were given – *The Devil's Disciple* and *Carrots* – an English version by Alfred Sutro of the play by Jules Renard – in which the new leading lady played the persecuted boy.

On 8 November we find Bernard Shaw writing to tell Ellen Terry: 'News this morning that the incontinent youth Johnston Forbes-Robertson is going to be led to the altar by his leading lady, Miss Gertrude Elliott. I foresaw it, and wanted to put a clause in the contract against it. However, he might do worse. She is a nice American woman and will mend his extensively broken heart.'[1] In fact this was in Forbes-Robertson's own words 'the prelude of nothing less to me than a supremely happy life.' The Forbes-Robertsons had four daughters, all of whom inherited some of their father's talent, and one of whom, Jean, became famous in his profession.

As an actor Johnston Forbes-Robertson scarcely had a failure in any part he played: he was admired by everyone from the ordinary play-going public to the most exacting of the critics. We find Bernard Shaw writing: 'Forbes-Robertson, acting stupendously well . . . while Max Beerbohm, speaking of his performance in *The High Bid*, said: 'The words could not have been more perfectly uttered than they were by Mr Forbes-Robertson. We realised at once to whom *he* beautifully belongs. It is to Mr Henry James.' No words could be higher praise from this critic. Of his performance in *Hamlet* to which he owes his place in history, Hesketh Pearson tells us in the calm of retrospect:

No literary criticism of Hamlet was worth twopence by the side of Forbes-Robertson's dramatic explanation of him. The whole thing was final in its exquisite simplicity. . . . Leaving entirely on

[2] Forbes-Robertson was now 43, his bride some 20 years younger.

one side the actor's extraordinary physical grace and the organ-music of his marvellous voice, he was the only artist of his time – I dare guess of any time – who was Hamlet in gesture and speech. He lived in the period and spoke its language. . . . Forbes-Robertson's Hamlet was the only Shakespearean performance one could see twenty times (and twice in one day) yet wish to go on seeing it twenty times twenty.

While speaking of Tree's Hamlet, Desmond MacCarthy said: 'We much preferred the fastidious, scholarly, airy-gallent Hamlet of Forbes-Robertson.'

As a manager Forbes-Robertson's name was never connected with a particular London theatre in the way Irving's was with the Lyceum and Alexander's with the St James's. He spent a very great deal of his time on tour, some of it in the English provinces, even more in America and Canada, and in over twenty years he played only four seasons in London. He was often away for a year or more at a time and he was as well known in New York as in London, in Winnipeg, Montreal, Toronto, Washington, Chicago, Philadelphia as in Liverpool or Manchester. 'We visited [he said of the American tour of 1903] all the leading cities in the east, to the south as far as Richmond . . . and westwards to the restless and energetic city of Chicago.' Owing to the American custom of morning performances he was sometimes forced to play Hamlet nine times a week and during the course of his visits he watched many of the cities of North Americas change from one night stands to places where his company could perform for a week. When he planned his farewell tour to all the towns where he was known, he found that it would take four years to perform it.

His productions were noted, as might be expected, for their scholarship and taste. His chief Shakespearian productions apart from *Hamlet* were of *Romeo and Juliet*, *Macbeth* and *Othello*. In none of these roles was he transcendent, the temperament of the classical actor being less suited to these parts.

In the discovery and production of new plays, he seems to have had neither better nor worse judgment than that of the other actor-managers and his appreciation was neither so fine nor so literary as to bring about a division between his tastes and those of the public he had to please. He chose his plays, as every manager must, to suit this public, but he chose them, too, as every actor must, to suit himself. He had no difficulty in reconciling the two, nor was he lacking in a straightforward business sense. Among the plays to which he gave their first performance the only ones of interest today are *The Devil's Disciple, Caesar and Cleopatra, The High Bid*, a dramatised version of *The Light that Failed* – a play that caused Max Beerbohm to ask himself whether perhaps Rudyard Kipling was the pseudonym of a woman – and a curious play, forgotten today but with which, after *Hamlet*, his name was most often associated, called *The Passing of the Third Floor Back*.

Caesar and Cleopatra was written for Forbes-Robertson but Bernard Shaw could not persuade him to produce it for several years. In 1899 he wrote to Ellen Terry: 'Forbes-Robertson has given up Caesar. "Can't run the risk of such a heavy production." Is going on tour next Sept. instead of opening a new theatre – wants the last act of *The Devil's Disciple* altered into an English victory. I have cut him off without a shilling.' When Forbes-Robertson finally produced it, he did so at the Amsterdam Theatre, New York, and then took it on tour in America and Canada. It is an interesting fact that after being very well received in all these places, it failed at a subsequent production in London. Forbes-Robertson says that in some places it was said that the reason it succeeded in New York and failed in London was that the New York audiences were less sophisticated – a view, he adds, that was highly amusing to those who knew America's theatre-going public. That this amusement was justified seems to be proved by the fact that *Caesar and Cleopatra* had far more success in London when he played it again at Drury Lane in 1913.

Caesar was, after Hamlet, Forbes-Robertson's greatest role. Hesketh Pearson tells us: 'There has been nothing to compare with it on the stage of my time: a great classical actor interpreting to perfection a self-inspired classical part. . . . There was not a movement or an inflection in his Caesar that could have been bettered.'

The High Bid was written by Henry James originally for Ellen Terry, but when it became clear that she would never put it on the novelist re-wrote it as a short story and called it *Covering End*. Forbes-Robertson, reading this story, was struck

by how admirably it might suit the stage. He wrote to James
asking if he would be willing to have it turned into a play and
James sent him *The High Bid*.[3] Forbes-Robertson gave the play
some performances in the provinces but he did not at the time
take it to London. He opened instead at the St James's Theatre
in Jerome K. Jerome's play *The Passing of the Third Floor Back*.
The story of this play is of a lodger in a boarding house in
Bloomsbury who so influences the minds of his fellow-lodgers
that they are translated to a higher plane of thought and feeling
and where they find peace, love and contentment come to them.
The Passing of the Third Floor Back was held by some to be
blasphemous, by others to be merely puerile, but it was one of
the greatest successes of its time and, after *Hamlet*, made more
money for Forbes-Robertson than any other play. After rebuk-
ing the actor-manager for not bringing *The High Bid* into
London, Max Beerbohm wrote:

Appparently in doubt whether Mr. James be good enough for the
metropolis, he gives us Mr. Jerome Klapka Jerome. This tenth-rate
writer has been, for many years, prolific of his tenth-rate stuff. But
I do not recall, in such stuff of his as I have happened to sample,
anything quite so vilely stupid as 'The Passing of the Third Floor
Back.' I do not for a moment suppose that Mr. Forbes-Robertson
likes it one whit more than I do. And I wish his pusillanimity in
prostituting his great gifts to it were going to be duly punished. The
most depressing aspect of the whole matter is that the play is so
evidently a great success.

But Max Beerbohm was wrong in thinking Forbes-Robertson
prostituted his gifts. On the contrary, when Forbes-Robertson
read the play he was at first dismayed because he felt that in
the ordinary sense it was no play at all. He says, however,
that he gradually became deeply impressed by the elevating
character of the theme. He discussed the matter with his wife
and they both agreed that although some people might like this
play very much these would not be enough to make it profit-

[3] On 27 March 1908 when Forbes-Robertson performed *The High Bid* for the first
time at Edinburgh he received a telegram from Ellen: 'You have my play!' Forbes-
Robertson writes: 'We then discovered that she did not consider she had parted with
her acting rights when agreeing to its being published in story form. It was a most
unfortunate misunderstanding, soon, however, cleared up, but embarrassing for me
at the time'.

able : it was unlikely to draw. Yet in spite of this they decided
that they must produce it. 'The long and short of it was, we were
both in love with the high motive of the play, and decided to
produce it solely on that score. As time proved, we were well
rewarded for our enthusiasm.' They were rewarded in England
and all over America and Scotland. *The Passing of the Third
Floor Back* turned out to be one of those plays that could be
revived again and again and used as a stop-gap when some
other play failed.

In June 1913 Johnston Forbes-Robertson received a knighthood. In the same year, although not quite sixty, he started
on his long farewell tour of England, Scotland, Canada and
America. After playing three months at the Theatre Royal
Drury Lane, three months in New York, a month in Chicago and
visiting Indianapolis, St Louis, Kansas City, Denver, Salt Lake
City, Los Angeles, and San Francisco, he burned all his scenery
except that of four plays because from now on he would play
in no town long enough to need more. In Portland, Tacoma,
Seattle, Victoria, Calgary, Edmonton and Winnipeg he found
himself in the midst of preparations for war but he continued
on his nomadic way, playing in the last year of his tour only
one-night stands.

Here are the words with which this flawless actor, who
entered the theatre in response to an invitation and who, almost
alone in the ranks of leading actors, never had to struggle for
place or admiration, summed up his career :

I stripped myself of Hamlet's garb with no sort of regret, but
rather with a great sense of relief, for not only was it my last
appearance in a part which cost me a vast amount of mental and
physical strain, but the last of theatrical management, the gambling
nature of which had always been abhorrent to me. On looking back,
it seems to me that I was far more nervous on the last performance
of *Hamlet* than on the first. It is said that nervousness is a necessary
attribute for the actor, and that he who does not suffer from it is
rarely of much account in his art. It may be so, but all I can say is
that as far as I personally am concerned, it has been nought but a
shackling handicap. Never at any time have I gone on the stage
without longing for the moment when the curtain would come
down on the last act. Rarely, very rarely have I enjoyed myself in
acting. This cannot be the proper mental attitude for an actor, and

I am persuaded, as I look back on my career, that I was not temperamentally suited to my calling.

He lived for more than twenty years, until 1937, happy in retirement.

Sir Herbert Beerbohm Tree
1853-1917

Sir Herbert Beerbohm Tree succeeded Sir Henry Irving as leader of the theatre. A natural leader of men as well as a great actor, he was born to this role and he revelled in it. He had the grand flamboyant manner and, unlike Irving who was pontifical and awe-inspiring, an irresistible charm. On his death his half-brother, Max Beerbohm, who had grown to dislike biographies of actors, decided against this form of memorial and, saying that Tree was 'many-sided, impressing different people in different ways', he collected together instead a book of short pieces by those who knew him best under the title *Herbert Beerbohm Tree*. Any doubts one might entertain as to the quality of this man are here set at rest by the giftedness of those who testify to it.

He was indeed 'many-sided' and it is possible for his daughter, Viola, to tell us convincingly that he was 'absolutely natural and unaffected' when it is clear from other people's accounts that he exaggerated certain qualities – an absent-mindedness, a whimsical vagueness – and put them to the service of his wit, his privacy and his need to cajole and persuade. But he was in a large way unaffected. Blithely romantic at a time when romanticism was becoming old-fashioned, he carried this off by the size of his undertakings and his own personality: friendly and sensitive, he was, nevertheless, completely self-absorbed. Desmond MacCarthy spoke of his 'restless, dream-glazed eyes which looked at objects in a steady, imperceptive way as though staring at his own thoughts, and that bar above them, which it is said, tends to lift its possessor an inch or two above the solid ground.'

Viola Tree inherited much of her father's nature and she succeeds probably best of anyone in the difficult and delicate task of creating on paper a unique, lively and credible human being. She tells us that Tree 'bore no resemblance to fathers as a race'. He was 'a never-failing excitement, a surprise, an event'. She remembers him best leaning on something, 'always with his hat on and wearing a big, flamboyant coat and carrying some very tall walking stick'. He never entered a room or the garden without called 'Viola!' or 'Children!' which had, she said, the effect of a flourish of trumpets.

He was very dominating, 'almost domineering', 'even to the point of casting out fear'. Thus, when she was rehearsing *The Tempest*:

As his prospective Ariel . . . I had to try the wires . . . and was timidly discussing with the professional on which foot to take off. The wire was, I remember, uncomfortably hooked into my strait waistcoat when he walked on to the stage. 'I always know about these things, dear; don't argue: fly!' and he gave the order to the mechanic up above to let go. Without a murmur I flew, my feet dangling high above his head, and tingling like telegraph wires at the sudden vibrations of his voice. 'Very good, dear; now sing!'

But although he was so dominating, he always thanked his children for being with him. 'So lovely, dear, your being with me.'

Tree was known to be very diffident about his looks and when he went to sit for his portrait to Sargent, who was 'terribly shy and modest about his work', his daughter feared that left to themselves they would never start. So the moment Tree stepped on the dais she called out: 'Look towards the window Daddy.'

He did so. Mr. Sargent became covered with confusion. 'Don't strain, don't strain; you will never be able to keep that pose'. My father seemed surprised and answered: 'No, no, it's quite natural.' This defiant turn of head and illuminated look was normal to him, before whose mind's-eye processions of popes, jugglers and sinister servants holding peacocks in the leash passed continuously to the accompaniment of music, sad, strange or grotesque.

And in a further passage, she says:

I think I shall always remember the last act of *Richard II* as my best time with him, because in it we did not seem to be on the stage – we were showing what we really felt about things: that there was an audience looking on didn't seem to matter. I played the Queen – very badly, except for the one scene, in which I became myself. I had to wait for his coming (Act V, Scene 1. A Street) with Aumerle:

> The Queen: This way the King will come; this is the way
>   To Julius Ceasar's ill-errected tower—

After this I looked instinctively to see my father come out, very simply and rather tired, dressed in black, and each time it seemed as if he were surprised to see me standing there, and as if we were really to say good-bye to each other for the first and last time. Then I fell on his neck, and said my speech sobbing, because at that moment I was not Richard's Queen but my father's daughter – all alone on the great isolation of the stage, for Aumerle and the super halberdiers had vanished like shadows to the dark corners. He never could begin his speech at once – he was so worried by my tears, as I looked at him through blinded eyes. By and by I put my head down on his shoulder so that he might begin – then only his voice came loud and ringing like a clarion:

> Join not with grief, fair woman do not so,
> To make my end too sudden. . . .

Today shame would intervene between us and such large, spontaneous expressions, but in the Trees they rose unrestrainedly to the surface.

There are many references to Tree's imaginative self-absorption. Bernard Shaw said that when his feelings were engaged he was human and shrewd and tenacious but that 'you really could not lodge an indifferent fact in his mind'. This quality, he said, was enormously valuable to Tree as an actor because he avoided staleness by always hearing the other performers' lines as though for the first time. At a certain point in *Pygmalion* Mrs Patrick Campbell had to throw a pair of slippers in Tree's face; and at rehearsal Shaw took great trouble to provide Mrs Campbell with a very soft pair, because being very dexterous she was a dead shot. Nevertheless, when the scene was reached the effect was appalling. Tree had totally forgotten that there was any such incident in the play; 'and it seemed to him that Mrs Campbell, suddenly giving away to an impulse of diabolical wrath and hatred, had committed an unprovoked and brutal assault on him. The physical impact was nothing; but the wound to his feelings was terrible.'

Tree was gradually reassured by Mrs Campbell and by the entire personnel of the theatre crowding solicitiously round him 'explaining that the incident was part of the play, and even exhibiting the prompt book to prove their words'. But, Shaw wrote, since it was clear Tree would be just as surprised and upset every time this happened, Mrs Campbell took care never to hit him again, and 'the incident was consequently one of the least convincing in the performance'.

Johnston Forbes-Robertson tells us that once in the street outside the theatre stage-door Tree was describing to Edward Sass, a fellow actor, how in his performance of the death of King John, he swept the crown from his head: 'Suiting the action to the word he swept off his hat, then, pointing to it lying in the gutter, and while Sass was spellbound by this unusual proceeding on the part of a distinguished actor in the public street, he asked: "Whose hat is that?" '

These incidents go near to an impression of the aprocryphal or of a great actor play-acting. This occurs again and again in anecdotes about Tree because it was absolutely natural to him to extend reality into the realm of make-believe. Discussing his equipment as an actor, Desmond MacCarthy speaks in a brilliantly explanatory phrase of his 'comprehension of the shifting connection between the heightened pose and the genuine feeling underneath'. An unfortunate result of this smudging of the boundary between the real and the fantastic is that Tree has been over-quoted. It is the duty of all who record the sayings and doings of public men to compensate by rigorous selection for the loss of the powerful personality, the exhilarating charm, behind which in life, as by sleight of hand, the exuberant failures slipped away; but it is a duty too seldom observed. It should have been particularly binding on those who wrote about Tree because of a characteristic Edmund Gosse has described in the following passage:

He was whimsical by nature and his wit was an offshoot of his whim. He tossed his arrows up into the air and sometimes they hit the bull's-eye miraculously; sometimes they did not. I have heard him say things that were deliciously apropos, and with a rapidity of mind that was exhilarating; but I have also heard him murmur things that were almost fatuous; and he seemed to lack personal criticism in this respect. . . . There was always debate behind his back whether Herbert Tree was 'clever' or merely silly, the truth being that he could be both.

Gosse adds, however, that if a quip of his was accepted Tree was pleased, if scornfully rejected 'not less pleased'. His object was 'never to instruct but to stimulate interest'. But the quality which above all made Tree irresistable is described in the following incident: Max Beerbohm tells us that once he was standing on the doorstep of his mother's house with another man when Herbert Tree arrived in a taxi. 'How are you, Mr Tree?' Beerbohm's friend asked. 'I?' said Herbert, shaking the proffered hand and gazing around him. 'I? Oh, I'm radiant.' Later Max's friend remarked to him that from any other man the epithet applied to himself would have seemed absurd, but that Tree's use of it was right and proper. 'He looked radiant, it was obvious that he felt radiant, and he told the simple truth in saying that he *was* radiant.'

It is tempting to speculate on the mature relationship of the two gifted brothers – the exuberant, romantic, popular actor who inevitably produced a broad if 'radiant' impression, and the flawless, perfected Max. Johnston Forbes-Robertson tells us that Tree once said to him: 'There is only one thing I have against Max, it is born in on me that in after years I shall come to be remembered only as Max's brother.' And Max himself encourages speculation, without doing anything to satisfy it, in the following passage:

I am afraid that as the years went by, and the gap between our ages was accordingly contracted, each of us found himself even more shy in presence of the other than he was wont to be with people at large. An old friend of Herbert's once said to him and me, in the course of a dinner in the 'Dome' of His Majesty's: 'You two, when you're together, always seem to be in an attitude of armed neutrality.' I suggested to Herbert that 'terrified love' would be a truer description.

Julius Beerbohm came to London in 1830 at the age of twenty and became a corn merchant. He was a German whose mother was of Slavonic descent and he married an Englishwoman,

Constantia Draper. This couple had three sons, Ernest, Herbert and Julius, and, when Constantia died at under the age of thirty, Julius married her sister Eliza and produced four more children as closely related to the first family as, except for full brothers, it is possible to be. Three of these children were girls and the fourth was Henry Maximilian Beerbohm – the incomparable Max. Nowhere in the history of either the Beerbohm or the Draper families is there anyone to account for the fact that both sisters bore Julius a son of such exceptional talent.

Herbert Draper Beerbohm was born in 1852 and educated partly at schools in England and partly at a school at Schnepfeuthal in Thuringia, where the discipline was of the ruthless cruelty known to us through accounts of German schools at the time. This experience has been held responsible for Herbert Beerbohm growing up to believe that all education was useless and that 'As humour is above wit, so is intelligence above intellect and instinct above knowledge.' But this kind of thought is very common among talented people to whom it is naturally attractive.

Julius Beerbohm became well-established as a corn merchant and, as they grew up, put each of his sons into his own business. None wished to remain there. Ernest, the eldest, departed to become a sheep farmer in Cape Colony where he married a coloured woman, known in his family as a 'brunette', and Julius, the youngest, also went abroad to Patagonia, about which he later wrote a book. Only when his second son announced his wish to become an actor did Julius draw the line. The life of an actor, he said, was all very well if one reached the top of the tree – a remark which is said to have suggested to his son the name he was later to take – but a disreputable and miserable business for everyone else. Herbert, therefore, alone among his sons, remained in his office for eight years, until he was twenty-five.

During his time, like so many of his contemporaries, he taught himself the rudiments of the art of acting in amateur dramatic companies.[1] As can be seen from his photographs he had strange looks, not obviously suited to his chosen profession. He was over six foot tall, his hair was bright red and his

[1] In an amateur society called the 'Philothespians' Tree met two other young city clerks – George Alexander and Lewis Waller.

eyes very blue with pale lashes. He was a natural mimic and he early became known for his imitations of leading actors of the day. For eight years he exhausted himself and his salary travelling about to rehearse and perform in plays, living, as his half-brother described it, in a 'whirl of amateur theatricals'. By February 1878, when he made his first professional performance in a touring company at Folkestone, he had already made some name for himself, and his father reluctantly gave his consent to it. From this time onwards he was always in work, sometimes in London, often on tour, but for several years he made no particular mark. His biographer, Hesketh Pearson writes: 'The oddity of Tree's personality did not appeal to everyone, and in spite of his occasional successes in London no one would have prophesied for him a brilliant future. The managers preferred the type of actor whose appearance and personality attracted women, such as H. B. Conway, who became a *jeune premier* at the Lyceum under Irving and an idol of female playgoers.' And he quotes the lessee of the Vauderville Theatre writing to his acting-manager as follows: 'And now, my dear Smaile, please understand me, I will give Tree £15 a week – not a penny more. H. B. Conway can have £25, as I think he will draw it, but £15 is every shilling as much as Tree is, or ever will be, worth.'

In 1881, when he was twenty-nine, Herbert Tree met Miss Maud Holt, a girl of eighteen who was studying and teaching Latin, Greek and mathematics at Queen's College, Harley Street and intending to go on to Girton. Miss Holt was also very much interested in amateur dramatics and had played Ophelia and Beatrice with amateur companies. A year later Tree asked her to be his wife. The course of this love affair, although it was to last all Tree's life, was not entirely smooth. A number of the letters he wrote her during the course of their engagement survive and have been quoted very fully in Hesketh Pearson's biography. From these it appears that Maud Holt was a strong-willed young lady and one who was inclined to disapprove of the ways of the members of the profession she wished to join. Tree wrote a spontaneous and natural prose and his replies to her strictures are not spoiled, as the letter of his contemporaries so often are, by pompous phraseology. His letters seem tender, solicitous and straightforward.

When he offended his fiancée by giving a scarf to Myra Home (who married Pinero) on her birthday, he wrote to her:

Oh, pray don't think seriously what you spoke hastily, dearest – Only it is so difficult to act strictly according to the cruel letter of what is considered the right thing to do. I assure you most solemnly that I have not broken through the spirit of what is right in doing what I have done – Indeed my only reproach is that I should make you unhappy.

And he tells her that he will pass her house that night after the theatre at about a quarter past eleven. 'If you would see me for only a minute, dear, I should be much happier.'

When Miss Holt spoke of the rumours she had heard about his life before he had met her, he begged her not to be too much influenced by narrow-minded advisers.

I was foolish – perhaps weak – but not vicious or dishonour-able. – I gave you to understand, when I first asked you to care for me, that my past life had not been entirely unworldly. I repented what I had done, and you forgave me. I have endeavoured to make every reparation for the error committed before I knew you, and I have been true and loyal to you. – There was never at any time the slightest claim upon me, and I have recently taken steps to remove even the possibility of a shadow in the future. Can I do more? Have I hitherto been impatient of your reproaches, and the attacks of your friends? – To whom do you owe your allegiance – to them or to me? It is for you now to say – I do not care to enter into competition with them – nor will I allow you to despise me, as you would grow to despise me, did not I demand your entire trust, and a love which is not regulated by acquaintances.

One is inevitably reminded of the young Irving writing to Florence O'Callaghan: 'Say of her to me, Flo, what you will – I willingly accept it but sayings or opinions of others keep back – especially expressions of condescension. These I cannot endure.' And: 'I hope my dearest with all my soul that when the day is past an end will be put to all reproaches from you or mis-understandings by me. . . . You still love me as you did – don't you my darling? *Answer this.*'

The situation of the two young men was very different because Tree and Maud Holt sincerely loved each other and theirs was to be a lifelong partnership in marriage and on the stage; but there is a dignity and a proper wilfulness in the letters of each which adds nobility to their relations with the two rebellious young women, and which allows us to comprehend why, in turn, they were to head their profession.

Tree's letter was written while Maud was away in Aix-les-Bains looking after a sick sister. Before he had time to post it he received a telegram from her saying: 'Come if like directly.' He then enclosed what he had written with another letter in which he said: 'Since writing this, I have received your telegram. I shall come to you at once. Nevertheless, I think it right to send this letter.' He then hurried to Aix where in his agitation he wrote rather incoherently:

Perhaps you do not want me after my last letter. – Anyhow, it may be that it would be preferred that I should not see you. If this is so I will not trouble you – I will not inflict myself on you, and if you will only give me a hint I will leave by the very first train. . . . Anyhow I only intended making a very short stay. – I did not wish to be unkind in saying what I did in my last letter to you – but it will be much better for us all not to be undecided any longer. . . . I don't know what to do or say – I wish the two hours of suspense were over. Don't hesitate to do whatever you think for the best. H.

This touching appeal could hardly fail in its effect and the two spent happy days in Aix together. Later, however, Maud Holt took exception to Tree's friendship with E. W. Godwin, the architect and stage designer, whose many amorous affairs had come to her ears. Once more Tree issued an ultimatum; once more she accepted it, and it was not long before the little half-brother waited under the rustic arches to act as best man. 'When at last he appeared . . .' Max wrote later, 'he looked so pale and excited that I gasped out instinctively: "Have you lost the ring?" I felt, god though he was, that it would be rather like him to have lost the ring.' And for proof that marriage brought tolerance to the bride, we have a letter from her husband written when she was away from home in which he remarks casually: 'The guests, Vezin, Godwin and Claud Ponsonby, have just departed. – We have had a pleasant chatty evening – plenty of scandal, you may imagine. – The corpses of soda water bottles and those of departed spirits are strewn around me, and I am alone.'

It was the custom to say of Tree that as an actor he remained

an amateur all his life. By this was meant not that the effects
he achieved were amateurish but that he could not repeat them
again and again. Henry Irving was self-taught, as Tree was,
but he acquired a control that enabled him to seize on and fix
a movement or a tone of voice, so that, without recapturing the
emotion that first inspired it, he could reproduce it every night
for weeks. Tree seems never to have wished to learn this
technique and he approached his parts afresh every night. This
must have made him a difficult actor to play with but it saved
him, as Bernard Shaw said, from staleness and provoked in
him, as in Viola Tree's account of his scene with her in *Richard
II*, a spontaneous response to the other actors in the play. This
lack of technique unfitted him for certain parts as for instance
where long sustained passages made it necessary to devise and
then learn a method of breathing, but it did nothing to diminish
the impact he made on the stage. Max Beerbohm who, in his
capacity as dramatic critic to the *Saturday Review*, never wrote
about his brother, tells us in his memoir that even as a child he
could see 'the enormous difference between him and the
ordinary "sound" actor, and why it was that his fame was so
great, and always becoming greater.'

Tree was pre-eminent as a character actor because he had
the ability to transform his whole personality and appearance
so that it often happened that he came on to the stage unrecognised. He did this without tremendously heavy make-up but by
a mental and physical, an internal and external, assumption of
the role he was to perform. Louis Parker says that when it
became known that Tree would play Beethoven many people
doubted his ability to do it because of the physical differences:
Beethoven was short and stocky with dark eyes. Then he says:
'I shall never forget our gasp of surprise when Tree made his first
entrance at the dress-rehearsal: a short, stocky, square-set little
man, with dark eyes. His head was Beethoven's head. I have
two portraits before me as I write: one of Beethoven and one
of Tree in the part, and it is difficult to tell which is which.'
However Bernard Shaw did not admire Tree as a character
actor and he once wrote:

His *tours de force* in the art of make-up do not impose on me:
any man can get into a wicker barrel and pretend to be Falstaff, or

put on a false nose and call himself Svengali. Such tricks may very
well be left to the music-halls: they are altogether unworthy of an
artist of Mr Tree's pretensions. When he returns to the serious
pursuit of his art by playing a part into which he can sincerely
enter without disguise or mechanical denaturalization, may I be
there to see! Until then let him guard the Haymarket doors against
me; for I like him best when he is most himself.

The evidence is very strong, however, that this critical treatment of Tree as a character actor was due to a want of appreciation in Shaw rather than to a failure in Tree. Max Beerbohm
wrote to Hesketh Pearson:

Shaw's remark about Herbert's *métier* being 'straight parts' seems
to me to be great nonsense. I remember he once said to me that
Herbert wasn't really a comedian, but a romantic actor – a theory
which I flatly rejected. Herbert had of course a strong element of
romance, but the main thing about him was that he was an
immensley versatile and *richly creative* comedian.

And after quoting this passage Pearson adds: 'The truth is
that Tree was equally successful in character comedy and quiet
pathos. Where he failed completely was in purely romantic
work, of which he gave the worst example in 1892 when he
produced *Hamlet*.'

Desmond MacCarthy's account of Tree acting is by far the
best, most sympathetic and most perceptive account left to us.
He tells us that Tree was essentially 'a romantic actor, perhaps
the last exuberant descendant of Romanticism flowering on the
English stage'. And again that 'in judging his talent and in
placing him among his predecessors and contemporaries, it is
important to think of him as an actor trailing with him into
the twentieth century clouds of romanticism, from which, for
our eyes, the glow and colour had in a measure departed.'
Then he goes on to say that, if Tree was pre-eminently a
romantic, the next thing to note about him is that he was a
character actor. 'A character actor is one that does not excel
chiefly in playing certain recurring situations, but in building
up before our eyes a definite human being. Tree possessed the
power of conceiving character in a very high degree. Of all his
contemporaries he had the largest share of this author's gift.'
But he goes on to say that an actor must have also the faculty

of representing the characters he understands and that Tree's power of understanding character often outran his power of representing it.

He could make himself look like Falstaff; he understood and revelled in the character of Falstaff, but his performance lacked fundamental force. Hence the contradiction in his acting: his performance as a whole often fell short of high excellence, yet these same impersonations were lit by insight and masterly strokes of interpretation, which made the spectator feel that he was watching the performance of the most imaginative of living actors.

MacCarthy tells us that Tree was always better in representing weakness than strength – 'failure whether of the faithful or ignoble kind' – and that he was 'admirable in the expression of that irony which is the revenge of the beaten or the refuge of the helpless'.

One characteristic of his acting – and it distinguished him from most of his eminent contemporaries – was that he always acted from his imagination. He flung himself neck and crop into his parts. Sometimes the results were disasterous, but even on these occasions there was always discernible that effort to become entirely the part which is the foundation of good acting.

And, most revealing of all, Desmond MacCarthy tells us this:

He was pre-eminently a social man, not a solitary one. He had that temperament which saves a man from becoming a crank, but at the same time makes it hard for him to trust those slight evanescent promptings which must be listened for and obeyed, if he is to find himself completely as an artist. Although he had obviously plenty of confidence and courage in undertaking the most diverse parts, I doubt if he had in him that hard kernel of arrogance which has made it easier for less gifted, less original men to get the best and only the best, out of themselves.

Herbert Tree made his first big hit as the Rev. Robert Spalding in *The Private Secretary*. He was under contract to a man named Edgar Bruce who let his theatre and his company with it to Charles Hawtrey. Tree was outraged at having to play this part and as a protest he deliberately burlesqued it, inventing much business and many gags. But these were so successful that they were taken over by W. S. Penley, the actor who afterwards played the part again and again and later became the original Charley's Aunt. Tree himself left *The Private Secretary* to play an Italian spy in a thriller, and with his performance of this very dissimilar part, his reputation was made.

Unlike Forbes-Robertson, who went into management because he felt it forced upon him, or Irving who did so to produce the plays that gave him the greatest opportunity as an actor, Tree was attracted to management for its own sake and remarking that 'Everything comes to him who doesn't wait', he took a theatre of his own at the earliest opportunity. In 1887, at the age of thirty-five and with the financial backing of a friend, he opened in management at the Comedy Theatre in Panton Street in a play called *The Red Lamp*. Tree played Demetrius, the head of the secret police, and when he came on to the stage made up to represent this character he did so unrecognised. 'Ripened judgment [Max Beerbohm was later to write] has not inclined me to think *The Red Lamp* the greatest play ever written. But I thought it so on its first night – the first night of Herbert's management. And I saw it seventeen times, without changing my opinion.'

Following the success of *The Red Lamp* Tree took the Haymarket Theatre and there followed one of those long settled periods, like the period of the Bancroft management, which has made this historic theatre one of the most famous in London.

Tree was beyond everything else a man of the theatre, one of those who find romance and fulfilment quite as much in the long stone corridors to the dressing-rooms, the voice of the call-boy, the mechanism of the scene shifts and the lighting, the vaulting shadows behind and the artificial brilliance in front of the sets, all the paraphernalia of stage-craft, as in the applause of the audiences. Consequently, his first allegiance was to the theatre, not to himself, and, unlike Irving, who required only 'table legs' to support the central figure, he engaged the best actors and actresses he could find and gave them the greatest opportunity. Bernard Shaw, in a letter to Ellen Terry, wrote that Tree 'surrounds himself with counter-attractions and lets them play him off the stage to their heart's content as long as he takes the money at the doors'. And, although Ellen Terry characteristically replied: 'You think Tree "lets the rest of his company play him off the stage"! I'd like you to see what is written in his heart upon that subject,' he insisted that Lewis

Waller, playing with Tree, was 'ten times as good as the very best man you have supporting Henry at the Lyceum. He has authority, self-respect, dignity, and often brilliancy: you do not see him dodging about the stage with one eye on "the governor".'

Tree also had a greater literary taste than was common in the theatre at that time. He was always on the look-out for plays of some real quality; it was he who produced *Beau Austin*, and who suggested to W. E. Henley and Robert Louis Stevenson that they write a new version of the old melodrama *Robert Macaire* – plays which caused Max Beerbohm to give the whole of one week's article in the *Saturday Review* to the problem: What precisely was Mr Henley's share in the plays done jointly by Robert Louis Stevenson and himself? His speculations upon the point, as on all others, should be read for themselves. What is certain is that Tree as well as Henley had some share in the new version of *Macaire*.

> I suggested to them [he wrote] to make Robert Macaire a philosopher in crime. . . . I made a number of suggestions for the play and they wrote it, offering that I should be a part author. . . . This I declined – as I had done nothing. . . . I had occasion to regret my modesty, for when we came to produce the play I wanted to make some alterations, as I considered the construction somewhat faulty. My suggestions were pooh-poohed. The play was produced and the notices given to my performance were more flattering than were the references to the play. . . . Henley wrote to me somewhat violently, saying I had evidently done the butter-slide trick with the play; to which I replied that if he would not cease his correspondence I would do the play no more. . . . Still I have always liked him in spite of his bludgeonesque manners. One day I met him in the street in Edinburgh. He asked me, 'Why did you not come to see me?' To which I replied, 'My dear Henley, I forgot for the moment that we were on speaking terms.'

Hesketh Pearson said of Tree that he was 'the father of the repertory movement'. Quite early in his management he gave a series of Monday evening and Wednesday afternoon performances of plays – such as *Beau Austin* – which he thought could not be played as a commercial proposition. In spite of Irving's many successes it was still believed that 'Shakespeare spells ruin' and Tree originally put on *The Merry Wives of*

Windsor at one of these extra performances. In 1888, however, it went into the evening bill and was so frequently revived
that Falstaff became one of Tree's most popular parts.

'When is repertory not repertory?' he asked. 'When it is a
success.'

With the great success of *The Merry Wives of Windsor* it
became apparent that Tree was becoming a potential rival to
Irving. It was commonly believed that Irving watched the
advance of the younger man with jealousy and several rather
grim stories are told as evidence that he entertained this
unbecoming emotion. In a play called *The Village Priest*, produced at the Haymarket, an actor named Charles Allan, who
had been a member of the Lyceum company, made a single
entrance and spoke the words 'Allons! Marche'. When Irving
went round to see Tree after watching the play he talked lightly
for some time and on taking his leave said with obvious
embarrassment: 'Good-night – hm – Allen   excellent – hm –
God bless you!' And ten years later a friend of Irving's
described sitting with him while, at the close of Act 2 of a play
called *Herod*, Tree in the leading part ascended an imposing
bronze staircase, reciting the names of the places recently
added to his dominions.

> Hippo, Samaria and Gadara,
> And Gaza unto these, and Straton's tower.
> And high-walled Joppa, and Anthedon's shore,

'Well,' Irving's friend asked, 'What do you think of that?'
And Irving replied:

'Ah! Hm. . . . A very fine flight of steps.'

It is probably, nevertheless, an over-simplification to describe
the emotions Irving felt as jealousy. When he went to see his
own son H. B. Irving play Hamlet, a production in which a
brazier was placed on the battlements, the only thing he could
find to say was: 'I see – me boy – the streets are up in Elsinore.'

And, although in one case he was watching one of the leading actors of his day and in the other the early efforts of a
youth who was to become a good but never a great actor,
it seems likely that to Irving they were both men whose performances to his embarrassment he could not praise. It is very
common for interpretative artists, musicians as well as actors,

to be unable to see any merit in the performance of a contemporary. Having, after long years of study and experience, achieved a rendering of a role or a piece of music which, while giving the greatest play to their own talents, adds the sum of these talents to the genius of the composer, they cannot consider a rendering which is quite different equally valid and illuminating. A certain integrity to their art forbids them praising what they cannot like and makes them feel resentful that anything so unworthy should be successful. In many artists this impervious shell or arrogance is a constituent of the single-minded devotion which enables them to give the fullest expression to their own gifts. Irving was undoubtedly one of these. He seldom visited the theatre, often giving offence because he failed in the courtesy of going to see foreign actors in London.

However, Irving had no reason to be jealous of Tree's Hamlet, which was generally regarded as a failure. Tree had neither the technique nor the temperament for Hamlet and he surprised the more intelligent play-goers even of his own day by returning unseen by Ophelia after the scene in which he rages at her to kiss a tress of her hair.

'I never saw anything so funny in my life,' W. S. Gilbert said of his performance, 'and yet it was not in the least vulgar' (a phrase which Hesketh Pearson believes led to the common form 'funny without being vulgar').

In 1895 Tree was responsible for the first production of *A Woman of No Importance* and, when he gave a matinée of *An Enemy of the People*, for the first performance of an Ibsen play by a leading West End management. The second of these plays was sufficiently well-received to be revived occasionally and the first was very successful. Desmond MacCarthy says of *An Enemy of the People* that it was an example both of his weakness as a producer and of his gift for comprehending character. To liven up the play he introduced some completely inappropriate foolery, but his own acting as Dr Stockmann was 'masterly and subtle'.

He was perfect in the impassioned, indignant harangues, in representing Stockmann's incredulous distress of mind, his readiness to drop any number of points if only people will listen, a readiness which looks so like want of dignity but springs from sincerity. . . . That Tree comprehended his character completely was shown in the way he brought out to perfection that rare and touching humour which expresses itself in ways and words so like those of a person who has no humour, that people without a sense of character do not see the difference.

And Hesketh Pearson tells us that Tree was very good as Lord Illingworth in *A Woman of No Importance*, liking the part so much that he began to throw off his own witticisms in the same style. 'Every day,' Wilde remarked, 'dear Herbert becomes *de plus en plus Oscarisé*; it is a wonderful case of Nature imitating Art.'

Pearson says, too, that Wilde and Tree were in some respects very much alike. Both possessed happy natures, enjoyed life and revelled in nonsense. Both laughed at their own jokes as much as at other people's and both loved good food, good wine and good company. One might add that both were kind and both possessed an element of fantasy in their wit, in pursuit of which both could be very silly.

In January 1895 Tree took his company to America. Here, although he and Mrs Tree had an overwhelming social success, he was not immediately acclaimed by the critics and the public as Irving had been. He had a slightly guttural accent and eccentricities of manner and the American public did not take to him completely until he was nearing the end of his life. This did not in any way affect his own enjoyment or his liking for the place. Max Beerbohm accompanied him on this first tour as his private secretary with salary. ('But my mission was rather a failure. The letters that I wrote in his stead were so carefully thought out and worded that many of the letters sent to him could get no answer at all.') He has recorded that his brother was instantly responsive to the magic of New York.

While Tree was playing in Philadelphia a very successful dramatic version by Paul Potter of George du Maurier's best-selling novel, *Trilby*, was being played at one of the other theatres. Tree sent his brother to see and report on this. Across the supper-table that night Max reported to the effect that 'the play in itself was utter nonsense and could only be a dismal failure in London'. Six weeks later in New York, having one free evening before he sailed, Tree went to see *Trilby* himself.

At the end of the second act he left his box, found Paul Poter and purchased the English rights of the play. The name *Trilby* was to acquire the same association with that of Tree as *The Bells* with that of Irving; and, although Tree's American tour had not been a great financial success in itself, he carried home with him, like the scrip of shares in a gold mine, the foundation of a fortune.

Trilby, which in George du Maurier's own version is a minor classic, is the story of a girl who, though possessing the chest and vocal cords of a singer – the instrument of a voice – is totally unmusical and unable to sing in tune. She comes under the influence of Svengali, a musician and a hypnotist, and under his spell becomes a world famous singer. 'Svengali's make-up is marvellous,' W. S. Gilbert wrote to Maud Tree. 'We could *smell* him.' Hesketh Pearson gives the following account:

It was astonishing how Tree with the utmost economy of means could alter the entire appearance of his face. 'It takes father far less time to make himself ugly than it takes mother to make herself beautiful!' said Viola. No one could account for the celerity with which it was done or the amazing effectiveness of the result. While Irving used to spend an hour or more to make himself look like another edition of Irving, Tree transformed himself completely in ten minutes. Yet, though the Svengali disguise was remarkable, the performance was an epitome of Treeisms: the quick slinking walk, the flashing eyes, the hand on hip, the fluttering fingers, the foreign gestures, the slightly guttural accents: in this part even his faults were turned into virtues, and the total mesmeric effect, as if Trilby's singing entirely resulted from Svengali's power, was a triumph of suggestion.

George du Maurier had himself illustrated his novel and the public had a perfectly clear idea of what Trilby should look like. Tree had to find a young actress who must be tall and beautiful and sufficiently like the du Maurier drawings. From the start everything boded well for this venture and an eighteen-year-old girl named Dorothea Baird was discovered who, although inexperienced, was almost ideal for the part.[2] *Trilby* had an immediate success at its first production in Manchester, ran for many months at the Haymarket, was revived again

[2] Dorothea Baird married H. B. Irving and was the mother of Sir Henry Irving's biographer, Laurence Irving.

and again and was an enormous money-maker. Tree had himself written two of the scenes for the London version and, as Hesketh Pearson has already pointed out, Shaw showed his acuteness in immediately picking out one of these. 'I derived much cynical amusement from this most absurd scene; but if I were Mr du Maurier, I should ask whether the theatre is really in such an abject condition that all daintiness and seriousness of thought and feeling must be struck out of a book, and replaced by vulgar nonsense before it can be accepted on the stage.' This lends interest to Tree's often-quoted estimate of the play, given to someone who praised it to him. 'Hogwash,' he is said to have replied. But it is very doubtful whether an actor can successfully write and play in scenes which to his taste are hogwash. It seems likely that Tree, who revelled in his part and in the play, took his intellectual estimate of it from, among other people, his brother, Max.

Tree's liking for management for its own sake became predominant in his character as he grew older. He had the reckless magnificence and the comprehensive creative ambition of the true impresario. Every day as he arrived at the Haymarket he could see on the other side of the street the site on which Sir John Vanbrugh had once designed and managed a theatre, at present occupied by an old opera house which was shortly to be demolished. Even before the success of *Trilby* he had determined to acquire this site and build his own theatre there, and the fortune made by this play enabled him to put £10,000 into the enterprise. Others who put up money were Sir Ernest Cassel and Lord Rothschild.[3]

Her Majesty's Theatre (renamed His Majesty's after the death of Queen Victoria) was built in Portland stone by C. J. Phipps with interior decorations by Romaine-Walker, and when it was finished Bernard Shaw wrote:

It rises spaciously and brilliantly to the dignity of art; and if its way of doing so is still elegantly rhetorical and Renascent in conception, yet that style is not altogether the wrong one for a theatre;

[3] Hesketh Pearson tells us that the enterprise was financed by a company called The Playhouse Ltd, the capital consisting of debentures, and that Tree's debentures ranked after the others for the payment of interest. He says that Tree paid just under £6,000 a year ground rent and the building, estimated at £55,000, cost very little more.

and it is wonderfully humanized and subtilized by the influence
of modern anti-Renaissance ideas on the decoration. . . . The
Lyceum and Drury Lane, old as they are, would, if they were destroyed, be regretted as the Garrick and Daly's would never be
regretted, but not more than Her Majesty's, which has as yet no
associations.

Her Majesty's Theatre was for Herbert Tree the richest
reward of his life. It realised his dreams, and it became not
merely the scene of his creative triumphs, the spur of his
ambition, but his solace from pain, his refuge from society,
and at times his home. He built two rooms for himself in the
great dome, one of which was, like the Beefsteak Room at the
Lyceum under Irving, the scene of magnificent hospitality and
small intimate dinners, the other a study and bedroom combined. Viola Tree tells us that he hoped the bronze dome would
turn green. They used to look up at it together from the top
of the Haymarket and one or other of them would remark: 'I
think it's a little greener today, don't you?'

The banqueting hall under the dome was a high room ending
in rafters. The small inner room had a frieze running round it
with scenes from *Twelfth Night*, *The Tempest* and *The Taming
of the Shrew*. Underneath these were bookshelves containing,
his daughter says, 'great big useful books' and a mass of hopeless presentation copies bearing such titles as 'Shakespeare
Through an Old Stagers' Spectacles', while the interesting books
and papers were piled up on chairs, sofas, desks. And she tells
us he loved the theatre.

He loved the place, and never could keep away from it for long.
Even on my wedding day, when we were driving to St. Martin's
Church, I very typical and rather sedate (for me), with veil and train
poised ready for my spring on to the red carpet, he turned to me
suddenly in Regent Street and said, 'Will you drive me down to the
theatre, first, dear?' And so at the stage-door I, the bride, sat watching his beloved figure – flamboyant coat-tails, hat, stick and all –
vanish through the swing doors, only to return a few minutes later
having found out that all was well. I was so glad afterwards, as it
would not have seemed natural for me to be driving with him and
not to stop there.

And Iris Tree wrote at the same time:

Theatres have lost their meaning for me now – I have known one theatre so well, and have loved it so long, it has run through the chain of all my memories, but now the link is broken. When I was a child the theatre was a refuge from lessons, mutton and rain, a place whose mystery was never dimmed by familiarity, a place of sliding curtains and endless doors, a corridor of echoing adventures.

Her Majesty's is a big theatre – too big many people thought to suit the subtle delineations of human sensibility and emotion in which Tree excelled. In it he gave vent to the exuberant and theatrical side of his nature which made him so much enjoy management. Although he produced many plays by other authors, his years at Her Majesty's were chiefly notable for his Shakespearian productions, and these for the magnificence and extravagance of detail with which they were presented. Hesketh Pearson wrote, in a comparison scarcely complimentary to either actor: 'In the presentation of Shakespeare, as opposed to the exploitation of an actor's individuality, Tree must be given the palm. His acting versions were as much like the original texts *as the elaborate scenery allowed.* whereas Irving's had been arranged to exhibit the leading actor.[4]

In defence of both actors it must be said that they drew crowds into the theatre to see Shakespeare at a time when he was held to 'spell ruin' – something no one else would attempt in the West End of London until 1925, when John Barrymore proved once more that it could be done by playing *Hamlet* to full houses at the Haymarket.[5]

Tree's first Shakespearian production at Her Majesty's was of *Julius Caesar*. The scenery and costumes were by Laurence Alma-Tadema and the acting of a quality to inspire Shaw's remarks to Ellen Terry quoted on p. 153. Tree played Antony, and there was general agreement that it was both the most magnificently mounted and the best acted production of Shakespeare within living memory. It was fifty years since *Julius Caesar* had been seen in the West End and it ran for five months and made a profit of £11,000. *Twelfth Night*, Pearson tells us, was Tree's most satisfactory Shakespearian production, Olivia's garden being copied from a photograph in *Country Life* and

[4] My italics.
[5] Barrymore, John, 1882–1942. The cast for his *Hamlet* at the Haymarket included Constance Collier as Gertrude and Fay Compton as Ophelia.

being both beautiful and realistic. Tree played Malvolio with much invention of comic business and with four little Malvolios who followed him about and lined up behind him whenever he spoke. This business was sufficiently successful for Tree's half-brother to write to his biographer after his death: 'His Svengali and his Malvolio abide in my mind as two of his especial triumphs.'

In the opening scene of *The Tempest* a ship rocked on a realistic sea, the waves splashed and the wind roared; in *Antony and Cleopatra* the text had to be re-arranged to suit the scenery, the return of Antony to Alexandria, which is the occasion of one speech in the text, being illustrated by a tableau in which excited crowds and dancing girls were a prelude to the arrival to music, first of Cleopatra, then of Anthony. In *Richard II* real horses were introduced in the Lists at Coventry, and Tree as Richard entered London on a horse in place of the speech in which the Duke of York merely describes this happening.

The result of all this accumulation of commentary and illustration [Desmond MacCarthy wrote] however ingenious or lavish, round a play was often to slow down its action intolerably; and while attempting to interpret Shakespeare to the eye, the production too often failed to interpret him to the mind. Thus it was that, in company with several other critics, I found myself, when Shakespeare was on at His Majesty's, shouting: 'Sir Herbert Tree's carriage stops the way!'

But the public continued to fill the theatre and Tree to be unmoved by criticism. People who did not like theatrical illusion, he said, need not come to the theatre. 'The bookworm has always his book.'

When Tree was a young man Dion Boucicault expressed surprise that he should know so well the tricks of the trade.

'Mention one trick,' Tree said.

'You allow the gestures to precede the words.'

'Do I?' said Tree. 'Well, I'm sorry you told me, for now I shall probably do it all wrong.'

And he said once: 'I have not got technique. It is a dull thing; it enslaves the imagination.'

It is strange that a man who believed these things should

have been the founder of the Royal Academy of Dramatic Art.
In 1904 Tree took and furnished two houses in Gower Street
and started a school which taught elocution, dancing and fenc-
ing. He then lent his theatre for public performance by the
students, gave advice when asked for it and jobs to the most
promising pupils. His academy filled a much felt need and it
prospered so greatly that it soon became a national institution.

At the same time he initiated an annual Shakespearian
festival at Her Majesty's putting on six plays in six days in
all the splendour of their original productions. In 1909 he
received a knighthood for his services as an actor and manager,
and in 1910 he put on *Henry VII*, which was generally regarded
as the most magnificent of all his productions and which in
the early days of the war was finally to ensure his complete
triumph over American audiences.

It would be wrong, however, to conceive the programme of
plays put on at Her Majesty's in terms of one Shakespearian
production after another, because Tree, like everyone else, produced a great many purely commercial plays that have no
abiding interest and a few – such as the Henley-Stevenson
Macaire, *Trilby*, *Beau Austin*, a version of *Oliver Twist* in
which he made a marvellous Fagin and a Christmas play by
Graham Robertson called *Pinkie and the Fairies* – which some
people still remember. The only plays still regularly performed
to which he gave a first performance are *A Woman of No
Importance* and *Pygmalion*.

Rehearsals under Tree's management were well known for
their chaotic character. An unmotivated anarchy reigned,
people came in and out of the theatre, sat and talked to Tree,
who every now and then produced a witticism at which he and
all his henchmen laughed, the stage staff rushed about in all
directions, people bellowed at each other and stood distractedly
about. At one rehearsal, overcome by the attempts of his stage-
manager to impose some order on the scene, Tree knelt and
prayed: 'Dear Lord, do look at Bertie Shelton *now*.' There is
no explanation of what magic ultimately restored order in
time for the curtain to go up on the vastly complicated and
magnificent scenes for which this theatre was famous. Tree
was not at all quarrelsome by nature, but he quarrelled at
rehearsals with Henry Arthur Jones (who quarrelled with a

great many other people), with Mrs Patrick Campbell (who
sometimes managed to drive him screaming from the stage),
and he went very near quarrelling with Shaw. Shaw said afterwards that he could never bring himself to hit Tree hard enough
– 'whereas no poker was thick enough, no brick heavy enough,
to leave a bruise on Mrs Campbell'. He said also that the effect
of rehearsing under Tree's management became apparent to
him only when he saw some photographs of himself after the
first night. He suppressed these but he sent one to Mrs
Campbell saying 'Are you not ashamed?' and another to Tree
saying 'This is your work.'

Tree made £13,000 out of the first production of *Pygmalion*;
he took it off when it was still making a great deal of money
because he was bored with it and wanted a holiday, and also
because Shaw's lack of interest in his performance irritated
him. Out of self-preservation Shaw refused to see the play until
the hundredth performance, when he discovered without surprise that Tree had introduced a happy ending by throwing a
bunch of flowers to Eliza in the interval between the end of
the play and the fall of the curtain.

'My ending makes money: you ought to be grateful,' said
Tree afterwards.

'Your ending is damnable: you ought to be shot,' Shaw
replied.

All this happened in the summer of 1914.

Tree had a talent for neat little aphorisms with which he
amused himself so much that he would sometimes call out to
his secretary to make a note of something he had just said, or,
when reminded of some earlier saying, cry delightedly: 'Did
I say that? Did I say that?' Too many of his sayings which
require the occasion and the glowing personality for a just
appreciation have been preserved in print. But in addition to
wit Tree had the masculine virtues of tolerance and generosity
which are reflected in the following endearing examples of
these sayings:

It is better to drink a little too much than much too little.

And of marriage:

Which is the victim – he or she – She was, he is.

The second of these has a sad truth which, while of general application, had a particular reference to his own case. For Tree was as incapable of fidelity as his wife was of condoning infidelity.

The picture that is left to us of Maud Tree is less attractive than she may have been in her lifetime. In the first place we have the series of letters written to her by Tree during their engagement which show her in a harsh and puritan light, in the second she had not the gift of easy self-expression which he possessed and passed on to his children. Consequently, the long essay she wrote in the collection of memories of her husband is not only the least satisfactory in the book but probably does less than justice to herself. For if it is true that writers with the gift of style can preserve for us the quality and individuality of men long dead, it is equally true that a false picture can endure through the lack of it.

There are varying accounts of her ability as an actress, but Bernard Shaw suprisingly tells us that she was a natural comedian. She seems also to have been a wit and some of her sayings, like those of her husband, have been the rounds. Of these the most apt was when Tree, having persuaded Mrs Kendal and Ellen Terry rather late in the careers of these two great actresses to appear as Mistress Ford and Mistress Page to his Falstaff, came into the theatre together with them.

'Look at Herbert and his two stars,' someone remarked.

'Two ancient lights,' Maud Tree replied.[6]

The Trees' married life had to survive the difficulties caused by her acting in his company.

'*Why* Marion Terry? *Why* not me?' she asked him once. And received the reply:

'You see, the part needs extraordinary sympathy.'

But Tree's great kindness, generosity and affection might have been enough to appease her for his lack of prejudice as a manager had he not transgressed so audaciously and so frequently as a husband that, feeling herself too much sinned against, she failed in all those qualities of sweetness, good temper and tolerance in which he so conspicuously shone.

---

[6] The story is also told of Irving who, passing the theatre and seeing on the bills Mrs Tree's name together with Mrs Kendal's and Ellen Terry's, remarked to his companion: 'Three little meds [maids] – eh! Three little meds.'

This classical situation was completed by Tree's unequivocal resentment when Lewis Waller fell in love with his wife, and for a few years the Trees did each other so much damage when together that they seldom met. Then Maud Tree, out for a drive with Lewis Waller (whose love, it was believed, she accepted with gratitude but did not return), had an accident and broke her jaw. This spoiled her appearance and ended her career. She suffered deeply, and in this situation Tree's sympathy and affection were so necessary to her and so overwhelming that she ceased to do violence to his angelic qualities in an effort to retain a monopoly of them. She reconciled herself to the fact of his natural sons and learned to make jokes about his susceptibilities. Tree adored his children and in all ways but the one was a family man. 'Be sweet, dearest Viola,' he wrote to his daughter, 'during all the years, as you have been to me during all the years that have passed. Your fond Father. And do remember to spell holiday with one "l"!' During his last years he managed to enjoy the society and affection of all his loved ones and, when his daughter Iris was to meet one of her half-brothers, it was her mother whom Tree asked to explain the situation to her.

The Great War of 1914 sent audiences into the theatres with a taste for only the lightest of fare. After two failures in London Tree went to Hollywood to make a film of *Macbeth*, letting His Majesty's Theatre to Oscar Asche. Asche produced a musical play called *Chu Chin Chow* which occupied the theatre for five years – at that time the longest run in history. Tree put on a Shakespearian season in New York, playing *Henry VIII*, *The Merchant of Venice* and *The Merry Wives of Windsor*. He had an enormous success and wrote to his wife: 'They want me to have a theatre here in the autumn and call it the Tree Theatre.' He made speeches from the stage and elsewhere in aid of the Allied cause and on one occasion he gave a performance of *Oliver Twist* for the benefit of the Red Cross in which the Artful Dodger was played by Charlie Chaplin. Then he made a triumphant tour of all the leading cities of America with his Shakespearian productions, making speeches wherever he went and earning from the *New York Times* the title of 'unofficial ambassador extraordinary'. In 1916 and again in 1917 he faced the hazards of an Atlantic crossing to visit England.

Max Beerbohm believed that in the last years of his life his brother grew to care less for acting.

His versatility had ranged over so vast a number of diverse interpretations. What new thing was there for him to do – for him, to whom the notion of marking time was so utterly repugnant? Especially after the outbreak of the War did I notice in him an impatience of his work. The last time we met was at my mother's house, just after his return from America. He was looking, as usual, splendidly well, and was full of animation. But in all his talk there was not a word about acting.

In the summer of 1917 Tree was staying at Epple Bay in Birchington when he slipped and fell down the stairs. He had a successful operation on his knee but blood clots formed as a result of it. He died at the age of 64, his personal radiance undimmed. He was a very great actor and one of the last truly romantic figures. Stick in hand and coat tails swinging, he dominated the theatrical scene for many years. For all who can remember his name the very words 'actor-manager' recall it. 'Irving,' one says, 'and Tree.'

Sir Gerald du Maurier
1873-1933

Gerald du Maurier was a fine late flowering of the genus, highly and subtly developed. In point of time he has no place in this book because, although he started his career on the stage in the nineteenth century, he did not go into management until 1910. Yet, although a man of the twentieth century, more precisely one who took colour from both and gave it to the period between the wars, his affinity to the Victorian actor-managers was unquestionable. During his long period at Wyndham's he was not a manager in the true sense of being responsible for the finance of the theatre. He entered into an arrangement with Frank Curzon by which the latter supplied him with a theatre, a fixed income and a percentage of the profits. Curzon took all the financial risks but did not interfere with the policy or the choice or presentation of the plays. For twenty-five years Gerald du Maurier's name was connected with Wyndham's Theatre, as Irving's had been with the Lyceum, Alexander's with the St James's and Tree's with Her Majesty's.

Du Maurier was the subject of one of the most famous biographies in theatrical history, written by his daughter, Daphne, soon after his death. Chiefly remembered for a style which, very individual and in itself short-lived, killed forever the old romantic style of acting, he was, nevertheless, the last of the romantic heroes of the theatre.

He was born unusually well-equipped for the stage. His lean, brown, rather crooked face with the jutting chin and the brushed-back hair was oddly beautiful, witty, sensitive and rather cruel; formed, as Shaw said of Ellen Terry's, in a unique mould. He recalled no other person, conformed to no general type. He put his natural elegance to the service of his casual, throw-away manner, partly invented, partly absorbed from the trivial manner of the day, but this did not diminish the impact of his personality. He had all the magnetism and easy dominance of his great predecessors.

The son of a man whose fame, although not earned in the theatre, had spilled over into it, Gerald du Maurier acquired no added grace from a pseudonym. He bore easily and artlessly the name of a French family of minor nobility and it was not until after his death that Miss Daphne du Maurier discovered and published the fact that he owed it to one of the many fantasies of his great-grandfather. Robert-Mathurin Busson came to London at the time of the French revolution, not, as he pretended, to escape the fate of an aristocrat, but after suffering one prison sentence for fraud and in fear of another. He was obsessed with social status and delusions of grandeur and in London, where poverty in an emigré family was not unusual, he was able to invent for himself a claim to nobility. He began to sign himself Busson du Maurier and, when he discovered that there was a real Comte du Maurier living in La Sarthe, he fabricated a story of relationship and intermarriage between the Aubreys, the family of the real counts, and the Bussons, so that the chateau at le Maurier and the family living there made his stories seem more rather than less probable to later generations.

Robert-Mathurin Busson was the father of six children, of whom one, Louis Mathurin, married an Englishwoman named Ellen Clarke, the daughter of a famous Regency courtesan who was mistress of Frederick, Duke of York. These two were the parents of George du Maurier.

George du Maurier, born in 1834, lived part of his childhood in London, part in Paris. Thus the duality of his inheritance was repeated in his environment. As a young man he studied art but owing to the loss of the sight of one eye had to give up any idea of working as a painter and to earn his living as an illustrator. This was at a time when illustration was regarded as an art requiring specialised talents and du Maurier, who was on the staff of *Punch* with Charles Keene and John Tenniel, first made his name with his drawings. Later in life be began to write novels and his second book, *Trilby*, was the first 'best-

seller' in England and in America. He was an admirable artist
in both mediums. His *Punch* drawings are a major source for
social historians and, if the enormous sales of *Trilby* can be
accounted for more by the Svengali theme than by the wit
and charm of the earlier part of the book, Svengali had sufficient
originality and power to become an authentic literary figure.
The gift of romantic, rather sentimental story-telling is an
important part of the heritage of the du Maurier family.

George du Maurier was very light-hearted and gay in society
and a tremendous talker. He had a really fine tenor voice and a
talent for singing French songs. Nick-named Kicky, he was very
much loved and a list of his friends and well-known
acquaintances would be a list of the artists and literary figures
of the period. At the same time, his biographer tells us, 'his
status as a gentleman was quite secure, and he was able to mix
in the best society'. He was a close friend of Henry James.

When he first joined *Punch* he received instructions from
Mark Lemon, a famous editor who understood the talents of his
contributors. 'I was particularly told not to try to be broadly
funny, but to undertake the light and graceful business, like a
jeune premier.' Among the talents which the highly talented
Kicky was to pass to his talented son, that for 'the light and
graceful business' was supreme.

Yet he suffered from what his latest biographer describes as
the 'aching nostalgia' to which Ruskin was also prone. She
states that: 'Continual backward looking was a central feature
of du Maurier's personality, the cause of much personal
unhappiness, but also the source of his later creative power as
a novelist.' And she quotes from *Peter Ibbetson*:

Oh, surely, surely, I cried to myself, we ought to find some means
of possessing the past more fully and completely than we do. Life
is not worth living for many of us if a want so desperate and yet
so natural can never be satisfied. Memory is but a poor, rudimentary thing that we had better be without, if it can only lead us to
the verge of consummation like this, and madden us with a desire
it cannot slake.

Because of his eyes he could never escape from the dread of
poverty and even after *Trilby* had made him a rich man he
continued in fearful parsimony. In the same way when he

became the author of a popular best-seller, his success terrified him. Leonée Ormond writes:

Like a mole, searching for dark and familiar places, du Maurier shied away from the limelight, and the public exposure to which he was subjected. The apparatus of publicity and public success, which had no note of jubilation for him, seemed to undermine his health and his confidence, to tear him from the secure and familiar patterns of his life. He was certainly suffering from fatty degeneration of the heart, but it is impossible to escape the conclusion that *Trilby*, to a very large extent, was the cause of his death.

Yet it is emphasised that it was only with the publication of *Peter Ibbetson* that the dark and melancholy side of du Maurier's nature began to be understood. Daphne du Maurier makes it plain that even his children were quite unaware of the true nature of this man.

George du Maurier married Emma Wightwick, a striking beauty but one who was always uneasy in society and cared only for her husband and her children. These she loved and tended with an anxious, passionate devotion. The du Mauriers had five children – Beatrix, Sylvia, Louise, Guy and Gerald. Gerald was the youngest and the most indulged. He was referred to in his own family as the 'ewee lamb'. He was an extremely bright, precocious child who learned very early to get his own way by playing on his mother's anxieties.

By the time of his birth in 1873 the du Mauriers were living at Hampstead, and a year later they moved into New Grove House, where they were to remain for twenty years. During almost the whole of his life Gerald du Maurier lived in Hampstead. His father used him and his brother and sisters as models for his drawings and, even when he was not drawing them, worked placidly with the five children running about in his studio.

Gerald was educated at Harrow where he did surprisingly badly in his work, his letters to his mother containing a mixture of fairly light-hearted apology for being low in his form and self-confident requests for food. 'Look here, I'm awfully sorry about tenth place but I really will do better and in the meantime will you be a darling and send down at once a large square tin of milk biscuits, a cake from Buzzards, some Cadbury's chocolate, a Roll tongue, chicken and ham sausages, two tins of sardines, some more jam and honey, and anything else you like.'

From the earliest age he mimicked the people who came to the house, and although his sisters turned away from these exhibitions remarking: 'Don't look at Gerald; he's showing off,' his father could never disguise his amusement. As he grew older he began to entertain the boys in his house at Harrow as well as his father with imitations of Henry Irving. Yet, when he left school, although he was immediately in demand for amateur theatricals, he was put to work in a shipping office. His period there was short, however, and following it he enjoyed himself for some time merely in a social way, going to dances and house-parties, always much in demand as an amateur actor. Since it soon became clear that he was not likely to make much success of anything else, his parents began to weaken in their opposition to the idea of his going on the stage. It was at this time that Henry James remarked that if Gerald really wanted to go on the stage he didn't see how his parents could prevent it.

To this du Maurier responded: 'That's all very well, James; but what would you say if you had a son who wanted to go into the church?'

Lifting both hands in horror, Henry James replied: 'My dear du Maurier, a father's curse.'

Once Gerald's parents were reconciled to the idea there was no further difficulty. George du Maurier merely applied to his friend John Hare to take the boy, and Gerald gave his first public performance in January 1894 at the Garrick Theatre as a waiter in *An Old Jew*, a comedy by Sydney Grundy. He stayed with Hare for six months, during which time he persuaded everyone of his natural talent, and then he went on tour with Forbes-Robertson, playing among other parts that of Algy in *Diplomacy*. At the end of this tour he signed a contract with Tree, with whom he stayed for two years. Much of this time was spent playing Dodor in *Trilby* since this was the period of the phenomenal success of this play. He opened with Tree in Manchester in September 1895, and after the riotous success of the provincial tour, played the part in London, in a second tour of the provinces and in America. Alternating with it, he played Gadshill in *Henry IV*.

At this time he was enormously high-spirited and full of zest, enjoying life with a light-hearted fervour. He encountered pain for the first time when his father died. The du Mauriers were an unusually close and devoted family, bound together by ties far stronger than any they achieved with the outside world and suffering acutely when separated. Immediately after his father's death he went to America with Tree on his first and rather unsuccessful tour. He found it expensive and he did not care for the people.

He began now to exhibit a susceptibility to women which showed itself in two abortive engagements – the first to a young French actress named Marguerite Sylva, the second to Ethel Barrymore. Later, when he left Tree, he joined the management of Mrs Patrick Campbell at the Royalty Theatre and remained with her, playing in London and on tour, for two years. Daphne du Maurier wrote:

There was no peace with her, no quiet moment; it was either heaven or hell, ecstasy or despair. When you were with her you wanted to be away, out of sight, alone; and when she was gone it was torture until you heard that voice again, rather full, rather sullen, the voice of Athalie or Phèdre. You adored her and hated her in turn. You sat at her feet and worshipped, or rushed from her presence slamming the door and calling damnation upon her name. She was disturbing and possessive and impossible, but it was better to be frowned upon by her than ignored.

Also she taught one to act.

Much of his charm, his delicacy, his ease of manner, and his assurance he owed to her. She worked tirelessly, taking infinite pains with him. . . . There were scenes, of course, blistering rows and fierce reconciliations, days of sulky silences and days of riotous successes. And in this weird mixture of excitement, anger, and frequent disillusion, Gerald developed his mind, his intuition, and his little grain of genius.

'I have taught a clown to play Pelleas,' said Mrs Campbell.

Then suddenly in the autumn of 1901 the company broke up: Mrs Campbell went off to New York and du Maurier at the age of twenty-nine, rather changed and showing for the first time the streak of bitterness which his later associates were to recognise as a part of his nature, returned home.

For a while he rested, playing in a comedy called *The Country Mouse* but taking life easily. Then in the following summer he was engaged to play the juvenile lead in Barrie's new piece *The Admirable Crichton*. Playing opposite him was a young actress named Muriel Beaumont.

Muriel Beaumont – known for the rest of her life as Mo – had much of the temperament of her mother-in-law, a temperament necessary to the du Maurier men. From the time that she married Gerald, she sank her own life in his, caring for no one but him and his children. In return, in spite of a susceptibility to women which caused his children to speak of the 'stable' and bet on the runners, he loved no one but her. Only when one of the runners, misunderstanding the situation and believing that she might seriously endanger the position of his wife, acted on this assumption, did his succession of love affairs impinge in any way on Mo's life.

The year following du Maurier's marriage saw the first performances of *Peter Pan*, which was written for his nephews (his sister's children), the Llewelyn Daviases. Du Maurier doubled the parts of Mr Darling and Captain Hook. Daphne du Maurier wrote of his first performance:

When Hook first paced his quarter-deck in the year of 1904, children were carried screaming from the stalls, and even big boys of twelve were known to reach for their mother's hand in the friendly shelter of the boxes. How he was hated, with his flourish, his poses, his diabolical smile! That ashen face, those blood-red lips, the long, dank, greasy curls; the sardonic laugh, the maniacal scream, the appalling courtesy of his gestures. . . . Gerald *was* Hook. . . . He was a tragic and rather ghastly creation who knew no peace, and whose soul was in torment; a dark shadow; a sinister dream; a bogey of fear who lives perpetually in the grey recesses of every small boy's mind. All boys had their Hooks, as Barrie knew; he was the phantom who came by night and stole his way into their murky dreams.

Thus he reverted for the last time to the melodramatic past, to the world in which he himself had grown up, to the imitation of Irving and Tree in which he had so long excelled. The following year he appeared in *Raffles*.

Raffles was a gentleman and a cricketer but a cracksman. This was the first play about a crook and it was the first example of 'naturalistic' acting. To quote Daphne du Maurier once more: 'He brought something to it that was personal and unique – a suggestion of extreme tension masked by a casual gaiety – making of Raffles someone highly strung, nervous, and finely drawn, yet fearless and full of a reckless and rather desperate indifference, someone who by the force of high spirits had developed a kink in his nature.' This might be a description of du Maurier himself; it was the part he was to play for the rest of his life both on and off the stage. How much of it was natural, how much 'naturalistic', no one would ever know. His critics, most of whom have arisen since his death (unlike Kean and Irving who had to wait on posterity for complete recognition, Gerald du Maurier won great appreciation in his lifetime), quite rightly insist that there is a difference between the two. Whether in the theatre this difference is always clear is another matter. Ultimately the art of acting – as also the art of writing plays – is to seem to be rather than to be, and styles that to one generation seem natural may to the next seem naturalistic. Actors often appear to be playing a part and, when one enters a room and hears a voice on television replying to the questions of an interviewer, one can normally tell when it belongs to a member of the acting profession. The timing is invariably too good, the modesty – so desirable on television, yet so difficult to achieve – too easily handled, the lines thrown away in a manner impossible to the ordinary man. Spending all his professional life in impersonation, the actor finally loses his own identity and becomes naturalistic rather than natural – a tendency which becomes more obvious as fashion and mannerisms are no longer in the style of the day. Now that actors of the past can be seen on film or television, great talent reveals itself, more than in any other way, by the extent to which the mastery of the performer transcends the inevitable changes of fashion.

Gerald du Maurier has two great claims to fame. The first is that he invented the 'naturalistic' manner, and in doing so killed the melodramatic manner which had become an obstacle to the presentation of the 'new' drama and even to acceptable portrayal of the classics. He put the modern meaning into the theatre word 'ham', and, although he has been followed by actors who have been able to adapt his technique to the requirements of the classics – even high tragedy, a feat he never attempted – it remains true that he made a vital contribution to the development of acting.

His second claim to fame is that, within the limits he imposed upon himself, he was a master. Beloved by the public, he was nevertheless an actor's actor. Only another actor is fully aware how difficult is the style he made his own and, just as people say of Picasso that he can draw and paint in the traditional style when he wishes, so everyone in the theatre knew that du Maurier could play every part to perfection. He left behind him one convincing record. He was one of the first to appear in a 'talking' film when the technique had been sufficiently developed to leave behind something like a true impression. An extract from his film, *Lord Camber's Ladies*, made in 1932, produced by Alfred Hitchcock and directed by Benn Levy, was shown in 1969 in the television programme *Omnibus*. Watching this extract and asked to comment on it were Sir John Gielgud, Dame Edith Evans, Donald Sinden and Vanessa Redgrave.

Du Maurier played the part of a doctor and held a glass in his hand.

'Give me the nitric acid,' he said to Benita Hume, playing opposite him, and when she did so he dropped it into the liquid in the glass and asked her if she could see it cloud.

'No,' she replied after an interval.

'Neither can I.'

Miraculously, in the last three simple words, their impact undiminished, were all the wit, style and individual timing which had made du Maurier supreme in his day. Commenting, Dame Edith Evans said:

He was a very, very fine actor indeed. He could do every part Better than they did. But he chose to be the sort of originator of the rather throw-away style, which when it didn't have the guns behind it, which it had when he did it. . . . A lot of people copied him; all they did was throw away, but they didn't throw anything away, do you see. I'd great admiration for him.

His success in *Raffles* was the turning point in his career. He followed it with *Brewster's Millions*, *What Every Woman Knows*, *Arsène Lupin* and *Alias Jimmy Valentine*. Most of these were trifling plays, poorly written, but the public, who still preferred great acting to great plays, filled the theatre to see du Maurier. The pattern of the future was set.

In 1909 he produced, although he did not play in, his brother Guy du Maurier's play *An Englishman's Home* at Wyndham's Theatre, under Frank Curzon's management. *An Englishman's Home* was one of those extraordinary pieces of timing for which generation after generation of du Mauriers have shown such flair. It was the story of what happened to a middle-class Englishman and his family, untrained to bear arms, when England was suddenly and unexpectedly invaded by enemy troops. Mr Brown refuses to leave his home, is found with a gun he is unable to use competently, is captured and shot by the enemy after a foolish, useless but gallant display of patriotism. Three or four years later *An Englishman's Home* was as dead as if it had never been written, but at the time of its production it touched some response of fear and horror in the audiences and, received with a frenzy of enthusiasm, was regarded by those responsible for England's defence as the finest piece of propaganda ever written.

In 1910 du Maurier joined Frank Curzon in management at Wyndham's Theatre and with only one break remained at this theatre for most of his acting career. The break was occasioned by the war.

He was a natural leader of men and his skill as a producer has been testified to again and again by the leading actors and actresses of his day. He could play each part in every play – in *The Dancers* it was said he vaulted backwards and forwards over a bar at rehearsal while instructing two of the younger members of the cast – and his natural manner and faultless sense of timing became part of the technique of modern acting and could be seen not merely in his own performances but also in those of actors like Ronald Squire and actresses like Gladys Cooper, Tallulah Bankhead, Celia Johnson, and hosts of small part players who owed their style to hours of patient coaching at Wyndham's Theatre.

Nevertheless, the thing that most distinguishes him from every other actor-manager of his eminence is that during the whole of his career he was responsible for no production of any historical interest whatever. He introduced no play which has remained in the repertory of English theatre and he neither acted in nor produced any of the classics. He said of himself that he was the lowest of the low-brows and this was the simple truth. The age in which he lived was inexplicably philistine, the tastes of audiences returning to the level of the audiences of the early nineteenth century – 'the winter solstice' of the British drama. From Tree to Barrymore no one dared to risk Shakespeare in the West End of London, no reliable public existed for opera, which was put on only at the expense of philanthropists, musical comedy replaced light opera because even this proved too strong a diet for popular consumption, and the word 'highbrow' was adopted in denigration of anyone whose tastes were other than the most trivial. An analysis of the underlying causes of such a situation is a matter for social historians but in such circumstances it is not entirely surprising that the great gifts, the extraordinary stage presence of the leading actor of the day, should all have been wasted on productions of purely commercial drama.

The most notable production of his career was that of Barrie's *Dear Brutus*. The story of the artist who is given a second chance in life but wakes to find this a dream appealed to something in du Maurier's own nature and Daphne du Maurier wrote of his performance in this play:

Those who watched Gerald as Harry Dearth in 1917 saw, not a performance of an imaginary character, but the revelation of a living man, his hopes, his fears, his little ghosts and dreams, what he might have been, what he might yet become, a challenge and a confession in one. . . .

It was very moving and very terrible; he concealed nothing, and laid himself bare to the gaze of the world with a ruthless disregard of his own privacy, putting himself in pillory, to be looked upon by the curious as though in some sudden and desperate need of salvation.

But this was a rare occasion. For the most part du Maurier put his talents to the service of light entertainment.

Whether a sense of the triviality of his professional career contributed to the discontent and despair which finally overwhelmed him it is impossible to say, because this inability to enjoy life is so often the price paid for creative talent. It can be found in the melancholia of Dr Johnson and Evelyn Waugh, the aching nostalgia of George du Maurier and Ruskin and heard in Graham Greene's confessions of boredom. In Gerald du Maurier it caused a strain of bitterness and self-pity to develop in what had been in youth a purely joyous nature.

During the war years when Tree went to America, du Maurier naturally took his place as leader of the theatre. He became President of the Actors' Benevolent Fund and during the whole of the war he performed valuable services for charities as well as providing in his professional capacity entertainment for the wartime population and the soldiers on leave. His wartime productions included *The Ware Case* by George Bancroft, the son of Squire and Marie Bancroft and *A Kiss for Cinderella* by J. M. Barrie. Then in the summer of 1918, at the age of forty-five, he joined the army. His military service lasted only a few months but this could not have been foreseen at the time he joined and the unnecessary, almost Wildean masochism of the act did not diminish its gallantry. As an example to the profession of which he was the head the gesture was entirely wasted and he seems to have been a very bad soldier. His daughter wrote of this period in his career:

It was impossible to teach him; he would not concentrate, and, as he had done at Harrow thirty years before, he was inclined to shrug his shoulders at authority and make humorous remarks at serious moments. The instructors found it easier to ignore him than to waste precious time in expounding theories which obviously meant nothing to him, and which he did not grasp.

Yet one cannot help believing that if one of his instructors had been called in to Wyndham's Theatre to guide its leading actor in the impersonation of a young cadet he would have found a lively intelligence which responded quite easily to instruction.

Luckily the ordeal was soon over and du Maurier returned to Wyndham's Theatre, to *The Choice*, *The Prude's Fall* and *Bulldog Drummond*. In January 1922 he received a knighthood for his services to the Theatre and to the Actor's Benevolent Fund.

These were the days of the luncheon parties at Cannon Hall the beautiful house in Hampstead where, because he could never be alone, the du Mauriers entertained every weekend. People were asked to lunch because they could play tennis, or because they were old friends or because he had been in the mood to ask them when he met them in the street, but they all had one quality in common. In some way they were connected with the theatre. Du Maurier had no interest in social life as such, and neither aspired to nor could be cajoled by what remained of high society. People flocked in and out of Cannon Hall all day on Sundays but the only conversation that could ever be heard concerned in one way or another the theatre.

At the centre of these conversations, at the centre of this world, du Maurier reigned as Irving and Tree had reigned. He had all the intense magnetism of his great predecessors, all the natural charm; he was lightly malicious, restless, bitter and discontented. He was adored by the men and women who surrounded him, adored and feared.

Among these was the playwright Frederick Lonsdale. Younger than du Maurier and coming from a world which gave him none of the actor's natural advantages, he was always in thrall to the older man. As a youth he had made a name for himself as a writer of musical comedy, and du Maurier with a characteristic mixture of affection and malice, usually referred to him as 'the muck writer'. Nor when Lonsdale began his enormously successful career as a writer of drawing-room comedies did he appear to be much more impressed. The sensitive relationship between these two men was the immediate cause of a break in theatrical tradition.

In 1923 du Maurier had a great success with a play called *The Dancers* which he wrote himself in collaboration with Viola Tree. Two previously unknown young actresses, Tallulah Bankhead and Audrey Carton, appeared with enormous success and together with du Maurier drew audiences for over a year. But this was the last of the great Wyndham's successes and du Maurier for the first time in his life had a serious run of failures. He was badly in need of a play to restore his fortunes when Frederick Lonsdale arrived at Cannon Hall to read him his new play, *The Last of Mrs Cheyney*. The two men dined together with Mo and after a good dinner and a glass of port retired to du Maurier's library where Lonsdale, settling down by the fire, began to read his play. Presently he looked up in expectation of intercepting some reaction from du Maurier to find that his host had fallen asleep.

He was not the first, nor, in all probability, the last man to fall asleep during the reading of a play, well known to have a disconcertingly soporific effect. The trouble in this case was that Lonsdale, who valued du Maurier's opinion above all else, did not believe he had fallen asleep. He believed him to be staging an insult. Furiously he rushed from the room and down the stairs, with Mo after him explaining that du Maurier was tired and ill, begging him not to break up a friendship of so many years, and, getting into his car, drove off to London. Unable to forgive du Maurier he gave *The Last of Mrs Cheyney* to Gladys Cooper who, in conjunction with Gilbert Miller, put it into rehearsal at the St James's Theatre.

There are two equally good male parts in this play and Ronald Squire was engaged for one of them. The part of Lord Arthur Dilling had not yet been cast when to everyone's astonishment a message was received from du Maurier saying he would like to play it. So *The Last of Mrs Cheyney* opened on 22 September 1925 with a quite exceptional array of stars and ran for 514 performances. The significance of the incident was that the play made a fortune, a fortune that but for du Maurier's slumbers might have revived the management at Wyndham's. His sleep closed his long career there, and with it the whole of an era. The great days of the actor-manager were drawing to a close and nothing could for long have prolonged them. *The Last of Mrs Cheyney* might have done so for a few more years.

Frank Curzon died soon after, however, and even more serious, so did T. B. Vaughan, his business manager. Without a theatre, without a partner or a business manager, du Maurier had to fend for himself. At various theatres during the next years he produced *Interference* by Roland Pertwee and Harold Dearden which was a financial success, a moderately successful revival of *Dear Brutus* and another of *Peter Pan*. He went back to Wyndham's for a short time, where he turned Edgar Wallace into a playwright by the education he gave him while producing *The Ringer*. With the money he made from this he bought the house at Fowey where his wife lived after his death. He produced a play called *Cynara* with Gladys Cooper in which Celia Johnson made a great success and he went on tour with George Bancroft's play *The Ware Case*, a tour during which he made little money for himself but over £100 in every town for

the Actor's Benevolent Fund. As late as 1932 he acted in
Diplomacy, first put on by the Bancrofts in the 1880s. But every-
thing now was an effort and success obstinate and grudging.
Daphne du Maurier writes:

For the first time, Gerald began to look a little older, a little
weary, a little worn. He complained of not sleeping, of feeling
eternally tired, of having 'Mummie's pain' under his heart. . . . He
spent much of his time pottering in the drawing-room and looking
through old letters of Guy's, old sketches of papa's. It was as
though he wanted to soak himself in the past and shut away the
present and the future.
Fewer people came to the Sunday lunches. He began to appreciate quiet days. . . . Here he was, at the head of his profession, nearly
sixty and sick to death of acting; frittering away the days in doing
nothing, in lunching with a pal, in having a yarn, in hanging about;
wondering at the back of his mind why he was alive at all, and if
there was any riddle in the universe after the long day was over.
And, in spite of everything, he had to go on acting because he could
not afford to retire.

He could not afford to retire because, like so many people
after him, now that he was into the lean years he began to
receive tax demands for money made in the fat years. This was
a new and unexpected hazard in a profession already too
hazardous. He felt trapped and to earn money he began to
play small parts in talking films.

Nowadays, when one sees an old, beloved and respected actor
or actress playing bit parts in films, one rejoices that, for a
few weeks' work each year he or she is making enough
money to live on. No longer the one-night stands, the long
train journeys, the desperate attempts to play men or women
the age of one's grandchildren. For a few weeks, up much too
early, standing about all day, speaking a few lines – then peace
and security. But when du Maurier played the doctor in *I Was
A Spy* and a valet in *Catherine the Great* audiences held their
breath in pain to see the mighty so fallen. 'He loathed every
poisonous moment, it was something that had to be endured. . . .
He did it because he could not at the moment bring himself
to consider any other means of making money; it was one stop-
gap after another, one more straw floating on the surface of
the water.'

Then the day came when Sybil Beaumont, his sister-in-law and secretary, presented him with a new tax demand. 'I can't be bothered with income tax, Billy dear', he replied. 'They're probably quite decent fellows. Write and tell them I haven't any money.' He began to drink too much brandy and his gaiety was almost gone. In 1933 he died. He had struggled too hard to carry on a tradition which in the conditions of the day was already out of date. He left very valuable property in Cannon Hall and the house at Fowey and, when all was settled, it was found that Mo was sufficiently well provided for.

Epilogue

In 1969 the Arts Council Grant to the National Theatre was £340,000 and to the Royal Shakespeare Theatre Company £200,154. The Royal Shakespeare Theatre Company reported a deficit of £161,126 and stated that they faced the biggest financial crisis since they started in 1928. No moral can be drawn from this except that expressed in Tree's elliptical definition: 'When is a repertory not a repertory? When it is a success.' (He meant that the only way the expenses of a repertory company can be met is by abandoning the policy every time a play is sufficiently successful to be kept on for a run.) Nevertheless, if it is financially no easier to run a repertory of serious plays today, this makes an interesting point from which to review the achievement of the actors who managed the theatres of London for fifty years or more.

Without either patron or state aid, they had to please the public if they were to keep their theatres open. They were scolded by the critics for a lack of adventure in their choice of plays and for a lack of taste in their productions. They refused to put on Ibsen and they caused Shaw to invent the word 'bardicide' and to accuse Irving and Tree of turning to Shakespeare as to a forest out of which literary scaffolding 'could be hewn without remonstrance from the landlord'. Nevertheless, from Bancroft to Tree they kept Shakespeare on the boards of the theatres and gave production to such new English playwrights as came their way. The Bancrofts gave memorable productions of *The Merchant of Venice* and *The School for Scandal* and Irving of *Much Ado About Nothing*. Irving and Forbes-Robertson gave distinguished performances of Hamlet and Tree

put on an annual Shakespeare festival at Her Majesty's
Theatre. Alexander gave the first production to plays by Wilde,
James and Pinero, Tree to plays by Wilde, Bernard Shaw and
Pinero.

They kept the theatre alive in the provinces, touring themselves in the summer and keeping first class companies touring
all the year. (In addition to the leaders of the theatre, Sir John
Martin Harvey and Sir Charles Wyndham toured regularly in
the provinces and Sir Nigel Playfair had a glorious reign at the
Lyric Theatre, Hammersmith.) Irving, Tree and Forbes-Robertson travelled extensively in America.

Very few parallels with today can be drawn because the
conditions were so different, but certain principles for the
management of a commercial theatre emerged. In this book the
aspect of management has been dealt with only in relation to
dramatic productions because, while there was no universal
financial system and a high degree of financial chaos, the success
of a theatre depended then as now only secondarily on the
competence of the business management which was usually
carried on by a paid employee. Trying to explain how it was
possible for a theatre to be successful under Tree's inconsequent
management, Shaw said: 'Theatre business is not like other
business. . . . A London West End theatre is always either making such an enormous profit that the utmost waste caused by
unbusinesslike management is not worth considering, or else
losing so much that the strictest economy cannot arrest the
process by a halfpenny in the pound.'

The first rule for success in the Theatre is to choose a play
the public will pay to see. The second, equally simple and early
discovered by Bancroft, is not to run it too long. A. E. W.
Mason says:

Alexander was quick to understand when a play was sagging
because of one of those temporary depressions which once or
twice or even more often in a year afflict the theatres of London,
or whether it was dying. If it was dying he was no less quick to
whip it off before its vitality was quite exhausted. It was characteristic of the Grand Panjandrum that the gunpowder ran out of the
heels of his boots. That is nothing to the money which runs out of
a theatre when a play is kept on after its popularity has gone.

The third rule of the nineteenth-century theatre was that

in a star theatre the star must appear. Alexander could no more keep a theatre running profitably than Irving could when he was prevented by illness from acting himself.

Perhaps the last of these three rules accounts for the fact that, while there are few parallels with the present day, there is one curious parallel between the lives of so many of these actor-managers. With the single exception of Irving, they all became bored with the theatre. The Bancrofts retired in their middle forties and lived as long again in retirement without apparently wishing to return except occasionally to the stage; Forbes-Robertson retired at sixty and lived a private life for twenty years without regrets; Alexander continued to manage his theatre until his last illness but turned increasingly to politics; and Max Beerbohm noticed in Tree 'an impatience of his work'. Gerald du Maurier suffered a more embracing boredom – he was bored with life. It seems most likely that they were all exhausted by the everlasting need to entertain a capricious public.

The actor-managers were vital to the development of the English drama. By the strength of their personal characteristics they brought the middle and upper classes back into the theatre and changed the conditions and status of their profession. They introduced new standards of production and of acting, and without state aid kept a repertory of classical plays in production, while also putting on the stage the work of English playwrights of talent. They set up schools for dramatic art and established a benevolent fund for the members of their profession. They added colour to the social scene and invested the theatre with magic.

Bibliography

Archer, William, *Henry Irving, Actor and Manager*, Field and Tuer, 1883.

Arthur, Sir George, *From Phelps to Gielgud*, Chapman and Hall, 1936.

Bancroft, George Pleydell, *Stage and Bar*, Faber and Faber, 1939.

Bancroft, Squire and Marie, *The Bancrofts On and Off the Stage, By Themselves*, Richard Bentley, 1888.

Bancroft, Squire and Marie, *The Bancrofts*, John Murray, 1925.

Beerbohm, Max, *Around Theatres*, Rupert Hart-Davies, 1953.

Beerbohm, Max, *More Theatres*, Rupert Hart-Davis, 1969.

Craig, Edward Gordon, *Henry Irving*, Dent, 1930.

Craig, Edward Gordon, *Ellen Terry and her Secret Self*, Samson Low, Marston, 1931.

Dark, Sydney and Grey, Rowland, *W. S. Gilbert. His Life and Letters*, Methuen, 1924.

Dent, Alan, *Mrs Patrick Campbell*, Museum Press, 1961.

Du Maurier, Daphne, *Gerald, A Portrait*, Gollancz, 1934.

Forbes-Robertson, Sir Johnston, *A Player Under Three Reigns*, T. Fisher Unwin, 1925.

Great Acting, ed. Hal Burton. BBC. 1967

Gielgud, Sir John, *Early Stages*, revised edition, Falcon Press, 1953.

Hatton, Joseph, *Henry Irving's Impressions of America*, Samson Low, Marston, Searle and Rivington, 1884.

Henry Beerbohm Tree. Some Memories of Him and His Art, ed. Max Beerbohm, Hutchinson, 1920.

Irving, Laurence, *Henry Irving: The Actor and His World*, Faber and Faber, 1951.

Irving, Laurence, *The Successors*, Rupert Hart-Davis, 1967.

James, Henry, *The Complete Plays of Henry James*, ed. Leon Edel, Rupert Hart-Davis, 1949.

James, Henry, *The Scenic Art*, ed. Allan Wade, Rupert Hart-Davis, 1949.

MacCarthy, Sir Desmond, *Drama*, Putnam, 1940.

MacCarthey, Sir Desmond, *Theatre*, MacGibbon and Kee, 1954

Manvell, Roger, *Ellen Terry*, Heinemann, 1968.

Mason, A. E. W., *Sir George Alexander and the St James's Theatre*, Macmillan, 1935.

Menpes, Sir Mortimer, *Henry Irving*, Adam and Charles Black, 1906.

Ormond, Leonée, *George Du Maurier*, Routledge and Kegan Paul, 1969.

Pearson, Hesketh, *Beerbohm Tree: His Life and Laughter*, Methuen, 1956.

Pearson, Hesketh, *The Last Actor-Managers*, Methuen, 1950.

Pearson, Hesketh, *The Life of Oscar Wilde*, Methuen, 1946.

Pemberton, T. Edgar, *The Life and Writings of T. W. Robertson*, R. Bentley, 1893.

Playfair, Giles, *Kean*, Reinhardt and Evans, 1950.

Robertson, Graham, *Time Was*, Hamish Hamilton, 1931.

Rowell, George, *The Victorian Theatre*, Geoffrey Cumberledge, Oxford University Press, 1956.

Scott, Clement, *From The Bells to King Arthur*, John Macquean, 1897.

Shaw, Bernard, *Our Theatres in the Nineties*, Constable, 1932.

Steen, Marguerite, *A Pride of Terrys*, Longman, 1962.

Terry, Ellen, *Ellen Terry's Memoirs*, preface and notes by Edith Craig and Christopher St John, Gollancz, 1933.

Terry and Shaw, *Ellen Terry and Bernard Shaw. A Correspondence*, ed. Christopher St John, Constable, 1931.

The Oxford Companion to the Theatre, ed. Phyllis Hartnoll, 3rd edition, Oxford University Press, 1967.

Wilde, Oscar, *The Letters of Oscar Wilde*, ed. Rupert Hart-Davis, 1962.

Index

Figures in italics refer to illustrations

A Nation
Forged in Fire

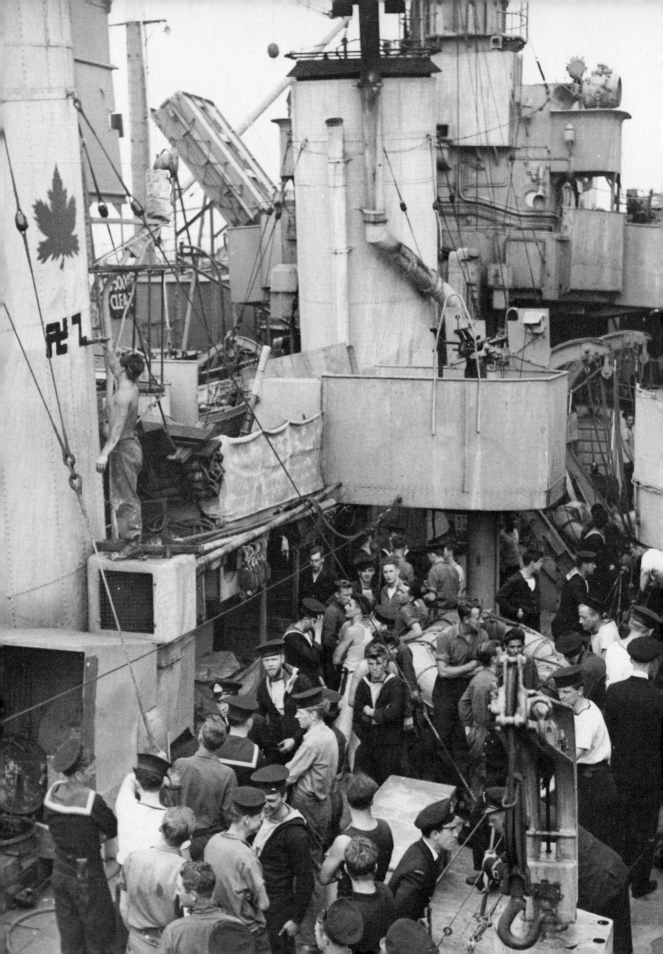

A NATION
FORGED IN FIRE

Canadians and the Second World War 1939–1945

J. L. Granatstein and Desmond Morton

LESTER
&ORPEN
DENNYS

PUBLISHERS

FIRST EDITION

Canadian Cataloguing in Publication Data
Granatstein, J.L., 1939-
  A nation forged in fire

Includes index.
ISBN 0-88619-213-7 (bound)   ISBN 0-88619-215-3 (pbk.)

I. World War, 1939-1945 — Canada. 2. Canada — History — 1939-1945. I. Morton, Desmond, 1937-
II. Title.

D768.15.G73 1989   940.54'0971   C89-093060-0

Design by Don Fernley
Picture research by Jim Burant
Maps by Jonathan Gladstone, j.b. geographics

Typeset in 11 pt. Aster by Alpha Graphics Limited
Printed and bound in Canada by Metropole Litho Inc.

Lester & Orpen Dennys Limited
78 Sullivan Street
Toronto, Canada   M5T 1C1

Page I: Infantrymen of Les Fusiliers Mont-Royal move warily down a Falaise street behind a tank of the Sherbrooke Fusiliers, hoping against hope that the Sherman will provide some protection and not merely attract enemy fire.

Page II: On board the destroyer HMCS *Chaudière*.

Page III: The Lancaster was the mainstay of Bomber Command, the plane that blitzed Germany into rubble. This veteran Lanc, its missions chalked up on its nose, came back to Malton, Ontario in mid-1945 to inspire the workers at Victory Aircraft Ltd. Note the vengeful doggerel about the Pacific war.

CONTENTS

While official war artists documented the struggle overseas, civilian artists used pleas, threats, and exhortations to enlist the support of the public at home; this poster is by the well-known painter Philip Surrey.

ACKNOWLEDGEMENTS

Readers of this book will recognize that our primary debt is to all those who let us share their memories. We have tried to tell the story the way it happened, the way those Canadians who fought and experienced the war lived it. To this end, we advertised widely for letters, unpublished accounts, memoirs, and memorabilia, and many veterans of the Second World War and their wives, children, and friends sent us boxes of treasured material. We are immensely thankful to all those who assisted us with these first-hand accounts and anecdotes.

We have benefited again from the careful editing of Gena Gorrell, who has caught us out in more errors than we care to contemplate. Any that remain, we regret to admit, must be pinned on us alone.

Finally, this book is dedicated to the able teachers in history and political science we shared a long time ago when we were both young cadets at the Royal Military College. George Stanley, Richard Preston, Ezio Cappadocia, Donald Schurman, and Fred Thompson constituted the superb history department, while J. Murray Beck singlehandedly professed political science at RMC. They made us interested in our country's past and its government and, despite our best efforts to resist, turned us into historians and scholars. We remain grateful for the example of careful and conscientious scholarship they set us.

J.L.G. and D.M.
April 1989

Royal Canadian Engineers pause for a brief prayer with a chaplain just before boarding their landing craft for the D-Day invasion.

INTRODUCTION

Patriotism for the British Empire was high fashion in Canada in the early years of the twentieth century. But the Canadians who so cheerfully marched off to Armageddon in 1914 in defence of that empire found a war they could not have expected. Many of those who returned home after the Armistice on November 11, 1918 swore that neither they nor their sons would ever go to war again. The "war to end war" did not, however, and the bitterness and unresolved conflicts it left soon brought the world back to the brink. In September 1939 — hesitantly and without enthusiasm — Canadians again went to war. Once more, armies were mobilized, men learned to fly fighters and drop bombs, and sailors went to sea to fight the elements and escort convoys through the North Atlantic to Britain. Once more, conscription tore apart the fragile links between French and English Canadians, though less violently than in 1917.

But the Second World War was very different from the Great War. The conflict spread over more of the globe, and the battles were on a larger scale; no longer were great campaigns waged for patches of worthless European ground. This was a war of movement, of armoured vehicles and close air support, of thousand-bomber raids and vast flotillas of aircraft carriers and battleships. The intensity of the fighting for infantrymen was, if anything, greater than in 1914–18, the potential for loss and suffering for all the combatants — and the civilians living behind the lines — greater still. Britain, France, the Soviet Union, Germany, Italy, and other nations that became battlegrounds suffered huge losses of fighting men and civilians. North Americans happily saw their cities spared but, as in the First World War, the losses of men were heavy. And the horror that befell Japan in 1945 still haunts the world, a spectre of future wars.

The fear of that spectre has resulted in a powerful anti-war movement around the world. But while the quest for peace and global harmony is a noble one, it should not blind us to the lessons of history. The war that Canada and its allies fought from 1939 to 1945 was a war for survival against powerful enemies that embodied genuine evil. With Hitler, Mussolini, and Tojo seeking to enslave the world, Canadians were forced to take up arms once more. They did so without joy, but with ample courage and resolution. And while the fires of war inflicted terrible sufferings on many Canadians, they also forged a stronger, surer, and more sovereign nation.

I
TO WAR ONCE MORE

Ottawa, September 3, 1939. The Minister of National Defence urgently summoned a staff officer to the Privy Council offices, where the Cabinet had just learned of Britain and France's declaration of war on Germany. Ian Mackenzie, the minister, told the chiefs of staff to put all defence measures into effect. The Canadian armed forces, he later recalled, could "fire on any blinking German who came within range of our guns...." But, he added, "we were not at war." The minister was absolutely correct, however puzzling his words may have sounded, for Canada was still neutral and would remain so for another week. Not until Parliament met and formally decided to participate in this war was Canada a belligerent.

A quarter-century before, when Canada had been brought into the conflict immediately on Britain's declaration of war, people had turned out by the thousands to shout and to cheer the prospect of war, to hail militia men in uniform, to sing "God Save the King" and "Rule, Britannia" with a fervour as great in Montreal as in Toronto. But that was before the boys went overseas to the horror of the trenches. That was before the casualty lists swelled to fill pages in the daily newspapers. And that was before the survivors of the carnage in France and Flanders came home with their terrible wounds in body and mind. Canadians remembered all this, and this time there were no cheering crowds in Halifax, Montreal, Toronto, or Vancouver. There were few Canadians who gloried in the coming of the second German war.

THE RISE OF THE DICTATORS

If the mood on the streets was sombre, there were many who believed that the job had to be finished this time, as the British Empire, France, Italy, and the United States had not completed it in 1918. The battles of the First World War had left Germany's territory physically unravaged, although the 1919 Treaty of Versailles had imposed heavy and humiliating burdens on the defeated nation, giving German territory to Poland and Czechoslovakia and even obliging the Germans to admit guilt for starting the war. The treaty's punitive clauses soon began to seem almost "unfair", however, as the British, French, Americans, and others tried to forget the long, hard struggle in a search for amusement and profit.

But the Germans did not forget their humiliation. The government that came into existence after the 1918 abdication of Kaiser Wilhelm was a shaky creation. The great inflation of the early 1920s wiped out the savings of the middle classes, and the Depression that began in the fall of 1929 caused the same widespread unemployment in Germany as elsewhere. And the Germans — much like the Italians, Spaniards, and others — saw the economic crisis lead to burgeoning growth on the left wing of the political spectrum. Everywhere, socialists and Communists argued that capitalism had broken down and that only they had the answers. Workers flocked to march under their party banners.

Not all German workers went to leftist parties, however. Tens of thousands joined parties that called for a rebirth of German pride and strength and for an end to the rearmament limitations the Treaty of Versailles had imposed on Germany. Ominously, many among the middle class and the industrialists — frightened of Communism for economic reasons — also turned to the right-wing parties. The great beneficiary was the National Socialist German Workers' Party, led by a mesmerizing orator named Adolf Hitler. Hitler's speeches played on people's fears, pointed to scapegoats, and promised every true German a place in the sun.

The Führer, as Hitler was adoringly called by his followers, was thought to be radical on social questions, but the sober right-wing industrialists were sure that he could be controlled by sensible men like themselves. Early in 1933, as the result of backroom political manoeuvring, the Nazi party took power, with Hitler being made chancellor but with conservatives holding some of the key portfolios. The new chancellor, however, quickly demonstrated that he was not a politician like the others. He began to consolidate his party's domestic power by officially sanctioning a policy of anti-Semitism and by crushing the political opposition of the Communists and socialists. Opponents were murdered or jailed in concentration camps, and the free discussion of ideas was frozen into fearful silence. At the same time, the Nazis began to test the restrictions the Versailles treaty had placed on rearmament. Hitler, it was becoming clear, sought total control in Germany. His followers, marching in their disciplined and goose-stepping ranks, sang "Today Germany, tomorrow the world", and throughout Europe the fear was that the Nazi stormtroopers meant exactly what they said.

Worse, the victorious Allies of 1918 were far from united. They had split asunder under the strain of imperial rivalry and economic competition in the 1920s, and the divisions between them increased in the next decade as the Great Depression savaged their industries and trade. In the dog-eat-dog world of the depressed 1930s, there seemed no will to act for peace. The United States professed little interest in Europe's affairs, and in 1935 President Franklin Roosevelt signed the American Neutrality Act, banning shipments of war materiel to nations at war; a 1936 amendment also prohibited loans to such nations. The boneless League of Nations, so ineffectual that Joseph Stalin's tyrannical Soviet Union often appeared as the staunchest supporter of collective security and freedom, certainly could do little to rally the democracies. Among the dominions only the smallest, New Zealand, was staunch for collective security. It was easily ignored. The seizure of Manchuria by Japan's militarist government early in the decade had drawn only the lightest of slaps on the wrist from the League. In the fall of 1935, Italy — under its fascist leader, Benito Mussolini — invaded and annexed the African nation of Ethiopia; the League responded with mild, ineffective economic sanctions, and further attempts to help Ethiopia were aborted by Britain and France. Clearly the League, and the collective will it was meant to embody, were faltering. Had there been unity Hitler might have been stopped early in his career: perhaps in 1936, when he sent his troops into the demilitarized Rhineland from which they had been barred by the Versailles treaty; or in 1938, when he marched his army into Austria and united it with Germany.

Canada had played its small, discreditable part in all this. Its representative to the League had actually congratulated Japan for bringing stability to Manchuria, and in 1935 the government had disavowed the oil sanctions against Italy proposed by its permanent representative in Geneva. Successive governments had argued against any attempt to bind League members to act against aggressors. Entry to the League of Nations in 1919 had been one of the steps on the road to national autonomy, but the Canadian record there and in the world had shown more attention to symbolic steps towards nationhood than willingness to work to keep the peace or to put teeth into collective security.

Through the mid-1930s, domestic issues continued to attract more interest in Parliament and press than foreign squabbles. In the First World War there had been bitter divisions over conscription, and the memory of that rankled still, especially in Quebec. Now politicians argued that Canada was "a fireproof house far from inflammable materials", as Senator Raoul Dandurand had told the League in the 1920s — delicately implying that the rest of the world should put its house in order and leave North America to get on with the business of making money.

Canada, in other words, had turned its back on the world's problems. The 1920s had not been a boom time for the whole country. There had been terrible drought in Alberta and widespread unemployment in much of the country. There was interest in international trade, and those in political circles worried about events that affected the British Empire, but there was very little ambition, among either politicians or populace, to play a world role. Mackenzie King, the Liberal prime minister from 1921 to 1926 and 1926 to 1930, had taken that view, and so too had R.B. Bennett, the Tory prime minister from 1930 until his defeat by King in October 1935. But by the late 1930s outside events at last began to force themselves into the Canadian consciousness. Hitler, Mussolini, Stalin, and the generals who exercised enormous influence in Japan compelled attention. The drumbeats of war were beginning to resound in many quarters.

There was conflict in the Far East, where since 1937 Japan had been busily engaged in swallowing as much of China as it could grab. There were bloody purges in the Soviet Union in the last years of the decade, as Stalin slaughtered generals, politicians, intellectuals, and ordinary citizens wholesale; those who did not die were sentenced to the Gulag. And there was civil war in Spain, where the social-democratic government, supported by the Soviet Union and by volunteers from around the world, was under assault by fascistic army officers led by General Francisco Franco and backed by the fascist regimes in Italy and Germany.

The Spanish war stirred many Canadians. Roman Catholics in Quebec and throughout English Canada overwhelmingly supported Franco, the man who would rescue the Church from the attacks of the left. But others saw the Loyalists as a democratic government under attack and Spain as the first real test of democracy against fascism. Thousands of Canadians — most, but not all, Communists — overcame the roadblocks placed in their way by Ottawa and joined the International Brigades formed to resist Franco. The Canadian Mackenzie–Papineau battalion (named after the rebel leaders of 1837) fought long and hard in the losing effort to save Spain, while a Montreal doctor, Norman Bethune, pioneered techniques to give the wounded blood transfusions right on the battlefield. (In 1938 Bethune turned his attention from Spain to China, and went to work with Mao Zedong's Red Army in its fight against Chiang Kai-shek and the Imperial Japanese Army; he died of septicemia in 1939.)

But it was Hitler's Germany that attracted most attention. There the Nazis were launching increasingly violent pogroms against Jews and imposing ever tougher restrictions to make their lives impossible. And always, Herr Hitler made his shrill demands for the return of territories and peoples that had been lost in the 1919 treaty — demands that focused on Czechoslovakia and Poland. A superbly efficient and completely mendacious propaganda machine, skilfully directed by Joseph Goebbels, turned the Führer's demands into psychological weapons. If repeated often enough, "the big lie" became something to be believed, however ludicrous it may have been. At the same time, Field Marshal Hermann Goering's air force was expanding, the army was growing, and the navy was building submarines and pocket battleships as fast as the North Sea shipyards could turn them out. Germany had rearmed its militant population with a powerful ideology and modern weapons, while the world watched and worried.

The dictatorships had their supporters in Canada. Home-grown fascists, stirred by visions of themselves as Aryan supermen, dressed up in black shirts and denounced Jews and foreigners. Parades and occasional riots disrupted Toronto and Montreal. Fascist leader Adrien Arcand in Quebec was even given financial assistance by R.B. Bennett's Conservative Party. The Communists, following orders issued by Moscow, had their members working in the trade unions and in the Depression's relief camps, and Communist Party leader Tim Buck almost won a martyr's halo when he narrowly escaped assassination in Kingston Penitentiary. The Japanese consulate in Vancouver spread propaganda about Japan's "civilizing mission" in its war against China, and many old-timers in the Japanese community listened. Italo-Canadians felt much the same about Mussolini's war in Ethiopia. At last Canada was caught up in the political ferment. Radio, still less than twenty years old, brought direct reportage on the events of the day to Canadian living-rooms. The world out there was at the boil, and everyone knew it.

All the same, some people tried to hide their heads in the sand. After 1935 the Mackenzie King government made tentative efforts to begin military preparations for the war that many could see coming, but these were bitterly resisted. The Québécois remembered all too well the way Anglo-Canadians had pressured them during the 1914 war; Liberal politicians had won election after election by promising that never again would anyone be conscripted for a British war. There was a small pacifist movement whose supporters believed that any war for any cause was insane. There were advocates of collective security and the League of Nations. There were imperial loyalists, ready to follow Britain wherever she led, whether to war or to appeasement. And a great many people were simply isolationists, convinced that Canada was as safe as any place on earth if only the sentimental links to London and the European vortex could be cut.

In this whirl of argument about war and peace, one fact was clear: the Canadian armed forces scarcely existed. Defence appropriations for 1937–38 were $36 million (up $10 million from three years before), and for 1939–40 the budget forecast for the three services was $64.6 million, sums that allowed only the tiniest of forces. The Royal Canadian Navy in 1939 had a regular-force strength of under 2,000, ludicrously small but almost double its size three years before. The fleet consisted of four modern destroyers, two older ones, and four minesweepers. The Royal Canadian Air Force was equally weak, despite its role in survey work and mercy missions in the inter-war period. In 1939, regular-force strength was 298 officers and 2,750 airmen, and there were eight squadrons. The RCAF had 270 aircraft of 23 different types, but only 37 were even remotely combat-worthy.

The Canadian Army was no better off. Up-to-date equipment was woefully lacking: in 1939, for example, the army had four anti-aircraft guns, five mortars, eighty-two Vickers machine guns, ten Bren guns, and two light tanks. Even trucks were in short supply. The Permanent Force had only 4,261 all ranks in mid-1939, every unit being under strength.

If the regular forces were pathetically weak, so too were the reserves — the Saturday-night soldiers, airmen, and sailors. The militia had a strength of 51,000 in armouries in countless small towns from Prince Edward Island to Vancouver Island, where units were often the focus of social life. Officers used their pay to help their units attract and hold volunteers. In many regiments, even men in the ranks gave their pay to unit funds. This was patriotic but it did not make the militia more warlike. With equipment in short supply, the militia was ill prepared for anything like modern war, but its members had the rudiments of military training. The figures were equally depressing for the air reserve, with its total strength of 1,000 organized into seven auxiliary squadrons. The Royal Canadian Navy Volunteer Reserve had a strength roughly equal to that of the Air Force auxiliary. That the men of the regular and reserve forces were game, no one doubted; that they would not survive two minutes (assuming their ammunition lasted that long) against a first-class foe was equally certain.

As the situation in Europe grew blacker, Canadians still hoped against hope that war could be avoided. Canada's influence on the issues was limited, but that influence, such as it was, was exercised in support of peace and appeasement. When Britain, France, Italy, and Germany met in Munich in September 1938 to discuss Hitler's demands for the return of the Sudetenland to Germany, and when the Great Powers pressured Czechoslovakia into acquiescence, there was relief all across the country — and the world. Instead of war there would be ''peace in our time'', the dessicated British prime minister, Neville Chamberlain, said after he returned from Munich. Meet Germany's ''just'' demands, in other words, and Herr Hitler would prove a reasonable man. Mackenzie King had met the Führer in 1937, and he shared Chamberlain's views, adding his own gloss to them by noting Hitler's deeply spiritual nature and desire for peace. Like Mackenzie King, Hitler had loved his mother.

In April 1939, with the ink on the Munich document scarcely dry, Hitler's army, the *Wehrmacht*, invaded the rest of Czechoslovakia. The full force of the Nazi propaganda machine was then turned on Poland, and the ''Corridor'' that gave the Poles an outlet to the sea at Danzig and divided Germany in two. Appalled at this turn of events, Britain quickly offered guarantees of military support to Warsaw, without consulting Canada and the other dominions. Chamberlain's abandonment of appeasement horrified the Canadian prime minister, who was informed of the guarantee only after it had been made. But King knew that his options were limited.

AN AUTONOMOUS NATION?

The Statute of Westminster of 1931 had made Canada autonomous in foreign policy, an independent nation within the British Commonwealth. But without sources of diplomatic information, and with only a tiny foreign service, Canada could scarcely be expected to create an external policy of its own. The Statute of Westminster, in other words, was only a paper statement of independence, and psychologically Canada remained the colony it had legally been in 1914, when the British declaration of war against Germany had committed Canada as well.

Moreover, Mackenzie King *wanted* Canada to go to war if Britain did. Usually seen as an isolationist, the strange, dumpy little man who ruled Canada was a sentimental Anglophile, an imperialist and a monarchist, one who believed fervently that Britain stood for the ideals of democracy and godliness that he cherished. It was Mackenzie King who brought George VI and Queen Elizabeth to Canada in the spring of 1939 to be cheered by loyal subjects from the Atlantic to the Pacific, and it was King who gushed in his diaries about the great qualities of Canada's monarchs. How could Canada let down such splendid people if it came to war?

What of Quebec? Although the royal couple had been hailed in Quebec City and Montreal, there was no desire in *la belle province* to send troops overseas again, to go into another war that would see the conscriptionists demanding their tithe of blood from French Canada. Here King was helped by his great colleague Ernest Lapointe, the Minister of Justice. A big man, Lapointe was trusted as was no other Quebec political figure. In the months after Munich, he and King performed a delicate ballet to calm public opinion and to satisfy those who still hoped Canada might be able to stay neutral in a European war. One day the prime minister would declare that it was "madness" to assume that Canada would send troops to Europe every twenty years to rescue a continent that could not govern itself. The next day Lapointe would maintain just as strongly that there could be no doubt of the Canadian response if there was a prospect of an aggressor raining bombs on London. And the day after, the prime minister would subject the British high commissioner in Ottawa to a tirade against London's policy, which aimed at dragging Canada into a war over Eastern European issues. What did it all mean?

It meant that King and Lapointe were manoeuvring, however reluctantly, to bring a united Canada into war through a decision of Canada's Parliament. "Parliament will decide" had been the prime minister's invariable answer to questions about his foreign policy, and King actually intended this. That only one decision would be possible was another matter. For Quebec it was essential that Canada actually have a choice — but the province's concerns about conscription also had to be satisfied.

And they were. At the end of March 1939, the prime minister pledged that if war should come, there would be no conscription for overseas military service. The leader of the Conservative Party, Dr. R.J. Manion, echoed that promise. The sigh of relief in French Canada was almost audible. The Liberal Party, dependent on Quebec, surely could not betray its promises, particularly so long as Ernest Lapointe was there.

King had thus laid the groundwork to take Canada into war. And by August 1939 war was fast approaching. As German pressure on Poland mounted, and as the Poles prepared to send their cavalry squadrons against the Nazi tanks, Germany and the Soviet Union — hitherto bitter enemies — signed a pact on August 23. The public clauses talked of friendship; the secret ones divided Poland between the Nazis and the Soviets. With one of his enemies bought off, Hitler hoped that Britain and France would draw back.

By this time, however, it had become all too clear that appeasement was a failure. Sooner or later, the Germans would have to be stopped. And so, when the Panzer divisions of the *Wehrmacht* crossed the border into Poland on September 1, the British and French issued an ultimatum. On September 3, they declared war.

Technically, Canada was still at peace. The Statute of Westminster had given the King of Canada the right to declare war on behalf of his dominion, but Parliament had not yet decided. A special session called for September 7 heard the prime minister say that "We stand for the defence of Canada; we stand for the co-operation of this country at the side of Great Britain; and if this house will not support us in that policy, it will have to find some other government to assume the responsibilities of the present." And Mackenzie King justified his tortuous course on foreign policy by noting that he had made it "the supreme endeavour" of his leadership "to let no hasty or premature threat or pronouncement create mistrust and divisions between the different elements that compose the population of our vast dominion, so that when the moment of decision came all should so see the issue itself that our national effort might be marked by unity of purpose, of heart and of endeavour."

The prime minister also repeated his pledge against conscription for overseas service: "No such measure will be introduced by the present administration." That reference to "the present administration" was a delicate reminder that other parties, whatever they said now, might not be as trustworthy. As four years had elapsed since the last general election, a contest at the polls could not be far off.

The special war session lasted only three days. J.S. Woodsworth, the leader of the Co-operative Commonwealth Federation and a genuine pacifist, was heckled when he spoke out against the war, and one or two Quebec MPs, voicing the real concerns of French Canada, called on Canada not to participate in this British war. Those lonely voices aside, Parliament voted $100 million for war expenditures (double the amount voted twenty-five years before) and decided to enter the war at Britain's side. George VI signed the proclamation on September 10, and Canada was at war with Germany — one week after Britain.

Why? Did Canada go to war because Hitler represented an unspeakably evil regime or because Poland was a democracy worth the saving? Hitler *was* evil, but in 1939 few had heard of concentration camps, and the "final solution" of the "Jewish problem" was not yet Nazi policy. There was some talk of atrocities, but after the popular exposés that had debunked most Great War claims of Germans cutting the hands off Belgian priests or crucifying Canadian soldiers, people were skeptical. And the Poles themselves ran a tyrannical regime marked by authoritarianism and anti-Semitism. A few months before, in fact, Warsaw had insisted on its territorial share of Czechoslovakia. Poland was no democracy. Czechoslovakia had been one, but the British and French had abandoned it (and its efficient army and armaments factories) to Hitler a year earlier.

In other words, Canada went to war in September 1939 primarily for the same reason as in 1914: because Britain went to war. Not for democracy, though that was crucial. Not to stop Hitler, though that mattered. Not to save Poland, though that was the ostensible reason. Canada went to war only because Neville Chamberlain felt unable to break the pledges he had made to Poland in March 1939. Had he slipped free, as he tried to do, Canada would have sat by and watched the Reich devour Poland without feeling compelled to fight. Some Canadians knew that Hitler had to be fought; in 1939, however, that motive was not as powerful as the old loyalties.

The much-trumpeted autonomy that Canada had won was, therefore, irrelevant in the face of a war involving Britain. Ties of sentiment, blood, and culture had foreclosed every option but one. The simple truth is that the English-Canadian majority wanted Canada to fight because of the link to the mother country, not because of any understanding of the issues at stake. Ethnic Canadians were generally cooler, but acquiescent. French Canadians were willing to allow English Canadians to volunteer, so long as the threat of conscription no longer existed. The decision to go to war may have been the only possible one, but large numbers of Canadians were not enthusiastic about the prospect.

Marching As to War

Enthusiastic or not, Canada was now in the war. Plans had to be made for the volunteers who were starting to queue up at militia armouries and naval stations. The prime minister, fearful of casualties and of the impact of another conscription crisis on his country and party, was hoping that Canada could wage a war of "limited liability" — like a cautious insurance company protecting itself against undue risk. He was delighted to be told by London twice in the first week of September that the defence of Canada was the first and major charge on his government. Once Canada was at war, however, London began pressing the Canadian government to send troops overseas.

Cabinet met on September 15 to prepare the war program. The ministers were horrified when the chiefs of staff presented plans for the first year that would cost $491 million, almost as much as the country's entire peacetime budget. That sum, they decided, had to be cut back to $314 million. The army's plan for three divisions was reduced by one — a saving of approximately 20,000 men. But there was to be an expeditionary force, despite Mackenzie King's reluctance. One of the infantry divisions was to go overseas as soon as possible, and the second was to be recruited and trained in Canada for dispatch if necessary. In command of the First Division was Major-General

Andrew G.L. McNaughton, a very successful artillery officer in the Great War, a respected scientist, and the head of the National Research Council. Mackenzie King liked Andy McNaughton because he thought the general was against conscription; moreover, because the general had been close to Prime Minister Bennett, some thought he was a Tory, so no one could claim that the Liberal government was playing patronage games with the army!

While those decisions were being implemented, London proposed the establishment of a giant air training plan, as well. The British had been trying for some years to persuade Canada to allow the training of Royal Air Force pilots in its great open spaces. Although a small project had been agreed on in April 1939, the war had intervened before the first trainees had reached Canada. Now the idea was to train some 20,000 pilots and 30,000 air crew in Canada each year. The British Commonwealth Air Training Plan (BCATP), as it came to be called, had been suggested by the Australian high commissioner in London and by Vincent Massey, the Canadian high commissioner, and had been seized upon by the Air Ministry.

King initially liked the idea, but the more he thought about it, the angrier he became. If the British had produced this scheme at the outset, it could have been Canada's major contribution and might have made an expeditionary force unnecessary. He and his ministers were worried about the financial costs, as well as the political complications. The war program decided upon in mid-September had been based on their assessment of the maximum Canada could do.

In the end — after difficult, often bitter negotiations with a British mission and dominion representatives — the BCATP was created. The total cost was set at $607 million, with the Canadian share being $353 million, a vast increase on the original budget fixed for the first year of war. The RCAF was to administer the BCATP, and some Canadian graduates were to be placed in RCAF squadrons. The agreement, signed in the early morning hours of December 17, 1939, was announced in a national radio address by Mackenzie King. That day, not coincidentally, was his sixty-fifth birthday.

The military side of the war effort was beginning to take shape, but there was opposition in the country. In Quebec, Premier Maurice Duplessis, whose Union Nationale party had been in power since 1936, looked on the unease created by the war as an opportunity to seek re-election. Duplessis's government had not been a notable success, and the province's creditors were unhappy about the worth of provincial bonds, but his snap election call on September 25 caused near panic in Ottawa. The premier was "a little Hitler", King wrote, and his election announcement a "diabolical act". The concern was genuine: Ottawa's carefully constructed national unity could be jeopardized by the acrimony certain to be created by a provincial election, and if

Duplessis won, his government would be a thorn in the federal government's side.

The solution came when King's Quebec ministers decided, over his initial opposition, to enter the provincial contest. "They took the view," King wrote in his diary, "that if Duplessis carried the province, it would be equivalent to a want of confidence in themselves as Federal ministers, and that they would feel it necessary to withdraw from the Cabinet as having lost all influence...." Moreover, the ministers campaigned on the issue of conscription: if Duplessis won and they resigned, then French Canada would have no voice in Ottawa, making conscription a certainty. That argument had force. By calling for provincial autonomy in the face of Ottawa's wartime centralization, Duplessis put himself on the defensive. The election saw the Liberals take 53 per cent of the popular vote and 69 seats in the Legislature.

Duplessis had argued implicitly that Canada was doing too much, but the reaction in parts of Ontario was precisely the opposite. The Liberal premier, Mitchell Hepburn, had been fighting with his federal cousins for years, and King's half-hearted support for the war intensified Hepburn's distaste for the prime minister. In the Ontario Legislature on January 18, 1940, Hepburn moved and easily carried a resolution "regretting that the Federal Government at Ottawa has made so little effort to prosecute Canada's duty in the war in the vigorous manner the people of Canada desire to see." Mackenzie King was appalled at this challenge from the most populous province, but he quickly saw the potential advantages. Parliament was due to reassemble for a partisan and bitter pre-election session. Hepburn's accusation offered the perfect excuse for a sudden election.

The MPs and senators gathered to hear the Speech from the Throne on January 25 sat stunned when the governor general announced the dissolution of Parliament. It was trickery to force a sudden election because of Hepburn's move, to be sure, but — aside from the outrage on the Opposition benches — few in the country seemed to object. The election campaign that followed, taking place during the "Phony War" that left the European front uneasily calm for seven months, was quiet. The Conservatives promised to form a government of the "best brains" in the land and unwisely dubbed themselves the "National Government" party, a name that stirred recollections in Quebec and elsewhere of the Union Government that had been created in 1917 to enforce conscription. The CCF, torn by the pacifism of its leader and many of his followers, was ineffective. Only the Liberals, pledging no conscription and promising a sound war effort, had the experienced men Canada needed in wartime, or so Grit propaganda claimed. The people believed them, and on March 26 they gave the Liberals 51.5 per cent of the popular vote and 181 seats, a huge majority in a House of 245. The Tories were slaughtered wholesale, even Manion losing his seat. The CCF's Woodsworth was barely re-elected. Social Credit dropped from 17 seats to 10. It was a Liberal triumph, and Mackenzie King was again firmly in command.

BUILDING THE FORCES

With politics temporarily out of the way, the business of preparing for war continued slowly. War production, eagerly sought by the government as a way of putting the still-large numbers of unemployed men and women back to work after ten years of Depression, began at a glacial pace. The British firms that held the patents on modern machines of war were reluctant to give the rights to produce guns, tanks, and bombs to Canada. The strictly limited federal budget did not allow for many new factories to be built or for industry to convert from peace to war production. In Ottawa's war of limited liability, not many businessmen or politicians wanted to take risks either.

Some Canadians stepped forward, though, and put more than their money or careers on the line. On September 1 — the day Hitler invaded Poland — Father Mike Dalton, a Roman Catholic priest in Windsor, Ontario, telegraphed Ottawa to volunteer: "If you are called upon to furnish Chaplains for the Service, I shall be ready on land or sea or air." There were more like him, too. In September 1939, 58,337 men and a few nursing sisters enlisted as volunteers in the army's active service force for the duration of the war. That was just about the same number that had enlisted in the first five months of the Great War. In fact, there were more men lining up outside the headquarters of militia units than the authorities could handle, and many "old sweats" from the previous war tried in vain to re-enlist. Farley Mowat recounts the story of the veteran who had his son drive him to the nearest headquarters of the Hastings and Prince Edward Regiment:

> he could not drive himself, having lost most of his sight and most of his lungs to mustard gas in 1918. He wept when they turned him away. But the Regiment did not forget him, for the son enlisted before the two returned to their farm that night.

There were many like that veteran. But there were also those parents who dreaded the thought of their sons enlisting. One father wrote the RCMP to try to stop his boy from joining up:

> My son Noah Summers has volunteered to go overseas and I feel I need him here. I lost one leg in the last war and had another one come back disabled.... Now I am not as young as I used to be and I need my boy each

fall to help me, I have farm lands which I have to go back and look after each fall.... You will do me a great favour if you turn him down I feel I've done my duty for my country and you know those boys have to be fed over there I am a Sask wheat farmer and have had plenty grief the last few years.

Still, there were thousands who had been unemployed for so long during the Great Depression that the prospect of a private's pay of $1.30 a day (and dependants' allowance of $60 a month plus $12 for each child), three squares a day, and a warm greatcoat looked pretty good, particularly with winter only two months away. Patriotism was the motive force for many; for some, the war offered a chance to escape from a life of relief, bread lines, skimpy food, and no money; for others, it was a simple desire for adventure or a chance to flee an unhappy marriage.

But after the imposition of stern fitness standards ("Men perfectly fit, mentally and physically, for all active service conditions of actual warfare in any climate, who are able to march, can see to shoot, and hear well") and admonitions from Ottawa to go slowly in recruiting those with dependants, the flood of volunteers turned into a trickle. There was no equipment and little barrack space. One Winnipegger who enlisted in the artillery in September remembered being issued a Great War uniform of "breeches, long puttees, brass-buttoned tunics, bandoliers — and boots that we dyed ourselves with thick, black army issue coloring. We had no barracks and lived out." Only 64,902 had been enrolled by the end of 1939 and just 20,000 more were taken on strength in the first four months of 1940. There were not enough uniforms even for those.

Recruiting for the navy was slower yet, only a few handfuls being enrolled. By the end of the first month of the war, only 3,000 sailors were in uniform all told, and waiting lists swelled across the country. Small as it was, however, the RCN quickly got its destroyers ready for war service. HMCS *Fraser* and *St. Laurent* steamed out of Esquimalt immediately after fighting broke out on August 31 and arrived via the Panama Canal to join the other ships at their war station at Halifax on September 15. Already, harbour defences were in place at the great port from which the convoys were starting to go forth.

The Royal Canadian Air Force too struggled to get ready. Thirty-five modern aircraft from the United States barely managed to get over the border in the week after September 3, before Canada declared war and the American Neutrality Act came into effect. The regular and auxiliary squadrons went on full-time service on September 3, their ancient Wapiti aircraft and their few modern Hurricanes cranking up for action. Over the next two weeks, the reserves mobilized and recruiting began.

But it was the army that attracted the press coverage in the first months of war. The 1st Canadian Division, including such famous infantry units as the Royal Canadian Regiment, Princess Patricia's Canadian Light Infantry, the Royal 22e Regiment (the "Van Doos"), and the Seaforth Highlanders, began its move overseas in December 1939. In contrast to the situation in 1914, this time the division's officers and men were wholly Canadian. Almost 7,500 officers and men left Halifax on five great liners on December 10. One soldier remembered that these ships that eventually carried thousands of troops at a time "now carried only hundreds. It was a classy way to travel.... State rooms were allotted on a first-come, first-served basis....the ships still had their peacetime crews, and...they wouldn't let us do anything." Other ships were less grand. Robert Fulton of the Army Service Corps sailed on an old liner, the ss *Armonda*, and lived in the hold. "Top tier was in hammocks, second tier slept on top of the mess tables and third tier slept under the mess tables. And you prayed that the guy above you didn't get seasick."

Two additional convoys brought Canadian army strength in Britain to 23,000 by February 1940. The division was largely untrained, about half of its men never having served even in the militia before the outbreak of war. Training before embarkation had concentrated on foot and rifle drill, and only the most rudimentary tactics had been practised. The coldest winter of the century hampered training in England ("sniffles, coughs, frozen winter pipes, plugged toilets, largely unheated barrack rooms," one soldier remembered it), and not until April could more advanced training take place. Each infantry battalion spent time in a model trench system learning the patrolling and raiding techniques with which the Canadian Corps had won the Great War, and although vehicles were in short supply, units could pool their transport for mobile exercises.

One private in the Royal Canadian Army Service Corps, Jack Ainsworth of Calgary, wrote to his parents on May 6 about the monotony of training: "We're going for marches and doing rifle drills same as we did when we first joined up and all in all we aren't doing a thing new but just seeming to stand still." Worst of all, Ainsworth said, "I've finally found out what's missing over here. There's no place we can get a hamburger...." Still, as one British woman remembered, "all the girls were on Cloud 9 if they could go out with a 1st Div. Canadian."

Herr Hitler was unwilling to let the division get ready for Great War–style trench warfare at its own pace. In April, the Phony War suddenly came to an end. Germany invaded Denmark and Norway, and most of the 2nd Brigade of the 1st Canadian Division left for Scotland on April 18 to await embarkation for northern Norway. Those orders were changed the next day: British units were sent into the cauldron, and the disappointed Canadians returned to their camp at Aldershot. They had been spared a hopeless campaign, as Denmark fell at once and Norway held out only into May.

The one bright spot in this increasingly serious military situation was that Neville Chamberlain was out of power in London on May 10. Toppled by revolt on the Tory backbenches, caused by the poor planning and disastrous results of the Norwegian campaign, Chamberlain had been replaced by a different sort of leader. Winston Churchill was a fighter, an innovator, and a man to inspire a nation at war. Mackenzie King had little confidence in the new prime minister, noting in his diary that Churchill was "tight most of the time". Perhaps it was true, but better Churchill drunk than Chamberlain sober. Britain soon was to need all the inspiration it could find.

On May 10, the same day Churchill took power, Hitler let loose his Panzer divisions in a *Blitzkrieg*, or "lightning war", against the Low Countries and France. The Germans used their tanks and mechanized infantry in a revolutionary way, large units bypassing pockets of French resistance and sweeping into the lightly manned rear areas. The *Luftwaffe* added to the panic and confusion caused by the Panzers with carefully co-ordinated dive-bombing attacks on enemy units; their Stukas were equipped with sirens to increase the terror, and the combined effect was to create chaos and spread despondency. The Dutch were overrun in a few days, and when the British and French forces left their prepared positions along the Franco-Belgian border to move forward to assist the Belgians, they and the Belgian army were cut off by a German thrust through the Ardennes forest and across the Meuse River. By May 20 the Germans were at Amiens and by the next day the Panzers, incredibly, had reached the English Channel near Abbeville, trapping the retreating British Expeditionary Force in a pocket. Only the miracle of Dunkirk — when a great flotilla made up of ships of the Royal Navy and hundreds of small civilian craft evacuated 338,000 British and French soldiers, while the *Wehrmacht* inexplicably sat by — would prevent the war from being lost completely before the end of May.

The situation in France had turned critical in less than two weeks. A desperate War Office called on General McNaughton and his Canadian division to support the beleaguered troops. McNaughton went to France on May 23 to study the battlefield, and while he was there his troops moved to Dover — but then he advised London that there was no prospect of his division rescuing the situation, and the men were sent back to Aldershot. Anxious to get into the fight, the Canadians sat discouraged and unhappy in their barracks while great events transpired at Dunkirk. "The Great Retreat from Dover" or "the Plymouth Panic", the troops called their abortive mission. The miraculous rescue of most of the British Expeditionary Force (but not its equipment) could not hide the magnitude of the disaster. Yet — despite the critical situation in France, and the collapse of the once-mighty French army — there was still wishful thinking in Churchill's London about the possibility of constructing a fortified Anglo-French redoubt in the Breton peninsula.

The Canadians were fated to be key players in this scheme, and on June 12 and 13 one brigade of infantry and a regiment of artillery — or about 5,000 men all told — landed at Brest, on the western tip of France. When Mackenzie King learned of the plans to send the division to France, he wrote in his diary that "it was like sending our men into a fiery furnace to be devoured in whole, almost in their first encounter." Fortunately, the fires were postponed this time. On the 14th, the Germans marched into undefended Paris, and although most of the Canadians had already moved inland by truck and by train, wiser heads concluded that there was little point in seeing the division thrown away for no prospect of gain. The troops were ordered to return to the coast and to abandon their vehicles and guns. The commanding officer of the Royal Canadian Horse Artillery, Lieutenant-Colonel J.H. Roberts, flatly refused to destroy his precious guns and brought them back to England. His war diary bitterly noted, "Although there was evidently no enemy within 200 miles, the withdrawal was conducted as a rout." The guns were more than welcome in an almost undefended England; the trucks, 216 of which were run off a cliff or set on fire, might also have been rescued had there been less panic.

The grumbling over the fiasco was very pronounced, the soldiers bitching that CASF, the initials of the Canadian Active Service Force, really meant Canadians Almost Saw France. In fact, the providential order to withdraw had saved thousands from death or capture; with the French capitulation, nothing was going to stop the *Wehrmacht*, certainly not the Canadians scattered across France. Six men were left behind in the rush to disembark: one was mortally injured in a road accident, four were interned but subsequently made their way back to England, and one became a prisoner of war. Given the chaos, the losses were remarkably small. Inevitably, the returning soldiers told tall tales about the French girls they had met, and one (probably apocryphal) story persisted of a Canadian who had managed to contract venereal disease during his brief excursion on the Continent.

But no one could see anything funny in Britain's situation in the summer of 1940. Hitler now controlled western Europe and the French shore of the English Channel and, although most of the British forces in France had been rescued at Dunkirk, there was only one division in England that was reasonably well equipped: McNaughton's Canadians. From being a slightly reluctant partner in a war of limited liability, Canada had suddenly become Britain's ranking ally in a war for survival.

While Canadian leaders wrestled fruitlessly with the Depression, the dictators of Europe had greater success. Here Hitler and Mussolini (foreground right and left) are clearly in step. While Hitler put Germans back to work (or in the army) and drew the frenzied adulation of his countrymen, Mussolini gave the Italians a policy of foreign aggression and imperial grandeur which for a time satisfied most. Behind and between the two is Rudolf Hess, who would parachute into Scotland in 1941 in a bizarre personal "peace mission"; the smiling figure left of Mussolini is Hermann Goering.

The Great Depression was the central fact of most Canadians' existence in the 1930s. This young unemployed worker is "tin-canning" to raise pennies for food and shelter in Vancouver; in a few years he would be expected to enlist and risk his life for a system that, in the eyes of many, had failed.

One testing ground for the clash between dictatorships and democracies was Spain, where a vicious civil war pitted General Franco's fascists (supported by Italy and Germany) against the legitimate government (supported by the Soviet Union). These two Canadians are among those who defied Canadian law to fight fascism with the Mackenzie–Papineau battalion. Labelled "premature anti-fascists", Mac–Pap veterans suffered discrimination during and after the Second World War.

Mackenzie King offered no bold standard for Canadians to rally around during the pre-war years. The fussy little man, destined to be Canada's longest-serving prime minister, thought the world would be a safe place if only Europeans and Asians resolved matters the way Canada and the United States did. When he addressed the League of Nations in 1936, King poured Canadian cold water on the flickering hopes for collective security to resist aggression.

In 1936 Hitler sent his ill-equipped and untested army into the demilitarized Rhineland, to the cheers of its inhabitants. The British and French were not amused, but failed to act. A chance to stop Hitler was lost.

OFFICERS AND COMMANDER-IN-CHIEF OF LOCAL FACISTS

Although Canada had its own homegrown Nazis, fascists, and racists — including these (misspelled) followers of Quebec's self-proclaimed *führer*, Adrien Arcand, who proposed exiling Canadian Jews to the Hudson Bay region — the emotional link to Britain remained strong.

The ties were reaffirmed when George VI and Queen Elizabeth paid a timely visit in 1939. Even Montreal's popular and corpulent Mayor Camillien Houde, who would be interned for most of the war for opposing national registration, seems to bask in the imperial glow as the royal couple sign the city's guest book. The prime minister looks on from the rear.

When war broke out in the early hours of September 1, 1939, recruiting began at once. Artillerymen seeking volunteers in Montreal were spiffily turned out (in Great War style), and all across the country men queued to be sworn in.

As headlines blared out the news, the *London Free Press* — a Conservative paper convinced that when Britain went to war, Canada was automatically included — was one week early in its proclamation.

If ever a nation was unready for war, it was Canada in 1939. The armed forces were tiny and ill equipped. The cadets at the Royal Military College, Kingston, would prove to be effective wartime officers, but their bayonet drills and instruction harked back to the Great War.

Even the tanks at Camp Borden were inadequate, too small and undergunned, and in any case there were too few of them.

Because barracks had yet to be constructed, many found themselves sleeping on
straw in fairground horse palaces. These soldiers at Toronto's Exhibition
Grounds staged a mock funeral for Hitler in the last days of the Phony War:
"Hitler thinks he's got a laugh; God help him when he gets this draft." Note that
two soldiers have Great War ribbons; almost none who had served in 1914–18
would be deemed fit enough to go into action in this new war.

The 1st Canadian Division arrived in Britain before the end of 1939. Six months later came the desperate evacuation of Dunkirk, and some Canadian units were sent off on a futile and short-lived attempt to stabilize a front in France's Brittany region. Almost all the men made it back to England, but the equipment abandoned in their withdrawal was a serious loss.

Meanwhile domestic politics continued much as usual. The prime minister and premiers met in 1941 to discuss revenues; as this glum picture suggests, nothing came of the meeting. Note the body language of Ontario's Mitchell Hepburn (front, second from left) as he turns away from his hated fellow Liberal Mackenzie King. Behind King (third from left) is Manitoba's John Bracken; at the right rear is Alberta's "Bible Bill" Aberhart.

II
WAR AT HOME AND ABROAD,
1940–42

The calamitous events in France stunned Canada. The six-million–strong French army had been thought to be the most powerful in the world, and the pride of its vaunted generals had collapsed like a pricked balloon. The confusion and muddle that had bedevilled the British Expeditionary Force were apparent despite the press censorship, but there was a curious kind of relief in Britain and Canada. The untrustworthy French (for so the British had always seen them) were gone, and now Britain and the Commonwealth could carry on all the better for being alone. "Chin up, there'll always be an England," said one lapel button sported by Canadians in the summer of 1940. Most Canadians agreed that, so long as the Royal Navy remained intact, Britain would survive and ultimately prevail.

That was a slim chance at best, and Ottawa realized it. A limited-liability war was no longer possible for Canada, and the only question now was what could be done. In April 1940, even before the *Blitzkrieg*, the government had agreed to the formation of an overseas Canadian Corps of two divisions. The prime minister persuaded his cost-conscious colleagues that this was owed to General McNaughton for his work in creating the 1st Division.

That seemed a feeble response after the middle of May. Under increasing public pressure, the government announced a series of measures to accelerate the war effort, including the early despatch of the 2nd Division overseas, the stationing of infantry in the West Indies and Iceland, and a greater financial commitment to the war and to Britain. King admitted to his caucus on May 23 that he almost feared to tell the country that the war effort would cost more than a billion dollars a year. The entire pre-war federal budget had amounted to about half a billion dollars; after less than a year of war, defence expenditure was already twice that much. "We had to consider whether that would not occasion a run on the banks...."

Some provinces thought Ottawa was weak and half-hearted. In Saskatch-

28

ewan, where pro-Nazi organizations had been active before the war, Attorney-General J.W. Estey created the Saskatchewan Veterans Civil Security
Corps in early June. The corps was to help the police by acting as a deterrent
against defeatism and subversive talk, and to bring "comfort and assurance
to our people in isolated areas, especially where Anglo Saxon settlers are in
the minority." Immigrants might well become a fifth column — or so the
attorney-general believed. Estey was not alone in the panicky summer of 1940.
His corps soon had 7,500 men mobilized to watch for troublemakers and to
check out rumours of Nazi sympathizers. In September, for example, a man
at Nipawin was reported to have served the Kaiser in the Great War and to be
an "open admirer of Nazi progress". Checking, however, demonstrated that
the suspect was "loyal to Canada and very thankful to be living in a free
country."

For many people, the sign of a serious war effort was conscription. The
Canadian Legion, the biggest veterans' organization, began deluging Ottawa
with telegrams calling for the complete mobilization of the manpower, financial, and industrial resources of the country, and the newspapers were beating the drums. Aware that many thought him completely unacceptable as
prime minister during a total war, King was sensitive to the demands. On the
other hand, as a realist, he had to consider what might happen if Britain was
knocked out of the war. Canada had to keep "our own defences strong; possible danger arising later on," he wrote in his diary. "... up to a few weeks ago,
our thoughts were all with respect to cooperation overseas. Today we would
have to turn them to possibilities of internal troubles to be dealt with in
Canada."

The answer might be conscription for home defence only. And by the middle of June, King had persuaded himself that this was the right course. On
June 18, he himself drafted a bill, subsequently known as the National
Resources Mobilization Act, and presented it to Parliament that day. The bill
conferred "upon the government special emergency powers to mobilize all
our human and material resources for the defence of Canada". To calm Quebec, still nervous about conscription, the prime minister affirmed that the
NRMA related "solely and exclusively to the defence of Canada on our own soil
and in our own territorial waters." As a first stage, a national registration was
ordered, but King stated that "no measure for the conscription of men for
overseas service will be introduced..."

In Quebec the NRMA drew worried looks. The bill seemed only the first bite
at the cherry of conscription. After all, had not registration in 1916 preceded
conscription in 1917? But the three leading Quebeckers in the Cabinet —
Ernest Lapointe, Charles G. "Chubby" Power, the Minister of National Defence (Air), and P.J.A. Cardin, the Minister of Public Works — spoke strongly

for the bill, and it passed into law on June 21. Even so, before the registration took place on August 19, 20, and 21 the populist mayor of Montreal, Camillien Houde, urged his people not to register. Ottawa moved with swiftness and Houde was interned for his foolish comments, a deliberate step to *encourager les autres*. The registration took place without further difficulty, and Houde remained behind barbed wire for four years.

The results showed that there were almost 8,000,000 men and women over the age of sixteen, and 800,000 civilian men who were single or childless widowers between the ages of twenty-one and forty-five — a number that had been reduced slightly by the race to the altar following the government's announcement that only those wed before July 15 would count as married. As of August 27, single men became liable for military service.

The first home defence conscripts called up under the NRMA reported for training at camps across the country on October 9, 1940. There were 30,000 new trainees in the group, all between the ages of twenty-one and twenty-four, and the plan was to train 240,000 men a year. But the term of service was only thirty days, which could have little military value; at most, the drill and sports might help get the conscripts into better physical shape. "Trainees reporting Friday are urged to bring along any basketball or badminton equipment they have available," one press notice in Toronto actually said. Officers commanding the camps thought the discipline of the NRMA scheme would help overcome the effects of "twenty years of pacifist debauchery." But if the government's purpose in creating the NRMA was to persuade men to go on to volunteer for active service, it got off to a slow start; the army initially forgot to create any system of enrolment.

In fact, the army was short of equipment and instructors, and had all it could do to handle the home defence soldiers. Even so, General Harry Crerar — the Chief of the General Staff and, like many senior officers, a graduate of the Royal Military College and a veteran of the trenches — soon was pressing the government to extend the training period to a more useful four months. The Cabinet eventually agreed, and announced its decision in February 1941. Now, the "R" recruits called up under the NRMA would take their basic and advanced training with the "A" recruits, who had enlisted voluntarily. Two months later, when unemployment had disappeared across the country and the pool of twenty-one–year–olds was starting to dry up, the King government moved to keep NRMA men on service for the war's duration, thus freeing volunteers serving in home defence units for overseas. For the first time in the war, manpower pressures were starting to pinch just a little. Moreover, Canada now had two armies: one of volunteers willing to serve anywhere, and one of conscripts limited to service in Canada.

To its credit, the government resisted substantial public opposition and permitted conscientious objectors to refrain from military service. Ottawa established various forms of alternative service that "conshies" could do, including working in national parks for fifty cents a day. Jehovah's Witnesses in particular refused to recognize the authority of the state and almost 200 Witnesses were prosecuted. In all 10,851 men opted for alternative service during the war.

MR. KING AND MR. ROOSEVELT

By late 1940, the threat Hitler posed to the survival of freedom was all-consuming. If Britain fell, Canada's physical security would be threatened as never before, and only the United States would be able to guarantee it. Striking an alliance with the United States was essential. President Franklin Roosevelt was as supportive as he could be, given the necessities of American election-year politics, his quest for an unprecedented third term, and the strong current of isolationism that ran through the United States. The patrician Roosevelt, a shrewd political tactician and an inspiring leader, had won sweeping election victories in 1932 and 1936, and he had given hope to a nation that had been shattered by the Depression. He and Mackenzie King, both Harvard graduates, were friendly, and their governments had co-operated in 1935 and 1938 to negotiate and sign trade agreements that lowered tariffs and greatly increased the movement of goods across the border. And Roosevelt had been helpful in persuading his officials to get aircraft to Canada in that crucial week before Canada officially joined the war.

Even so, the United States had hung back while France went through its death agonies in May and June 1940. The Americans were beginning to fear that the Western hemisphere might have to become self-sufficient in a world in which Europe was under German sway while Japan increasingly controlled the Pacific. What would Canada's place be in such a world? What would happen to the remnants of the British Empire if Britain itself was swallowed by Nazi tyranny? In particular, what would happen to the Royal Navy? With the great fleet in German hands, in addition to the smaller but powerful German navy, North America would be in grave jeopardy.

Much to his discomfort, Mackenzie King found himself having to convey Roosevelt's thinking on the world situation to the new British prime minister. Churchill was tough, combative, and aggressive, and King "felt something of a sinking feeling" when he realized what message Roosevelt wanted delivered: the fleet had to be kept in action as long as possible and then dispersed to the Empire — even if that meant the occupation of Britain and destruction comparable to that visited upon Poland or France. Otherwise Japan was sure to have a virtual free hand in the Pacific to build its captive "Greater East Asia Co-Prosperity Sphere" while Germany and Italy would swallow all of Britain's colonies. Mackenzie King blanched at the thought of delivering this message. It seemed to him, he recorded in his diary, "that the United States was seeking to save itself at the expense of Britain.... That the British themselves might have to go down. I instinctively revolted against such a thought. My reaction was that I would rather die than do aught to save ourselves or any part of this continent at the expense of Britain."

Nonetheless, King delivered the message. His reward came when Churchill told the Westminster Parliament that

> We shall never surrender, and even if...this island or a large part of it were subjugated and starving, then our Empire beyond the seas, armed and guarded by the British fleet, would carry on the struggle, until, in God's good time, the New World, with all its power and might, steps forth to the rescue and liberation of the old.

Even though some of the telegrams from London struck a less forthright note, it was one of Churchill's greatest orations in a summer of magnificent speeches. Oratory was almost the only weapon Britain had.

Meanwhile Mackenzie King was looking to Canada's own defences. The one effective RCAF squadron and the tiny resources of the RCN had been sent to England in late May 1940, and Canada's coasts were now more or less naked. There was some prospect that Roosevelt might be able to get around the confines of the Neutrality Act by swapping surplus American destroyers for British bases in Newfoundland and the West Indies; that would ease the strains on the hard-pressed Royal Navy. But it would do little to defend Canada directly. Moreover, studies by the Bank of Canada showed that the defeat of Britain would cripple the Canadian economy, creating massive unemployment as much of Canada's overseas trade disappeared at a stroke. In the face of such dangers, Canada had to look to Washington for help. It had only one card to play: the necessity for the United States to plan a continental defence of which Canada was an integral part.

Roosevelt took the initiative on August 16, 1940, inviting Mackenzie King to meet him at Ogdensburg, New York, the next day. King accepted at once and the conversations between the president and the prime minister altered Canada's history. The two leaders agreed to establish a Permanent Joint Board on Defence to study defence problems and recommend ways the two governments could resolve them.

The PJBD agreement guaranteed that Canada was safe from invasion so long as the United States remained a great power. The Ogdensburg Agreement — the first the United States had signed with a belligerent — was a major gain for the Allied cause because it tied Washington and Canada closer together and meant that Canada could continue to send men and material overseas.

Those were entries on the asset side of the ledger. On the other side, the Ogdensburg Agreement was a clear demonstration that the world had changed and that Ottawa realized it. Britain could no longer guarantee Canadian security, and Canada had been forced to turn to the south. No Canadian government could have done otherwise. Churchill, however, was unamused at what he saw as Canada's scuttling to save itself and telegraphed King that "there may be two opinions" about Ogdensburg. "Supposing Mr. Hitler cannot invade us...all these transactions will be judged in a mood different to that prevailing while the issue still hangs in the balance." Convinced that he had done his bit for the Empire, King was shattered at Churchill's carping. Not until the old British lion (prompted by his high commissioner in Ottawa) sent him a telegram congratulating him for "all you have done for the common cause and especially in promoting a harmony of sentiment throughout the New World" did King recover.

A few Canadians could not accept the new defence relationship. Arthur Meighen, the former Conservative prime minister, was furious at King and Roosevelt. "Really I lost my breakfast," he wrote a friend, "when I read the account this morning...and gazed on the disgusting picture of these potentates posing like monkeys in the middle of the very blackest crisis of this Empire." And Frank Underhill, a noted Canadian historian, was almost fired by the University of Toronto when he told a conference at Lake Couchiching that the Ogdensburg Agreement showed that "we can no longer put all our eggs in the British basket." The historian was saved, in part, by Ottawa's efforts to persuade the university that the Americans might misunderstand his firing for such statements. The new world reality took time to sink in.

Canada's physical defences were secured by the new alliance, but its economy was in danger because of its efforts to assist Britain. Every ship or truck or airplane that was made in Saint John or Windsor or Montreal and sent to Great Britain contained parts imported from the United States. There was nothing wrong with that; indeed, it had been true in peacetime. The difference was that the war had forced Britain to put controls on its currency, ending the easy convertibility of pounds into dollars. Canada's exports of war materiel built up huge reserves of pounds sterling in London which could not be converted into the American dollars needed to cover its trade deficit with the U.S. At the same time, the extra imports required to meet the demands of war production had to be paid for in full. Canada was caught in a double bind: every effort to help Britain forced the nation deeper into a hole with the United States.

This problem was minor compared to Britain's. As early as December 1940, the British ambassador to Washington had told the press, "Boys, Britain's broke. It's your money we want." And it was true. The costs of fighting a second world war in a single generation had quickly swallowed up Britain's currency reserves. The necessity of paying for purchases in the United States forced London to sell off most of Britain's remaining American holdings. But while Roosevelt was a tough bargainer with an eye on post-war commercial advantage, he was also committed heart and soul to the Allied cause, and he came up with the brilliant idea of lending or leasing munitions and supplies to the Allies; "repayment" could be "in kind or property, and any other direct or indirect benefit which the President deems satisfactory." At a stroke, Britain's financial crisis disappeared.

But at the same time, lend-lease increased Canada's financial problems. While it had extended generous assistance to Britain, Ottawa had not been handing over supplies without charge. Instead, British-held Canadian stocks and bonds had been taken in payment for the wheat, flour, bacon, cheese, and munitions shipped overseas. If Britain could now get everything it needed on lend-lease from the U.S., why should it pay for goods from Canada? Then what would happen to the Canadian economy and to the full employment the war had brought? The answers were all too clear.

Canada could have sought lend-lease aid itself from the Americans as a way out of its difficulties. Led by James Ilsley, whose transparent integrity made him one of the few popular ministers of finance in Canadian history, the finance department wisely decided not to do so — especially after it learned that one American demand was for Canada to sell its holdings in the U.S. It was one thing for Britain, separated from the Americans by an ocean, to take lend-lease, whatever the conditions. It was another for Canada, with its common border and with the already large American stake in the Canadian economy. Who knew what concessions the Americans might demand after the war in return for their largesse?

Even with lend-lease ruled out, Mackenzie King and his officials were equal to the challenge. In mid-April 1941, the prime minister travelled to Hyde Park, New York, Roosevelt's family home, to talk about Canada's financial problems with his friend. Meeting on what Roosevelt called a "grand Sunday", the two struck a deal that resolved Canada's difficulties.

The president agreed that the components Canada had to import for munitions intended for Britain could be charged to the British lend-lease account.

In addition, Roosevelt undertook that the United States would purchase more raw materials and supplies from Canada to offset Canada's increased wartime purchases in the U.S. The Hyde Park Declaration signed by the two men anticipated that Canada could "supply the United States with between $200 million and $300 million worth" of defence articles such as ships and aluminum. It was a triumph for King, one that ended his country's financial difficulties for the duration of the war. And once freed of the problem posed by the shortage of American dollars, Canada was able to do far more for Britain. In January 1942, the government announced a gift of a billion dollars' worth of materiel, an indication of the country's burgeoning strength — and an effort to keep employment and production up in Canada. There would be further gifts as the war wore on.

Meanwhile, King's government had launched a series of fund-raising campaigns at home. Beginning in January 1940 and running through the duration of the war, nine War Loan and Victory Loan campaigns produced an astonishing $8.8 billion for the war effort. Every device of publicity was employed, from celebrities buying bonds (the five-year–old Dionne Quints took $20,000 in January 1940) to entertainments, speeches, and magazine advertising. All the stops were pulled. One advertisement for the Second Victory Loan in 1942 showed two tiny blond tots asleep with their teddy bear. "Let's Keep Our Canada a Happy Land for Them," the headline read.

Pinky-white Dimples; a button of a nose; wee, slender fingers clutching at your coverlet — what kind of world is this to which you will awake?

Your life, we hope, will be rich in love and laughter. God forbid that your Canada should ever come under the heel of ruthless barbarism, where babies are born to be the future shock troops, or the mothers of a brutal military race.

We promise that you shall inherit a Canada blessed with the promise our fathers bequeathed to us....We will buy Victory Bonds to the very limit....

The advertisements worked.

THE WAR ECONOMY

The Victory Bond results were but one sign of Canadian war prosperity. Workers had money because every factory in the country was going full blast. C.D. Howe, the hard-charging Minister of Munitions and Supply who had made his fortune building grain elevators, co-ordinated the production effort. Soon, Canadian plants and workers were producing the goods in completely unparalleled fashion. From a standing start in 1939 (war orders to the end of December amounted to only $60 million), production accelerated year by year. In 1941 it passed the billion-dollar mark, and the next year the total reached $2.5 billion. Considering that the gross national product in 1939 had been just over $5 billion, the growth in war industry was phenomenal.

By sector the gains were equally impressive. Before the war Canadian shipbuilding had been insignificant, but between 1939 and 1945, 391 cargo vessels, 487 escorts and minesweepers, and 3,600 specialized craft came down the ways. The story was the same for military vehicles: at the peak of production in 1944, 4,000 trucks and 450 armoured vehicles a *week* were built. In the aircraft industry, production went from near zero to 4,000 military airplanes a year, including huge four-engined Lancaster bombers. The same kind of increases were visible in every area of war production, from ammunition to guns to radar sets, and much of the money to help build the new war plants — $750 million between 1939 and 1944 — was put up by the government. Howe's department itself created at least twenty-eight crown corporations to produce everything from rifles (Small Arms Limited) to synthetic rubber (Polymer Corporation) to wood for aircraft (Veneer Log Supply Limited).

To staff the factories, hundreds of thousands of new workers were needed, a serious problem when the army, navy, and air force took most fit men from the labour force. The result was jobs for everyone. Families that had had no one gainfully employed during the 1930s now had father overseas, mother working in a munitions plant, and grown children, male and female, bringing home good wage packets each week from aircraft factories or shipyards. There was all the overtime work anyone could want, and Canadians suddenly had plenty of money. In the first week of January 1942, the Unemployment Insurance Commission offices in Halifax announced that not a single claim had been filed.

Moreover, the war created new opportunities for women — even if those opportunities only lasted for the duration. Beginning in 1941 women were enlisted into the army and air force; the next year, the navy followed suit. CWACS (Canadian Women's Army Corps) and Wrens (Women's Royal Canadian Naval Service) and WDS (Women's Division, RCAF) enlisted in large numbers. Over 17,400 served in the RCAF in Canada and overseas, as parachute riggers, wireless operators, clerks, and photographers. In addition to nursing sisters, the army enlisted over 21,600 women — and grudgingly opened up mechanics' jobs, among others, to them. The RCN signed up over 7,100 Wrens. No women in any of the services performed combatant duties, though some came under enemy fire.

In an era when the double standard was very strong, rumours about loose morals among CWACS, Wrens, and WDS spread widely and wildly. There were even stories of troopships returning from England to North America full of pregnant CWACS. While there were single CWACS who became pregnant (about thirty-five per thousand per year), such exaggerated stories were lies, apparently fostered by soldiers who resented women encroaching on the traditional masculine preserve of the armed forces, or by scandalmongers at home. The whispering campaigns in no way diminished the value of the services performed by women in the military, although they likely hurt recruiting and caused pain to families in Canada.

Traditional male jobs opened up at home, as well. Women drove buses, taxis, and streetcars in the streets of Halifax, Toronto, and Vancouver for the first time (they had only been allowed to collect streetcar tickets during the Great War), and found work in factories. "Roll Up Your Sleeves for Victory!", one advertisement seeking women for war work called, and in September 1942 the government registered all women born between 1918 and 1922, a clear sign of the growing scarcity of labour. At the peak of wartime employment in 1943–44, some 439,000 women worked in the service sector and 373,000 in manufacturing. In the aircraft plants, 30 per cent of the workforce was female; in factories manufacturing artillery pieces, almost half were women. In October 1943, for example, 261,000 women — usually dubbed "Rosie the Riveter" by the press — were working in munitions industries, garbed in overalls or jumpsuits and with their heads swathed in the mandatory bandanas or turbans to keep long hair from getting caught in the machinery. There were even 4,000 women construction workers. Women's wages rose more in wartime than did men's, perhaps in an early and tentative recognition of the principle of equal pay for work of equal value.

Women without war work helped the national effort as much as they could. Many worked in servicemen's canteens, making sandwiches or pouring coffee. Others rolled bandages for the Red Cross or donated blood ("Make a Date with a Wounded Soldier...and KEEP IT!", the ads said). Still more knit socks, sweaters, and scarves for servicemen. Mothers, sisters, and wives wrote letters to loved ones overseas — sometimes putting their emotions and fears into words, more often hiding them in a forced cheerfulness. Letters from servicemen were read by military censors, and sometimes arrived with whole sections snipped out or blacked over. "Careless talk costs lives," the posters warned, and careless letters were dangerous too. Whole families tended Victory gardens to produce vegetables and fruit for canning. Women ran salvage campaigns, gathering metal scrap, tin cans, and bones and fats. They tried to cook supper with the minimum use of scarce electric power, and scrambled to produce nourishing meals in the face of shortages.

For the first time, the woman worker was important enough that the governments of Canada, Ontario, Quebec, and Alberta agreed to co-operate to set up a few day-care centres in the factories, thus freeing young mothers from the house. Social workers worried about older children "who wander about the streets" creating "a sudden upward leap in the statistics of juvenile delinquency." *Canadian Forum*, a left-wing monthly, called for action to "prevent the indiscriminate employment of young mothers where other labour is available." But where was that other labour to be found?

Some was on the farms. Farm daughters and sons, tired of milking cows at 5 A.M., were powerfully attracted to better-paying jobs in the cities. Since large numbers also enlisted, the burden of farming then fell on the farmer and his wife. But somehow they did the job and harvested bumper crops during the war. The climate co-operated. Canadian wheat, hard-hit by drought, dust storms, and grasshoppers during the Depression, now poured forth in huge quantities from prairie farms, and prices were good. Butter, eggs, cheese, bacon — everything that could be produced could be sold overseas to hungry Britons lining up for their pitifully small rations. As the U-boat gauntlet reached its peak of deadly efficiency over the winter of 1942–43, delaying and destroying precious supply ships, Britain's travails made boom times for Canadians.

Boom time or not, there was little that Canadians could do with their dollars. They could save them. They could buy Victory Bonds. But there was not much else to buy. Factories that had produced automobiles, radios, or refrigerators before the war now made army trucks, wireless sets, and field kitchens. Consumer goods dried up, and imports from Europe or Asia disappeared completely. A black market flourished in such things as tires and whisky, and Canadians were urged to report profiteers and speculators. The police used these tips to crack down on the black marketeers, sending 253 to jail, prosecuting 23,416, and collecting $1.7 million in fines. Still, everyone "knew someone who knew someone" who was getting rich illegally, and the rumours rippled through society, making the problem seem worse than it was.

The Wartime Prices and Trade Board, created at the beginning of the war to monitor prices and shortages, had played a minimal and largely advisory role until late 1941. Then inflation began spiralling as too many people with too much money chased too few goods. The government responded by slapping a freeze on prices and wages. After December 1, 1941, no one was allowed to sell "any goods or supply any services at a price or rate higher than that charged...during the four weeks from September 15 to October 11...." Donald Gordon, the hard-drinking Scottish-Canadian banker who headed the WPTB, became one of the most powerful figures in wartime Canada.

Gordon's agency also controlled wages, despite the objections of organized labour. Unions had looked to the war as a heaven-sent chance to recover ground lost in the 1930s. "No employer in Canadian industry or commerce may, without permission, increase his present basic wage rates," the WPTB decreed. To ensure that no one suffered unduly, Ottawa created a cost-of-living bonus to ensure that wages kept pace with prices. The bonus was eventually fixed at 25 cents a week for each one-point rise in the cost of living index, for those earning more than $25 a week. At the end of 1941 most workers still earned less than $25 a week, but by 1946 — the WPTB notwithstanding — the average wage for production workers had increased from $975 a year in 1939 to $1,516; for office and supervisory employees, it had gone from $1,746 to $2,305.

Labour made other major gains during the war. In June 1940, the government had recognized labour's right to organize and bargain collectively in industries subject to federal jurisdiction, though it did almost nothing to enforce those rights. Even so, union membership rose substantially, 200,000 new workers being added to the rolls in 1941 and 1942 alone. Manufacturers in established industries such as steel continued to take a tough line against union recognition, however, and the tension in these industries grew apace. There were major strikes in some critical wartime industries, most notably in the steel mills in Sydney and Sault Ste. Marie at the beginning of 1943. When politicians glumly concluded that locking up strikers would not produce steel, the government had to recognize the need for change.

By late 1943 the government had begun to consider the problems of postwar reconstruction — and King and his ministers had also started to consider their own political survival. One product of this contemplation of the future came in February 1944, when the King government passed an Order in Council, PC1003, that recognized the right of all employees to organize, bargain collectively, and strike, rights earned a decade earlier by American workers. Most of the provinces that had not already given unions their rights duly followed Ottawa's lead. Even the Steel Company of Canada, the hardest of hard-line anti-union bosses, was forced to the bargaining table once the company's steelworkers' local was certified. PC1003 was Canadian labour's Magna Carta. The wage controls took some of the gloss off the measure until after the war, but for the first time Canadian labour unions had their rights in place.

From Ottawa's point of view, if not that of every businessman or worker, the freeze on wages and prices was completely successful. The cost of living had risen by 17.8 per cent from September 1939 to October 1941, but from October 1941 to April 1945 the increase was a mere 2.8 per cent. The cost of fuel and light actually fell by about 5 per cent, while the cost of clothing and home furnishings was stable. Only food rose modestly in price.

Unquestionably, however, the quality of goods produced under the price controls for the domestic market grew shoddy. Leather shoes fell apart if they got wet. Clothing manufacturers used cheaper fabrics as a way around the price freeze. And to save cloth, the government declared the two-pant suit illegal and forbade cuffs on men's trousers. (By 1943, zoot suits — with wide lapels, overlong jackets, and draped pants — somehow began to appear on tough teenagers flaunting their defiance of wartime regulations.) No woman's dress could have more than nine buttons — and bloomers were forbidden for the duration! There was no elastic to hold them up, in any case.

Food rationing began in 1942, when the government introduced coupons for sugar, coffee, tea, butter, and gasoline, and ration books became an essential part of weekly shopping. It became illegal to trade rationed goods — housewives could not swap a pound of butter for a pound of coffee, nor could a rationed commodity, such as sugar, be given away. Even at its most draconian, rationing never pinched very tightly. Still, housewives had to learn to manage with less sugar than before the war, and some foodstuffs became very scarce on the shelf. Clark's Soups told shoppers that "When the Japs give in, we'll get more tin...supplies are low, short of tin, you know." The butter ration allowed six ounces per person per week, and housewives stretched that by mixing butter with gelatine and evaporated milk. Still, the weekly meat ration (secured from butchers by presenting small blue tokens) was never smaller than one to two and a half pounds (depending on cut) per person.

After April 1943 non-essential automobile users were entitled to 120 gallons of gasoline a year, enough for some 2,000 miles of pleasure driving. "A gallon a day keeps Hitler away," the slogan went, and drivers were urged to slow down and ease up on the brakes to conserve scarce rubber. The Garden Taxi Company in Halifax got around the shortage by putting tires made of birchwood on one of its cars. The noise "is something awful", people complained. "You can tell the car is coming by the squeaks and groans." But the truth is that, thanks to relatively good wages and full employment, almost all Canadians ate and dressed far better than during the dreadful decade of the 1930s.

Even children were pressed into the service of the state. Schoolkids brought their nickels and dimes to class to exchange for War Savings Stamps which they stuck in special booklets for post-war redemption. They collected bottles, cans, fats, and bones. They sang "God Save the King" every day and "O Canada" less frequently, watched National Film Board shorts from the *Canada Carries On* series, and studied war poetry and the events at the front.

They gathered metal scrap and picked milkweed pods for processing into oil in an abortive National Research Council project. They read "Canadian whites", comic books printed in black and white, instead of full-colour American ones, which were barred to save scarce U.S. dollars. These comics featured super-heroes like "Johnny Canuck", who was "Canada's answer to Nazi oppression", "devoting his time to the destruction of Hitler's war material factories in the Berlin area." They and their parents went to the movies to be thrilled by Jimmy Cagney in *Captains of the Clouds* because it was set in Canada and featured the RCAF, to laugh at *Abbott and Costello in the Navy*, and to weep with Irene Dunne in *The White Cliffs of Dover*. They listened to the CBC news read in the doom-laden voice of Lorne Greene. Boy Scouts, Girl Guides, Brownies, and Cubs thought of themselves as junior soldiers on the home front, memorizing airplane silhouettes or building airplane and ship models. Boys still followed the National Hockey League, though the older ones complained knowingly that the war had diluted the League's quality, so many hockey players having enlisted.

Children were also seen as a potential national resource, in part as a reaction to the relatively low state of general fitness that armed forces recruiting examinations had uncovered. Vitamins were deemed critical to health, and children began each day with a spoonful of vile-tasting cod liver oil, swallowed down with gasps of outrage and a firmly pinched nose. Dinnertime had its admonitions to "eat your carrots", supposedly to improve night vision and build better fighter pilots. High-schoolers tried to master arms drill in cadet corps commanded by teachers who had served in the 1914 war. At the universities, officer training corps prepared men for their future obligations. For the only time in Canadian history, the whole nation was organized, involved, and mobilized in a grand effort.

DISASTER IN HONG KONG

The national mobilization that marked the later years of the war was no sentimental response: the stupendous demands posed by the war required nothing less. After installing his puppet Vichy regime in France in June 1940, Hitler had turned his attention across the English Channel and unleashed the savage air war of the Battle of Britain. At the same time the Italians, who had joined the German cause in June, attacked British possessions in North Africa; control of the Mediterranean and the Suez Canal hung in the balance. By the end of 1940 Hungary, Romania, and Bulgaria had all cast their lots with the Axis. Germany seemed unstoppable.

For a time it appeared that Yugoslavia might manage to maintain neutrality. In the spring of 1941, however, the *Wehrmacht* turned to Yugoslavia and easily conquered it, although the brutality of the Nazis spurred Serb nationalists, and a guerrilla war led there by a Communist named Tito would turn into the war's most successful people's struggle. Next Hitler sent his legions into Greece to rescue his Italian allies — who had invaded the country in October 1940 — from their own military ineptitude. Churchill ordered British and ANZAC (Australian and New Zealand) troops to leave their North African bases to assist Greece, but once again the Germans' skill and daring swept them aside.

Then Hitler, his ambition unbounded, made the greatest mistake of the war: on June 22, 1941, he sent the *Wehrmacht* into the Soviet Union. The non-aggression treaty of August 1939 was just another scrap of paper now, and the Russians were instantly embraced by Great Britain as they reeled under the massive Panzer assault. By late fall, as the weather turned cold, the Nazis were at the outskirts of Moscow. There, to the surprise of almost everyone in the West except die-hard Communists, the Soviets held — greatly assisted by "General Winter", an old Russian ally.

Supplies for Marshal Stalin's Red Army went by convoy to Murmansk, or by air from Canada through Alaska to Siberia. The casualties in the Russo–German war were enormous, so much so that some Canadians actually felt guilty that Russia was suffering while Canada, thus far, had faced little fighting. Still, Canada did its bit for the Soviets. Pre-war outrage at Stalin's purges and chagrin at Russia's invasion of Finland in 1939 were forgotten as the Canadian Aid to Russia Fund mobilized business and society leaders to raise money and to collect food and clothing. Canada-Soviet Friendship Societies sprang up, with patrons including premiers and bishops. The war made strange bedfellows; as Winston Churchill said, if Hitler had invaded hell, he would at least make a favourable reference to the devil!

While all these great events occurred in North Africa, the Mediterranean, and Russia, the Canadian army was still training in England. There was a lot to learn about modern war, as one armoured regiment commander noted. Major Bill Murphy, placed in command of the British Columbia Dragoons, wrote to his parents about his regiment:

...my command consists of something like 600 all ranks.... Naturally with temperamental monsters such as tanks you must have very skilled men to run them and their equipment, and it takes lots of work to train men for these jobs. The driver must not only know how to drive, where to drive, and how to get there without being knocked out, but he must also be able to do a great deal of repair work.... In short he must be a skilled soldier and also a skilled mechanic. Then in each tank we have a driver operator. He is the man who operates the radio set in each tank, and also acts as loader of our guns.... Then you have a certain number of gunners.... Ruling the roost you have a crew commander who commands the tank. In the regiment also are experts from the signal regiment to assist with the sets and a Light Aid Detachment from Ordnance — skilled mechanics who also help to keep vehicles on the road and repair them.

Add to that the administrative side, and the trucks carrying food, gasoline, and ammunition, and the complexity of the task of readying a regiment of under 1,000 men for combat becomes apparent. A division of 20,000 involved much more, of course — and all this was to be commanded by officers who in peacetime had never even seen a full-strength battalion.

The Royal Canadian Air Force also trained in Britain, but once its pilots were deemed fit to fight, they saw action almost every day in RAF or RCAF squadrons. The fighter pilots took their toll of *Luftwaffe* raiders while bomber crews perfected the night-bombing techniques that would eventually reduce Germany to rubble. By the end of 1941, the RCAF had had 1,199 members killed; while that was a heavy loss, compared to the carnage of 1917 it seemed tolerable. At sea, the U-boats were sinking merchant ships by the score, while occasionally the RCN's corvettes and destroyers depth-charged a Nazi submarine into submission — often in co-operation with the RCAF's long-range aircraft. Again, the losses of merchantmen, escort vessels, and officers and ratings — 439 by late 1941 — were heavy but sustainable. There was no comparison with the toll after two years of fighting in the Great War; at the 1916 battle of the Somme alone, for example, Canadians had suffered over 24,000 casualties.

Soon there was action enough to satisfy all but the most bloodthirsty, as the war became truly world-wide. On December 7, 1941, Japan capped its years of aggressive expansionism in China by attacking Dutch, British, and American possessions in the Pacific. The United States Navy suffered huge losses as much of its Pacific Fleet was caught at anchor at Pearl Harbor in Hawaii. American aircraft in the Philippine Islands were destroyed on the ground, leaving that great archipelago almost defenceless. And the Japanese struck at the British possessions of Malaya and Hong Kong. The only bright spot after a day of unparalleled disaster was that the United States Congress declared war against Japan and, responding to Hitler's declaration of war on Washington, against Germany and Italy.

Among the defenders of the crown colony of Hong Kong were two battalions of Canadian infantry. The Pacific theatre was not a natural one for

Canadians, Eurocentric as they had always been. But British generals in London, convinced that the Japanese army was inefficient and weak and might be deterred by even a small show of strength, had persuaded themselves that a Canadian reinforcement for the colony's British and Indian troops would have "a very great moral effect in the whole of the Far East". No one in London believed that Hong Kong could be defended against a serious attack, but the Minister of National Defence in Ottawa did not know this, and it was difficult to turn the War Office down. The units sent to the Far East in October 1941 were the Royal Rifles of Canada, a bilingual unit originally from the Quebec City area, and the Winnipeg Grenadiers, a battalion that had served on garrison duties in Newfoundland and Jamaica. The Chief of the General Staff apparently considered that Hong Kong service would be similar. Neither battalion was among the best trained in Canada at the time.

Under the command of Brigadier J.K. Lawson, a Permanent Force officer, the Canadians arrived in Hong Kong on November 16. They had scarcely had time to acclimatize themselves when Japan's powerful 38th Division left its staging area near Canton in occupied China and fell upon them on December 8. The 14,000-man British garrison had no air cover, and insufficient artillery and motor transport, and the Canadians' vehicles had been diverted to the Philippines. Soon there were shortages of food, water, and medicine. The British planners' notion that Japanese soldiers had difficulty operating at night was overturned when the ferociously effective Japanese overran the mainland defences called the Gin Drinkers' Line. The morale of the population and the military never recovered.

On December 18, the Japanese launched an amphibious assault on Hong Kong island, rapidly establishing themselves ashore in force with the aid of fifth columnists who cut the barbed-wire entanglements on the beaches. The Canadian troops, split up among their own commanders and British officers, found themselves engaged in hand-to-hand combat against heavy odds. For a dreadful week, they shared in a succession of hopeless counter-attacks against superior forces and grim defensive actions in the face of well equipped and heavily supported enemy units.

One of the many casualties was Company Sergeant-Major John Osborne of the Grenadiers, who led the survivors of his company in an attempt to retake Mount Butler. Osborne directed the attack, picking up and throwing back enemy grenades. There were only a handful of his men left when a grenade landed just out of his reach. Osborne shouted a warning and threw himself on top of the explosion. He was posthumously awarded the first Victoria Cross won by a Canadian in the Second World War. Another of the dead was Brigadier Lawson, whose headquarters were overrun at 10:00 A.M. on December

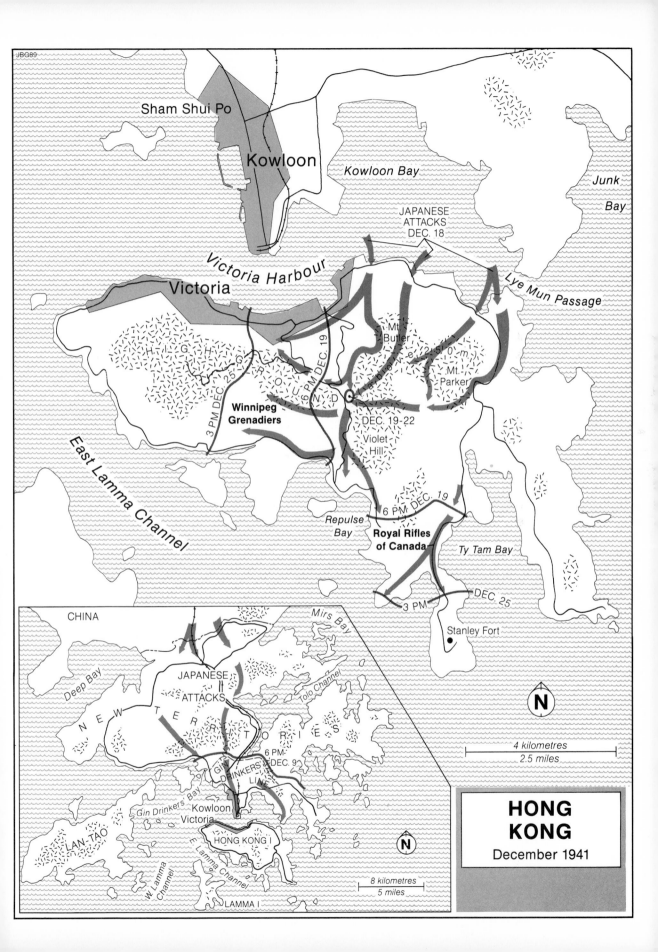

Sham Shui Po

Kowloon

Kowloon Bay

Junk Bay

Victoria Harbour

JAPANESE
ATTACKS
DEC. 18

Lye Mun Passage

Victoria

Mt
Butler

East Lamma Channel

H I G H   G R O U N D

3 PM DEC. 25

6 PM DEC. 19

Mt.
Parker

**Winnipeg
Grenadiers**

DEC. 19-22
Violet
Hill

Repulse Bay

6 PM DEC. 19

**Royal Rifles
of Canada**

Ty Tam Bay

3 PM

DEC. 25

Stanley Fort

JBG89

CHINA

Mirs Bay

Deep Bay

JAPANESE

ATTACKS

Tolo Channel

N E W   T E R R I T O R I E S

6 PM
DEC. 9

GIN   DRINKERS   LINE

Gin Drinkers Bay

Kowloon

Victoria

LAN-TAO

HONG KONG I

N

4 kilometres
2.5 miles

W Lamma Channel

E. Lamma Channel

N

8 kilometres
5 miles

LAMMA I

**HONG
KONG**

December 1941

19. Lawson told General Maltby, the Hong Kong commander, by telephone that he was "going outside to fight it out" with a pistol in each hand. A Japanese colonel later said, "We wrapped up the body in the blanket of Lieutenant Okada, o.c. No. 9 Company, which had captured the position. I ordered the temporary burial of the officer on the battleground on which he had died so heroically."

That was almost the only chivalry shown by the Japanese. When the defenders, their position completely hopeless, finally surrendered on Christmas Day, the victors engaged in an orgy of brutality. The wounded in hospital were murdered, nurses were raped and slaughtered, and soldiers attempting to surrender were maltreated and sometimes butchered. "They took us," one private later wrote, "ripped off our insignia, took our shoes, belts, pictures, and wristwatches. We walked with our hands up and they nicked us in the back with bayonets. They took out DeLaurier and two or three others and used them for bayonet practice all night long. We could hear them."

The last message to reach Canada from Hong Kong arrived after the surrender: "Situation critical. Canadian troops part prisoners residue engaged casualties heavy.... Troops have done magnificent work spirit excellent." It was all true. The Canadians had suffered terrible losses in the fighting — 23 officers and 267 other ranks killed and 28 officers and 465 other ranks wounded, or 40 per cent of the 1,975 Canadians on the island. Survivors faced harrowing experiences in the brutal North Point and Sham Shui Po prisoner of war camps (where Canadian POWs suffered the special attentions of Kanao Inouye, a Canadian-born Japanese known as "The Kamloops Kid"). Later, many were moved to Japan to work twelve-hour days in the mines and on the docks at Niigata, on a ration of 800 calories a day. Many of the soldiers who returned to Canada after the Japanese surrender in August 1945 were so broken physically that they never recovered. The government's policies, otherwise generous in monetary and rehabilitation terms, failed to meet the special needs of the Hong Kong veterans.

The events in the Pacific had major repercussions at home. About 22,000 Canadians of Japanese origin lived in Canada, most in British Columbia, where they were largely fishermen, loggers, and market gardeners, with a smattering of young professionals. Racism against Orientals had been endemic in British Columbia for decades. Japanese-Canadian support for Japan's war with China, the coming of war in the Pacific, and reports (sometimes very exaggerated) of Japanese espionage and fifth-column activities in Pearl Harbor, Malaya, and elsewhere all combined to bring panic to the surface.

Egged on by municipal and provincial politicians, the public and press demanded action, and the federal government acquiesced. Male Japanese citizens were ordered off the B.C. coast on January 14, 1942. On February 26, days after the Japanese army had captured the supposedly impregnable British fortress of Singapore, the order was extended to cover everyone of Japanese origin — male or female, Canadian citizen or not — living in designated "security areas" along the coast. "It is the government's plan," Ian Mackenzie, the Minister of Pensions and National Health and B.C.'s representative in the Cabinet, assured his province,

> to get these people out of B.C. as fast as possible. Every single man, woman and child will be removed from the defence areas of this province and it is my personal intention, as long as I remain in public life, to see they never come back here.

The government moved the Japanese Canadians inland to rudimentary housing, often in former ghost towns, and put men to work on road gangs or cutting trees. Later, Ottawa confiscated the property of the evacuees and sold it at sacrifice prices. The military necessity behind the decision to move the Japanese Canadians inland was at least arguable; there could, however, be no justification for judicial theft of property. Yet almost no one protested.

The disaster of Hong Kong set off a storm of political fury in Ottawa. George Drew, the Ontario Conservative Party leader, urged Canadians to "face the shameful truth" that untrained men had been sent to Hong Kong. The disaster was all the proof necessary for Drew and others who believed Canada was short of trained men. It was also proof positive that the voluntary system of recruitment had failed and that conscription for overseas service was needed immediately. Mackenzie King soon established a royal commission under the Chief Justice of Canada, Sir Lyman Duff, to examine the Hong Kong affair. Duff's report, released in June 1942, concluded that the expedition was neither ill conceived nor mismanaged. But, he said, there had been inefficiencies that had resulted in the Hong Kong force being separated from its transport; and he conceded that some of the men had not been completely trained.

CONSCRIPTION AGAIN

What was most significant about the Drew charges was less what they said about Hong Kong than what they signified about the resurgence of conscriptionist sentiment. Complaints were heard all across the country about the NRMA soldiers sitting safely in Canada. The "R" recruits, training with their "A" comrades, bore the brunt. In his novel *Home Made Banners*, journalist and editor Ralph Allen talked about the pressure at "Camp Salute", where camp badges and arm patches differentiated conscripts and volunteers. Subtle efforts were often used to persuade "R" men to go "active", but sometimes more open means were employed. Allen has his training company commander deliver the message:

> If good old Number Nine platoon can show a one hundred percent active service roster by Wednesday morneen, the whole platoon will leave on forty-eight hour passes at noon and I'm confident. It just means all pulleen together and talkeen it over among yourselves.... I know that no man in Number Nine would want to deprive his entire platoon of the last leave they'll be getteen for a long time....

As Allen described it, the platoon verbally and physically beat up the "R" recruits until all finally agreed to volunteer. The platoon got its leave.

In truth, there was no shortage of volunteers as yet — there scarcely could be, given the light casualties the Canadian army had suffered. But the government had caved in early in 1942 to demands from the generals for a "big-army" plan of five overseas divisions, organized into two corps and grouped in the First Canadian Army. To get the necessary men for that size of organization, better suited to a great power than to a nation of just eleven million, as well as the men for the RCAF and the RCN, and to sustain the vast industrial and agricultural effort at home, was bound to put severe strains on the country's human resources. But the public insisted that Canada do its bit in the war — and in early 1942 that war looked as if it was going to be lost. Japanese forces spread irresistibly across South-East Asia and the Pacific. Germans pounded at the gates of Moscow and at Britain's only major fighting front, Egypt, where the Eighth Army was being routed by General Rommel's Afrika Korps.

The critics of government policy, however, scarcely thought of the strain on Canada's human resources. To them, the fact that Canadian soldiers had not yet gone into action against Germany was just further evidence that men were lacking. To them, the fact that recruiting in Quebec lagged behind that in English Canada (although much less so than in the Great War) was proof that only conscription could make French Canada fight.

The leader of the campaign for conscription — or total war, as it was now called — was Arthur Meighen. The architect of the Military Service Act of 1917, Meighen had been brought back to lead the Conservative Party in November 1941. Bolstered by an extensive press campaign organized in Toronto, Meighen and his supporters bombarded the country with arguments for conscription. And with some in his Cabinet, most notably defence minister Colonel J. Layton Ralston, making similar arguments, the prime minister had to listen.

Yet those promises against conscription for overseas service had been made and repeated endlessly since March 1939. How could they be overridden? The answer came easily to King's fertile mind. A non-binding plebiscite would allow the government to decide to impose conscription — or not — at its discretion. The decision to ask the people to release the government from its pledges against compulsory overseas service was announced in the Speech from the Throne on January 22, 1942, and the ballot was scheduled for April 27.

In the intervening few months, Meighen's attempt to win a by-election in the Toronto constituency of York South was scuppered by the victory of a CCF schoolteacher, Joe Noseworthy. That was a body blow to the Tories and to conscriptionists, a relief for King, who now would not have to face his relentless and sharp-tongued opponent in the House, and a boost for the CCF. The defeated Meighen, still the nominal Tory leader, now could only rail at King from his Toronto home.

More important, French Canada quickly demonstrated that it did not choose to forget the promises King and Lapointe had made. Lapointe had died of cancer in November 1941, but his shade was mobilized to serve the Ligue pour la Défense du Canada, an anti-conscriptionist umbrella organization that captured the province with its campaign for a "Non" vote in the plebiscite. "Jamais, Jamais...a dit M. Lapointe," the posters said, and the result was an overwhelming vote of 72.9 per cent against conscription in Quebec. Six heavily French-speaking constituencies outside Quebec and such Ukrainian- or German-speaking constituencies as Rosthern, Saskatchewan, and Vegreville, Alberta, also voted no. But throughout the rest of the country, the vote was heavily in favour of giving the government the power it sought: in Prince Edward Island 82.4 per cent voted yes, in Ontario 82.3, in Alberta 70.4, and in partly French-speaking New Brunswick 69.1 per cent. The overall result showed 2.95 million voters in favour of conscription, 1.64 million opposed.

The strong rejection in Quebec shook Mackenzie King and confirmed him in his views against compulsion for overseas service. But what could his policy be after the plebiscite had settled matters? As King put it, his position was "Not necessarily conscription but conscription if necessary," a confusing but exact statement of his intent. If conscription became necessary to win the war, it would be imposed; but if conscription was not needed, it would not be. To the outrage of some in his Cabinet and many in the country, all King agreed to do was to delete Section 3 of the National Resources Mobilization Act, forbidding the use of conscripts overseas. P.J.A. Cardin resigned, claiming that

Quebec had been betrayed, and the defence minister, Ralston, threatened to leave the Cabinet because of the breach of faith with English Canada. He was dissuaded with difficulty, though King providently filed his letter of resignation. Quebec was angry but hoped against hope that conscription might not be necessary. English Canadians were convinced they had been gulled by the plebiscite. King was unmoved by the complaints from both sides. If he was in the middle under attack from both extremes, he must be right. In fact, for a time, the issue died.

DEBACLE AT DIEPPE

What helped weaken conscription's force as an emotional issue in the summer of 1942 was the national grief over the disaster at Dieppe. The little French resort town on the English Channel, with its stony beaches and its popular casino, had been a favourite summer vacation spot for Parisian bourgeoisie for decades. For the planners at Admiral Lord Louis Mountbatten's Combined Operations Headquarters in Britain, however, Dieppe seemed an ideal place to test out theories and equipment for amphibious warfare (the last major amphibious landing had been at Gallipoli in 1915) and to establish whether a fortified port could be captured.

At the top political levels, there were additional motives. The Americans wanted the earliest possible opening of a second front in Europe, but Churchill and his General Staff worried about the logistical difficulties and feared the horrible casualties that might result. An assault on Dieppe might demonstrate the feasibility or otherwise of a great cross-Channel invasion. Moreover, the Soviet Union needed all the support it could get; a major raid on the French coast would show Stalin that the western allies were in the war and would divert Nazi resources away from Russia. As well, people in the Allied nations were demanding help for the Russians. Finally, the Canadian generals — and some politicians — wanted action for their boys in England, who were bored and frustrated after training for almost three years.

At the end of April 1942, the British had suggested that Canadians make up the attacking force, and General McNaughton, commanding the First Canadian Army, and General Crerar, commanding I Canadian Corps, had agreed. Crerar designated the 2nd Canadian Division, under Major-General J.H. Roberts (the officer who had saved his guns in the chaos of France two years earlier), to provide the men. The assault on Dieppe was first scheduled for early July; this attempt had to be abandoned because of rough weather, and the troops returned to their bases, understandably disappointed and talking freely. That breach of secrecy should have ended the Dieppe project. But because Mountbatten's planners argued that the Germans, even if they had heard of the raid, would not now anticipate it falling on the same town, the amphibious assault was rescheduled for August 19.

The plan called for six squadrons of fighter-bombers overhead and eight destroyers and one gunboat offshore to provide covering fire while infantry from the Essex Scottish and the Royal Hamilton Light Infantry, accompanied by tanks from the Calgary Regiment, hit the beach in front of the town from landing craft. To the east, at Puys, the Royal Regiment of Canada and three platoons of the Black Watch were to land. On the western flank, the South Saskatchewan Regiment and the Queen's Own Cameron Highlanders were to go ashore at Pourville. British commando units numbering just over 1,000 men were to take out coastal batteries farther east and west of the main landings. The infantry of the Fusiliers Mont-Royal would form a floating reserve. The object of the raid was to capture and hold Dieppe just long enough to establish a perimeter so that dry docks, harbour installations, and "any other suitable objective" could be blown up. About 6,000 men, 5,000 of them Canadians, constituted the "Jubilee" force. The raid's celebratory code-name soon was to seem grotesquely inappropriate.

The complex plan went awry even before the Canadians began to go ashore. By chance, the raiders' ships encountered a German coastal convoy in the early morning, and the firing alerted coastal defences. Surprise may have been lost as a result. In any case, the German shore defences were at readiness, and almost no Canadians that August 19 found getting ashore a simple chore.

The assault at Puys saw the Royal Regiment and the Black Watch destroyed by withering fire from two platoons of Germans located in a fortified house and on a cliff to one flank of the beach. "At the instant of touchdown," about 5:10 A.M., one Canadian officer later wrote, "small arms fire was striking the [landing craft], and here there was a not unnatural split-second hesitation in the bow in leaping out onto the beach. But only a split second. The troops got out...and got across the beach to the [sea]wall; and under the cliff." There most stayed and died in "ten hours of unadulterated hell", unfortunately joined by their comrades of the second and third waves, who reinforced failure and landed despite the slaughter of the first wave. Gunner Joseph Dessureault, his fingers blown off, asked a friend to take his false teeth out of his pocket and put them in his mouth. "He said he didn't want to die without his teeth being in," the friend remembered. Though Lieutenant-Colonel Catto and a few men managed to scale the cliffs, most survivors clung to the beach. The surrender at Puys occurred before 8:30 A.M. One captured Canadian, Bob Prouse, remembered that "There wasn't one Jerry whose lips weren't trembling" when the victors rounded up the survivors. "Maybe, like us, it was their first time to meet the enemy face to face."

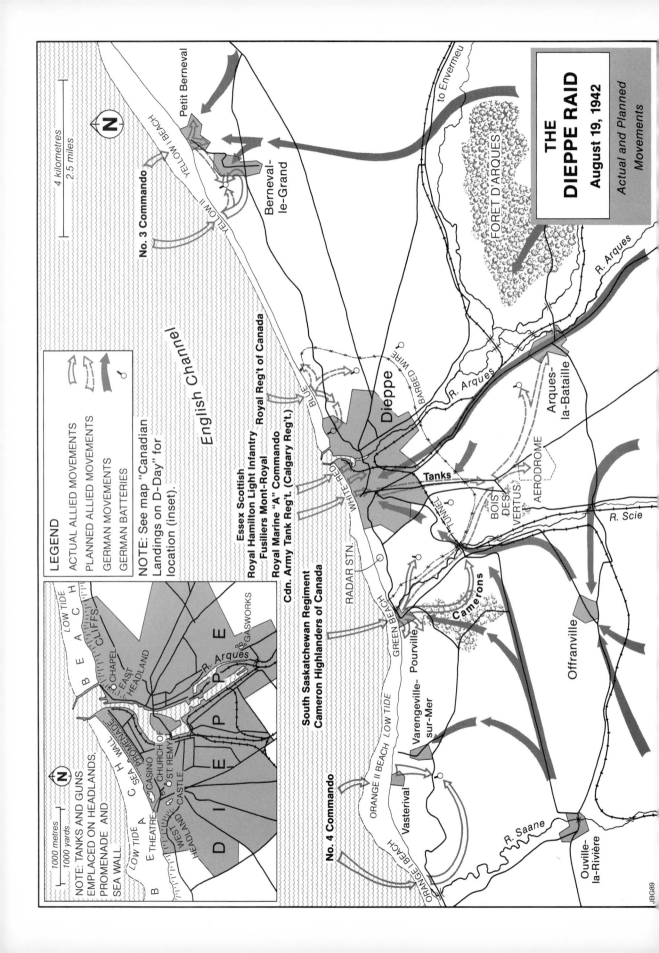

THE DIEPPE RAID
August 19, 1942

Actual and Planned Movements

LEGEND

- ACTUAL ALLIED MOVEMENTS
- PLANNED ALLIED MOVEMENTS
- GERMAN MOVEMENTS
- GERMAN BATTERIES

NOTE: See map "Canadian Landings on D-Day" for location (inset).

Essex Scottish
Royal Hamilton Light Infantry
Fusiliers Mont-Royal
Royal Marine "A" Commando
Cdn. Army Tank Reg't. (Calgary Reg't.)
Royal Reg't of Canada

South Saskatchewan Regiment
Cameron Highlanders of Canada

No. 4 Commando

No. 3 Commando

4 kilometres
2.5 miles

English Channel

YELLOW I BEACH
YELLOW II

Petit Berneval
Berneval-le-Grand

to Envermeu

FORÊT D'ARQUES

R. Arques

R. Arques

Arques-la-Bataille

BARBED WIRE

Dieppe

Tanks

AERODROME

BOIS DES VERTUS

TUNNEL

R. Scie

Camerons

Offranville

BLUE

WHITE — RED

RADAR STN.

GREEN BEACH

ORANGE II BEACH
LOW TIDE

Varengeville-sur-Mer

Pourville

Vasterival

ORANGE I BEACH

R. Saane

Ouville-la-Rivière

Inset:

NOTE: TANKS AND GUNS EMPLACED ON HEADLANDS, PROMENADE AND SEA WALL

1000 metres
1000 yards

D I E P P E

BEACH
LOW TIDE
CLIFFS
CHAPEL
EAST HEADLAND
R. Arques
GASWORKS

SEA WALL
PROMENADE
CASINO
CHURCH OF ST. REMY
THEATRE
WEST HEADLAND
CASTLE

LOW TIDE

JBG89

At Pourville, Colonel Cecil Merritt's South Saskatchewan Regiment and the Cameron Highlanders got ashore against relatively light opposition, but Merritt's force ran into heavy fire at the River Scie. The colonel repeatedly led his men across a bridge swept by fire — "Come on over, there's nothing to it" — earning a Victoria Cross, but the infantry, hooking to the left in an attempt to take Dieppe from the rear, were stopped short. Merritt's bridge and Merritt's courage were glorious events on a black day. "It wasn't human, what he did," one officer said. The Camerons advanced about 2,000 yards inland before the withdrawal orders came.

On the main front, where the assaulting force touched down half an hour after the Puys and Pourville landings, the disaster began at once. The well-placed Germans dominated the beaches with fire from a sheer cliff at the left of the landing beaches, destroying landing craft loaded with men and equipment before they grounded, and slaughtering those few organized platoons that managed to make their way up the beach. Because General Roberts had only faulty information on these events, the Fusiliers Mont-Royal went ashore at 7:00 A.M., its men adding to the toll. The Calgary Regiment's brand new Churchill tanks, intended to land with the first wave, arrived late. The first tank off the ramp sank in deep water. Those that got ashore provided little help, their treads failing to find purchase on the baseball-sized pebbles that made up the beach. Any that did manage to move found their way blocked by the seawall. Bogged down, the tanks became sitting ducks, while their light guns made little impression on the defenders.

There was much heroism at the charnel-house of Dieppe. The Royal Hamilton Light Infantry's padre, Captain John Foote, repeatedly dragged wounded men to an aid post set up in the lee of a landing craft, miraculously surviving amid the hail of fire. When the evacuation order finally came, Foote deliberately stayed ashore to look after those who were captured; he was a prisoner until 1945 and was awarded the Victoria Cross. Billy Field, an RHLI dispatch rider, remembered that the Germans seemed to be able to spot assault engineers, their packs loaded with high explosives. "Each one went off like a bomb. I tried to keep my distance." A few Canadians fought their way off the beaches and into the casino, where they battled the defenders from room to room. Others got into the town, shooting up Germans heading towards the beaches. It was magnificent but entirely futile. By 9:00 A.M. the raid was seen to be a disaster, but the evacuation did not begin until 11:00 A.M. Using assault landing craft, the Royal Navy took the survivors off, a few at a time. That operation, which finally ceased about 2:00 P.M., was an extraordinary feat.

The cost of the raid was high. Of the 4,963 Canadians who had set off from England, 2,211 returned, almost half of whom had never gone ashore. Only

300 to 400 men were evacuated from the main beaches in front of the town, about 600 from Pourville, and half a dozen at best from Puys. The fate of the remainder was death, wounding, or capture. First reports on the Essex Scottish were that only 44 of 550 had made it back; all the officers were lost. The invading Canadians had 1,946 captured in the raid (more than in the whole campaign in north-west Europe from June 6, 1944 to the German surrender in May 1945). So fierce was the fighting that only the Fusiliers Mont-Royal brought their commanding officer back to England.

One German after-action appraisal noted that the "Canadians on the whole fought badly and surrendered afterwards in swarms." That was too harsh. Another observed that the Canadian soldier "fought — so far as he was able to fight at all — well and bravely." One lesson was that an amphibious assault was not the best way to give infantry or armour its first taste of battle.

Overhead, the Royal Air Force and the Royal Canadian Air Force had ensured local air superiority, and only the strong air cover had allowed the evacuation to proceed. In all, 74 squadrons of fighters, day bombers, and reconnaissance aircraft had taken part. Missing had been the heavy bombers that might have neutralized the German defences. But even in the air the Germans had won the day, destroying 106 aircraft against a loss of 48. Total *Wehrmacht* and *Luftwaffe* losses amounted to 591 killed and wounded.

The Canadians taken prisoner at Dieppe suffered a further indignity after the raid. The enemy had found orders that called for captured Germans' hands to be tied to prevent destruction of documents. In retaliation, the *Wehrmacht* ordered Canadian POWs to be shackled. Inevitably, the Allies responded by chaining German prisoners in Canadian camps. At the POW camp in Bowmanville, Ontario, Canadian troops had to be called on to enforce the order; the result was 82 casualties, almost evenly divided between Canadians and Germans. At the camp at Gravenhurst, Ontario, 86 Germans easily removed their handcuffs and hid them, greatly embarrassing their captors. Soon, face became involved for both sides, and only sustained efforts by Swiss intermediaries finally ended the whole discreditable affair.

Dieppe was a costly lesson for the Allied high command. The idea of assaulting a fortified port now seemed mad, and the necessity for massive fire support became clear. Better training, communications, equipment, planning — all were now seen to be essential. Why no one realized the necessity for these sooner remains inexplicable, just one more example of the human inability to foresee the obvious. Nor is it clear why the planners failed to realize that every Dieppe beach was commanded by almost unassailable cliffs, and that tanks could not operate effectively on pebbled beaches. It was as if Dieppe were ten thousand miles from England, not a few miles across the

Channel. Yet planners needed Dieppe to learn the necessity for painstaking preparations, and for a huge diversion of resources into landing craft, radios, and supporting weapons. Dieppe's losses were part of the price of the Normandy landings almost two years later.

The day after the débâcle, as the Canadian army's official historian, Colonel Charles Stacey, wrote in his memoirs, Admiral Mountbatten turned up at American army headquarters "with a bushel basket of decorations for the small detachment of U.S. Rangers" who had gone to Dieppe. "I, in my simplicity, asked why Lord Louis should be so interested in sucking up to the Yanks." The reply was that "He wants to be a Supreme Commander." A year later, Mountbatten was just that, in India.

In countless towns across Canada — in Windsor, where the Essex Scottish had been raised, or in Weyburn, Estevan, and Bienfait, whose men had filled the ranks of the South Saskatchewans — the casualty lists with their grim tale of suffering and death shook everyone. The Germans seemed more formidable than ever.

The beautiful Canadian military cemetery at Hautot-sur-Mer, a few miles inland from the Dieppe beaches, holds the remains of 656 victims of the abortive raid. Of them, 121 could not be identified, one testimony to the ferocity of the fighting; their headstones say only "A Soldier of the Second World War — A Canadian Regiment — 19 August 1942." For the others, cut down in their prime, the headstones — marked with crosses and the occasional Star of David — stretch on, row after row.

The fall of France made it clear that there might not "always be an England" and Canada started looking elsewhere for help. In August 1940, King met Franklin Roosevelt (left), here in the back seat with U.S. Secretary of War Henry Stimson (right), at Ogdensburg, New York. The Permanent Joint Board on Defence they created was the first military alliance between the two nations.

Clarence Decatur Howe — the American-born Minister of Munitions and Supply — bullied and cajoled Canadian industry into a massive war effort. Here, looking more manic than determined, Howe sits behind the wheel of Canada's 500,000th military vehicle.

Britain's plight during the blitz stirred individual Canadians to action. Thousands offered to open their homes to evacuated British children like these two schoolboys clutching their gas masks.

Hundreds of thousands donated money, clothing, and food for victims of the Nazi bombing. Here, Scouts in Toronto sort canned food in July 1940.

The benefits of war production were spread across the country. Above, the corvette HMCS *Edmundston* is launched in Esquimalt in 1941. *Edmundston* served off British Columbia until September 1942 and on Atlantic convoy duty for the rest of the war.

Although rationing was limited to a few foodstuffs— like butter, sugar, and meat— there was pressure to conserve everything.

One of the sacrifices Canadian children made was to give up full-colour American comic books, which were banned to save scarce exchange; in their place came Canadian "whites" featuring heroes such as Johnny Canuck. It was less of a sacrifice to join a public-school cadet corps, like this one in Toronto, to wear a scarlet tunic and march through the streets to the cheers of onlookers and the admiration of even smaller children.

The Pacific was an unnatural theatre of war for Eurocentric Canadians, but at British request two battalions of infantry were sent to strengthen the garrison of Hong Kong. They arrived in November 1941 and, three weeks later, were fighting for their lives.

The attack on Pearl Harbor and Japan's stunning military successes raised fears of invasion in British Columbia, and the Japanese — like the Nazis — were portrayed as barbarians and vermin.

As anti-Japanese feeling intensified, Ottawa succumbed to the pressure to remove Japanese Canadians from the coastal defence zone, and herded men, women, and children into camps in the interior.

As the armed forces and industry expanded, men became a scarce resource. That, as well as women's demands to have a chance to do their part, led all three services to set up uniformed women's branches to take over non-combat work and "Relieve a Man for Active Service", as the sign behind these CWAC recruiters in Winnipeg urges.

In Britain, the Canadian infantry divisions continued their training. General "Andy" McNaughton, their popular commander, was a shrewd publicist, but this 1941 photograph of him and Prime Minister Winston Churchill plotting the war's strategy together strains credulity.

The Canadian army in Britain received its baptism of fire on August 19, 1942, when the 2nd Division staged a raid on the French port of Dieppe. The result was a slaughter, with two-thirds of the attacking force being killed, wounded, or captured.

MEN of VALOR
They fight for you

"When last seen he was collecting Bren and Tommy Guns and preparing a defensive position which successfully covered the withdrawal from the beach." — *Excerpt from citation awarding Victoria Cross to Lt.-Col. Merritt, South Saskatchewan Regt., Dieppe, Aug. 19, 1942*

At home the Dieppe catastrophe was turned to propaganda purposes, as in this poster celebrating the courage of Lt.-Col. Cecil Merritt, commanding officer of the South Saskatchewan Regiment. Erect and bare-headed, his helmet swinging from his wrist, Merritt had led his men across a long and heavily defended bridge.

III
ACTION STATIONS: THE WAVY
NAVY AT WAR

She was short and stout, the corvette. Under 1,200 tons fully loaded, about 205 feet in length, the "Patrol Vessel, Whaler Type" could cover a range of 4,000 miles at twelve knots. Her maximum speed was only sixteen knots, but she was manoeuvrable. Her main armament was depth charges, dropped off the stern or fired over the side, although there was one 4-inch gun, a two-pounder "pom-pom", one or two 20mm Oerlikon guns, and a few machine guns. The standard crew for this little vessel, first proposed in 1938 by William Reed of Smith's Dock Company in England, was forty-seven officers and men, and the estimated cost of building and equipping one was £90,000. The corvettes were, in Winston Churchill's words, "cheap, but Nasties". Exactly.

The corvette was the main fighting component of the Royal Canadian Navy, the ship in which most of Canada's war at sea was to be fought. Food, munitions, aircraft, and tanks — almost all the materiel that North America produced for the European war had to cross the sea in convoys — vast arrangements of tankers, freighters, troopships, and other supply and escort vessels that could occupy as much as thirty square miles of ocean and could travel no faster than their slowest ship. The convoys were vital to the Allied cause, but they were desperately vulnerable to attack, and their defence would depend mainly on Canadian corvettes.

BUILDING A FLEET

The Royal Canadian Navy, like the army and the air force, had survived the inter-war years in penury. The RCN had in fact had to fight against being disbanded in 1933 as an unnecessary luxury. It had survived but in a strictly attenuated form.

Just thirteen ships. That was the fleet when the Second World War began. There were *Saguenay*, *Skeena*, *Fraser*, *St. Laurent*, *Restigouche*, and *Ottawa*, six destroyers, the oldest being eight years old. (Arrangements for acquisition of a seventh had been under way some months before the outbreak of war, and in October 1939 *Assiniboine* was added to the navy.) There were four modern minesweepers, all built in Canada in 1938, a training schooner and a training ship, and a trawler. Even that roster was a marked improvement over 1922, when the navy had been able to put only one destroyer and two trawlers to sea on each ocean. In January 1939, Mackenzie King's Liberal government had announced an expansion plan intended to produce eighteen destroyers, sixteen minesweepers, and eight anti-submarine vessels — enough to defend the Atlantic and Pacific coasts — but that plan was effectively scrapped in May.

Just 2,673 officers and ratings. That was the RCN's manpower after the outbreak of war, once the regulars and reserves had been called to duty. There were 1,990 officers and ratings of the regular navy, 145 of the RCN Reserve — made up of officers and men who made their living from the sea, largely as merchant sailors — and 132 officers and 406 ratings of the RCN Volunteer Reserve, the Wavy Navy, so called from the thin wavy stripes RCNVR officers sported on their sleeves. It was the RCNVR officers — lawyers, accountants, recent college graduates — who ultimately commanded most of the RCN's wartime vessels. There was no shortage of hyperbole, even if men were scarce. The *Victoria Daily Times* in November 1939 hailed Canada's "jolly, well-behaved sailor boys...splendid young blue jackets...[who] face the world and its troubles with a grin." Unfortunately, it would take more than a grin to win the Battle of the Atlantic.

The pre-war fleet was completely insufficient for the demands of wartime. Ports had to be defended, and to do this the RCN "persuaded" other government departments to turn over auxiliary vessels, sixty of which, along with most of their crews, were incorporated into the navy by the end of 1939. In late 1939 and early 1940 the government also purchased a number of rich men's yachts for conversion into escorts, and three liners from Canadian National Steamships were turned into "armed merchant cruisers". Later in 1940 the RCN received six old American four-stack destroyers. This was part of the "destroyers-for-bases" deal made between President Roosevelt and Prime Minister Churchill in the summer of 1940, in which fifty destroyers were exchanged for 99-year leases to bases in Newfoundland and the West Indies, a bad deal at any time — except in the desperate days of summer 1940. The RCN christened these new ships *Annapolis, Columbia, Niagara, St. Clair, St. Croix*, and *St. Francis*. These obsolete, spartanly equipped destroyers rolled fiercely in rough weather, especially when low on fuel, and were hated by their crews.

A major burst of wartime construction got under way in February 1940 when the government placed contracts for sixty-four corvettes with Canadian shipyards, intending to take twenty-four — and possibly an additional ten — into the RCN; the remainder were being built for the Royal Navy. Contracts were similarly let for twenty-four Bangor-class minesweepers. Further contracts followed in a flood as the war went against the Allies after June 1940.

Building ships for war was a major challenge for Canadian shipyards, which had little experience of naval construction. Most yards had never been required to supply machinery, fittings, and materials of naval standard. Now fifteen tiny shipyards on the east and west coasts and on the St. Lawrence and the Great Lakes set out to build corvettes, each of which required 700 tons of steel plate, 1,500 valves, and 39 tons of copper wiring. There was not enough yard space, too few skilled workers, and insufficient equipment. Soon there would be shortages of steel, copper, rubber, and guns to contend with. Factories somehow had to produce ship and engine parts to specification, and all the parts had to be put together in the yards. Over the course of the war naval ship-building expanded to ninety yards employing 126,000 men and women.

The first corvettes slowly took shape, and before 1940 was over, 14 of them had made their way to Halifax. They were late, not completely equipped, undermanned, and had no armaments; but they could move through the water, though they "rolled in a heavy dew". The first few set off for England in December 1940, armed with wooden dummy 4-inch guns, there being none of the real thing available in Canada. One story, probably apocryphal, has it that a Royal Navy admiral saw the drooping wooden weapons on *Windflower* and *Mayflower*, the first two corvettes to reach the British Isles, and expostulated, "My God! Since when are we clubbing the enemy to death?" But however unprepared the first corvettes may have been, they and their successors — and in all, 122 corvettes came off the ways in Canada — eventually packed a wallop.

So too did the volunteers who were slowly joining the navy. Slowly, not for lack of interest or enthusiasm, but because both the government and naval headquarters were cautious about expansion. By the end of 1939, RCN regulars had increased by only 60 since the onset of war, RCNR by 719, and RCNVR by 1,590. The rate of growth remained glacial: in January 1941, total strength was only 15,000 — most of it among those who enlisted in the RCNVR for "hostilities only", or until the defeat of Germany.

Initially, and for some time afterwards, medical qualifications were very high. Peter Dankowich, a naval recruit at the Lakehead, remembered, "I joined with three other fellows, and one had something wrong with his eye, one didn't have enough education, one passed his medical with me and joined the Air Force." Good eyesight was deemed the most important attribute for officers and ratings, and the largest number of rejections were for imperfect vision. The basic educational standard was Grade 8; after March 1942 intelligence tests were employed to screen out those with deficient capacities to learn. Later in the war, all three services would be less scrupulous in accepting volunteers.

In fact, the RCN never had much difficulty in recruitment, and it was by far the most popular of the services; it enlisted over 100,000 men and women during the war. The force was at its peak in January 1945, when 87,141 men and 5,300 women were carried on strength — a number approximately equal to Britain's Royal Navy in 1939.

One widespread myth was that the RCN drew especially heavily on prairie farmboys who had never seen the sea. It was said that many desperately wanted to join the navy — like Earle Johnson, who "had never seen sea water before" and said the war provided an opportunity. Moreover, Johnson claimed, "prairie boys made good sailors because it seemed like hardly any of them were seasick!" In fact, most naval recruits were from the twenty cities that had naval reserve divisions. HMCS *Discovery* in Vancouver, referred to as a "ship" like all RCN shore stations, drew more than three-quarters of its 7,221 recruits from that city, and *Donnacona* in Montreal found 70 per cent of its 8,125 there. The three prairie provinces produced just over 20 per cent of the recruits for the RCN, almost exactly their share of the male population from eighteen to forty-five years of age.

Early in the war, new entry training took place at the naval reserve divisions. Its object was to help a novice sailor adapt to living and working with a large group of men. Training aimed to begin the process of instilling discipline, to adapt civilians to an authoritarian military system. Training also aimed to make men fit and to teach some of the basic skills of the sailor, including seamanship, knot-tying, and the proper way to wear the arcane uniform of jumper and bell-bottom trousers. None of this was very sophisticated. Norm Lilly, who enlisted at HMCS *Griffon* at the Lakehead in 1940, remembered that the training there was "*basic...*more or less to get [recruits] so that they knew how to march, so you could march them down to the station and put them on the train" to the coast — that is, to *Stadacona* and, after 1942, to *Cornwallis* in the east or *Naden* in the west for further training.

By 1941, the training curriculum had expanded and become more relevant to the actual duties sailors had to carry out. The basic training, however, remained much as it had always been. Cliff Webber, a new naval recruit from Brantford, Ontario, wrote to his friends at home in July 1942 of his daily routine at *Cornwallis*:

Get up at six have P.T. By eight we are marching on the training field. Stay there till about half past eleven and come back for dinner. At one we start marching again until half past four and have our supper and that finishes the day.

Webber added that there was nothing to do in Nova Scotia, "only go to a show. There's nice girls down here but you don't know what you're going around with. If you get what I mean." That was unfair. Halifax was a good-sized city. The dance floor of the Silver Slipper attracted many servicemen; so did the good food at Norman's. If young sailors wanted to swap tales with old salts, they could always try the Allied Merchant Seamen's Club on Hollis Street, and after 1942 beds could be found cheaply at the Navy League's Hollis Street hostel.

In 1942, women were at last allowed to join the newly established Women's Royal Canadian Naval Service. Training of the Wrens, as they were universally known, took place at *Conestoga* in Galt, Ontario, a shore station called — like every Wren barracks — the Wrennery. Mary Kraiger, who enlisted at Port Arthur, Ontario, joined up when she was seventeen. It was an exciting time. "It made women out of us. It was fantastic, the discipline and everything that went with it. Especially in basic [training]. That's where they either made you or broke you. So I guess most of us were made." In all, over 7,000 women signed on with the RCN; they did most kinds of work at shore establishments, notably in offices and as wireless operators, and served in Canada, Britain, and the U.S.

THE WAR FOR THE CONVOYS

The RCN's operations in the first days of the war were ruled by the government's order to "cooperate to the fullest possible extent" with the Royal Navy. But that proved less than satisfactory, and early in 1940 the Cabinet War Committee approved a recommendation from Naval Service Headquarters in Ottawa to put all the RCN's destroyers under the operational control of the Admiralty. Only the British had the capacity to see the global naval situation and to ensure that each ship was used to best advantage. Thus in late May 1940, as the situation at the front in France turned towards disaster and as naval losses mounted rapidly, the Admiralty urgently requested that RCN destroyers be sent to help protect the British Isles against invasion.

To its credit, the King government abandoned its rigid insistence on autonomy. The Cabinet saw the situation as one of "extreme emergency", and the RCN put all its resources, except for the bare minimum needed to carry out duties on the coasts, at the disposal of the Royal Navy.

Immediately, three destroyers set out for Britain. Two more were in refit and would not be ready until mid-June; another was due for refit; and yet another was en route to Bermuda but was instead diverted to England. By June 3, four RCN destroyers were at Plymouth, and soon they were fighting E-boats (torpedo boats) and U-boats (submarines) and assisting in the evacuation of Allied soldiers from parts of France not yet under German control. HMCS *Fraser* picked up the Canadian minister to France, Lieutenant-Colonel Georges Vanier, from *Le Cygne*, a sardine boat, off Arcachon on June 21 as the French capitulated at Compiègne. (Never, said Vanier later of the tub from which he was rescued, "never have I seen a boat which looked less like a swan in line or in colour.") Four days later, *Fraser*, whose captain had had one night's sleep in the last ten, was rammed by the British cruiser HMS *Calcutta*. So crushing was the impact that the whole forepart of the Canadian destroyer was ripped off, leaving the bridge — and the *Fraser*'s captain — on the cruiser's bow. *Fraser* was lost, along with forty-seven of her crew and nineteen British sailors.

As the Germans took over French ports and airfields on the Bay of Biscay, the cruising range of the U-boats and the *Luftwaffe* increased. The convoys from Halifax, hitherto largely unmolested except in the near vicinity of the British Isles, now were exposed to attack for a much longer period of time. With France out of the war, and Britain in desperate straits and fighting with only the Commonwealth at its side, those convoys now were all the more important.

Inevitably, as the British Isles came under threat of invasion, the Royal Navy had to concentrate in home waters. Escort vessels were taken from the convoys, and the merchant ships, to a terrible extent, were left to their fate. For the U-boats, the summer of 1940 was the first "happy time", with months of fat pickings from the almost unprotected convoys. But the Royal Air Force's victory in the Battle of Britain halted Hitler's invasion plans. The RN still had to keep strong forces in British waters, but as the fear of invasion lessened, escort vessels again became available for the convoys.

In the North Atlantic, the worst was yet to come. Admiral Karl Dönitz, Commander-in-Chief U-boats, had been developing the idea of the "wolf pack" since 1935. He had tested out the concept in pre-war exercises and had even published a book about mass submarine attacks on convoys, in January 1939. The theory was simple: a line of U-boats was stationed at right angles to the usual convoy routes. The first U-boat to spot a convoy radioed its location to Dönitz's headquarters and shadowed the supply ships. Headquarters then directed all U-boats in the vicinity onto the convoy, each submarine captain attacking independently. There were potential problems in this method, not least the number of wireless transmissions required to operate the system and the potential target offered to the defenders.

But in September 1940, when the first wolf-pack attacks began, the odds were in favour of the Germans. The U-boat commanders and their crews were professionals who had absorbed the lessons of the Great War, and they were backed by a first-rate intelligence and cipher system that could read many British naval codes. Their boats were equipped to remain at sea for an amazing three months or more, and they carried up to twenty-one torpedoes, which could be fired on or below the surface at ranges up to nine miles. Their one vulnerable point was the necessity to surface to recharge batteries or to send signals. Even so, under air or naval attack the German submarines could "crash dive" in thirty seconds, and within a minute the U-boat could be as much as 700 feet from where it had dived.

The RN and RCN were operating at a severe disadvantage. Both were desperately short of convoy escorts, air cover was strictly limited — and impossible over much of the North Atlantic, thanks to inadequate aircraft range — and anti-submarine expertise had yet to be gained. Moreover, the asdic used to locate U-boats under water was still primitive and subject to a variety of confusions that could result from water temperature, shipwrecks, and schools of fish; radar to find U-boats on the surface was in its infancy; and anti-submarine weaponry to sink them was primitive. (Asdic was named for the Allied Submarine Detection Investigation Committee that had been formed in 1918 to devise sound-locating devices; the American term, "sonar", has since become the NATO standard.) The Royal Navy's intelligence resources also were limited. Ultra, the great secret operation by which codebreakers operating from Bletchley Park in England worked to decipher German Enigma-coded messages, could not be used unless the encoding machine's key was known. Not until a U-boat's Enigma machine was captured intact along with the papers detailing its settings — on May 8, 1941, by a boarding party from the Royal Navy destroyer *Bulldog* — could the British predict German submarine deployment. In the terrible winter of 1942–43 that advantage was lost for a time when the key was changed. The German navy, on the other hand, had cracked the British convoy code and used this knowledge with success until the ciphers were changed in June 1943.

Fortunately, the Germans had relatively few U-boats in the beginning — their construction program only began to produce them in quantity in 1942. Even so, in March 1941 alone the Nazis sent more than 200,000 tons of shipping to the bottom.

The defenders tried desperately to redress matters. British and Canadian troops occupied Iceland in May and June 1940; at that time the North Atlantic island was still closely tied to Denmark, which the Germans had overrun in April. Air bases soon went into operation there to extend the range of air cover. Allied scientists worked feverishly to upgrade the effectiveness of asdic

Recruits Wanted, Orville N. Fisher. Military District No. 3 embraced all of Eastern Ontario. By 1941, when this was painted, the rush of recruits had ceased there; jobs in munitions factories were plentiful, and the armed forces had to scramble for volunteers. "King and country" slogans still drew them, though not nearly as successfully as in the Great War. (CWM 12584)

Corvette Entering St. John's, Newfoundland, Tom Wood. The RCN's little corvettes, just over 200 feet long, bore the brunt of the U-boat war, and St. John's, with its superb harbour, was their refuge. (CWM10554)

Convoy under Attack, Tom Wood. By 1943, Flower-class corvettes were armed with one 4-inch gun, one pom-pom, and two 20mm Oerlikon guns, along with 70 depth charges and a hedgehog mortar — better weapons to counter the deadly tactics of the U-boat wolfpacks. (CWM10553)

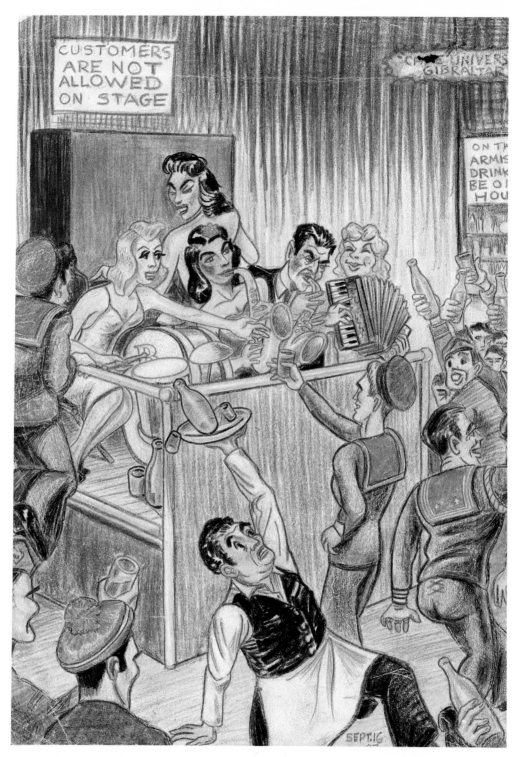

"Beat the drum, Blondie, I'll buy you a drink!" This sketch by RCNVR telegraphist Jack Muir, an *unofficial* "war artist", portrays one of Gibraltar's best-known characters, the blonde drummer at the Universal Bar. "The boys used to buy her drinks. These she would pour into a pail as soon as the donor wasn't looking, and instead drink coloured water. At the end of the evening she turned the full pail in to the barman, getting a commission." This was conservation carried to extremes. (Courtesy of Jack Muir)

STAR WEEKLY   TORONTO APRIL 3, 1943   10 CENTS

CONVOY WINS THROUGH

The Canadian public was eager for war news, and especially so for tales of Allied victories. This 1943 cover illustration from the *Star Weekly* illustrates the sinking of a Nazi raider by Allied battleships. By then, surface raiders had been driven from the sea and battleships only rarely saw a convoy. (Metropolitan Toronto Library Board)

Canadians on the home front continued to be bombarded with appeals for volunteers. This simple and effective effort makes its point bluntly. (NAC C- 19281)

The Spirit of Total War, F.B. Taylor. Pro-conscriptionists demanding "Total War" attacked the Mackenzie King government's reluctance to implement compulsory service overseas. But the phrase also suggests the complete mobilization of the civilian population, as evoked in Taylor's painting unabashedly glorifying the workers. E.P. Taylor, the artist's better-known brother, also served the war effort, as one of C.D. Howe's "dollar a year" industrial advisers. (CWM72073)

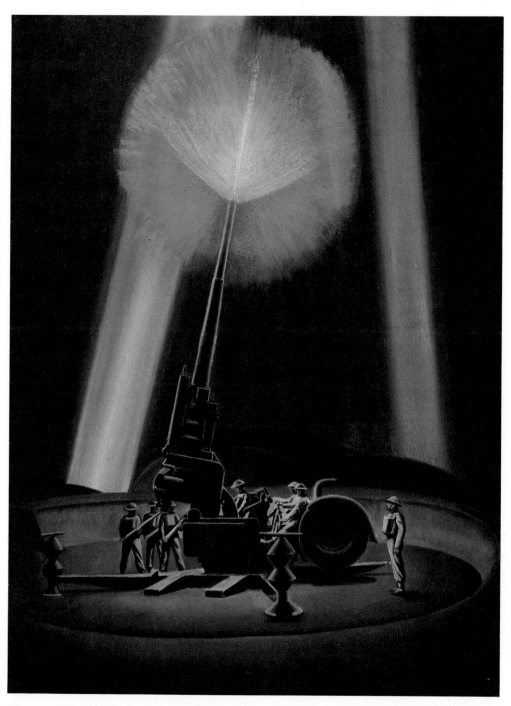

Heavy "Ack-Ack" in Action, Orville N. Fisher. The threat of a Japanese attack on the British Columbia coast kept thousands of servicemen in Canada, including these men manning a 3.7-inch anti-aircraft gun. The gun could fire to a maximum height of 39,600 feet; happily, it never had to prove itself on Canadian soil. (CWM12525)

and radar. And the captains and crews of escort vessels slowly learned how to defend their charges more effectively.

The Canadians were learning too. In May 1941, the RCN accepted an Admiralty request to assume responsibility for convoy escort in the area of the British colony of Newfoundland and, as much as possible, to use its own resources for this purpose. St. John's, located well along the great circle route from North America to Britain, was the logical site for the Newfoundland Force to be located. Under Commodore L.W. Murray, RCN, seven corvettes arrived in St. John's on May 25. They were soon joined by two Royal Navy destroyers and the RCN destroyers that had been serving in British waters. Murray, a Nova Scotian who had joined up in 1911 as a fifteen-year-old and had served in the Royal Navy until he returned to the RCN in the Depression, set up headquarters on the top floor of the Newfoundland Hotel, and St. John's, or "Newfyjohn" as it was universally known, was to become a huge base and a more popular posting than Halifax. The number of RCN officers and ratings stationed in the city rose from 900 in 1941 to 5,000 three years later.

The Newfoundlanders, Signaller Don McEwen remembered, were "great people, wonderful people", a common reaction to the way ordinary Newfoundlanders pitched in to look after the RCN, inviting sailors home for dinner and organizing dances and parties. The Caribou Club catered to the ratings while the Crowsnest, an old loft reached by a high staircase (lethal after too many drinks), looked after officers. The ties forged during the war, and wartime prosperity brought by servicemen's spending, likely helped lead to support for Confederation once peace came.

St. John's was a long way from Ottawa, however, and simple administrative messages, let alone intelligence, seemed to take a long time to arrive. Moreover, the naval stations and air bases were widely separated, hampering co-ordination, and the bad weather in the area made matters worse. From the beginning of Murray's command, communications, climate, and distance conspired against the effective achievement of his task.

Nonetheless, convoys leaving Halifax now were accompanied by escort ships based there or in Sydney to a rendezvous point where the Newfoundland Escort Force took over. Murray's ships had sole responsibility to 35° west, where ships of the Iceland Escort joined them. At 18° west, British-based ships assumed responsibility for the final leg. This system, in effect by July 1941, meant that convoys had continuous naval escort; air cover, provided by RAF Coastal Command and the RCAF, was also complete except for the "black hole", a 300-mile gap in the middle of the North Atlantic, the RCN's sector.

The RCAF's air strength on the Atlantic coast was strictly limited — five

obsolete and slow Douglas Digbys in Newfoundland; in Nova Scotia, ten Digbys, nine relatively new but completely inadequate Stranraer flying boats
with a speed of 105 mph and an effective range of only 300 miles, and fifteen
more modern two-engine Hudson bombers with a range of 350 miles. Moreover, the RCAF had almost no experience in conducting far-ranging ocean
operations and absolutely none in anti-submarine operations. Not until the
spring of 1941 were long-range Catalina flying boats devoted to patrols in the
western Atlantic, and they were so few in number that they were insufficient
to help the struggling, straggling convoys much.

In August 1941 President Roosevelt and Prime Minister Churchill held their
first wartime meeting, off Argentia, Newfoundland. The resulting Atlantic
Charter propounded a series of international aims, such as self-government
and freedom from fear. That had an impact on morale, especially in Britain.
Of more immediate import was the way the summit affected the anti-
submarine campaign. Although the United States was still neutral, and would
be so until the Japanese attack on Pearl Harbor that December, U-boats had
been attacking American cargo vessels sporadically since 1940, and the president had decided that this could no longer be tolerated. Under his direction
the U.S. Navy secretly agreed to assume responsibility for the western Atlantic in September 1941. A United States Navy officer at Argentia, one of the
leased Newfoundland bases, now took control of the northern part of the
western Atlantic. The Newfoundland Escort Force thus fell under command
of the USN. These changes, instituted by Britain and the U.S. without any con-
sultation with Canada, naturally produced some hurt feelings.

The new command structure was window dressing, however, to the real war
that was fought at sea between the lumbering merchant ships and their
escorts and the U-boats. Under command of its commodore, usually a retired
naval officer, a convoy moved in columns a thousand yards apart, each ship
some six hundred yards from the ones ahead and behind. There might be ten
or more columns, each of five or more ships. Thus a convoy filled a substantial block of ocean — a ten-column convoy would have a frontage of roughly
six miles.

In 1941 alone, over 5,000 ships were convoyed east across the Atlantic. The
ocean space covered by each convoy was enormous because the loads carried
by the freighters were huge. One convoy in July 1944 would carry a million
tons of cargo — 85,000 tons of grain, 85,000 of sugar, 38,000 of molasses,
50,000 of other food, 35,000 of lumber, 37,000 of iron and steel, 310,000 of oil,
80,000 of tanks and other military vehicles, and 250,000 of other military supplies. All Britain — and all the Allied armies training there — ran on the goods
transported by the convoys.

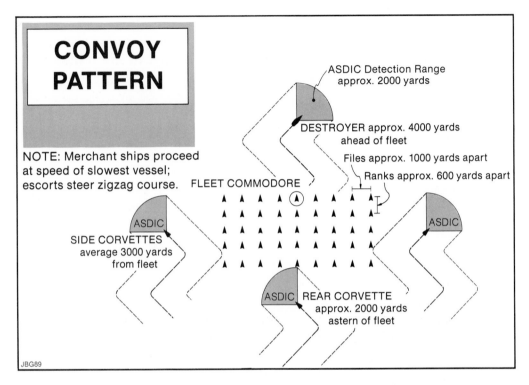

CONVOY PATTERN

NOTE: Merchant ships proceed at speed of slowest vessel; escorts steer zigzag course.

ASDIC Detection Range approx. 2000 yards

DESTROYER approx. 4000 yards ahead of fleet

Files approx. 1000 yards apart

Ranks approx. 600 yards apart

FLEET COMMODORE

SIDE CORVETTES average 3000 yards from fleet

ASDIC

ASDIC REAR CORVETTE approx. 2000 yards astern of fleet

JBG89

Around the convoy were the naval escorts, ordinarily corvettes or destroyers. While the merchantmen ploughed straight ahead, the escorts took up station on each side of the block, zigzagging back and forth to cover as much ocean as possible with their asdic sweeps, trying to pick up the tell-tale "ping" that would indicate the presence of a U-boat.

In winter the waves washed over the deck and the escorts iced up. Spud Graham of Thunder Bay, Ontario, remembered that a ⅜-inch stay could measure five inches around as it iced up. "You had to get rid of that, because there was a lot of weight up there. Lots of times, we went chop, chop, chop. If you didn't, you'd be liable to turn over."

That work was tremendously tiring. So too was the perennial seasickness, the shortage of sleep, the overwork, the pounding the body took from the constant rolling and pitching, and the lack of privacy in crowded conditions. Corvette crews had increased in number as new equipment was squeezed into the tiny hulls. From the original forty-seven, crews grew to fifty-eight, then to eighty and ninety-three. Some corvettes late in the war had more than a hundred men aboard. That crowding meant acute shortage of "slinging space", places to hang hammocks. New seamen on corvettes simply didn't get space and were obliged to wait until crew members left and they moved up in the "hammocking order". The unlucky just slept where they could, most often on the deck.

The food supply was frequently a problem; Vic Cousins remembered one crossing when Christmas was celebrated with dehydrated cabbage and potato, and the crew resorted to eating the lifeboat rations. In *A Bloody War*, Hal Lawrence remembered how awful it could be on a corvette in a gale:

> ...it is impossible to keep food on the galley stove. The bread grows green mould. The cockroaches pit-pat around the decks and bulkheads energetically. The rats grow bolder as they become hungrier. Dry clothes are forgotten. In the foetid, crowded messdecks exhausted men sleep where they can.... Wretchedly sick men...lie in their vomit until the bosun's-mate hauls them up to push them on watch again.

All that held the crews together in such circumstances was their youth. The average age of RCN sailors was around twenty-two years, and most of the corvette captains were no more than five years older. The daily rum ration also helped ward off the North Atlantic's chill, even if it had to be tossed down as soon as it was dished out. Abstainers received six cents a day in lieu of the tot of grog to keep them warm. Cigarettes were also cheap at ten cents a pack — and in England they could be picked up free. "Welcome to Canadian Overseas Forces", cards tucked into cartons said. "These cigarettes have been sent to you with the compliments of the Ontario government.... George A. Drew, Prime Minister of Ontario." Humour helped too. The ship's badges painted on the gunshields became exercises in ingenuity and word play. HMCS *Wetaskiwin's*, for example, showed a queen sitting in a puddle — a wet-assed queen.

The logistics of riding herd on a convoy were also wearing, however neat the theory. In practice, the convoy blocks were often less than symmetrical. Ships straggled. Skippers accustomed to keeping their distance from other vessels in peacetime found it hard to keep station in calm seas and almost impossible in storms. In the North Atlantic, especially in winter, it was far from uncommon for seas to be so rough that waves swept right over the deck, even on large ships. Vessels broke down and had to be abandoned to make their way when and if repairs were effected. There were language difficulties, since the merchant crews were often Norwegian, Dutch, Greek, or any of twenty other nationalities. English was the common language, but understanding varied.

The "black hole" in air cover in the mid-Atlantic also helped the Germans. Various devices to remedy this problem were tried. One was Catapult-Armed Merchant ships (CAMS), equipped with Hurricane fighters that could be hurled into the air by catapults, to fend off long-range *Luftwaffe* bombers. Flying one of those Hurricanes was like playing Russian roulette; if the bomber didn't get the pilot, chances were that a crash landing in the ice-cold ocean would. There was no way of landing the aircraft back on the ship; ditching or escape by parachute were the pilot's only options.

Another self-defence measure was the gun mounted on some merchantmen. One RCN naval gunner wrote a friend in July 1941 that he was aboard a 1,500-ton Norwegian freighter which was a DEMS — Defensively Equipped Merchant Ship — to direct the operations of its single gun. "I am the only rating aboard and have quite a lot of equipment besides the big gun. I had a really smart crew coming over," he added. "I lead a good life aboard as I am my own boss with my cabin to myself and my meals with the officers. Of course, in the danger zone I have to stand watch from 9 a.m. to 10 p.m., but I don't mind as I can't sleep much anyhow. I had less sleep in Toronto." The gunnery rating concluded by noting that the submarines were "bothersome, but we came through unscathed." He was not so lucky on his next trip. That letter was his last.

The merchant sailors on the 456 Canadian merchantmen also suffered enormously in the North Atlantic struggle. Working for $75 or so a month and a war risk bonus of $44.50, Canadian merchant seamen, some making crossing after crossing, had 68 Canadian ships sunk from underneath them; 1,148 men died, blown up by torpedoes, burned by exploding fuel, or drowned in the icy waters. It was a small fraction of the total loss of seafarers.

THE FATE OF SC-42

The fate of convoy SC-42 in September 1941 illustrated the dangers faced by merchant seaman and their naval escorts. SC-42 (the initials stood for "slow convoy") had sixty-four vessels arranged in twelve columns, and its escort consisted of the destroyer *Skeena* and the corvettes *Orillia, Alberni*, and *Kenogami*. None of the ships had radar; the *Kenogami*, commissioned in Montreal on June 29, 1941, was on its first tour of sea duty. The cargo ships, wallowing ahead at little more than five knots, were south-east of Greenland on the evening of September 9 when a wolf pack of at least eight U-boats fell upon them.

The first sign of attack was the "whump" of the explosion produced by a torpedo hitting the fourth ship in the outside port column, the SS *Muneric*, which sank immediately without survivors. The corvette on that side of the block, *Kenogami*, commanded by Lieutenant "Cowboy" Jackson, RCNVR, launched its asdic sweep without significant success, but then saw a U-boat on the surface. An attack with its 4-inch gun was unsuccessful, the U-boat getting away. *Skeena* came to assist, but was called away by word of a submarine near the front of the block. By this time, merchantmen were reporting numerous U-boat sightings, and the convoy commodore was ordering emergency course changes. Two more ships were hit by torpedoes, this time throwing survivors into the water as they went down. The last ships in the columns, although designated as rescue ships, were reluctant to linger very long to pick up survivors; the corvettes did what they could, but their task was to protect the surviving cargo ships. As a result, many survivors of the initial attacks had to wait a long time for rescue — if rescue came at all.

Two hours later the U-boats struck again, hitting two ships; one of them sank. *Kenogami* and *Skeena* moved out and searched in vain for the attacker, though a few depth charges were dropped on suspected contacts. *Orillia* now began to take a disabled tanker in tow, effectively removing it from the rest of the struggle. *Alberni* was the only corvette remaining with the convoy, and as the convoy commodore changed course, it found itself surrounded by merchantmen and unable to check out U-boat sightings. For some hours the convoy proceeded unprotected, before the escort pattern was resumed, but fortunately no attacks came in this period.

A merchant ship loaded with grain was torpedoed near dawn, the escorts again failing to find the enemy. Attacks continued during the daylight hours, another merchant being hit, and the defending destroyer and two corvettes staged an attack at a sighted periscope. "Charge after charge rained down on the U-boat, held now by asdic," Hal Lawrence wrote. "A large bubble of air rose to the surface, along with some oil. Asdic contact faded. A probable hit? A possible, anyway." *Skeena*'s captain, Lieutenant-Commander Jimmy Hibbard, RCN, declared the U-boat sunk.

That night, after two more ships had been hit by torpedoes, the convoy escort received reinforcement when the corvettes *Chambly* and *Moose Jaw* arrived. The two came in from the dark side, hoping to catch surfaced U-boats silhouetted against the southern sky. *Chambly*, under Commander J.D. Prentice, RCN, soon picked up a definite contact, closed with it, and dropped depth charges. *Moose Jaw* was close behind when the wounded U-501 surfaced. "Stand by to ram," *Moose Jaw*'s captain, Lieutenant Frederick Grubb, RCN, ordered. The corvette fired at the submarine with its guns, preventing the submariners from manning their deck gun. At this point, as the U-boat and the corvette were a few yards from each other, the German captain leapt from his bridge onto the fo'c'sle of the *Moose Jaw*. "See what he wants" Grubb said. The U-boat captain identified himself, and surrendered. The *Chambly* came alongside as the U-boat crew gathered on deck and put a boarding party aboard to search for code books. But the sub began to sink, and the boarding party withdrew — except for one Canadian, Stoker W.I. Brown, who was

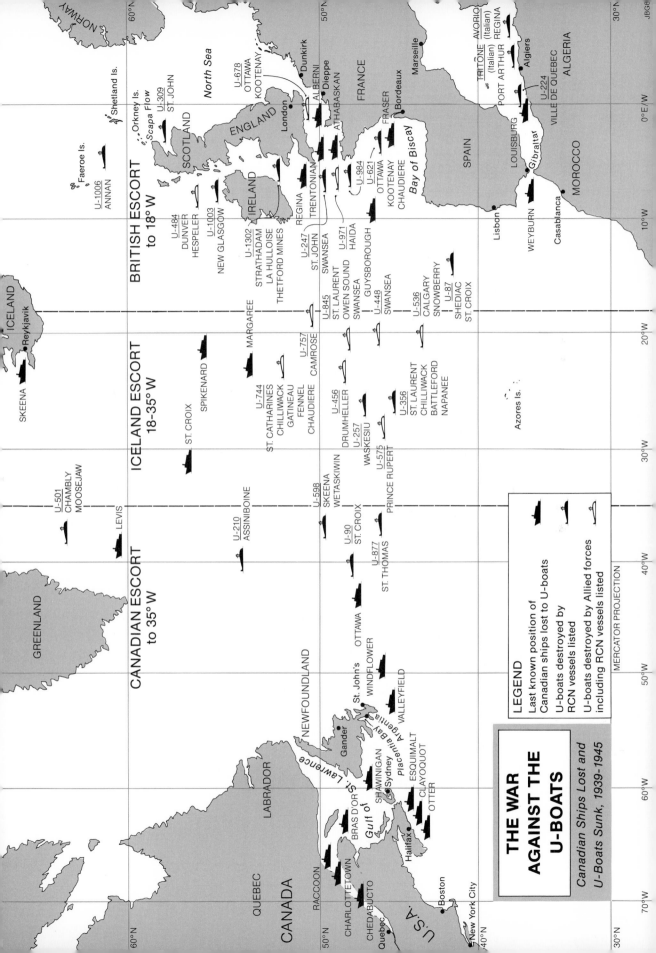

THE WAR AGAINST THE U-BOATS

*Canadian Ships Lost and
U-Boats Sunk, 1939-1945*

LEGEND

Last known position of
Canadian ships lost to U-boats

U-boats destroyed by
RCN vessels listed

U-boats destroyed by Allied forces
including RCN vessels listed

MERCATOR PROJECTION

CANADIAN ESCORT
to 35° W

ICELAND ESCORT
18-35° W

BRITISH ESCORT
to 18° W

trapped inside along with eleven Germans. U-501 was the first confirmed kill of the war for the RCN.

That was the navy's only success that night. Five more vessels of SC-42 were sunk before the convoy was reinforced by nine ships on September 11 and came under effective air cover from Iceland. All in all, SC-42 lost sixteen of its sixty-four ships to the wolf pack.

That convoy disaster was one of the war's worst. Subsequent evaluations of the battle agreed that a four-ship escort was simply inadequate to protect a large convoy from a wolf pack. Another lesson was that the escort groups had to be better trained to operate as a group, and that escorts could not be detached to shepherd crippled ships to safety or search for survivors in the midst of an action. Hard lessons, those, and paid for in lives. In November 1941, after another convoy received a thrashing from U-boats, the RCN concluded regretfully that most corvette captains knew very little of the fundamentals of anti-submarine warfare. Better training could be given, and time would give experience. Radar would also help, and it soon made its appearance on the escorts — by the end of the winter of 1941–42 every escort had some form of radar. Often those sets, produced in Canada to Canadian design, were almost useless in the rigorous conditions of the North Atlantic, but they improved as the war went on. More effective weaponry was also needed, and it became available in 1943; the forward-throwing "hedgehog" that launched an intricate circular pattern of 65-pound bombs 230 yards ahead of the corvette would be the most effective anti-submarine weapon. That helped mightily, as did HF/DF, the "Huff-Duff" High Frequency Direction Finding sets that pinpointed nearby U-boats by triangulation.

New weapons and equipment seemed to reach the RCN long after Royal Navy ships had them. There was a natural tendency for the British to fit their own ships first with the newest equipment, but sometimes the very conservative Naval Service Headquarters in Ottawa was to blame. Officers there considered some types of equipment — HF/DF and hedgehog were only two examples — "unproven" and refused to press for their installation on RCN ships. Scientists, engineers, and politicians all played their roles in a serious technological failure. Since the main victims, as in SC-42, were foreign merchant seamen, Canadians have been blessedly indifferent to their naval failure.

WAR IN HOME WATERS

Although the attack on Pearl Harbor on December 7, 1941, brought the U.S. into the war, that did not relieve the pressure in the North Atlantic. The USN had to move much of its strength to the Pacific to make up for the losses caused by the surprise Japanese attack and the disasters that followed. That left the Atlantic defences much under strength, and the u-boats extended their operations westward. Also, the United States Navy unaccountably failed to impose a convoy system along the Eastern seaboard; with the great cities along the coast still lit up at night and silhouetting passing ships, American waters provided a perfect hunting ground for the u-boats. Heavily laden oil tankers, travelling alone up the coast, were slaughtered wholesale. In the first six months of the year, 3 million tons of Allied shipping were lost. Eventually, the Americans put a convoy system into effect and the losses eased.

That changed the anti-submarine role of many RCN ships. Now they went on "the triangle run", sailing eastward from Halifax and Sydney until they handed over the convoys in mid-ocean. They refueled at St. John's before picking up a westbound convoy for Boston or New York; then it was another convoy to escort to Halifax. The triangle run — with its pleasant spells of leave on Broadway and in the fleshpots of Manhattan, mixed in with too frequent spells of horror at sea — became the war for a large part of the RCN.

The u-boat war had also come to Canada in the spring of 1942. The Gulf of St. Lawrence, hitherto an area of safety where convoys were thought unnecessary, suddenly became a theatre of war. The first sinkings in the gulf occurred on the night of May 11, when two cargo ships were destroyed by torpedoes. The RCN quickly put convoys into operation and formed a scratch St. Lawrence Escort Force from minesweepers, armed yachts, and motor launches. This undermanned anti-submarine navy had special difficulties as the peculiar qualities of the gulf and river distorted asdic signals, something the u-boat skippers quickly realized. The submariners found air attack more frightening and deadly; the RCAF mounted bomber patrols that repeatedly forced u-boats to submerge in unnerving crash dives that often made it difficult to recharge batteries. Nonetheless, by the end of 1942 two escorts and fourteen merchant ships had been lost in the St. Lawrence. More were to follow, and there was such panic among the politicians in Ottawa that the government closed the St. Lawrence to merchant vessels for much of the remainder of the war and moved substantial numbers of troops into the area. The experience that many Gaspé communities had of helping oil-soaked survivors ashore brought the war home to Quebec — in a spring when Bill 80, to authorize the use of conscripts overseas if necessary, was being debated.

Another disaster occurred farther afield when u-69 sank the ss *Caribou*, the passenger ferry plying its regular way from Sydney, Nova Scotia, to Port-aux-Basques, Newfoundland, on October 13, 1942. The submarine fired one torpedo, scored a direct hit, and dived to evade the attack of the minesweeper

Grandmère. On the *Caribou*, there was chaos as mothers scrambled to find their children. One woman, witnesses said, was so frenzied that she threw her baby over the side and jumped after it; both died. Another baby, fifteen-month–old Leonard Shiers of Halifax, was lost in the sea three times that night but was saved each time by a different rescuer. An RCN Nursing Sister, Margaret Brooke of Ardath, Saskatchewan, struggled all night to keep Nursing Sister Agnes Wilkie on the overturned lifeboat to which they clung; Wilkie was washed away just after daybreak. In all, 137 died in that disaster, many of them women and children. Angus L. Macdonald, Minister of National Defence (Naval Services), said that if "there were any Canadians who did not realize that we were up against a ruthless and remorseless enemy, there can be no such Canadians now." It seemed small compensation that between July and November 1942 the RCAF had sunk three U-boats and the RCN four.

The Battle of the Atlantic, of which the St. Lawrence war was only a small subsidiary, was now intensifying. In the fall of 1942, New York City outstripped Halifax as the main convoy port, and the U-boats concentrated in the Greenland air cover gap for a massive effort to stop the steady flow of men and supplies to Britain. The German submarine fleet had suffered considerable losses of boats and crews, but thus far their extraordinarily efficient production lines still turned out U-boats faster than the Allies could sink them. During 1942, for example, strength rose from 91 operational U-boats to 212. That led to heavy merchant losses — in November 1942 the U-boats sank 119 ships, in February 1943 they sank 63, and the next month 108. The loss of merchant ships was staggering, almost unsustainable, and Canadian ships were part of the problem. For a time RCN escorts were pulled out of the fight in the North Atlantic for retraining and re-equipping on the easier Gibraltar–United Kingdom run, after the Royal Navy observed that four-fifths of the merchantmen recently sunk had been lost while being escorted by RCN ships.

But the tide of the battle slowly began to turn. In March 1943, the RCN, RN, and USN held the Atlantic Convoy Conference in Washington to decide how best to combat the U-boats. One decision, much desired by the Canadians, was to put the RCN and RN in complete charge of convoys on the northern route. As a result of the forceful arguments of the Canadian representative, Rear-Admiral Victor Brodeur — a sturdy nationalist — Canada got its own operational sector. Admiral Murray took over as Commander-in-Chief Canadian Northwest Atlantic, responsible for the Atlantic from 47° west and south to 29° north. To be out from under the command of the Americans was enormously gratifying to RCN officers. One senior officer, the magnificently named Captain Horatio Nelson Lay, had earlier noted that the USN's "general attitude appears to be that they consider the R.C.N. as purely a small part of their own fleet...." That had rankled, as had the USN's doubts — probably justified — about Canadian efficiency and effectiveness. The new command arrangement was just one sign of the stature the RCN had begun to earn in the war. A further sign came in 1944 when the RCN assumed responsibility for *all* North Atlantic convoys. In four years, the tiny Royal Canadian Navy had somehow become the third-largest Allied fleet.

Far more important than this shuffling of command, however, were the steady modifications in equipment — corvettes were improved enormously through structural alterations, rewiring, and new weapons — and an exponential growth in the number of ships. Canada alone produced 70 frigates — twin-screw super-corvettes especially designed for anti-submarine work, with better speed and armaments — over the course of the war; the United States launched 379 destroyer escorts in 1943. This meant that convoys had more protection from the moment they set sail; it also meant that support groups, unattached to particular convoys, could be called on for assistance. The 300-mile gap in air cover was closed by the entry into service of long-range Liberator bombers, and thanks to the Convoy Conference even the RCAF managed to get its hands on some. By November 1942, the RCAF had four anti-submarine squadrons based in Newfoundland and five in the Maritime provinces, and bore the responsibility for all air cover north and east of Newfoundland.

Moreover, small escort carriers, their flight decks built on merchant ship hulls, now sailed with support groups, bringing heavy concentrations of air support to convoys under attack. And newly developed MACS — Merchant Aircraft Carriers, tankers or grain carriers equipped with a flight deck and three or four aircraft — also began to sail with the convoys.

The Germans countered these measures with the "Gnat" — a new acoustic torpedo that homed in on the noise made by ships' screws. An early victim was HMCS *St. Croix*, a destroyer. The survivors, picked up by two British ships, fell victim again to another acoustic torpedo and a sole Canadian survived. Among those lost was Mackenzie King's nephew, a naval surgeon. Acoustic torpedoes were in turn defeated — within seventeen days, so responsive were Allied scientists — by the development of "Cat gear", a simple noise-making device towed behind each vessel to deflect the torpedo harmlessly. Later the Germans developed the snorkel and equipped their bigger and faster new submarines with it. This breathing device let U-boats stay submerged for as long as ten days, and charge their batteries during that time, a great advantage given the Allies' air superiority and advanced radar. Hitler's navy was also moving rapidly towards putting very effective hydrogen peroxide–fueled submarines to sea — boats that could dive deeper, stay submerged longer, and attack from a submerged position with an array of sophisticated weaponry. These would be true submarines, instead of diving boats. Happily, the war ended before significant numbers of them saw action.

The sinkings continued right up to May 1945 in this increasingly scientific war. By war's end the u-boats had sunk a total of 12 million tons of shipping. But now they paid a heavy price in return. In May 1943 alone, 41 submarines went to the bottom — and stayed there. Even so, in March 1945 the Germans had an impressive 463 u-boats in service.

The RCN's escorts played their full part in the struggle for the sea lanes. Canadian ships provided half the escorts for the North Atlantic convoys, and the RCN, often aided by the RCAF, destroyed or shared in the sinking of twenty-seven German or Italian submarines; seventeen of those sinkings took place after November 1944, a testimony to the length of time needed to make Canadian sailors into truly effective specialists. But they finally mastered the necessary anti-submarine arts and they came to excel at them. And now, when the RCAF and RCN sang the unofficial anthem of the anti-submarine war, they did so knowing that they had the upper hand. "The North Atlantic Squadron" had many verses, almost all unprintable except for the chorus:

> Away, away, with fife and drum,
> Here we come, full of rum,
> Looking for women to peddle their bum,
> In the North Atlantic Squadron.

As Admiral Murray said, "The Canadian Navy did not win the Battle of the Atlantic by itself, but without it the battle could not have been won."

THE BIG SHIP NAVY

By late 1943 the Royal Canadian Navy had turned into more than just an anti-submarine force. In the middle of that year Canada and Britain agreed that the RCN would take over a variety of ships from the Royal Navy, including escort and light fleet carriers, cruisers, frigates, landing craft, and destroyers. That greatly pleased the navy's senior officers, who, in truth, had never really considered that anti-submarine warfare was what a "real" navy did. Sometimes that attitude had had serious effects. When Naval Service Headquarters insisted on building big Tribal-class destroyers in Halifax in 1942, the impact on yard space and scarce resources of skilled manpower was such that repairs and modifications to corvettes had to be slowed. Ultimately, that probably meant that merchant ships went to the bottom for want of escorts, and men and supplies were lost.

At the end of 1943 the RCN had 306 operational warships, 71,549 officers and ratings, and 4,553 Wrens. The six destroyers with which it had begun the war had been joined by the six received from the USN in 1940 (and two received subsequently) and four new Tribal-class destroyers acquired in 1942–43, as well as eight more turned over by the Royal Navy. There were losses too, of course. The *Ottawa* and the *St. Croix* were torpedoed in the North Atlantic and the *Margaree* sank after colliding with a freighter.

Some ships, like the *Haida*, under Commander Harry DeWolf, earned a fearsome reputation; this Tribal destroyer (now moored in Toronto harbour as a memorial to the men and women of the RCN) participated in the sinking of two German destroyers, a minesweeper, a submarine, and fourteen other ships of war. The *Haida* and the *Athabaskan* were chasing three enemy destroyers off the French coast on April 28, 1944, when the *Athabaskan*, hit by a torpedo fired by one of the German ships, sank. Commander DeWolf kept his ship picking up survivors as long as he could. The *Haida*'s historian, William Sclater, described the scene as the destroyer came alongside a raft.

"Take the wounded first," said the men on the raft, and the wounded were helped out.

It was slow work for they could not help themselves. Many were burned. The last of them were just coming up when the ship started gently ahead. She went very slowly at first, and the men on the nets worked desperately to get the survivors inboard.

From somewhere at the back of the raft a voice was heard to call, "Get away, *Haida*, get clear." A sailor said it was the voice of the young Captain of the *Athabaskan*. Other survivors said he had swum to a raft and rested his arms on it, as if they were burned, and had encouraged them to sing.

Haida rescued 44 of her sister ship's crew; another 83 were captured by the Germans; 129 officers and men, including Lieutenant-Commander John Stubbs, the young captain, were lost.

The new navy operated all over the world. It ran motor torpedo boats out of England, and minesweepers that served from Canadian and British ports and helped clear the Normandy approaches for the D-Day landing. Flotillas of Canadian landing craft took part in the invasions of North Africa, Sicily, Italy, and Normandy, where they carried Canadian infantry ashore in all but the first of those landings.

But it was the big ships that most sharply differentiated the new RCN from the old. The very idea that a navy which had begun the war with a handful of men in a tiny fleet of ships would have the capacity four or five years later to man two aircraft carriers engaged in the complex task of air operations at sea was almost unbelievable. But true it was, and Canadians manned the *Nabob* and the *Puncher* (except for their air crews), though both carriers remained on the rolls of the Royal Navy. The *Nabob*, commanded by Captain Lay, RCN, was on only her second operation when she was hit by a torpedo in the Barents Sea in August 1944. The Germans had transferred most of their U-boat operations to the Norwegian fjords, and there they based their one remaining pocket battleship, the *Tirpitz*. Thanks to luck and sound seamanship, *Nabob* made her way the 1,100 miles to the Royal Navy base at Scapa Flow in northern Scotland under her own power, despite a hole in her side 50 feet by 20 feet, but the carrier was considered so badly damaged as not to be worth repair. *Puncher* saw a few months of action, sending her Barracuda and Wildcat aircraft against German shore installations in Norway, then was converted to a troop carrier to return Canadian servicemen home from Europe.

The RCN also acquired the cruisers *Uganda* and *Ontario*, in 1944 and 1945 respectively. As part of its commitment to the Pacific war, the government agreed to contribute two light fleet carriers, two cruisers, the armed merchant cruiser *Prince Robert*, rearmed as an anti-aircraft ship, ten destroyers, and fifty frigates and corvettes. As it turned out, however, only one cruiser and the *Prince Robert* reached the Asian theatre before the Pacific war's end.

On the west coast, the RCN had to protect communications off British Columbia, an important task after Japan entered the war. By January 1942, the navy had two armed merchant cruisers, three corvettes, five minesweepers, and a number of smaller ships on patrol. One freighter, SS *Fort Camosun*, was torpedoed and shelled by a Japanese submarine on July 19–20, 1942. The next night, the same submarine shelled the lighthouse at Estevan Point, B.C., helping greatly to increase the alarm and fear of invasion in that province. Fortunately no Japanese invasion attempts occurred, though the British and American Joint Chiefs of Staff and Canadian planners did not discount the threat for another year.

The growth of the Royal Canadian Navy during the war was extraordinary by any standard. It played a vital role in a critical area of the war and acquitted itself well. Its teething troubles, complicated by sometimes weak command arrangements and vicious fighting between admirals and politicians, were inevitable. There were technical problems aplenty in learning how to fight the U-boats, especially in the early years. But the RCN's record was highly creditable, all the more so for being accomplished by volunteers who learned their tasks from scratch. The "Wavy Navy" won Canada's war at sea, though the price of naval inexperience and unpreparedness was enormous.

The peaceful appearance of this convoy, formed up in Halifax's Bedford Basin, is deceptive. The thousands of cargo ships that kept Britain supplied with munitions, food, and other vital war materials had to be co-ordinated, not just with each other, but with trucks and trains for loading and unloading. Factory schedules, troop movements, and even the strategy of the war were timed around the arrival of convoys — and the intricate system was at the mercy of weather and U-boat wolf packs.

Most of the protection for convoys was provided by corvettes like HMCS *Halifax,* built in Montreal in 1941. The design was based on that of a whaling ship; whales, like U-boats, were fast and elusive under water, and whalers were seaworthy, cheap, and easy to build.

Winter weather conditions in the North Atlantic varied from dreadful to appalling. Waves washing over the deck deposited ice faster than the crew could hack it off, making vessels almost unmanageable; if the weight of ice became too great, the ship could capsize. Here, the corvette *Wetaskiwin* comes into St. John's harbour in December 1942.

Living conditions at sea could be horribly cramped. On corvettes like *Kamsack* (above), hammocks were slung everywhere, and those who could not find slinging space slept on seat cushions or on the deck. Since washwater had to be distilled from the sea, little washing was allowed. One sailor remembered trying to sleep "while below me someone put sardines on toast, and the smells from the paint-locker and the heads fought the other smells, and the motion went on, and everything creaked and groaned and rattled." Facing: on the frigate *St. Catharines* some men resorted to sleeping in the open, while the fresh air and exercise of the cruiser *Uganda*'s "physical jerks" were a welcome break.

As the most tradition-bound of the services, the RCN was the least interested in enlisting women. But under pressure from Canadian women the navy eventually opened a variety of shore-based jobs to them. This Wren arriving in England in April 1945 is one of the thousand or so who managed to get postings overseas.

The unofficial crests that appeared on ship's gunshields were usually painted by amateur artists among the crew, and enthusiasm more than made up for any lack of finesse. This ferocious emblem adorned the corvette *Moose Jaw*; the minesweeper *Minas* booted the backside of a U-boat ("Oih! Min-as!") while the corvette *Baddeck* boasted five aces.

Submarine nets were placed around the entrances to vital harbours like Halifax, hung from booms and drawn apart by gate ships to let friendly traffic through. A skilled U-boat captain could follow a warship closely and penetrate the defences, as happened to the Royal Navy at Scapa Flow.

A single torpedo could do terrible damage to a freighter, as this burning Liberty ship shows.

Even crewmen who made it to the lifeboats had no guarantee of rescue; the convoy had to keep station, and under attack the escort vessels could spare little time for rescue efforts. The survivors of the torpedoed SS *Eurymedon*, coming alongside the destroyer HMCS *Ottawa* in September 1940, were among the lucky ones. Two years later, the *Ottawa* herself was torpedoed and sunk on convoy duty in the North Atlantic.

U-boats were not the only menace; the *Luftwaffe* also posed a threat to RCN ships venturing into the English Channel or the Mediterranean. One effective means of defence, mounted on such armed merchant cruisers as HMCS *Prince Robert* and *Prince Henry*, was the 20mm "pom-pom" gun, which could throw up a stream of 2-pound shells from its eight barrels.

RCN ships took part in operations other than escorting convoys. The destroyer HMCS *Algonquin* participated in attacks on the D-Day beaches; it also escorted carriers in the operations that heavily damaged the German pocket battleship *Tirpitz* and other targets in Norwegian waters in 1944.

HMCS *Haida*, shown under way and photographed from her sister destroyer HMCS *Huron*, sank torpedo boats, a minesweeper, a destroyer, and a submarine. Her captain, Commander Harry DeWolf, became one of the RCN's best-known fighting sailors as a result.

This catapult-armed merchant ship (CAMS) carries a single Hurricane fighter which was hurled from a launch mechanism. It was literally a one-shot defence: once his task was complete the pilot could only ditch the aircraft and hope to be plucked out of the sea.

After the Nazi surrender in May 1945, the surviving U-boats made their way to the nearest Allied port. The first to arrive in North America was U-889, here docking at Shelburne, Nova Scotia. The U-boat's captain — all of 26 years old — watches proceedings from the conning tower.

IV
PER ARDUA AD ASTRA: THE RCAF AT WAR

S ir Gerald Campbell, Great Britain's high commissioner in Ottawa, was
angry. Mackenzie King, he informed London on December 19, 1939,
was the "narrowest of narrow Canadian nationalists", a man full of
"mystical and idealistic talk of a crusade or holy war against the enemies of
civilization and democracy," and at the same time interested primarily in
"what the common cause can be made to do to help Canada."

Campbell was furious at the Canadian role in the negotiation of the British
Commonwealth Air Training Plan (BCATP), concluded just two days before. In
the high commissioner's view, King's government initially had reacted positively to the proposed training scheme

> because if they played their cards right, they could employ the essential
> features of the scheme for the greater honour and glory of Canada. It would,
> incidentally, be an effective weapon against the enemy, and this fact had its
> own value, since the Canadian people were pressing for effective measures
> on the part of their Government. But first things come first, and here was a
> plan which promised a far better return in the way of political capital than
> the despatch of a mere division or two to the Western Front.

That scathing telegram demonstrated all too clearly that the BCATP, quite possibly Canada's major contribution to the war against the Axis powers, was
conceived in bitterness and anger.

CREATING THE AIR TRAINING PLAN

The Canadian people had never doubted that their country would play a
major role in the air in the Second World War. After all, pilots such as Bishop,
Barker, Collishaw, and hundreds of others had distinguished themselves in
the air combat of the Great War. But the condition of the RCAF at the begin-

ning of September 1939 was not such as to inspire much confidence. The one squadron of the Permanent Active Air Force that was equipped with modern Hurricane fighters had only two of them. The Auxiliary Active Air Force had twelve squadrons, most dependent on the Tiger Moth. The reserves, pilots and air crew with flying experience, were soon called up, and men were slowly enlisted in the Special Reserve for wartime service. Canada had a flying heritage — but few up-to-date aircraft and only a tiny number of trained personnel.

There had been pre-war schemes to train pilots for the Royal Air Force in Canada's wide-open spaces, but they had never been implemented. In the days immediately after the war against Hitler had begun, however, Vincent Massey and Stanley Bruce — the Canadian and Australian high commissioners to London — put a proposal for an empire-wide air-training plan to the British government. London was delighted to accept and, on September 26, asked Canada to participate. What London wanted was a plan to train "not less than 20,000 pilots and 30,000 personnel of air crews annually." The British estimated that at least ninety flying schools would be necessary to produce that many air crew, and they said, selling the idea as hard as possible, that the "immense influence" such a plan could have on the war "might even prove decisive".

For Prime Minister Mackenzie King, this proposal came days too late. Had the telegram from London come before the Cabinet decided to send the 1st Canadian Division overseas, he would have been much happier. But London's request was on the table, and won a favourable response from his Cabinet, and King had to let matters proceed. Proceed they did, and a British delegation headed by Lord Riverdale, a blustering industrialist, arrived in Ottawa in mid-October for discussions. London had sent no forecasts of cost with Riverdale, and when these were produced in Canada, the Cabinet was stunned. The estimate for the plan's total cost over three and a half years was $888.5 million, of which the British proposed to make a "free contribution" of $140 million and hoped that Ottawa would pay half the remainder. Other dominions were to pick up the rest of the tab. But $370 million was a staggering sum for a country that had had a pre-war gross national product of $5 billion and a 1939 federal budget of $500 million. Mackenzie King said quickly that "it was not Canada's war in the same sense it was Great Britain's", a comment that infuriated the British team, adding that "he was afraid there could be no question of taking on responsibility for the scheme in the [suggested] proportion...."

That set the tone for the rest of the negotiations, as the Canadians and British argued bitterly with each other, using every economic lever to manoeuvre for advantage. At last, on November 13, the negotiators struck a deal: Britain was to pay $218 million, Canada $313 million, Australia $97 million, and New Zealand $21 million. Later changes raised the proposed Canadian share an additional $40 million. (In fact, the plan ultimately was extended into 1945, and the costs escalated far beyond the 1939 estimates. In the end, Canada paid $1.6 billion of a total cost of $2.2 billion.) We had gone further than intended, King said, but it was right "so that the British Government might feel that we had acted generously." But because King had insisted that the BCATP be recognized as taking priority over all other Canadian contributions to the war, London was furious at Ottawa.

There was more quarrelling to come between the great partners in the training plan. The question was what was to happen to the Canadian graduates — would they be organized in RCAF squadrons or would they be merged into the RAF? Mackenzie King, naturally enough, wanted RCAF pilots, observers, bombardiers, and wireless operators to be under Canadian control, just as the army's divisions and RCN's ships were. The British were troubled by this. In the first place, Canada expected London to pay the costs of RCAF squadrons overseas in return for its share of the BCATP's costs. Also, if Canadians were "segregated", the Australians and New Zealanders might demand the same. As both sides raced to reach a final accord that Mackenzie King could announce on December 17, the solution was to fudge the issue. The unresolved issue of "Canadianization" was to cause major problems down the road.

The plan agreed to in Ottawa called for Canada to become, in President Roosevelt's later phrase, "the aerodrome of democracy". There were to be three Initial Training Schools, thirteen Elementary Flying Training Schools, sixteen Service Flying Training Schools, ten Air Observer Schools, ten Bombing and Gunnery Schools, two Air Navigation Schools, and four Wireless Schools. Other administrative and training units brought the total to seventy-four schools or depots, and each *month* the BCATP was expected to graduate 520 pilots with elementary training, 544 with service training, 340 air observers, and 580 wireless operator–air gunners. The RCAF had the administrative responsibility for the plan, estimated to require 3,540 aircraft — or more than twelve times the number of military aircraft in Canada in September 1939. To staff the plan's schools, 33,000 air force personnel and 6,000 civilians would be needed. This was a gigantic plan, all the more so when the pre-war RCAF's tiny 4,000-man strength was considered.

THE BATTLE OF BRITAIN

While the RCAF scrambled to locate, construct, and man the airfields necessary to get the British Commonwealth Air Training Plan operating by the spring of 1940, the first RCAF squadrons were already proceeding overseas. In February 1940, 110 Squadron arrived in England to train for "army co-operation" duties. Intended to accompany the 1st Canadian Division to France, the squadron was supposed to provide combat ground support for the infantry and to carry out observation duties. No. 1 Squadron (later renumbered as No. 401) arrived in June 1940.

The summer of 1940 was to be the Battle of Britain — when the German air force set out to destroy the fighters of the RAF, clearing the way so *Luftwaffe* bombers could bring Britain to its knees by wreaking havoc on the cities. Huge air armadas of bombers and their escorting fighters would leave French bases each day, and each day the outnumbered pilots of the RAF would rise from their stations to meet them, with British radar guiding the interceptors to their targets, and providing that crucial extra minute or two of warning time.

Equipped with Hurricane fighters, No. 1 Squadron became the first RCAF unit to fly in combat when its pilots sortied on August 26. Three Dornier 215 bombers were shot down, but Flying Officer R.L. Edwards died when a Dornier downed his fighter. Five days later, the still untried Canadian pilots ran into experienced Messerschmitt pilots, and three RCAF aircraft were lost. By the end of October, when 1 Squadron flew to Scotland for a rest, its pilots had claimed thirty-one "kills" and forty-three "probables". But the squadron had lost sixteen of its eighteen Hurricanes in action; three of its pilots had been killed and ten more wounded.

Another squadron of Canadians was also flying, in the RAF. So many Canadians had gone to Britain before and just after the outbreak of war to join the RAF that the Air Ministry had created 242 Squadron entirely from Canadian pilots. Soon it was under command of Squadron Leader Douglas Bader, a famous RAF officer who flew with two artificial legs after losing his own in a flying accident in 1931. Flying Hurricanes from the Biggin Hill airfield south of London, the Canadians of 242 Squadron flew air cover over the Dunkirk evacuation and then played a distinguished role in the Battle of Britain.

On August 30, for example, nine Hurricanes of 242 Squadron met head on with a huge force of the attacking *Luftwaffe*. After one flight of three fighters had tackled the covering German fighters — a dangerous task as the Hurricanes (unlike the faster, more manoeuvrable Spitfires) were markedly inferior to the Messerschmitt 109s — the remaining two flights of 242 Hurricanes claimed twelve victories without loss to themselves.

Those numbers may have been inflated by the pilots — at 400 mph it was difficult to tell if a plane had been shot down or simply damaged — and then redoubled by the Air Ministry, which was desperate to keep up British morale in that dark summer. What is certain, however, is that more German than British and Canadian aircraft were destroyed; equally certain, every *Luftwaffe* pilot shot down over Britain was taken prisoner or killed, while RAF and RCAF pilots, if they bailed out successfully, could fly again. By the end of September, as the *Luftwaffe* slowed the tempo of the daylight attacks that had cost Field Marshal Hermann Goering's air force so heavily, it was becoming clear that the Battle of Britain had been won.

TRAINING AIR CREW

None of the pilots who flew in the Battle of Britain had been trained under the British Commonwealth Air Training Plan. Before long, however, the BCATP's graduates were arriving in Britain and North Africa and the Far East in large numbers, so large that in retrospect the great training scheme seemed to have sprung up full-blown after the signing ceremony in December 1939. In fact, the birth-pangs were long, the labour enormous.

The BCATP had to begin by building the necessary bases. The Department of Transport took on the task of organizing airfield construction, first inspecting the country's 153 airports (some little more than dirt strips with a tumbledown shack or two) and deciding which could be employed for training. The DOT decided that 24 existing airfields could be used if additional buildings were provided. Dozens of other sites for airfields, gunnery ranges, and supply depots were chosen, depending on climate, ground conditions, and water supply. Political considerations occasionally entered in as well — Mackenzie King's constituency of Prince Albert, Saskatchewan, was the site of an air observer school; other politicians also tried to press their ridings' claims. Even so, every province had an array of BCATP installations. Saskatchewan, flat and open, trained a fifth of the pilots and up to a third of some categories of air crew. To have so many Canadians from all across the country in the province, as well as thousands of British, Australian, and New Zealand airmen, undoubtedly made a mark.

Air crew recruits had to be physically fit and, initially, between 18 and 28 years of age. As the war went on, standards eased and the age range became 17½ to 33 for pilots and 17½ to 39 for air gunners. Medical standards were also lowered.

Recruits joined the RCAF as "Aircraftsmen 2nd Class" (usually called Acey-Deucey after the abbreviation AC2) and withstood the lengthy rigours of the manning depot. These included parade square training, spit and polish, lessons in military courtesy, and other measures to turn civilians into "uniformed raw material suitable for further training", as one BCATP graduate,

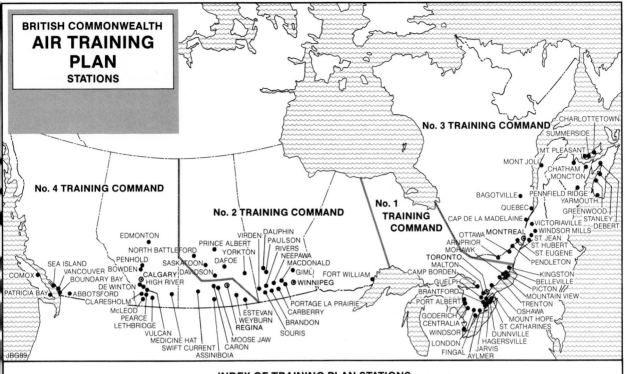

INDEX OF TRAINING PLAN STATIONS

NOTES

1) RAF Stations carry numbers over 30; those marked by an asterisk (*) were merged into the RCAF and are also listed under their later RCAF numbers (marked †) in the index.

2) Training Command number follows station location in brackets.

GENERAL FACILITIES

Training Command Headquarters
- 1 - Toronto (1)
- 2 - Winnipeg (2)
- 3 - Montreal (3)
- 4a - Regina (4), 1940-41
- 4b - Calgary (4), 1941-44

Initial Training Schools
- 1 - Toronto (1)
- 2 - Regina (4)
- 3 - Victoriaville (3)
- 4 - Edmonton (4)
- 5 - Belleville (1)
- 6 - Toronto (1)
- 7 - Saskatoon (2)

General Reconnaissance Schools
- 1 - Summerside (3)
- 31 - Charlottetown (3)

Operational Training Units
- 1 - Bagotville (3), EAC
- †3 - Patricia Bay (4), WAC
- 5 - Boundary Bay (4), WAC, Det, at Abbotsford (4) from Aug. '44
- 6 - Comox (4), WAC
- †7 - Debert (3), EAC
- †8 - Greenwood (3), EAC
- *31 - Debert (3), EAC, see #7
- *32 - Patricia Bay (4), WAC, see #3
- 34 - Pennfield Ridge (3), EAC
- *36 - Greenwood (3), EAC, see #8

PILOT TRAINING FACILITIES

Elementary Flying Training
- 1 - Malton (1)
- 2 - Fort William (2)
- 3 - London (3)
- 4 - Windsor Mills (3)
- 5 - Lethbridge (4) moved to High River (4), June '44
- 6 - Prince Albert (2)
- 7 - Windsor (1)

Elementary Flying Training, cont'd.
- 8 - Vancouver (4)
- 9 - St. Catharines (1)
- 10 - Mount Hope (1) moved to Pendleton (3), Aug. '42
- 11 - Cap de la Madeleine (3)
- 12 - Goderich (1)
- 13 - St. Eugene (3)
- 14 - Portage la Prairie (2)
- 15 - Regina (4)
- 16 - Edmonton (4)
- 17 - Stanley (3)
- 18 - Boundary Bay (4)
- 19 - Virden (2)
- 20 - Oshawa (1)
- 21 - Chatham (3)
- 22 - Quebec (3)
- 23 - Davidson (2) moved to Yorkton (2), Jan. '45
- 24 - Abbotsford (4)
- †25 - Assiniboia (4)
- †26 - Neepawa (2)
- 31 - De Winton (4)
- 32 - Bowden (4)
- 33 - Caron (4)
- *34 - Assiniboia (4), see #25
- *35 - Neepawa (2), see #26
- 36 - Pearce

Service Flying Training
- 1 - Camp Borden (1)
- 2 - Ottawa (3)
- 3 - Calgary (4)
- 4 - Saskatoon (2)
- 5 - Brantford (1)
- 6 - Dunnville (1)
- 7 - MacLeod (4)
- †8 - Moncton (3) moved to Weyburn (4), Jan. '44
- 9 - Summerside (3) moved to Centralia (1), July '42
- 10 - Dauphin (2)

Service Flying Training, cont'd.
- 11 - Yorkton (2)
- 12 - Brandon (2)
- †13 - St. Hubert (3) moved to North Battleford (2), Feb. '44
- †14 - Aylmer (1) moved to Kingston (1), Aug. '44
- 15 - Claresholm (4)
- 16 - Hagersville (1)
- 17 - Souris (2)
- 18 - Gimli (2)
- 19 - Vulcan (4)
- *31 - Kingston (1), see #14
- 32 - Moose Jaw (4)
- 33 - Carberry (2)
- 34 - Medicine Hat (4)
- *35 - North Battleford (2), see #13
- 36 - Penhold (4)
- 37 - Calgary (4)
- 38 - Estevan (4)
- 39 - Swift Current (4)
- *41 - Weyburn (4), see #8

Central Flying School
- 1 - Trenton (1)

Flying Instructor Schools
- 1 - Mohawk (1)
- 2 - Vulcan (4) moved to Pearce (4), May '43
- 3 - Arnprior (3)

Instrument Flying School
- 1 - Mohawk (1)

Operational Training Squadron
- 13 - Sea Island (4) moved to Patricia Bay (4), Nov. '40

AIRCREW TRAINING FACILITIES

Air Observers' Schools
- 1 - Malton (1)
- 2 - Edmonton (4)
- 3 - Regina (4) moved to Pearce (4), Sept. '42

Air Observers' Schools, cont'd.
- 4 - London (1)
- 5 - Winnipeg (2)
- 6 - Prince Albert (2)
- 7 - Portage la Prairie (2)
- 8 - Quebec (3)
- 9 - St. Jean (3)
- 10 - Chatham (3)

Air Navigation Schools
- 1 - Trenton (1) moved to Rivers (2), May '42
- †2 - Pennfield Ridge (3) 1941-42, Charlottetown (3) 1944-45
- 31 - Port Albert (3)
- *32 - Charlottetown (3), see #2
- 33 - Mount Hope (1)

Central Navigation School
- 1 - Rivers (2)

Wireless Schools
- 1 - Montreal (3) moved to Mount Hope (1), Sept. '44
- 2 - Calgary (4)
- 3 - Winnipeg (2)
- 4 - Guelph (1)

Bombing & Gunnery Schools
- 1 - Jarvis (1)
- 2 - Mossbank (4)
- 3 - MacDonald (2)
- 4 - Fingal (1)
- 5 - Dafoe (2)
- 6 - Mountain View (1)
- 7 - Paulson (2)
- 8 - Lethbridge (4)
- 9 - Mont Joli (3)
- 10 - Mount Pleasant (3)
- 31 - Picton (1)

Naval Air Gunners' School
- 1 - Yarmouth (3)

Flight Engineers' School
- 1 - Aylmer (1)

Murray Peden, put it. Another recruit, Syd Wise from Toronto — who was just eighteen in 1943 — remembered his surprise at "how totally your life was controlled by the junior NCOs." Hardest for some was accepting the complete lack of privacy. In his memoirs, Robert Collins wrote of his first day at the manning depot at Brandon, Manitoba:

> I am surrounded by 750 naked and half-naked men. Skinny men, plump men, Greek gods. Men in boxer shorts, dirty shorts, and no shorts. Men with body odor that would fell an ox. Men brooding silently on their bunks. Men shouting, laughing, punching biceps, breaking wind, cursing.... I know none of these people.

After basic training, air crew trainees received their white cap flashes. That mattered, said Wise: "one little distinctive symbol can make you feel first part of a group and then something special." Then they went to Initial Training School for a ground school lengthened, by 1943, to ten weeks, and so intensive that, as Peden was warned, "If you stop for a leak — you'll fall a week behind." The best and fittest ITS graduates then proceeded to an Elementary Flying Training School for an eight-week course. The less fit were routed to Observer or Wireless School.

In the first days of the BCATP, when pilot instructors were in scarce supply, elementary flying was taught by commercially organized and civilian-managed flying clubs. The RCAF watched over the instruction and provided the discipline, but civilian pilots did the teaching — under the maxim "There Are Old Pilots, and Bold Pilots; There Are No Old, Bold Pilots." Eventually, the RCAF took over the training as well. The pilot trainees, now AC1s, learned to fly on De Havilland Tiger Moth biplanes, and later on Fairchild Cornells (built by Fleet Aircraft Ltd. at Fort Erie, Ontario) which, despite their 122mph top speed, had flying characteristics closer to the military aircraft then in use. All Training Command aircraft were painted bright yellow for easy spotting. Trainees learned navigation and something about armaments; they worked on engines, airmanship, and the theory of flight.

A substantial proportion of trainees failed to qualify. One pilot recalled that nineteen out of forty-one in his class "washed out" in six weeks, including the apprentice pilot who couldn't land. "Thirty or more times he executed a beautiful approach, then climbed just before touchdown." An instructor flew up alongside to try to lead him to earth, but nothing worked. "Finally, just at dusk, the frightened boy dropped to the grass in a perfect three-point landing. Next day he was on his way to gunner's school."

The survivors — 856 trainees died in crashes during the BCATP's operation, and in 1943–44 the rate of fatalities was one for every 20,580 hours of flying time — then proceeded to Service Flying Training School, where the RCAF provided the instructors, and where students flew tricky, unforgiving Harvards or multi-engined Cessna Cranes or Anson IIs. There they began to master night flying, formation flying, and radio work, in a course that eventually was extended to twenty-one weeks. Those who passed received their wings. About a third were commissioned as pilot officers; the others became sergeant pilots. Training was not yet over, however. Pilots proceeded to Advanced Flying Units and then to Operational Training Units before being posted to squadrons, overseas or in Canada. Smart ones going overseas stocked up on the things, as Robert Collins remembered, "that wise men said would win the everlasting gratitude of British girls, all allegedly starved for North American sex and consumer goods...crimson nail polish, silk stockings, and two dozen malted milk chocolate bars."

The air crew trainees included a substantial number of Americans who crossed the border to get into the war both before and after their country did. At the time of Pearl Harbor, the RCAF had 6,129 Americans on strength. Trainees from abroad — 42,000 from the RAF, 9,600 from the Royal Australian Air Force, and 7,000 from the Royal New Zealand Air Force — lived and trained with the 72,835 Canadians. Like them, they made friends in small-town Saskatchewan, went to dances in Quebec, or sailed in the Maritimes. One air gunner training at Mont Joli, Quebec, remembered that his group of trainees included "a New Zealander, a Cockney, a Welshman, and a Yorkshireman whom no one could understand without an interpreter. A Jew from Cambridge University, two Scotchmen, a full-blooded Chippewa Indian, and an odd assortment of Canadians, including a schoolteacher and two ministers' sons, completed the list." In a curious yet heartwarming way, the war brought the Commonwealth together. Many of the friendships formed in Canada carried over to bomber crews in England.

The BCATP initially produced only pilots, air observers, and wireless operator–air gunners. But as the war went on and new and larger aircraft came into service, the training changed as well. By the wrap-up of the plan, eight air crew categories were being produced: pilot, navigator, navigator B (with bombing training), navigator W (with wireless training), air bomber, wireless operator–air gunner, air gunner, and flight engineer. In all, 131,553 graduated, more than 50,000 of whom were pilots. Canadians accounted for 55 per cent of the graduates.

There were far more Canadian air crew, in fact, than there were RCAF positions to absorb them. In January 1941, Ottawa announced that as a result of an agreement with London up to twenty-five additional RCAF squadrons overseas would be formed from BCATP graduates. Other RCAF graduates were to wear Canadian uniforms even if serving in RAF squadrons.

That 1941 agreement resolved some of the problems of Canadianization, though there were recurring difficulties between Ottawa and London. The Minister of National Defence (Air) was Charles G. Power, known as Chubby to everyone. Power was a decorated infantry officer of the Great War, a Quebec Catholic, and a professional politician — tough, hard-drinking, and very able — and he wanted his senior RCAF officers to get experience of command overseas instead of being fully engaged in running the BCATP. The British policy interfered with this. But over time Power got his way, and there was soon a Canadian bomber group, as well as fighter wings. Power also won agreement for all suitable Canadian graduates of the BCATP to get commissions, thus eliminating the arbitrary distinction between pilot officers and sergeant pilots. By the end of the war, the RCAF had forty-eight squadrons overseas, flying bombers, fighters, transports, and U-boat hunters.

Other administrative problems were harder to resolve. Power told the prime minister about a Montreal father whose son was shot down in 1941 while flying with the RAF.

> In May he received a notification from the R.A.F. that the boy was missing. Then followed a cable from the R.A.F. giving some of the circumstances of the tragedy, then a formal notice, the first to be received from Canadian sources, addressed to the boy's mother, that the dependants' allowance to which she was entitled was now cut off.

In other words, the furious Power complained, it seemed that "Canada's only interest in a Canadian boy was to save a paltry thirty dollars a month." The air minister worked hard to establish clearer lines of control and communication over Canadian airmen, wherever they served.

What should be added, however, is that most Canadians who served with the RAF and flew in bomber crews that often included Australians, New Zealanders, South Africans, and other men from dominions and colonies felt some reluctance to be remustered into all-Canadian squadrons. Their crews had bonded together and developed a mutual trust, and in wartime that was a critical factor. Moreover, they could get away with murder in British-commanded squadrons. Flight Sergeant Bill Eccles, serving in RAF Coastal Command and Bomber Command squadrons as a radar specialist, remembered being sent on course and subjected to a full kit inspection. Neatly folded on his bed was a pair of bright orange silk boxer shorts, a gift from his mother in Montreal. "What are these, Eccles?" the inspecting officer demanded with great disdain. "Canadian issue, sir," was the reply — and it was accepted, presumably on the grounds that nothing better could be expected of the RCAF.

Some BCATP graduates never did get overseas. Many, especially from the earliest training classes, were fed back into the BCATP to act as instructors. Still more were posted to the Home War Establishment to defend Canada. The first class of pilots, graduating in November 1940, had 7 of its members go to home defence squadrons and 27 join the BCATP. Of the 203 Canadian pilots trained in 1940, only 20 went overseas, while 165 became instructors. That was inevitable, but frustrating.

At the start of the war, the idea that Canada might need direct defence seemed little more than a joke: protected by two oceans, the North American continent was almost invulnerable. Almost, but not quite. Nazi U-boats began picking off fat merchantmen within months, and that meant the RCAF had to develop the skills to attack U-boats from the air. Some pilots learned well. Flight Lieutenant David Hornell, pilot of a twin-engine Canso amphibian operating from Scotland on June 24, 1944, came across a surfaced U-boat north of the Shetland Islands. The submarine's deck gun fired at the lumbering Canso, hitting the starboard engine, but Hornell pressed the attack, dropping four depth charges in a perfect "straddle" that blew the U-boat's bows out of the water and sank it. The Canso landed on the ocean without breaking up, thanks to Hornell's "superhuman efforts at the controls", but it sank shortly after, and it was twenty-one hours before rescue launches reached the eight crew members. "There was only one serviceable dinghy and this could not hold all the crew. So they took turns in the water, holding on to the side...." Two of the crew had already died of exposure, and Hornell, blinded and exhausted, failed to survive the trip back to Scotland. He received the Victoria Cross posthumously.

On the Canadian west coast, there was a great public fear of invasion after Pearl Harbor. Although the military chiefs in Ottawa discounted any risk of attack, being unwilling to divert men and equipment from the European war, the commanders on the coast were far less certain. Their fears, plus the understandable political necessity to protect the homeland first, led in March 1942 to the decision to create a Home War Establishment of forty-nine squadrons, twenty-five of which were to be located in British Columbia. In June 1942, the Japanese occupied Attu and Kiska, American islands in the Aleutian chain off Alaska, and for a time the threat of invasion seemed real enough that RCAF fighter and bomber squadrons went to Alaska to operate with the American forces there. The squadrons launched attacks on the Japanese-held islands on September 25, 1942, and Squadron Leader K.A. Boomer shot down an enemy plane; he would be the only RCAF pilot to score victories over both

Japanese and German aircraft. But in the same month that the Japanese took the islands, the United States Navy won the great naval air battle of Midway and began to take the offensive in the Pacific. The Japanese were driven from the Aleutians by the summer of 1943 and the threat to the west coast gradually receded; so too did RCAF strength on the home front.

WAR AROUND THE WORLD

By the summer of 1941, the RCAF had had five fighter squadrons in Britain. The *Luftwaffe*'s daylight raids had almost ceased, and when air raids had come it had been under cover of darkness. Released from the struggle against Messerschmitts and Dorniers over England, RAF and RCAF fighter squadrons had begun daylight attacks on occupied France, either on their own or as escorts for bombers. Rail and road traffic were targets, as were factories, airfields, enemy shipping, and gun positions. If the *Luftwaffe* rose to meet the attackers, that was an opportunity to tackle them as well. Hugh Godefroy, a pilot in an RCAF fighter squadron based at Biggin Hill, remembered one sweep over France in late October 1941 when the *Luftwaffe* jumped the Spitfires:

> ...suddenly I realized that the sparks were going forward not backward! "TRACER!" I pulled the stick back in a wild break out of the formation. Looking back, I was just in time to see Brian Hodgkinson behind me roll slowly over, flames pouring from his engine, and a Messerschmitt pass below me within yards of my tail, his nose and wings rippling with fire. Ten voices scream on the R/T at once:
> "For God's sake, break, 109s!"
> "I'm hit. I'm on fire."
> "Bail out, you fool."
> "My tail's gone. I'm bailing out."
> It was complete pandemonium, but it lasted only for a minute.

"This was no joust bound by the rules of chivalry," Godefroy said. "I had never witnessed such persistent savagery. They were out to kill us by any means possible."

While they had been bested over England, the enemy continued to be a strong and skilful force. When the Canadian raid went in at Dieppe in August 1942, for example, seventy-four Allied squadrons, including eight from the RCAF, provided air support. But the *Luftwaffe* shot down twice as many aircraft as it lost; it was the worst day of the war for the RAF. The RCAF lost thirteen planes and pilots on that black day.

Canadian pilots were having better success elsewhere. In the air battles over the Western Desert and in the disastrous British intervention in Greece, Flight Lieutenant Vernon Woodward had twenty-two kills against Italian and German pilots. The RCAF's 417 Squadron operated in the desert from the spring of 1942, first patrolling the Suez Canal and then providing air cover over the supply lines of Britain's Eighth Army as it advanced east towards Tunisia after the great victory of El Alamein in November 1942. In May 1943, the squadron moved to Malta to provide fighter support for the invasion of Sicily. Earlier at Malta, Pilot Officer Buck McNair shot down nine enemy aircraft in one three-month tour — two years later he was commanding an RCAF wing. The RCAF also operated three squadrons of radar-equipped night fighters from England after 1941, and provided Intruder squadrons of Mosquitoes and Mustangs.

Canadian airmen served in other theatres of war as well. Hundreds of Canadians served with RAF squadrons throughout the Pacific. Two RCAF transport squadrons, No. 435 and No. 436, flew out of Burma, dealing daily with Japanese interceptors, wholly inadequate facilities, and some of the world's worst flying weather. No. 413 Squadron was based in Ceylon in 1942 when one of its Catalina flying boats, flown by Squadron Leader L.J. Birchall, spotted a Japanese fleet heading for Ceylon on April 4. "We immediately coded a message and started transmission," Birchall said after the war. "We were halfway through our required third transmission when a shell destroyed our wireless equipment." Then the Catalina was shot down. Six of the nine crew members survived; Birchall himself, "the saviour of Ceylon", withstood brutal Japanese interrogation and more than three years in a POW camp. But his warning had given the British time to prepare for the attack, and it was driven off. Birchall won the Distinguished Flying Cross for his exploits.

The Canadian pilot who attracted the most attention for his feats in the air war, however, was George Beurling. Rejected by the RCAF before the war because he had insufficient education, "Buzz" Beurling was finally accepted into the RAF in 1940. Ill-disciplined, unsuited to formation flying, and totally fearless, Beurling was a natural flier and a skilled shot, not unlike Billy Bishop in the Great War. He had two kills before he was posted to Malta in May 1942, and there, flying a Spitfire, he improved his score to seven by July and to twenty-nine by October — the highest total by a Canadian ace. The Spitfire could attain a speed of 404 mph, and with its powerful Rolls-Royce engine it could climb to 20,000 feet in just over six minutes, so it was generally used against enemy fighters while Hurricanes dealt with the lower-flying bombers. In this deadly combat Beurling was a master, combining reckless flying with the uncanny eye of the dead shot. He described shooting down an Italian

Macchi aircraft: "One of my shells caught [the pilot] right in the face and blew his head right off. The body slumped and the slipstream caught the neck, the stub of the neck, and the blood streamed down the side of the cockpit." Although the chivalry that had graced many pilots in the First World War was now replaced by pragmatic ruthlessness, pilots rarely saw their opponents die. "You have to be hard-hearted," Beurling said publicly. "You must blaze away whenever you are in a position to get his oxygen bottles or gas tanks." But to his sister Gladys he said, "I see their faces."

Nonetheless, "These are the best years of my life," Beurling said, and when he was decorated by George VI at Buckingham Palace — he received the Distinguished Service Order, Distinguished Flying Cross, and Distinguished Flying Medal and Bar — he told the king that he had enjoyed every minute in Malta. After being shot down and wounded, Beurling came back to Canada for a publicity tour; then it was back to England for more action, this time with the RCAF, until, in January 1944, he was taken off operations for repeated insubordination. A brilliant lone wolf, Beurling seemingly could not accept the necessity for discipline in the air. He returned home, was again lionized by press and public (something he could not abide), and left the RCAF in August 1944; he died in an unexplained plane crash in Rome four years later, on his way to fight for the infant state of Israel.

Meanwhile, the Allies' preparations for invasion had started by the beginning of 1944. By this time, the *Luftwaffe* had largely withdrawn from French skies; Hitler needed the fighters at home as the Reich attempted to ward off devastating day and night bombing attacks launched by the United States Army Air Force and the RAF and RCAF. That meant that many Spitfires could be converted into fighter-bombers, able to deliver heavy attacks at German air bases, gun positions, or headquarters in France. That activity, in which Typhoon fighter-bombers also participated, increased enormously as the date set for the invasion neared.

By D-Day — June 6, 1944 — the Allies had achieved virtually total air superiority over the Normandy battlefield. The Canadian government, Air Marshal Harold Edwards (the senior RCAF officer overseas), and the senior commanders of the First Canadian Army had all assumed that No. 83 Group of the Second Tactical Air Force would work directly with the Canadian army in France, providing aerial reconnaissance and attacking ground targets. Fifteen of No. 83's twenty-nine squadrons and half its ground establishment of almost 10,000 men were Canadian. Such a powerful force of Mustangs, Spitfires, and Typhoons could respond quickly to calls for air support and roam over the rear areas behind the *Wehrmacht*'s lines, shooting up targets at will. But military exigency interfered with this plan; early in 1944 No. 83 Group was assigned to support the Second British Army because it would spear-head the landings. No. 84 Group, with few Canadians and less experience, was designated to provide air support for the First Canadian Army when it came to Normandy later. That caused hurt feelings, but it did not markedly affect the air support offered to either army.

The air forces' mastery of the air did not change for the rest of the war in Europe. American, British, and Canadian soldiers could be almost certain that aircraft overhead were friendly; the *Wehrmacht* had to consider every plane hostile. This edge was crucial in the struggle in Normandy in the sum-mer of 1944. In the first few days after the invasion, Panzer formations suf-fered delays in reaching the front as their columns were repeatedly attacked by rocket-firing Typhoons, which were very effective in a tank-killing role; the delays helped the Allies secure their beachhead. By August almost all of the tactical squadrons were operating from forward airfields on French soil, which devastated the Germans. RCAF wings alone estimated that they had accounted for 2,600 enemy armoured vehicles and trucks. And when the *Luftwaffe* did take to the air, its pilots, as one RCAF officer noted, were "not the experienced and daring *Luftwaffe* of old, thank goodness!"

The Germans still had tricks up their sleeves, however, as the Allies discov-ered soon after the invasion of France, when pilotless v-1 flying bombs began falling on British cities. Fortunately, the v-1s, or "buzz bombs", flew slowly enough that fighters could shoot them down. Those that eluded the intercep-tors and the anti-aircraft weapons flew on noisily until they started their descent — then the interval of silence before the explosion was heart-stopping. That was not the case with the v-2, the first guided missile, which appeared a few months later; it travelled faster than the speed of sound and exploded before those on the ground heard it coming.

The pilots of the RCAF ran up impressive totals of destruction in north-west Europe. No. 126 Fighter Wing claimed 361 enemy aircraft destroyed in more than 22,000 Spitfire sorties. No. 143 Wing, flying the fast, heavily armed Typhoons, dropped almost 6,500 tons of bombs on enemy defences and destroyed 16 bridges, and 3,600 railway cars, vehicles, or barges. The *Luftwaffe* had been driven from the skies and the *Wehrmacht* was virtually paralysed in its tactical movements; in all of this, the RCAF's fighter and fighter-bomber pilots had played their role.

THE BOMBER WAR

Canadians also played a substantial part in the destruction of the German homeland. Undoubtedly, most of the damage inflicted on the enemy by the

RCAF came from bomber crews. Most RCAF casualties were suffered by those same crews.

Although the pre-war strategic planners in the RAF had spent substantial time planning for a bomber war, and although the RAF had bigger and better bombers than the Germans when the war started, the bombing of Germany had begun in an amateurish way. The British bombers at the beginning of the war were slow twin-engined machines capable of carrying only limited bomb loads, and equipped with unsophisticated aiming devices and what would soon be thought to be quaint ideas of morality. Only military and naval targets would be hit, most often without much damage, and the British public was proudly told in such films as *The Lion Has Wings* that no civilians could be hurt in such raids. Yet fighter aircraft could inflict heavy losses on bombers attacking by daylight, as the *Luftwaffe* discovered in August and September 1940. The answer for both sides was night bombing; this made it much easier to get past the enemy's defences, but also meant that any pretence of hitting military targets alone disappeared. Only one in ten of RAF Bomber Command crews in 1941 dropped their payloads within five miles of their targets in the Ruhr.

The RCAF formed its first bomber squadron in June 1941, entirely from Canadians serving in the RAF, and within days the squadron flew its first missions, in twin-engined Wellington bombers (known as "Wimpeys") with a speed of 235 mph. The Wellington was no prize, as this air force song (to the tune of "Bless 'Em All") suggested:

Worry me, worry me,
Wellingtons don't worry me,
Oil-chewing bastards with flaps on their wings,
Buggered-up pistons, and buggered-up rings,
The bomb load is so effing small,
Four-fifths of five-eights of eff-all,
There'll be such a commotion when we're o'er the ocean,
So cheer up my lads, eff 'em all.

The next year, seven more RCAF bomber squadrons took to the air, though by this time the technology of the bomber war had begun to alter as scientists raced to improve direction-finding devices. The British now had increasing numbers of four-engined heavy bombers at their disposal. Each new plane could carry up to ten tons of bombs, and target-finding aids like "Oboe", "Gee", "H2S", and improved bombsights were major advances. Oboe used two radar beams, one to direct the bomber towards its target and the other to indicate the point at which the bombs should be dropped. H2S radar bounced an echo off the ground, producing a "map" of the area below on a screen in the bomber. Gee allowed a navigator aboard a bomber to determine his exact position by calculating the difference in travel time between three radio signals transmitted by "master" and "slave" stations on the ground. Pathfinder aircraft now flew ahead of the bomber streams, marking the targets and directing the bomber streams onto them. Pilots like Wing Commander Johnnie Fauquier won fame for their pathfinding work.

The result of these innovations and others was that massive bombing raids became possible by mid-1942. In the space of two years, RAF Bomber Command had gone from virtually undirected single-plane attacks on military targets to co-ordinated thousand-aircraft raids on cities. Moreover, the United States Army Air Force was now in Britain in strength, and its B-17 "Flying Fortresses" flew over Germany by day, their thirteen .50-calibre machine guns taking a toll of the *Luftwaffe* interceptors. The Germans endured the Army Air Force by day and Bomber Command by night.

Against the bombers, the Germans mustered a sophisticated radar network that directed interceptors towards the attackers. *Luftwaffe* fighters soon had effective airborne radar that became more so as the war went on. To counter German radar, the Allies developed "Window", simple strips of aluminum foil that were dropped from the air and appeared as bomber-sized "blips" on the screen. Simple and effective, Window for a time neutralized radar-directed interception. The powerful and accurate radar-controlled anti-aircraft guns that threw up tons of flak at the bombers were also fooled by Window. Only the searchlights raking the skies were unaffected by the aluminum strips, and they provided a terrifying feeling of exposure for night-flying crews.

Air Marshal Arthur Harris, commanding Bomber Command, had become convinced that three hundred bombers were insufficient "to saturate the defences of a major industrial town." By April 1942, the technology existed to direct larger attacking fleets, and on May 30 the first thousand-bomber raid struck Cologne with a monstrous blow that forced the evacuation of 200,000 people and left 6,500 acres of the city in ruins, its cathedral spire rising alone out of the rubble.

Bomber Command then attacked the great city of Hamburg with its population of 1.5 million on July 24, 1943; this was the first raid to use Window. About 10 per cent of the almost eight hundred Lancasters, Halifaxes, Stirlings, and Wellingtons that came at the city in a near-continuous stream were from the RCAF. The first bombers arrived just after 1:00 A.M. to find that the Pathfinders' markers were clearly visible. The German radar, paralysed by

Window, was ineffective; so too were the fighters and the flak, though Hamburg was, next to Berlin, the most heavily defended target in the Reich. The bombers dropped their loads of incendiaries and 4,000- and 8,000-pound blockbusters, and only twelve aircraft were lost. As the Germans would normally have expected to destroy fifty bombers from a force that large, the effect of Window was apparent. Three days later, Bomber Command was back in force, dropping more incendiaries into the still-smouldering ruins. This time a firestorm was created, the flames creating 150-mph winds that fanned the flames further. Howling winds sucked people into the air. Fires devoured the oxygen. People who jumped into rivers and canals for safety boiled to death. At least 50,000 died, 75 per cent of the city lay demolished, and a million survivors fled the ruin and carnage. A week later, Hamburg was hit a third time.

For the bomber crews, the morality or immorality of their task was not something that troubled many. They were under orders, and they had to carry them out. Of course, said Donald Schurman, an RCAF air gunner serving with Bomber Command and later a historian, "every airman who could think had some idea of what we were doing. Nobody was much fooled by talk concerning military targets around which civilian houses 'just happened' to be grouped...." However, he added, "we were very young and we thought it a good idea at the time to kill Germans." Significantly, though a few British clerics and parliamentarians protested the savagery of the bombing, none raised a voice against it in Canada. When Cologne was bombed by a thousand aircraft in 1942, the *Globe and Mail* commented that this was the best way to deal with the "Hunnish hive".

To Hitler, raids such as those on Hamburg were "terror bombing", a not inapt term. German leaders who now complained about area bombing had, of course, all but originated the concept in the Spanish Civil War, and had continued it in their attacks on Warsaw in 1939, Rotterdam in May 1940, and British cities such as Coventry and London in the blitz. But whichever belligerent had started the bombing of civilians, the Allies had brought the technique to perfection, and in the circumstances Hitler had to pull the *Luftwaffe* home to defend the cities and factories, and to urge his scientists to new efforts to counter Window. By 1944 bomber losses were climbing again. On March 30, when 702 aircraft attacked Nuremburg, 94 bombers were downed — an almost insupportable loss.

For bomber crews, the war was terrifyingly dangerous. Casualties were staggering. There was none of the glamour of the fighter pilots for the men in Bomber Command, just long periods of boredom interspersed with moments of sheer terror. Murray Peden, who flew as a pilot with 214 Squadron of RAF

Bomber Command and wrote the very best book on the air war, *A Thousand Shall Fall*, described what a trip or "op" was like:

> Once we hit the enemy coast, the ever-present strain mounted rapidly to the higher level that was the concomitant of being in the enemy's ball park, blindfolded by night. I always waited tensely for the first burst of flak to stab at us, hoping it would not be too close. Once that first burst came up...I breathed a little easier and began the game that every pilot had to play, changing altitude, course, and speed, to throw off the next burst....
>
> At a point about 20 minutes from the target we began to approach an outlying belt of searchlights which stood before us on either side of our intended track in two great cones. I feared and hated those baleful blinding lights more than anything else the Germans used against us.... A pilot trapped in a large cone had little chance of escape....the searchlights' accomplices, the heavy guns, would hurl up shells in streams....

Then there were the *Luftwaffe*'s night fighters, Messerschmitt 110s and, later, jet-powered 410s, firing cannon shells able to riddle the heavy bombers and send them, trailing smoke, to the ground. Some carried upward-pointing guns, and sidled underneath the unknowing bombers to deliver a nasty surprise.

Crews might be able to parachute to safety if their pilot could hold the bomber level long enough for them to jump. If not, they rode their flaming aircraft to almost certain death. If they jumped safely, they were over hostile Germany or occupied Holland or the bitter cold of the North Sea. If they were lucky, they survived the landing and the understandable hostility of German civilians, and made it to a *Stalag Luft*, a POW camp for airmen. If they were even luckier, they might land in Ireland, neutral in the war; though they were interned in the same camp as Germans, these airmen ate splendidly, could leave the camp at will on day passes if they promised to return, and got on well with their guards.

Once in captivity, even in Ireland, it was an officer's duty to try to escape. On March 24–25, 1944, seventy-six Allied airmen participated in the Great Escape from the *Stalag* at Sagan in East Prussia. Three made their way to safety, eighteen were recaptured and returned to Sagan, five ended up at Sachsenhausen concentration camp, and fifty were executed by the ss and Gestapo on Hitler's order. "I can see their faces now," remembered Wally Floody of Toronto, a fighter pilot and an architect of the escape. "The Gestapo and ss took the fifty out, two by two, and under the pretext of allowing them to answer the call of nature, dispatched them with shots in the back of the head." Six of those murdered were RCAF officers: flight lieutenants Pat Langford of Penticton, British Columbia; George McGill of Toronto; Jimmy Wernham of Winnipeg; Gordon Kidder of St. Catharines, Ontario; George Wiley of Windsor; and Hank Birkland of Calgary. After the war, the Allies hunted down and hanged fourteen Nazis for their part in this murder.

The main Canadian share in the bomber war was borne by No. 6 Group, formed January 1, 1943, with eight squadrons. At its peak, No. 6 included fourteen RCAF bomber squadrons. Based in Yorkshire, No. 6 Group's officers and men became part of the community, in between their night-time visits to German airspace. They learned to drink tea and to avoid the NAAFI (Navy, Army, and Air Force Institutes) canteens if they could, they took out local girls, visited pubs, and accepted invitations for Sunday dinners from Yorkshire families. They named their aircraft after girls back home. And they tried to avoid dwelling on the fact that less than one-third of them would survive their 30-ops tours. It was hard to escape that realization. Before takeoff, one crew member said, you looked around at the sun and the trees, and you "think about the folks at home and how they're going to feel if you go missing." For this, sergeant pilots drew $3.70 a day.

No. 6 Group suffered from serious problems in its first year of operations. There were more training accidents than the norm, and more operational losses too. Between March and June 1943, losses amounted to more than a hundred aircraft, a rate that virtually guaranteed that no more than one in eight crews would survive their tours. Part of the reason for the heavy losses was bad luck, part the old machines the group had to fly. A lot was due to the extra distance No. 6 Group's aircraft had to fly to reach Germany from their Yorkshire stations, and the high risk of fog, snow, and sleet in the Vale of York. Too much was due to inexperience at the top. Commanders lacked the skill or the will to motivate their crews to press on to the target and not to abort their ops before German airspace was reached or, as often happened, before takeoff.

When Air Vice-Marshal "Black Mike" McEwen, a Canadian ace of the Great War, took over the group in January 1944, training was stepped up and discipline was reinforced. McEwen enforced dress regulations and, more important, he went on operations — something few senior officers ever did — acquiring the status of a good luck charm. There were further heavy losses after he took over, but gradually his discipline and some good luck reversed the numbers, and morale in No. 6 greatly improved. By this time all the squadrons had acquired Lancasters or Halifaxes in place of Wellingtons, and that helped. The Lanc was a wonder to fly; it could go 272 mph, and was

almost as manoeuvrable as a fighter. It carried a seven-man crew and from
seven to eleven tons of bombs, and it had nine .303 machine guns for defence.
The Halifax, just slightly faster and with the same armament, had a record of
being able to absorb punishment and still get its crew home. The confidence
produced by those bombers was deserved. Then, as the D-Day invasion grew
near and targets were chosen in France rather than in well-defended Germany, losses dropped further.

Raw courage also helped boost morale, and some actions stood out even in
those areas where courage was the norm. Pilot Officer Andrew Mynarski, a
twenty-seven–year–old air gunner from Winnipeg, was aboard a Lancaster
from 419 Squadron when it bombed Cambrai six days after D-Day. Attacked
from below by a *Luftwaffe* fighter and set afire, the Lancaster spun out of control. The pilot ordered the crew to bail out. Mynarski left his gun turret and
went towards the escape hatch, but saw that the rear gunner was trapped. The
citation for Mynarski's Victoria Cross described what happened next:

> Without hesitation...Mynarski made his way through the flames in an
> endeavour to move the turret and release the gunner. Whilst so doing, his
> parachute and his clothing, up to the waist, were set on fire.... Eventually
> the rear gunner clearly indicated to him that there was nothing more he
> could do and that he should try to save his own life. Pilot Officer Mynarski
> reluctantly went back through the flames to the escape hatch. There, as a
> last gesture to the trapped gunner, he turned towards him, stood to atten-
> tion in his flaming clothes and saluted, before he jumped out of the air-
> craft.... He was found eventually by the French, but was so severely burnt
> that he died from his injuries.

The rear gunner miraculously survived the crash, and his account of Mynarski's courage led to the posthumous award of the VC.

No. 6 Group played a major share in the bomber offensive. Its aircraft flew
41,000 ops and dropped 126,000 tons of bombs. That was almost one-eighth
of the total dropped by all of Bomber Command. Those No. 6 Group bombs
accounted for a goodly portion of the 560,000 dead and 675,000 wounded
Germans.

In thirty months of action, No. 6 Group lost 3,500 men. Another 4,700
Canadians died while serving with other Bomber Command squadrons. Others were wounded, many suffering disfiguring injuries from burns; plastic
surgeons like Dr. A. Ross Tilley of Toronto won fame for their efforts in re-
creating faces for men whose ears and noses had been burned away. The victims called themselves "guinea pigs", and Tilley called them "a pretty tough

group....there was always someone worse. They never allowed one another to feel sorry for themselves." But in the dark of the night, the horror of their disfigurement must have been all-consuming.

How effective the bombing carried out at such human cost was at winning the war remains unclear, as the United States Strategic Bombing Survey, compiled after the German surrender, showed. Raids on cities such as Cologne, Hamburg, and Dresden wreaked havoc and forced tens of thousands of German survivors to live in great discomfort in the ruins of their homes. Undoubtedly that hurt morale; undoubtedly the loss of sleep hampered workers at their jobs. But there is also no doubt that German war production continued to rise almost to the end of the war. More tanks, for example, were produced in 1944 than in any previous year. How much greater the production would have been without the bombing is uncertain, although the factories would presumably have poured out even more weapons than they did. The German armies also continued to fight with great skill and savagery until May 1945; whether that savagery increased because of the bombing of civilians is a moot point.

The RCAF bomber crews — like the fighter pilots, transport crews, and ground crews — had done dangerous and difficult wartime jobs with increasing professionalism and skill. They believed that they had played a major part in the war's outcome, and their commanders thought the same. When Air Chief Marshal Arthur "Bomber" Harris said farewell to Canadian air crew going home in 1945, he told his boys that "when you come to dandle your children on your knee, and they ask, 'What did you do in the last war, daddy?' you can tell them that you won it, because you did."

In all, a quarter of a million Canadians served in the RCAF and RAF, with 94,000 going overseas. Of these, 17,101 failed to return. Mackenzie King had favoured the idea of the BCATP in 1939 because he believed that air casualties could never be so numerous as to lead to a cry for conscription. But RCAF deaths were almost exactly equal to army battle fatalities in the European theatre. War had changed between 1939 and 1945, and nowhere was this change felt so clearly as in the war in the air.

Biplanes today always suggest the dogfights of the Great War. But well into the Second World War, pilot trainees — like these BCATP students heading for their Fleet Finches at an elementary flying training school in Windsor Mills, Quebec — learned the basics of their new trade in the biplane.

In March 1940 — during the Phony War — the RCAF station at Camp Borden, Ontario, still looked the way it had in peacetime — few buildings, limited construction under way, and only a smattering of aircraft. But on May 10, seven weeks after this picture was taken, the *Blitzkrieg* replaced the "sitzkrieg", and soon Borden and 50 other stations were operating at maximum capacity.

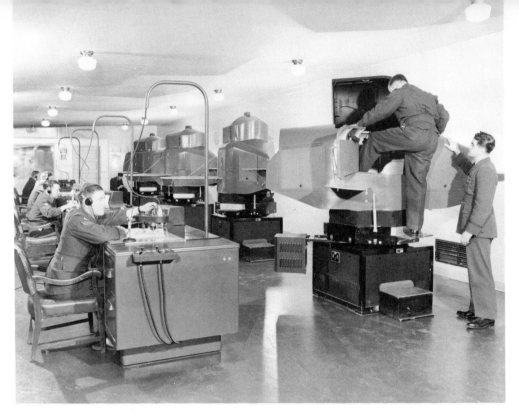

Student pilots received some training in the security of aircraft simulators like these ones at Virden, Manitoba, which could move in three geometrical planes to imitate the turn, bank, and pitch of real planes.

Soon, however, they had to venture into the air — and accidents were inevitable. The piggyback landing of these two twin-engine trainers produced no injuries, but BCATP trainees suffered 856 training fatalities, most the product of carelessness, disobedience, or pilot error.

Although the initial expectation was that Britain would supply most BCATP aircraft, the defeats of 1940 forced the British to keep every plane they could produce for their own defence. As a result, Canadian plants were converted to produce aircraft, such as these Avro Anson trainers on the production line at the Canadian Car and Foundry plant in Amherst, Nova Scotia, in 1942.

One of the best all-round aircraft of the war — and the most glamorous — was the Supermarine Spitfire. Its design had originated in the 1920s but was so fundamentally sound that, with ceaseless improvements, the plane maintained a margin of superiority over *Luftwaffe* aircraft throughout the war. This painting of a Spitfire IX is by wartime pilot R.W. Bradford, now director of the National Aviation Museum in Ottawa.

Canadian fighter pilots were popular figures, especially when they were as successful and good-looking as George "Buzz" Beurling, shown here beside his fighter marked with its impressive score of kills. Most of these came during the Battle of Malta; the Mediterranean island was a crucial British base until the victory in North Africa and the invasion of Sicily.

A Blenheim light bomber, one of the RCAF's pre-war aircraft, checks out a burning freighter, another victim of the U-boats operating in the North Atlantic.

RCAF ground crew from No. 413 Squadron service a Consolidated Catalina I flying boat in Ceylon in the spring of 1943. The year before, a powerful Japanese fleet heading for Ceylon had been detected by an RCAF Catalina which, though shot down, provided critical warning time.

The RCAF's major contribution to the air war was unquestionably the role it played in Bomber Command. This Halifax bomber at an RCAF station in Yorkshire was a tough, durable aircraft that carried a bombload of 13,000 lbs and had a maximum speed of over 280 mph at 13,500 feet.

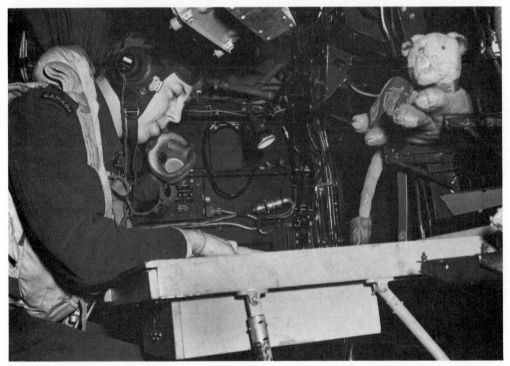

Getting the bomber to its target was the task of the navigator, here Flying Officer Gus Utas of No. 427 (Lion) Squadron — shown with his mascot, "Ruthless Robert".

Although war artist Paul Goranson described his subject as a dorsal gunner, he is in fact a waist gunner in a Wellington bomber. The twin-engine "Wimpey" had a fabric-covered metal geodetic structure, a maximum speed of 235 mph, and a bombload of 4,500 lbs.

This striking photograph shows a Halifax bomber from the RCAF's No. 6 Group over France. The Halifax first flew in action in 1941, and had the reputation of being able to absorb tremendous punishment and still get its crew home.

Germany and its people suffered terribly under the rain of high explosives. This photograph of the north German city of Bremen demonstrates how little of the city remained habitable by war's end.

But bomber crews paid a heavy price too; there is no sign of the crew bailing out of this Halifax bomber ablaze over a heavily bombed city. The RCAF's 14 bomber squadrons lost 6,164 dead and missing aircrew and 1,188 aircraft in operations.

Three members of No. 431 Squadron are debriefed after their D-Day mission. By 1944 the *Luftwaffe*'s fighters and flak were far weaker in France than in Germany, and missions over France were ordinarily "milk runs" — but the strain still shows.

V
SICILY AND ITALY

After the Dieppe débâcle in August 1942, the Canadian army in Britain had returned to its exercises, more than a little sobered by the casualties that had befallen the 2nd Division. The *Wehrmacht*'s reputation as near-supermen had been enhanced yet again. But so had the quality of Canadian training. Dieppe had forced a tough new realism, including live ammunition, in exercises for the once-jaded infantrymen.

By November of that year General Bernard Montgomery's Eighth Army had decisively defeated General Erwin Rommel's Afrika Korps at the battle of El Alamein, bringing nearer the end of the see-sawing campaign that had seen British and German-Italian forces alternately advancing and retreating across North Africa for two years. At almost exactly the same time as the victory of El Alamein, the Soviets surrounded the besieging German army at Stalingrad, cutting their supply lines and reducing them to starvation, and British and American forces landed in Algeria and Morocco and began moving east. Supermen or not, the Germans could be beaten.

By January of 1943 the German army at Stalingrad had been demolished, and by May the Germans had also been totally defeated in North Africa, crushed between Montgomery's army and the combined forces of the First British and Seventh U.S. armies led by General Dwight Eisenhower. What was to be next for the Allies? The decision had already been taken. At Casablanca in January 1943, Prime Minister Churchill and President Roosevelt and their military chiefs had agreed that the next operation should take place in the Mediterranean theatre, with the aim of forcing Mussolini's Italy out of the war. There was a range of possibilities: Italy itself could be invaded, or Sicily, Sardinia, or Corsica. Sicily was chosen, primarily because its capture would make the Mediterranean Sea virtually an Allied lake, and the two leaders quickly decided that Eisenhower would once again be in command. Under him would be General Harold Alexander, hitherto the overall commander of Britain's Middle East forces. In February, Montgomery and General George Patton, a successful American tank commander in North Africa, were placed in command of the invading British and American armies. On April 23, after discreet prior negotiations, the Chief of the Imperial General Staff, General Sir Alan Brooke, invited General McNaughton to contribute a Canadian infantry division and tank brigade to the invading force. Two days later, having consulted Ottawa, McNaughton accepted the proposal and named the 1st Canadian Infantry Division and the 1st Army Tank Brigade for the operation.

BLOODING IN SICILY

By April 1943 the First Canadian Army in Britain was a very substantial force. It included army headquarters, two corps headquarters, three infantry and two armoured divisions, and two army tank brigades — in all, almost a quarter of a million Canadian soldiers. These soldiers were for the most part young — about twenty years old on average. Half came from big cities, half from small towns and farms. Most were uneducated; many lacked even Grade 6 education. The army was full of Depression kids, those who had suffered the worst the "Dirty Thirties" had to offer. They might be young and untaught, but they were tough.

Their commander, the General Officer Commanding the First Canadian Army — Andy McNaughton — had vigorously resisted attempts by Whitehall and Ottawa to divide his command and employ the army in bits and pieces. The First Canadian Army was Canada's and his own, and McNaughton intended to lead it into battle as a great national force.

But by 1943, many units of the army had been in England for more than three years without hearing enemy fire. Training was an essential preparation for battle, but too much of it was hard on morale. Moreover, training was not the same as combat, and if the troops didn't get a taste of battle they might suffer grievously when they were finally dumped into large-scale action. There were also considerations of national prestige and self-respect. Was Canada's land force contribution to the war to be limited to Hong Kong and Dieppe?

A few hundred Canadian officers and NCOs had already been sent on a tour of duty in the North African campaign to get battle experience. When the British requested more troops for Sicily, Ottawa was quick to agree. Defence minister J.L. Ralston told the Cabinet War Committee that "he was 100 percent behind the decision. That it would give battle experience without which it was questionable whether the morale of the Army could be maintained."

The invasion of the Italian island, codenamed "Husky", was to be launched by the Seventh U.S. Army and the British Eighth Army in the second week in July. The 1st Canadian Division was to come under British command, and to be led by Major-General H.L.N. Salmon. But the division's first losses came well before it went into action; General Salmon and some of his staff died in an airplane crash on April 29 while en route to Cairo for briefings. Within hours, McNaughton had given the command to Major-General Guy Simonds, an RMC graduate, a former gunner, and at thirty-nine Canada's youngest general. Simonds had been one of the officers in North Africa under General Montgomery, an obvious advantage.

Simonds now had the job of getting his new division and the tank brigade ready for their role in Sicily. That meant training in Scotland for an amphibious landing and for mountain warfare, and issuing and breaking in new equipment including a rocket launcher called the Projector Infantry Anti-Tank (PIAT), and the U.S.-built Sherman tank. It meant that Simonds and his operations staff had to put the new commander's personal stamp on the plans already prepared for the Canadian landing. It meant that the divisional headquarters had to plan how to load each transport and troop carrier in a succession of convoys so that everything needed would be available at the right time and place. To carry the Canadian division, ninety-two ships would have to be organized into a fast assault convoy, a slow assault convoy carrying the bulk of the transport and supplies, and two follow-up convoys carrying the tank brigade — except for one armoured regiment which was to land with the first waves. The first, slow convoy left England on June 19; the last, the fast assault convoy, on June 28. Unluckily, three ships in the slow assault convoy were torpedoed in the Mediterranean with the loss of fifty-eight Canadians, five hundred vehicles, and some guns.

The Allied invasion plan targeted the south and south-west coasts of the island. The Americans were to land on the left from Licata to Scoglitti, the British and Canadians on the right from west of Pachino to Syracuse. Airborne forces would go in before the sea landing. No fortified port would be attacked — a lesson of the Dieppe raid — and heavy naval fire support would precede the assault.

The defenders included large numbers of Italian conscripts organized into weak coastal units, low in morale and poorly trained. The German forces, in strength in Sicily only since May 1943, consisted of two motorized formations, the 15th and 90th Panzer Grenadier divisions, and the Hermann Goering Panzer Division. All three were recently reconstituted divisions, full of untried reinforcements. They would fight and fight well, however, unlike Mussolini's dispirited and badly armed troops, and the rugged topography, traversed by narrow dirt roads and defiles and passes, made Sicily ideal for defence.

Simonds had been advised by intelligence reports that beach defences were fairly light in the Canadian sector, the extreme tip of the Pachino peninsula.

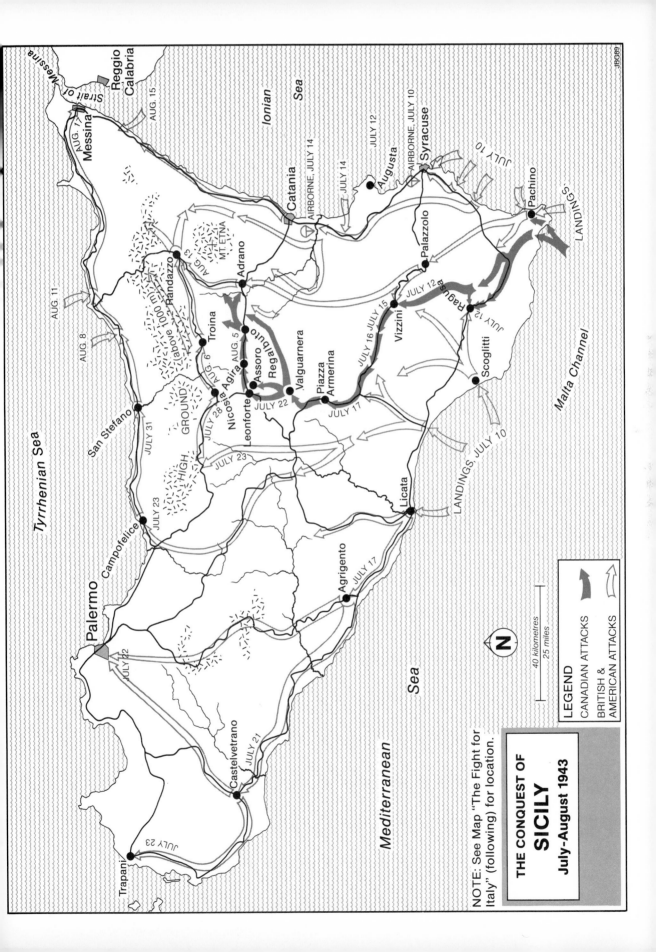

Reggio
Calabria

Strait of Messina

AUG. 15

AUG. 17 Messina

Ionian Sea

AIRBORNE, JULY 10

JULY 12

Syracuse

AIRBORNE, JULY 14 Augusta

JULY 14

JULY 10

Catania

Pachino

LANDINGS

Palazzolo

JULY 12 Ragusa

Vizzini JULY 12

JULY 15

JULY 16

AUG. 13 Randazzo

MT. ETNA

Adrano

Troina

AUG. 5 Regalbuto

Assoro

AUG. 6 Nicosia Agira JULY 22

Valguarnera

JULY 28 Leonforte Piazza Armerina

JULY 17

Scoglitti

(above 1000 m)

HIGH GROUND

JULY 23

LANDINGS, JULY 10

AUG. 11

AUG. 8

San Stefano

JULY 31

Campofelice JULY 23

Licata

Tyrrhenian Sea

Palermo

JULY 22

Agrigento

JULY 17

Castelvetrano

JULY 21

Trapani

JULY 23

Mediterranean Sea

Malta Channel

N

40 kilometres
25 miles

LEGEND

CANADIAN ATTACKS

BRITISH &
AMERICAN ATTACKS

NOTE: See Map "The Fight for
Italy" (following) for location.

THE CONQUEST OF
SICILY
July-August 1943

JBG89

The general's assault plan called for two brigades to hit the beach at 2:45 A.M. on July 10. Belated discovery of a sandbar in front of the Canadian beaches forced some hasty improvisations.

The major objective was Pachino airfield. That, like almost all the invading forces' objectives, was taken at negligible cost in the first hours of invasion, despite a storm that blew up a heavy swell. The sandbar forced some of the troops out of their LCA landing craft and into DUKWs — American-built amphibious trucks, made partially of wood, that could run on land as well as water. (General Montgomery, landing in Sicily aboard a DUKW, was said to have told his driver, "Steer away from the troops; if they recognize me they'll wonder why I'm not walking on water.") The port of Syracuse fell on the first day and three days later Augusta was taken. Patton's men struck out to the west and north-west, faced only by weak Italian opposition. Montgomery's Eighth Army moved northward along the coastal plain, the Canadians moving through mountainous terrain to hold the western edge of the British advance.

If any of the Canadians expected to find spaghetti and meatballs awaiting them in little trattorias, they were to be disappointed. Apart from purloined fruit and "liberated" livestock, food was the ubiquitous and much despised British "compo pack", here described by Lieutenant Farley Mowat of the Hastings and Prince Edward Regiment (Hasty Pees):

> ...the compo pack consisted of a wooden crate containing everything fourteen men were supposed to require for twenty-four hours: hard-tack biscuits in lieu of bread; canned yellow wax, misleadingly labelled margarine; tins of M&V (unidentifiable scraps of fat and gristle mushed up with equally unidentifiable vegetables); canned processed cheese which tasted like, and may well have been, casein glue; powdered tea, milk and sugar, all ready mixed; turnip jam (laughingly labelled strawberry or raspberry); eight (count them) tiny hard candies for each man; seven India-made Victory cigarettes which, it was rumoured, were manufactured from the dung of sacred cattle; six squares of toilet paper per man...; and one further item...a twelve-ounce can of treacle pudding that was an irresistible object of desire...we were starving for sweet stuffs.

British rations never reached a high standard, in England or in the field. But Private Mel Perrin of the 48th Highlanders was soon writing home to Toronto that "We have had quite a few ripe oranges, grapes, lemons, figs and so forth...." Even so, "I would give anything to be back buying those things...."

Others received food parcels from home. One soldier listed the contents of a parcel from his brother and sister-in-law: "One large tin of chicken, one tin of pork & beans, 3 pkgs of lemon, 1 tin of Kam, 1 small fruit cake, 5 bags of fruit drinks, 4 chocolate bars, 4 cubes Oxo, 1 pound cheese, 1 candy roll, 1 tin of lobsters" — and told his wife that three more parcels were on the way. "So, you see, Darling, I have quite a few things to eat."

The Sicilian roads were so bad that mule trains had to be improvised to haul food and ammunition forward over the hills. Private Jack Ainsworth of a Service Corps transport company told his parents how the mules had been rounded up. "We just took them where we saw them, on the road pulling wagons or in a field where we could catch them." One "old boy" had tried to say his beast was lame; "That didn't save his mule for him though." Incidents like that tended to turn the Sicilians, generally happy at the prospect of liberation, into bitter people who felt their fascist overlords had been replaced by equally uncaring foreigners.

By July 15, after a relatively untroubled advance (except for the hills, the dust, and the lack of water), the Canadians finally encountered the German defence — and it was skilful and well planned. The Germans' object was delay. As Brigadier Howard Graham of the 1st Brigade recalled, they would station "a minimum force of mobile troops and guns on half-track vehicles at innumerable strategic points at four- or five-mile intervals. By so doing, they forced us to deploy a force ten times their own numbers." The Allies expended time and energy and suffered casualties, and around the next bend in the road the entire exercise had to be repeated. By July 17 the Canadians had taken Piazza Armerina, in the centre of Sicily, after a stiff fight, but the battle had delayed their advance for a full twenty-four hours.

A few miles farther north lay Valguarnera, held in force by the 15th Panzer Grenadiers. Simonds decided to use two of his three infantry brigades in the attack. The 3rd Brigade led off with the Van Doos in front, riding in trucks. The Van Doos were temporarily stopped by a large crater in the road; they filled it in and continued in the moonlight until stopped again by heavy machine-gun fire from a German patrol. After repelling the patrol, they dug in for the rest of the night. The next morning, Brigadier M.H.S. Penhale sent all his battalions forward, taking the critical road junction en route to Valguarnera. Meanwhile Brigadier Graham's 1st Brigade had sent the Hasty Pees crosscountry over rugged terrain to the heights overlooking Valguarnera. While half the regiment shot up German vehicles, the remaining two companies fought off a German counter-attack, then retreated to firmer defensive positions. The Royal Canadian Regiment (RCR) was simultaneously attacking from the front, while the 48th Highlanders descended on the town from the hills to the south.

Valguarnera was a confused struggle, and a costly one. Canadian losses were 40 killed and 105 wounded. The enemy lost 280 captured and at least 200 killed or wounded. Field Marshal Albert Kesselring, the German commander, told Berlin that "troops trained for fighting in the mountains" had been encountered. "They are called Mountain Boys and probably belong to the 1st Cdn Division." That was almost a tribute.

Taking Leonforte and Assoro would also be difficult, thanks again to the terrain and stubborn defence. Assoro fell after the Hasty Pees, led by Major the Lord Tweedsmuir (son of a former governor general of Canada), scaled an astonishing cliff in the dark and, at dawn, found the German defenders below eating breakfast and washing, completely unaware of their enemies' presence. At Agira, Simonds put together a tremendous artillery barrage moving forward a hundred yards at a time; behind the exploding shells came the infantry. As often happened, though, the shelling had missed several enemy strongpoints, and the town was taken only after air attacks and bitter hand-to-hand fighting. Lieutenant John Dougan of the Loyal Edmonton Regiment had led his platoon behind the German lines when a German tank appeared at a bend in the road:

> Time seemed to stand still at that moment. Our PIAT man calmly and resolutely fired his anti-tank projectile — and missed! With the tank's gun now bearing almost directly on us, the PIAT man recocked his weapon and against all recognized procedures stood up and fired the gun from his shoulder. The recoil bowled him over but the projectile this time found its mark....

The PIAT was unwieldly and weighed thirty-two pounds, but was effective against virtually every German tank — if fired from close range.

By the end of July, the Canadians were pressing into Regalbuto, against heavy resistance and in the face of extreme mid-summer heat. The town fell on August 2 and by the 6th the Van Doos were knocking at the gates of Adrano. At that point — after twenty-seven days of hard fighting — the Canadians were pulled out of the line and into army reserve. Sicily would finally be in Allied hands after thirty-eight days.

Early in the Sicilian campaign, General McNaughton had arrived in Malta and had asked General Montgomery for permission to go to Sicily to see his 1st Division in action. Montgomery had refused; as he wrote in his memoirs, the division was just finding its feet and Simonds was "young and inexperi-

Night Traffic, Gander, Albert Cloutier. Goose Bay, Labrador, became a vital air station in the war against the U-boats. In 1941, the Newfoundland government leased the land to Canada for 99 years, and — in a remarkable engineering feat — Ottawa had the base in operation within months. The aircraft in the right foreground is a B-17 Flying Fortress; the others are B-24 Liberators. (CWM11001)

Coastal Command Harbour, Oban, L.R. Aldwinckle. The Short Sunderland flying boats, shown here being serviced in their Scottish harbour by small boats, carried the war to enemy submarines. Nicknamed the "Flying Porcupine", the heavily armed Sunderland had power turrets in nose and tail, each with four .303 machine guns. (CWM10651)

Air Raid on San Giusto, Pisa, Paul Goranson. Goranson was struck by the beauty that sometimes marked destruction. Bombers, searchlights, cloud, and fire combine to produce a scene suggestive of Dante's Inferno. (CWM11435)

Night Target, Germany, Miller Brittain. As soon as one searchlight found a target, several others would "steeple" it to pinpoint it for the ack-ack. Brittain, a New Brunswick painter who briefly served in the RCAF before becoming a war artist, marvelled at the eerie magic of the deadly searchlights: "A great red flare bursts and out of it come long silver streamers like some sort of enchanted tree." (CWM10889)

The Survivor, Eric Aldwinckle. Aldwinckle was
attached to Coastal Command and Fighter Command
and sometimes flew on operational missions to try to
understand the airmen he painted and admired.
"[They have] an awareness that is not found in
ordinary people," he said. (CWM10733)

Tank Convoy, Bruno Bobak. The youngest war artist, at 21, Bobak portrayed
Canadian armour moving through rugged Italian terrain. The advance was
awkward and dangerous; the many hills and rivers made progress slow, and
Allied tanks were completely outclassed by the *Wehrmacht*'s Tiger with its 88mm
gun and heavier armour. (CWM11992)

Above, *Battleground before Ortona;* below, *Hitler Line Barrage, Italy;* both by Lawren P. Harris. These almost surreal landscapes capture the utter devastation left by the war's passage. Harris' father, the famous Group of Seven painter, had been a war artist in the Great War. (CWM12657, CWM12694)

The Hitler Line, Charles Comfort. 1 Canadian Corps' breaching of the Hitler Line in May 1944 opened the way to Rome. Comfort's striking image suggests the strength of the *Wehrmacht*'s defensive works — and the resolution of the by-now battle-hardened Canadian troops. (CWM12296)

enced — it was the first time he had commanded a division in battle." More-over, Simonds' own response to the proposed visit had been "For God's sake keep him away."

By the time McNaughton paid his visit — after the fighting had ended — the division had marched 130 miles through the dust and heat, and had paid a heavy price: 2,310 officers and men, including 562 dead. All the same, the losses were not unusually high for a division in constant battle, and the division — often nicknamed the "Old Red Patch" for its distinguishing rectangular shoulder-flash — had faced a series of graduated challenges that prepared the Canadian formation for bigger tests to come.

UP THE ITALIAN BOOT TO ORTONA

While the Germans and the Allies battled over Sicily, events in Italy took their own course. Benito Mussolini's policies had brought nothing but disaster, and on July 25 Il Duce was toppled from power. On September 8, 1943, Marshal Pietro Badoglio, Mussolini's successor, announced that Italy had surrendered unconditionally, thus becoming the first Axis power to pull out of the war. Unfortunately, that changed little; the Germans simply took control of the country, put most of the Italian army in prisoner of war camps, and let loose the Gestapo to enforce Hitler's will. In Italy, as in Sicily, the Allies would have to advance against the entrenched and disciplined lines of the *Wehrmacht*.

Just before the assault on Italy, 1st Canadian Division headquarters issued its men a little booklet on Italy, mixing history, commentary, and crude stereotype. The Fascist Party, they were told, "is not in the least like our Conservative, C.C.F. or Liberal parties." The discipline of the Italian people was "generally slack" and they would "take to guns and knives instead of fists to settle a quarrel.... As to the women," the booklet said, more in hope than in expectation, "the less you have to do with them, the better."

The Allied plan called for the Eighth Army to cross the Straits of Messina on September 3 and surge up the toe of the Italian boot. The Fifth U.S. Army would land at Salerno, south of Naples, on September 9 and cut off the enemy's retreat. These landings were carried out as planned. Meanwhile the 1st Canadian Division landed just north of the port of Reggio Calabria and took it without effective resistance. Indeed, the Van Doos invaded a fort near Reggio only to find all its officers eating breakfast in their best uniforms while the fort's guns stood unmanned. "Seen very little of Jerry," a private wrote home

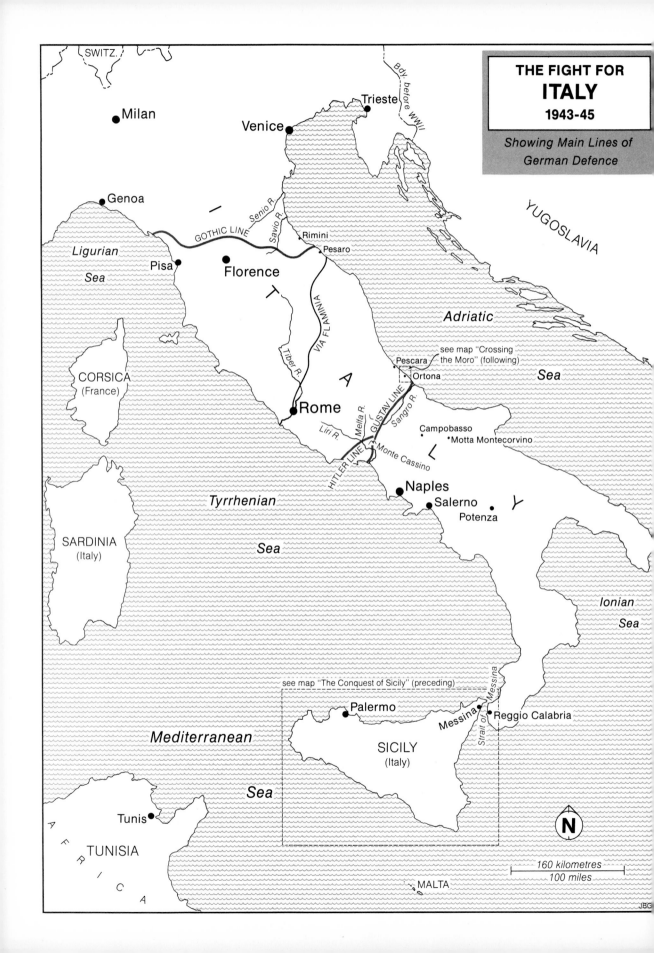

SWITZ.

Bdy before WWII

THE FIGHT FOR
ITALY
1943-45

Showing Main Lines of German Defence

Milan

Venice

Trieste

Genoa

YUGOSLAVIA

Ligurian

GOTHIC LINE

Senio R.

Savio R.

Sea

Pisa

Rimini

Pesaro

Florence

Adriatic

VIA FLAMINIA

Tiber R.

CORSICA
(France)

see map "Crossing
the Moro" (following)

Pescara

Sea

Ortona

GUSTAV LINE

Sangro R.

Rome

Liri R.

Melfa R.

Campobasso

Motta Montecorvino

HITLER LINE

Monte Cassino

Tyrrhenian

Naples

SARDINIA
(Italy)

Salerno

Potenza

Sea

Ionian

Sea

see map "The Conquest of Sicily" (preceding)

Palermo

Messina

Strait of Messina

Reggio Calabria

Mediterranean

SICILY
(Italy)

Sea

N

Tunis

TUNISIA

AFRICA

MALTA

160 kilometres
100 miles

JBG

to Canada on September 14, "and the Wop isn't worth bothering with." Within a week, in the face of *Wehrmacht* delaying actions, the division had pushed seventy-five miles forward.

After the Salerno landing, the Eighth and Fifth armies had to join up as quickly as possible. Montgomery ordered Simonds to take Potenza, a road junction fifty miles east of Salerno, and this was accomplished on September 20. Two days later, however, Simonds fell ill with jaundice and was replaced temporarily by Brigadier Christopher Vokes, a big, explosive peacetime soldier. On October 1, Naples fell to the Allies, and by that date the Canadian division — some of which had been operating along the east coast towards Taranto — was reunited in the centre of the peninsula, close to Campobasso.

By this time Hitler had ordered that Rome must be held at all cost, not only for its symbolic value but because its airfields were perilously close to Germany. The first sign of the new enemy resolve came at Motta Montecorvino, where the Royal Canadian Regiment and tanks of the Calgary Regiment ran into the 3rd regiment of the 1st Parachute Division, a *Luftwaffe* formation with a well-earned reputation as an elite force. The paras resisted fiercely for as long as possible, then withdrew without notice to the next defensible feature. The tactic was delay; the Germans had decided to move into a winter defence line fifty miles north of Campobasso, and south of Rome.

The delaying actions lasted for another month, and were costly to the advancing Canadians. Farley Mowat later wrote that he went out with the padre and a burial party to recover the bodies of some Hastings and Prince Edward Regiment soldiers killed a few days earlier. The bodies had bloated. "They did not look like men anymore. They had become obscene parodies of men.... For the first time I truly understood that the dead...were dead." At the time he wrote home to say that he wondered why it was Lieutenant Swayle and his men who had died. "Why him? Why them? And when will it be you? That's the sort of question you ask yourself."

Decisions were now being made that would determine the deaths and lives of many more Canadians. The original intent had been that the 1st Division would return to England after Sicily was taken. That, obviously, had not happened. Public opinion had been so positive about the fighting in Sicily that Ottawa was persuaded that Italy was a good place to send troops. Now, after several efforts by the Canadian government, the British agreed to send I Canadian Corps headquarters (some 8,500 men in all, including ancillary units) under General Harry Crerar to Italy, along with the 5th Canadian Armoured Division. The Canadian convoy was attacked by *Luftwaffe* JU-88s and one ship sank, though so slowly that there was no loss of life. Among the rescued were ninety-eight Canadian nursing sisters.

The defence minister, Colonel Ralston, had overridden General McNaughton's desire to keep the army together and had decided that the opportunity for a corps to fight and gain experience — and flattering publicity — was too great to pass up. General Alexander in Italy was unhappy that the decision had been made without consulting him. A raw armoured division was the last thing needed in Italy's steep hills and narrow valleys. McNaughton was furious that his cherished Canadian army would be split. The general's performance on exercises in England had led the British to doubt his ability to command the First Canadian Army in action, and now their concern — and his unhappiness — resulted in his enforced resignation from command by the end of the year. Having proved himself with the infantry division, Simonds took command of the 5th Armoured as of November 1 (although the division was not ready for action until the beginning of 1944). Vokes — whom Montgomery described as "a good rough cook" in comparison to the brilliant Simonds — was confirmed in command of the 1st Division.

The decision to split the army meant that Canada now had to maintain two supply and reinforcement lines — one to Britain and, once the invasion of France had taken place, to north-west Europe, and one through the Mediterranean to Italy. For a small nation this was a heavy burden, absorbing scarce manpower without any of the benefits of economy of scale. From that point of view, McNaughton's desire to keep the army together made eminent sense. But Ralston knew that troops had to see action and commanders had to gain experience. Also, ordinary Canadians felt that, without soldiers fighting, Canada was somehow out of the war. No number of bombers or corvettes could substitute for fighting divisions.

The Allies' advance on Rome was now blocked by the formidable obstacle of the Germans' winter line, which had its Adriatic base on the Moro river, two miles south of the town of Ortona. After stiff fighting on the upper Sangro River, Vokes' division was given the task of taking Ortona. As usual, the geography of the Italian peninsula favoured the defenders. First the division had to cross the Moro, an effort begun on December 6, 1943. The valley of the Moro was deep, cut by gullies and ridges, and, thanks to *Wehrmacht* demolitions, unbridged. The German defenders were the crack 90th Light Panzer Grenadier Division, famous from the desert war.

Initially the attack went well, infantry of the Princess Patricia's Canadian Light Infantry (PPCLI) fording the Moro at midnight without any covering fire. The enemy, surprised in their beds at Villa Rogatti, were driven out of the village. At San Leonardo the Seaforth Highlanders had more difficulty once the lead companies had waded across the Moro. Fifteen to twenty machine guns sprayed the attackers, who had only a small bridgehead after five hours' fighting. The morning brought the inevitable heavy counter-attack on the PPCLI, but that was driven off with the aid of British tanks. So was a second enemy effort, supported this time by Panzers. The German unit's war diarist praised the fire discipline of the Patricias, "who let our tanks approach to within 50 metres and then destroyed them." The Moro bridgeheads survived.

By December 8, the Canadians were ready for another major two-brigade assault across the river, supported by the troops who had won the bridge-head two days before. The soldiers were shivering from tension and cold weather, despite their long johns, wool shirts, khaki sweaters, scarves, and battledress jackets. Each man carried his rifle, several clips of .303 ammunition, an awkward and uncomfortable "tin hat" (worn now over a wool toque or balaclava), a shovel, a can or two of food, cigarettes, lucky charms and a few personal mementos, and extra socks. Most carried a grenade or two, and some unlucky souls were inevitably detailed to lug extra magazines of ammunition for the three Bren guns that each platoon of infantry had. The platoon commander's signaller had a heavy radio with a large aerial whipping back and forth. Soldiers waddled rather than ran; they could hardly do more.

Matthew Halton of the CBC watched the preliminary bombardment of the German lines over the Moro and recorded the scene for broadcast back to Canada:

> It's a terrific shelling. We get one or two enemy shells every minute on this position; the Germans get hundreds every minute on theirs. The valley of the Moro down there, through which our infantry have to attack, is one dense pall of smoke, and we can hardly see the town of Ortona, just a few miles away.

Led by the Royal Canadian Regiment and the 48th Highlanders, the division fought its way towards San Leonardo, greatly assisted by a field company of the Royal Canadian Engineers who built a bridge across the river despite heavy enemy fire. Tanks could now get across the Moro to beat back the enemy's counter-attacks, though mines and the terrain still posed enormous problems for the armour. Meanwhile the Seaforths, with tanks of the Calgary Regiment, were assisting in the battle for the town by pressing out of their bridgehead. One company of infantry riding aboard a squadron of tanks suffered heavily — two tanks rolled off a cliff and another blew up on a mine — but five tanks and the thirty-nine surviving infantry cleared the town. Lieutenant J.F. Maclean of the Seaforths led his platoon so effectively in silencing the German machine-gunners that he won the Distinguished Service Order, an award only rarely given to junior officers. It was "our first real battle on a

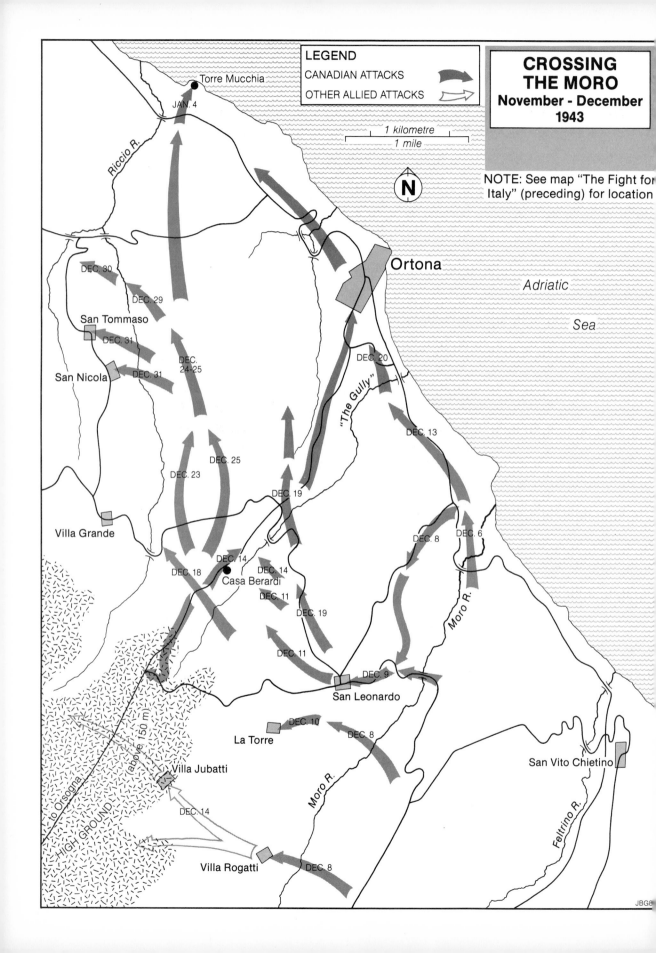

LEGEND

CANADIAN ATTACKS

OTHER ALLIED ATTACKS

CROSSING THE MORO
November - December
1943

1 kilometre
1 mile

N

NOTE: See map "The Fight for
Italy" (preceding) for location

Torre Mucchia

JAN. 4

Riccio R.

Ortona

Adriatic

Sea

DEC. 30

DEC. 29

San Tommaso

DEC. 31

DEC. 24-25

San Nicola

DEC. 31

DEC. 20

"The Gully"

DEC. 13

DEC. 25

DEC. 23

Villa Grande

DEC. 19

DEC. 8

DEC. 6

DEC. 18

DEC. 14

DEC. 14

Casa Berardi

DEC. 11

Moro R.

DEC. 19

DEC. 11

San Leonardo

DEC. 9

La Torre

DEC. 10

DEC. 8

San Vito Chietino

to Orsogna

(above 150 m)

Villa Jubatti

HIGH GROUND

DEC. 14

Moro R.

Villa Rogatti

DEC. 8

Feltrino R.

JBG8

divisional level with the Germans," the 1st Division's headquarters noted.

The Loyal Edmonton Regiment, who were in the thick of the fighting, had the grimness of the struggle eased by the presence within their lines of sheds full of hogsheads of maturing *vino*. "Most of these casks," the Eddies' padre remembered, "were being breached by 'stray bullets', shrapnel and 'other weapons'. There seemed to be a continuous party (with no cheese) interrupted by much fierce fighting against the enemy, they being only a short distance away."

Further counter-attacks by the *Wehrmacht* were beaten off, and the Germans finally conceded San Leonardo and withdrew to new positions. At the same time Field Marshal Kesselring, still trying to delay the Allies' advance at all cost, had the 2nd Battalion of the 3rd Parachute Regiment reinforce the *Wehrmacht* troops defending Ortona.

The Canadians had yet to reach Ortona. There was a lengthy and gruelling struggle around "The Gully", a long ravine that extended in front of the Ortona–Orsogna road. Here the mud was almost as much of an enemy as the Germans, impeding movement and engulfing the tanks and trucks. The Germans were dug into the forward slope of the ravine, fighting with a ferocity that was, for the Canadians, absolutely unprecedented. Not until December 13, when an attack by Seaforth Highlanders and the West Nova Scotia Regiment made some headway, was the defence breached. Then the Van Doos took up the charge, aiming at Casa Berardi, a grandly named cluster of farm buildings.

Defending the Casa were units of the 1st Parachute Division. At the van of the attack were the eighty-one men of the Van Doos' C Company, led by Captain Paul Triquet and backed by seven tanks of the Ontario Regiment. The Canadians jumped off at 7:00 A.M., after an hour of artillery preparation, and at first made good progress. But after they had gained a few hundred yards, the Germans counter-attacked with four tanks and a company of infantry. The exchange of fire came to an astonishing halt when an Italian woman and two children headed for the Canadian position. It resumed after they were under cover, and once a second Panzer had been destroyed the counter-attack fizzled out.

By this point, C Company had fifty men left. The surviving tanks tackled the machine guns that had caused most of the casualties, and Triquet carried on towards the farmhouses, still a mile and a half away. By noon, Triquet's command had shrunk to thirty men, and the Germans had effectively surrounded the little band. As Triquet told his men, "Never mind them, they can't shoot. There are enemies in front of us, behind us and on our flanks, there is only one safe place, that is on the objective." That seemed true, and by 2:00 P.M. Triquet had finally reached Casa Berardi, with fourteen men and the tanks. Casa Berardi was still occupied by the paratroopers, so Triquet had to clear the buildings while simultaneously beating off enemy attacks. The order of the day was "Ils ne passeront pas," and indeed the Germans did not pass. All through the rest of that day and into the night the Van Doos held their prize, until at 11:00 P.M. reinforcements arrived.

The battle continued all the next day. The reinforcing company of the Royal 22e suffered heavily, and additional reinforcements did not arrive until after midnight on the second day of battle. The Royal Canadian Regiment linked up with the Van Doos and consolidated the breakthrough on December 19. c Company by this point had nine men left including its commander. Triquet, thirty-three years old, was promoted to major and won the Victoria Cross, the first awarded to a Canadian in Italy.

Ortona, the anchor of the German line, now seemed open to the Canadians. But Hitler had put the highest priority on holding the town, and the Germans dutifully obeyed. By December 21, the Seaforth Highlanders and the Loyal Edmonton Regiment were clearing houses in the town, struggling forward house by house and street by street. The more experienced soldiers of the 1st Parachute Division had used demolitions effectively to channel the attackers into the main square, which they had selected as a "killing zone" and surrounded with machine guns and mortars. They also attempted to mousetrap the advancing infantrymen into houses wired with explosives, blowing up the house once the Canadians were inside. A platoon of the Edmonton Regiment was destroyed that way, except for one soldier who was found alive in the rubble after more than eighty hours. But the Canadians could play that game as well: infantry pioneers laid charges under two buildings occupied by the Germans, and an estimated two enemy platoons were buried by the simultaneous explosions.

Most of the struggle for Ortona took place in the row houses of the town. Mouseholing parties blasted through walls with explosives, then advanced with grenades and Sten guns clearing the path. It was brutal fighting, like a little Stalingrad. As General Vokes said, "Everything before Ortona was a nursery tale." Halton of the CBC told his audience, with wartime hyperbole, "The Germans were demons; the Canadians were possessed by demons. The more murderous the battle, the harder both sides fought...." Yet on Christmas Day, in the ruins of the Church of Santa Maria di Constantinopoli, Christmas dinner was somehow put together for the Seaforth Highlanders. "This was really a fantastic thing," Halton told Canada:

> not four hundred yards from the enemy, carol singers, the platoons coming
> in relays to eat a Christmas dinner — men who hadn't had their clothes off

in thirty days coming in and eating their dinners, and carol singers singing "Silent Night".

"Well," the padre of the regiment said, "at last I've got you all in church." For many of the Seaforths, this Christmas dinner was their last supper.

The 48th Highlanders had no Christmas respite — or dinner. They had worked their way behind the German defences on December 22–23 in an attempt to cut off the retreat of the paratroopers, and they spent forty-eight hours under constant fire. Not until Christmas night did reinforcements from the Saskatoon Light Infantry, a machine-gun regiment, make it to the 48th's lines; tanks of the Ontario Regiment got there the next night.

By December 27, the town was almost entirely in Canadian hands. That night the Germans simply disappeared in a well-managed withdrawal, all the more impressive for being staged when the Canadians were breathing down their throats. Ortona had been taken at last.

The 1st Canadian Division had lost 2,339 officers and men since the first attack on the Moro on December 8. Sickness or battle exhaustion had forced the evacuation of 1,600 more, including Brigadier Graham of the 1st Brigade. While reinforcements had been received, the division was still more than a thousand men below strength. Worse, every infantry battalion had suffered 50 per cent casualties in its rifle companies, the experienced men killed and wounded being virtually irreplaceable. The survivors were shaken and exhausted.

"Without a pause for reorganization," General Vokes said, "the offensive power of an infantry division was bound to become spent, not for lack of offensive spirit, but because the quality of team play within the rifle companies had deteriorated." That was true enough; indeed the entire Allied attack was grinding to a halt. Even so, Ortona had been a victory for the Canadians. "We smashed the 90th Panzer Grenadier Division," Vokes reported, "and we gave the 1st German Parachute Division a mauling which it will long remember." The 1st Canadian Division — and the widows and grieving mothers of its many dead — would remember it too.

NORTH TO THE SENIO

The Canadians got their respite, but the winter of 1944 was no Italian holiday. Although the front was largely static, patrolling and limited attacks continued. One private in the 48th Highlanders wrote on January 27 of "the whistling shells and whirr of bullets.... My nerves are not what they used to be and Jerry is really putting up quite a fight." But there were no major attacks and that allowed I Canadian Corps to go through a number of command changes. Guy Simonds left the 5th Canadian Armoured Division before it had seen much action to return to England and take command of II Canadian Corps for the upcoming invasion of France. He was succeeded by Major-General E.L.M. Burns, an intellectual but uncharismatic soldier who had served in the Permanent Force's signal corps. In March, Lieutenant-General Crerar returned to England to take over the First Canadian Army and Burns became commander of I Canadian Corps. Italy had been the training ground for Simonds and, less so, for Crerar. Montgomery, transferred to command the imminent D-Day invasion, would remember them both.

Despite the advances of the Allies, Rome remained in German hands, protected by heavy defences. The Americans had landed at Anzio, near the Italian capital, in January, but the Germans had quickly sealed off the beachhead. Farther south, the Eighth Army's advance had been blocked by the Gustav Line (and, a few miles behind that, the Adolf Hitler line). Over them all towered the massive bulk of Monte Cassino, impregnable and awesome, topped by the ruins of its great Benedictine monastery. During the early spring the Eighth Army — which, in addition to its Canadian divisions, had Indian, New Zealand, Polish, Greek, and British formations — was transferred secretly to the Monte Cassino area.

The battle for Rome began at 11:00 P.M. on May 11, when a thousand guns opened up on the defences of the Gustav Line. Tanks of the 1st Canadian Armoured Brigade participated in the opening battles in support of the 8th Indian Division. Brigadier Bill Murphy, in command of the brigade, wrote proudly, "My tanks were the first over the river.... Our losses in both tanks and personnel have been astoundingly light thank God and we are still full of fight." The 1st Canadian Division joined in on May 16, its actions helping to clear the way for the Poles who finally captured Monte Cassino on May 18. The Gustav Line had been breached; the Adolf Hitler Line was next.

I Canadian Corps moved into the action on May 23, Canadian soldiers fighting as a corps for the first time during the war. The French Expeditionary Corps had pushed through a lightly fortified part of the Hitler Line on May 17 and threatened the German rear, but the defences in front of the Canadian Corps remained strong. In a day-long and costly battle the Canadian 1st and 5th Armoured divisions cracked the Hitler Line, with its earthworks, pillboxes, bunkers, mines, and huge concentrations of concertina wire that hung up unlucky soldiers just as it had their fathers in the trenches of Flanders. The tanks poured through the gap carved out by the infantry. Lieutenant John Windsor, a troop commander in Lord Strathcona's Horse, remembered his regiment pushing forward up the Liri valley towards the Melfa River. "A mile, two miles, three miles, crashing through tangled woods and trim orchards." Others had been hit, Windsor said, "but I was indestructible." A moment later, a German shell crashed into his Sherman. It promptly burned, or "brewed up", and Windsor was left blind for life. His regiment's tanks crossed the Melfa, however, and with a company from the Westminster Regiment held their ground in the face of fierce counter-attacks. Major J.K. Mahony of the Westminsters led the Canadians' defence and, though twice wounded, held on, his men taking fifty prisoners, killing more Germans, and knocking out a Panther tank and three self-propelled guns. Mahony won the Victoria Cross, and the Strathconas' reconnaissance troop officer, Lieutenant E.J. Perkins, was awarded the Distinguished Service Order.

The same day, the Americans broke out of the Anzio bridgehead, and they soon linked up with General Mark Clark's Fifth U.S. Army (and its attached Brazilian Expeditionary Force) advancing northward. That threatened Rome, and the Allied advance turned into a pursuit of a shaken enemy. Peter Stursberg of the CBC reported on May 26 that "It's becoming a mad chase in blinding dust over bumpy mud roads to keep up with the Canadian advance now." Barry Rowland, the chaplain of the Irish Regiment of Canada (a Toronto unit in the 5th Armoured Division), wrote that "Our lads are doing a splendid job pushing Jerry right out of the war. They have taken a good number of prisoners and they are a poor lot." In fact, the inexperienced 5th and its corps headquarters contributed to a massive traffic jam in the narrow valley, making it easier for the Germans to get away. For General Burns, the ungenial Canadian commander, it was a first black mark. (A private in a 1st Division unit wrote home that "the censor would never let my opinion" of the 5th Armoured be sent in a letter.) On June 4, a few days after the Canadian Corps had been put into army reserve, the Americans liberated Rome, the first Axis capital to be taken.

Two days later, though, the Allies invaded France, and the Italian theatre became secondary in the eyes of the public and press at home. That hurt the soldiers still fighting in Italy; a Canadian killed there was just as dead as one killed in Normandy. Insult was added to injury when American-born Nancy, Lady Astor, the first British woman Member of Parliament, called the Eighth Army "D-Day dodgers", implying that its men were almost deliberately avoiding service in the "real war" in France. As a result, the bitter song "D-Day Dodgers" (sung to the tune of "Lili Marlene") became popular with the troops:

We are the D-Day Dodgers, out in Italy,
Always on the *vino*, always on the spree,
Eighth Army skivers and their tanks,

We go to war, in ties and slacks,
We are the D-Day Dodgers, in sunny Italy.

Lady Astor's contribution to morale did nothing to stop the advance. The Fifth and Eighth armies moved north from Rome, the Americans along the west coast towards Pisa, the Commonwealth forces towards Florence. Again the Germans used skilful rearguard actions and demolitions to buy time, but by August Florence was taken and, on September 2, Pisa. In August, however, three American and four French divisions had been pulled out of the line for an amphibious assault on the south coast of France. The shrunken Allied armies now prepared to assault the Gothic Line — a defensive barricade just north of the Via Flaminia that the Germans had been preparing since before Rome's liberation.

I Canadian Corps had had two months of rest, recuperation, and training. Most units were still below full strength (and there were complaints about the training of reinforcements), but they were ready to tackle the eastern end of the Gothic Line, anchored at the town of Pesaro.

The attack began on August 25. Six rivers lay between the Canadians and their objective of Rimini. Each was a major obstacle defended by a waiting enemy; each was crossed at heavy cost. The West Nova Scotia Regiment got caught in a minefield that the Germans skilfully covered with small-arms fire and turned into a killing ground. Nonetheless, by August 31 Canadians had a small foothold in the Gothic Line, obliging the shaken Germans — who had been surprised by the speed and depth of the Canadian penetration — to pull units from other sectors to check the corps's advance. That helped the Americans' progress, but slowed the Canadians, whose men were badly in need of a breathing spell.

The Germans also brought their 56-ton Tiger tanks into action in Italy for the first time. "We kept hitting it," a major in the 8th Hussars wrote of the first encounter his Shermans had with the Panzer, "but our 75mm shells just bounced off." If the Tiger's 88mm gun hit a Sherman, on the other hand, it was game over. However, as Brigadier Murphy wrote his family — in words that probably came more easily to a brigadier than to a tank commander — the differences in quality between the German and Allied tanks mattered less in Italy's close country than elsewhere. "We can use ground and creep up on him — manoeuvring until we can bring our guns to bear on a weak spot on his tank — all of which are known to us....we invariably heavily outnumber him. So we engage him from hull down positions with some tanks and creep up on him from the side with others."

Sometimes other methods had to be used to destroy the Panzers. In one action on the Savio River, Private Ernest Smith of the Seaforth Highlanders stood up in full view of an approaching Panther to fire his PIAT. The projectile hit the tank, but ten German Panzer-grenadiers dropped off the tank's back and charged at Smith. "Without hesitation," the Canadian official history said, "he moved into the centre of the road, shot down four of them with his tommy gun, and dispersed the remainder." A second tank now opened fire and more of the enemy began closing in on the Canadian, but Smith replenished his ammunition from a wounded Seaforth and fought off the Germans. Smoky Smith's raw courage was honoured with the Victoria Cross.

Not until September 22, after almost a month's heavy fighting that cost 2,511 casualties including 626 killed in action, did I Canadian Corps break through the Apennine barrier. They had savaged eleven German divisions — one German commander called them "right good soldiers" — and before them now stretched the great northern Italian plain.

Progress unfortunately was slow. The rains had come, turning the dust of summer into the mud of October and November. Tanks sank to their bellies in the ooze. The Germans, bruised though they were, remained "right good soldiers" themselves, and the *Wehrmacht* had lost none of its skill in defence. Every river required a major assault, hampered by the difficulty tanks had in operating in the mud. The new Eighth Army Commander, Sir Oliver Leese, had blamed Canadian delays on General Burns, a humourless officer with the ironic nickname "Smiling Sunray", and had removed him. His successor, brought from France, was no better loved by his men but had a shrewder grasp of Allied diplomacy. Lieutenant-General Charles Foulkes, a university-educated Permanent Force officer who had served in the RCR, took over I Canadian Corps on November 5.

The corps took Ravenna on December 4 and reached the Senio River by Christmas. After the new year the corps cleared the Senio area and fighting then largely ceased as both sides hunkered down to wait out an appalling winter.

There were still casualties, however. A major with the Seaforth Highlanders was wounded on January 4, 1945, after "13 months without a scratch — which is a pretty good record nowadays." He wrote a friend that "I rather expected something to happen this time, though — felt my luck was running low — yet I got a terrific shock when it happened. There's something very personal about a machine gun bullet." He added that "It was quite an experience — lying waiting for the stretcher bearers and thinking, the blood, the pain, then the morphine, the evacuation, the operation, the first bed pan, all the things you had watched others go through and never thought that one day you might be doing the same thing. Yet here I am. It all seems so damned natural."

As it turned out, the Senio operations were the last for the Canadians in Italy. In February 1945, after months of pressure from Ottawa, the decision was made to reunite all the Canadian troops under the First Canadian Army in north-west Europe. General McNaughton's dream of a Canadian army pointing the way to Berlin was at last to be realized, in March.

The casualties suffered by Canadian forces in Italy had been heavy. In all, 92,757 Canadians served in the Italian theatre and more than a quarter became casualties. There were 408 officers and 4,991 men killed; 1,218 officers and 18,268 men were wounded; and 62 officers and 942 men became POWs. Another 365 died from other causes, bringing the total to 26,254. As always, most of the losses fell to the "poor bloody infantry" — always in the forefront, always with the worst of tasks.

The Allies returned to Europe to stay in the summer of 1943. American, British, and Canadian forces invaded Sicily on July 10, and landed in Italy on September 3.

The weak Italian divisions posted in Sicily put up little resistance and the
Canadians advanced quickly through a landscape of heat, dust, and scorpions.
Farther inland, however, the inexperienced 1st Division met the Germans. The
Princess Patricia's Canadian Light Infantry is shown in a stiff action at
Valguarnera on July 20.

Regalbuto was a tougher nut to crack, for the Hermann Goering Division was firmly entrenched on the heights overlooking the town. But a careful, well-planned flank attack forced a German withdrawal and the town fell on August 2. Sherman tanks of the Three Rivers Regiment are seen moving through the ruins after the battle.

Once Sicily fell, the Allies crossed the Straits of Messina to the toe of the Italian boot. Initially the advance northwards was rapid as the Nazis fell back, but skilful German rearguards imposed as much delay as they could. Here a Sherman of the Calgary Regiment provides support to the West Nova Scotia Regiment's advance on the village of Potenza.

As the Allies advanced towards Rome, Nazi resistance stiffened. These soldiers of the Carleton and York Regiment are working their way through the bleak alleys of Campochiaro in the face of sniper fire.

When the infantry finally stopped their advance, all too often they had the backbreaking work of digging themselves slit trenches in the stony Italian soil. Digging, as this private of the Royal Canadian Regiment knew, was the best protection against the *Wehrmacht*'s artillery.

Commanding in Italy was General Bernard Montgomery (left), efficient, nasty, difficult. In command of the Canadian Corps was General Harry Crerar (centre). No great commander, Crerar was stiff, cautious, and sensitive to political realities — which, for him, meant Canada's Minister of National Defence, Colonel J. Layton Ralston (right) — a much-decorated battalion commander in the Great War.

General Guy Simonds (on the right, talking with one of his brigadiers) led the 1st Canadian Division through Sicily, and then took over the 5th Canadian Armoured Division on the Italian mainland. Simonds was resourceful, ingenious, and tough, and was the only senior Canadian officer to win Montgomery's regard.

Ortona — an ancient town perched on cliffs above the Adriatic — had a valuable
modern port, and in December 1943 the Canadians were ordered to take the town
without damaging the port's facilities. The desperate struggle involved the most
vicious fighting I Canadian Corps faced in Italy. Here, Canadians move an anti-
tank gun into position.

German mortar-fire has caught a Bren gun carrier and other vehicles in Ortona in
the open. As the Italian winter hit the Allied campaign, the Canadians began to
suffer heavy losses from "battle exhaustion", the new term for what an earlier war
had called "shell shock".

Men of the Loyal Edmonton Regiment stay close to the wall as they move cautiously down the dangerous streets of Ortona to the next bout of house-to-house fighting.

Other Edmontons escort captured German paratroopers. The *Luftwaffe* soldiers had set hundreds of booby-traps which killed many Canadians as they "mouseholed" their way from house to house.

This *Luftwaffe* sergeant from the Hermann Goering Division seems no more than a boy, like so many of the soldiers on both sides. The photographs, two of himself and one of the Führer, suggest either that the corpse was rifled for papers and valuables or that the photographer tried too hard to make a point.

Despite the carnage, a traditional Christmas dinner was served in Ortona's Church of Santa Maria. These officers and men of the 2nd Infantry Brigade headquarters seem well scrubbed and cheerful — but very little *vino* is in evidence, a reminder that a few hundred yards away the killing continued.

Facing, top: once the Gustav and Hitler lines had been cracked, Rome fell and the advance northwards speeded up. Since the commander of this Sherman tank of the Calgary Regiment is fully exposed in the turret, he must have known that San Pancrazio was clear of the enemy by the time this picture was snapped on July 16, 1944.

One of the most popular cartoonists in the *Maple Leaf*, the newspaper printed for the troops in Italy (and later in north-west Europe), was Bing Coughlin. His "Herbie" was always in trouble with officers, sergeants, and signorinas. This is Herbie's grudging tribute to Smoky Smith, a private in the Seaforth Highlanders who won the vc for (among other things) tackling ten Germans single-handedly on the Savio River on October 22, 1944.

"THERE HE GOES WITH THAT SMOKEY SMITH STUFF AGAIN."

VI
CHANGES AT HOME

By 1943, the succession of Allied defeats had ceased, and victory seemed more likely than it had a year earlier. For the first time, Canadians and their government began to think of what their future would — and should — be like.

There were differences of opinion between regions, parties, and individual ministers, but everyone agreed that the post-war world had to be different from the pre-war one. The Depression had put hundreds of thousands out of work and onto relief, destroying families and fostering political repression at home and fascism and Communism abroad. Opinion polls — begun in Canada during the war by the Canadian Institute of Public Opinion and also taken secretly by the Wartime Information Board, the federal government's new propaganda agency — suggested that people feared the return of depressed economic conditions. They wanted security: they wanted to know that there would be jobs for them, and for their children. They wanted the federal government to intervene in the economy to ensure that their wartime economic gains could be protected. The *laissez-faire* attitudes that had been so dominant in the country's pre-war history had been shattered by years of hardship. After all, the controls and rationing that had been imposed during the war had given Canadians a far higher standard of living. Why should controls and planning not work just as well in peacetime?

THE EMERGENCE OF SOCIAL WELFARE

The Co-operative Commonwealth Federation was one of the major creators and beneficiaries of this new mood. Since its formation in 1932, the CCF had failed to make much headway with the electorate. Bad times seemingly did not help a party with radical ideas. Nor had Woodsworth's pacifism helped the party in the 1940 election. But the war got the social democrats moving,

164

particularly after Joe Noseworthy's victory over national Conservative leader Arthur Meighen in the York South by-election of February 9, 1942. That result made the country sit up and take notice of the CCF, and the party's stock began to rise as Canadians digested its message of nationalization, social welfare, and social security. In August 1943 the party captured thirty-four seats in the Ontario provincial election, a dramatic rise from holding no seats to forming the Opposition. That same month, the party won two federal by-elections, one each in Manitoba and Saskatchewan. By September the CCF had 29 per cent of the country's support in the national opinion polls. For the first time ever, it was ahead of the Liberals and Conservatives — by one point. This was an astonishing ascent from oblivion, a tribute to the wartime effectiveness of the party's message.

The Conservatives were the first to react to the changed national mood. Badly battered in the 1940 election, the Tories had dumped Dr. Robert Manion, their leader since 1938, at the first opportunity. From May 1940 until Meighen took over in November 1941 they had been led in Parliament by Richard B. Hanson, a lacklustre New Brunswicker who had served briefly in R.B. Bennett's cabinet. After the York South débâcle, Hanson once more led the party in the House, while Meighen glowered from Toronto and observers speculated that the historic party was on its deathbed, its policies of high tariffs, *laissez-faire*, and the maintenance of the imperial connection all seeming outdated in the midst of the war.

The party put on a new face at a "thinkers' meeting" in Port Hope, Ontario, at the beginning of September 1942, and pushed its way into the twentieth century. The emphasis on tariffs disappeared, to be replaced by "a New National Policy" with social security as its goal. James M. Macdonnell, the businessman who had organized the meeting, argued that the state "had to see that every citizen is provided with employment at a wage which will enable him to live in decency." To colleagues who were dubious about reform, he put the point more bluntly: "Would you rather adopt a policy which will retain the largest amount possible of free enterprise or — hand over to the CCF? Half a loaf is better than no bread." The Tories then staged a national convention in Winnipeg in December and, under the influence of the "Port Hopefuls", selected Manitoba's long-time premier, John Bracken, as party leader. (One of the defeated candidates for leader was a little-known Saskatchewan MP named John Diefenbaker.)

A dour, silent man who had been a professor of field husbandry at the Manitoba Agricultural College before his selection as Progressive premier in 1922, Bracken had eventually turned himself and his provincial party into Liberal-Progressives. His only connection with the Conservative Party, some said, was that his father had attended John A. Macdonald's funeral in 1891. As a condition of taking the leadership, Bracken insisted on changing the party's name to Progressive Conservative, in an attempt to link the Tories to the still-powerful memory of the Progressive Party, the farmers' movement of the 1920s. Although humorists gibed that the "Pro and Con" party was going in two directions at once, the selection of Bracken and the new name demonstrated that the Conservatives, now publicly committed to social security, full employment, collective bargaining, medical insurance, and free enterprise, were in the centre of the political spectrum. The CCF was on the left, and Mackenzie King's Liberals, absorbed in running the war effort, were now the right-wingers.

Not for long. While the prime minister and the key ministers in the Cabinet War Committee reeled under the weight of their responsibilities, other ministers and the bureaucracy had been quietly preparing their plans to deal with the expected post-war slump. One major weapon was already in place. Unemployment insurance had won provincial consent early in 1940 and had passed through Parliament in the summer of that year. There was a certain cruel irony that unemployment insurance came into effect when the war had all but eliminated unemployment, but that was quite deliberate. As an insurance scheme, the plan had to begin in good times so that a healthy balance of funds could be accumulated before the claims began.

The Department of Pensions and National Health, under British Columbia's Ian Mackenzie, was also at work. In March 1941 the minister organized a Committee on Reconstruction to study the effectiveness of wartime controls and their applicability in peacetime and to consider trade problems and the conversion of war industry to civilian uses. The research director of the committee, Leonard Marsh, prepared the committee's major work, the "Report on Social Security for Canada". The Marsh Report analysed Canada's existing social legislation, suggested improvements, and laid down the principles to be followed to make social security work. It called for "provision for unemployment, both economically and socially", which was to include programs to combat unemployment at the end of the war, retraining programs, and a "national reserve program of public employment projects". In other words, Ottawa had to be prepared to create jobs to cushion the shock of the transition to peace.

The Marsh Report also looked at the "universal risks" of sickness and old age and suggested a national health insurance plan — an idea that Ian Mackenzie's department had been working on for years and that the Liberals had ostensibly adopted back in 1919. Marsh called for universal old age pensions of $45 a month for married couples, and for family allowances of approximately $7.50 a month for each child. As the report demonstrated, a couple with three children under twelve needed $122.85 a month to live; two-thirds of the male heads of city families and three-quarters of rural families were below that minimum income level in 1941. It was a shocking situation, the best proof of the necessity for schemes like those suggested.

There was only one problem: all these proposals would cost money — an estimated $900 million, or more than 10 per cent of estimated post-war National Income. "Pie in the sky," the critics said.

The Marsh Report's blueprint for the future drew enormous public interest, but the King government's initial response was indifferent or hostile. The prime minister, whose 1918 book, *Industry and Humanity*, had served as a charter for his long tenure of office, was an undoubted supporter of improvements in social welfare — when the time was ripe. But the time had never been ripe. A pay-as-you-go policy of war finance meant that taxes were very high during the war: in 1943, a married man with two children and earnings of $5,000 paid $1,062 in tax and was obliged to put $600 more into compulsory savings. Four years earlier, in 1939, tax on that income had been only $134. King feared that social welfare would carry high taxes into peacetime, and that, he thought, could only help the Opposition. Moreover, he told the Liberal caucus in Parliament, he would not buy the voters' support in wartime with their own money. King also warned his party that Marsh's social welfare proposals amounted to "a social revolution — a levelling down of those who were privileged.... That this could not be done in a day, but would take years." All of this was typical of the caution that characterized the prime minister.

After the CCF came from nowhere to run a close second behind the Conservatives in Ontario in August 1943, and after the CCF won two of four federal by-elections a few weeks later, it only needed the shock of the September opinion polls before King was ready to think again. Something had to be done to meet the popular desire for security or else the Liberals would be certain of defeat.

As a result, the National Liberal Federation called its first major wartime meeting at the end of September. The delegates enthusiastically voted for resolutions that promised massive benefits to veterans. They cheered resolutions proposing a "national scheme of social insurance" to include protection against privation resulting from unemployment, accident, ill health, old age, and blindness. They called for better old age pensions. They urged that family allowances be put in place. They pledged support for labour's right to collective bargaining. And they called for full employment through the efforts of both "public and private enterprise". The Liberals, in other words, were back in a political mainstream that had veered sharply to the left.

And the Liberals had one advantage the CCF and Progressive Conservatives did not: they were in power and could implement their promises. The Speech from the Throne that opened the new session of Parliament on January 27, 1944 largely ignored the war. Instead it set out the government's "reconstruction" plans. The "post-war object of our domestic policy is social security and human welfare," the governor-general read. "The establishment of a national minimum of social security and human welfare should be advanced as rapidly as possible." The government pledged to create "useful work for all who are willing to work", to upgrade nutrition and housing, and to provide social insurance. The three main areas of its post-war planning were the demobilization, rehabilitation, and re-establishment of veterans; the reconversion of the economy to peace; and insurance against major economic and social hazards. To this end, three new departments were created: Reconstruction, National Health and Welfare, and Veterans Affairs. Moreover, the Liberals promised to introduce family allowances, and they pledged to seek the agreement of the provinces for health insurance and a "more generous" contributory old age plan. It was a virtual social revolution.

The government carried out almost all of its Throne Speech promises, although health insurance and a national contributory old age pension took more than two decades to reach fruition. And, as was so often the case, the wily Mackenzie King saw the Tories play into his hands. The issue this time was family allowances.

One of the major reasons the government had come to support the idea of the "baby bonus" was to relieve pressure on the wartime system of wage controls, as the National War Labour Board had recommended in August 1943. If the government could not remove the freeze on incomes for fear of starting the inflationary spiral again, then "we can think of no other solution for the case of the head of the family who is receiving a substandard wage, than a system of family allowances." The Cabinet considered the board's report in September 1943, but the ministers worried about the political implications. Would not English Canadians see family allowances as a devious way of helping French Canadians with their large broods? The prime minister himself was again reluctant to hand out public money: "to tell the country that everyone was to get a family allowance was sheer folly.... Great care had to be taken in any monies given out from the Treasury...." But when King talked to one of the officials in his office and learned that the man had been raised and educated on a Great War widow's pension paid to his mother, he suddenly realized that a pension differed from a family allowance only in amount, not in principle. Reassured by this fresh perspective, he turned his great energies to getting family allowances into place.

To his surprise, the prime minister found that the Department of Finance was also in favour of the plan. The deputy minister told the Cabinet that without the baby bonus Ottawa would have to find huge sums "to make possible municipally managed low-rental housing projects.... With children's allowances on anything like an adequate scale, it should be possible to avoid such a program." The bureaucrats had also come to the conclusion that money had to be distributed to people who would spend it; only in that way would there be sufficient demand for goods and services to keep the economy running at the end of the war when the munitions factories shut down. In other words, it was better to give away money than to see the country slide back into a depression. Although some powerful ministers opposed the measure on the grounds of cost (and, as the recently converted King complained, because they "still think they can go out and shoot a deer or bison for breakfast"), the Cabinet went along. To many of the ministers, the argument that family allowances might actually help the nation's children to grow up healthier and stronger did not seem as important as the financial implications.

The bill proposing the baby bonus went to Parliament in the summer of 1944, suggesting $5 a month for children up to five years of age, and rising by steps to $8 for those from thirteen to fifteen. As important, the bill directed that the money was to be paid to *mothers*; for hundreds of thousands of Canadian women, this was the first money that did not have to be extracted from sometimes grudging husbands. (In Quebec, where the dependent status of women was enshrined in provincial law, protests from the provincial government forced Ottawa to pay the baby bonus to fathers!)

The family allowances were not to begin until July 1, 1945, after the next federal election. Some Tory MPs were outraged by the plan because they felt it was designed to bolster sagging Liberal fortunes in Quebec. One Toronto MP called it a device for "bonussing families who have been unwilling to defend their country. It was a bribe of the most brazen character, made chiefly to one province and paid for by the rest." He was ejected from the House of Commons when he refused to withdraw those words. Tory leader John Bracken also called the bill a "political bribe" while Conservative Premier George Drew of Ontario said that "one isolationist province" could not "dominate the destiny of a divided Canada". Even Charlotte Whitton, the Tories' leading expert on social welfare, added her two cents' worth:

> erratic, irresponsible, bewildered of mind, and socially incapable, feeble-minded and mentally affected parents are definitely the progenitors of many of our largest families.... payments of cash grants would perpetuate this menace.

Whitton went on to say that the baby bonus would extend "the uneven rate of natural increase" of Canada's newer racial stocks at the expense of less prolific British Canadians. Some Progressive Conservatives, such as John Diefenbaker, spoke in support of family allowances, and no Conservative voted against the measure on second reading, but the damage was done. For all the lofty aims of Bracken and the Port Hopefuls, the public perceived the Tory party as against social welfare, against Quebec, and against ethnic Canadians.

Family allowances did prove to be a very potent force in the elections, and it would be naive to assume that this was not anticipated by those who charted the bill's passage. But votes were not the only motive. The baby bonus was calculated to put almost $250 million a year into the hands of women who would spend it on their children. They would buy clothes and milk, medicines and books, cribs and carriages, and every dollar spent would help keep factories and farms producing. Family allowances were in this respect similar to veterans' benefits, to assistance to industry and farmers, to funds for the construction of housing. The Liberals had accepted the economic gospel of economist John Maynard Keynes, a creed that called for government spending in hard times to keep employment up. Everyone expected post-war times to be tough, and the King government had demonstrated that it was ready to act. When the boys came home from the war this time, they really would find a Canada fit for heroes. Or so the government desperately hoped.

ON THE WORLD STAGE

If the Liberal government had created a charter for the home front with its social security package, it was taking equally revolutionary steps in international affairs.

Canada had gone to war at Britain's side, and had solidified its relations with the United States at Ogdensburg and Hyde Park. But once the United States came into the war, the necessity for close and continuous strategic and economic planning between London and Washington tended to leave Canada and the other small allies out of the picture. This was profoundly disturbing to Canada's government; politicians, exerting themselves to the utmost to win the war, felt entitled to status and recognition.

But how could the King government's desire for a share in the war's planning be accommodated, given the need for swift and efficient action? If Canada had a place at the table, then Australia, Brazil, The Netherlands, and Czechoslovakia would be entitled to seats, too. Difficult as it was, the conundrum was not insoluble. The Canadians came up with an answer they called the "functional principle".

The functional principle took advantage of Canada's strengths in some key areas. It recognized that there was little point in demanding a share in strategic planning: Britain and the United States could never concede that — and, to be honest, Canada had little to contribute there in any case. On the other hand, the United States and Britain had created the Combined Food Board in January 1942 to allocate scarce food supplies. The United States was the greatest food exporter in the world and Britain the largest importer, so their right to take decisions on the CFB was unquestioned. But the second great food-producing nation on the Allied side was Canada, and justice and logic demanded that Canada have a share in the decisions that were to govern the distribution of food produced by prairie farmers. When other countries produced food in similar quantities, Canadians said, then they should have a place as well; until then, they could sit on the sidelines. The same situation existed in other areas under the aegis of the Combined Production and Resources Board and the Combined Munitions Assignment Board.

The Canadian government pressed its case in London and Washington. The Americans generally supported the idea of Canadian representation — if London agreed. The British were upset, however, at the upstart dominion seeking a share in decisions. The Combined Food Board, Whitehall argued, was not a decision-making body and could only make recommendations — it wasn't worth much, the message seemed to suggest. On the other hand, the British argued that Canadian representation "would not make for technical efficiency". That type of two-faced argument drove officials in Ottawa's East Block wild.

For the first time, the government had some cards to play and appeared willing to play them toughly. The country had given Britain a billion-dollar gift at the beginning of 1942 to pay for the food and munitions Britain so desperately needed. London could scarcely expect further gifts if it treated Canada "as a small boy to be relegated to the sidelines", or so the governor of the Bank of Canada told the British high commissioner in Ottawa. That was a threat — and one that had to be heeded. And it marked a revolution in Canadian foreign policy. The colony that had gone to war in 1939 still firmly attached to Mama's apron-strings was growing up.

The result was full Canadian membership on the Combined Food Board and the Combined Production and Resources Board, something no other Allied nation won. Buoyed by their hard-won success with the functional principle, the government detailed its claims publicly in a major address by the prime minister in Parliament on July 9, 1943:

> ...authority in international affairs must not be concentrated exclusively in the largest powers.... A number of new international organizations are likely to be set up as a result of the war. In the view of the government, effec-

tive representation on these bodies should neither be restricted to the largest states nor necessarily extended to all states. Representation should be determined on a functional basis which will admit to full membership those countries, large or small, which have the greatest contribution to make to the particular object in question....

Although that principle was never conceded by the Great Powers, it guided Canada's fight to get a seat on the directing committee of the United Nations Relief and Rehabilitation Administration, set up in 1943 to organize and run the great relief effort that would be necessary in Europe and Asia after the war. Ottawa's attempt failed, the Soviet Union proving no more amenable to Canadian claims of special status than Britain had been. But Canada did win a place on the UNRRA supplies committee, and a seat at the steering committee when supply questions were under discussion. That was more than might have been expected.

Moreover, Canadians were arguing their case in other areas. Civil air transport was going to boom after the war, and a whole series of agreements and regulations had to be worked out. Situated as it was, graced with thousands of wartime pilots, and with Trans-Canada Airlines and Canadian Pacific Airlines aspiring to world-class status, Canada demanded a role. To everyone's surprise, the country made a critical contribution to a 1944 conference in Chicago on air transport, mediating between London and Washington and drafting the charter that led to the creation of the International Civil Aviation Organization. The same thing occurred in discussions on post-war international finance: a Canadian draft plan was an important compromise document at the 1944 Bretton Woods Conference that laid out the shape of the post-war financial world. And Canada, represented by Lester Pearson and his colleagues in External Affairs, was in the midst of the fray in discussions leading to the formation of the United Nations Organization.

If Canada had bargained toughly with the Great Powers about the economic direction of the war, it did less well with the United States on continental questions. The beginning of war in the Pacific and the Japanese threat to North America had forced both Canada and the United States to pay attention to defence on the west coast. One result was American pressure for a road to Alaska, something that had been discussed in Washington and in British Columbia for years. Ottawa had resisted this intrusion onto Canadian soil, but the bombing of Pearl Harbor made it clear that both countries needed a way to move troops and equipment at will. The Americans got the go-ahead, and the all-weather gravel Alaska Highway — hastily bulldozed through some

1,500 miles of muskeg and swamp by 11,000 U.S. Army engineers and 16,000 Canadian and American civilians — was the result.

Soon there were airfields dotted across the north, helping aircraft and goods reach the beleaguered Soviet Union from North America. Oil developments at Norman Wells in the Northwest Territories, pipelines, and weather stations reflected U.S. initiatives. Over 15,000 American servicemen were in the north by the end of 1942. So large had their presence become that wits joked that the U.S. Army answered the telephone, "Army of Occupation"! But with the Japanese occupying some of the Aleutian Islands off Alaska from mid-1942, with submarines shelling West Coast installations and sinking merchant ships, the American presence had a comforting effect.

Some in Ottawa worried about the Yankee embrace, all the same. Prime Minister King fretted that the American presence "was less intended for protection against the Japanese than as one of the fingers of the hand which America is placing more or less over the whole of the Western hemisphere." But King, slow to act in almost all circumstances, had to be prodded into movement by the able and concerned British high commissioner in Ottawa. Malcolm MacDonald had served in Neville Chamberlain's Cabinet before Churchill sent him to Canada in early 1941. Two years later, he had visited the north and had been astounded to find no Canadian government representative there to watch the Americans or show the flag. For most purposes, he told Ottawa, the senior Canadian representative in the area was the secretary of the Alberta Chamber of Commerce, who was an unofficial representative of the Department of Mines and Resources.

Ottawa was finally stirred to act, and it did, appointing Brigadier W.W. Foster as special commissioner and giving him his own DC-3 aircraft to which the Red Ensign could be attached. Instructed that "no situation [must] develop as a result of which the full Canadian control of the area would be in any way prejudiced or endangered", Foster — who had directed the construction of the Canadian portion of the Alaska Highway — did his job quietly and competently. And at the end of the war, the Canadian government paid the Americans in full for every installation they had constructed in the north. Many thanks, the message was, and now go home. The Americans went, but just ten years later the Cold War would bring them back.

Even if the federal government's response to the implicit threat to its northern sovereignty had been slow and weak, something had changed in Ottawa during the war. A nation of just eleven million people, Canada had clearly come of age in a time when old and established nations were being crushed under the Nazi boot. Its diplomats moved in the corridors of power with a confidence bolstered immeasurably by the country's huge military, industrial, and agricultural contribution. Canadian representatives had new clout whenever they took their places at a bargaining table.

Moreover, the representatives Canada sent abroad to advance its interests were first class. The pre-war civil service had been small and not particularly efficient, but there were some outstanding officials in its ranks. Clifford Clark, the Deputy Minister of Finance, was a very able man; one of his key aides, Robert Bryce, was a leading Keynesian economist, and so hard-working that others stood in awe of him. The Department of External Affairs was full of men (but only a very few women) of ability: Norman Robertson, Hume Wrong, Lester Pearson, Escott Reid, and others had the respect of their British and American colleagues and the trust of their government.

The Cabinet ministers were no slouches either. C.D. Howe, the Minister of Munitions and Supply, had galvanized Canada's manufacturing industry into wartime production, and he dealt as an equal with ministers in Washington and London. J.L. Ilsley, the Minister of Finance, had a glowing reputation in Canada and abroad. Ralston, Crerar, Power, and Ernest Lapointe's successor, Louis St. Laurent, shared in one of the ablest governments Canada had ever seen in war or peace. And Mackenzie King — strange, incalculable man that he was — fought and argued for his country's place in the world. He did not always press as hard as his officials might have liked, but his experience and shrewd political sense invariably told him how far he could go. King was not cut out to be the bellicose ruler of a great power, but neither did he have the deferential acquiescence of a good colonial leader. Instead, he was ideally suited to be what he had become: the leader of the first of the wartime middle powers.

In August 1943, Churchill and Roosevelt (seated, right and centre) and the Combined Chiefs of Staff met at the first Quebec City Conference — called "Quadrant" — to plan Allied strategy in Europe and the Far East. Though Mackenzie King (seated, left) did not participate, he was on hand to play host and to pose for photographs. The empty chair was for the governor general, the Earl of Athlone.

"Quadrant" confirmed plans for the Normandy invasion, directed Eisenhower to accept Italy's surrender, and appointed Mountbatten to command in South-East Asia. Success was in the air; when the second Quebec Conference ("Octagon") met in September 1944, the principal subjects concerned the post-war period. Here Churchill is mobbed by admirers in Quebec City in 1943 as his car, also carrying Mackenzie King, passes by the Hôtel de Ville.

Traitors, spies, and saboteurs made for gripping novels and films and served other propaganda purposes. In fact, however, there was not a single proven instance of wartime sabotage in Canada.

While the North Atlantic was heavily patrolled by sea and air, the Pacific remained almost undefended. After Pearl Harbor there were real fears that British Columbia might be attacked: blackouts were taken seriously and every house had its heavy curtains or paper for covering windows. Early in 1942 plans were made for the evacuation of Vancouver Island in the event of a Japanese attack.

The United States had long wanted a road link to distant, vulnerable Alaska, and in the face of the Japanese threat the Mackenzie King government finally agreed. While more than 30,000 U.S. servicemen and civilians swarmed over the north building the Alaska Highway — as well as airfields, pipelines, and weather stations — Canadian politicians stewed over the threat to Arctic sovereignty. Top, a U.S. army construction camp near Fort St. John, B.C.; above, a signpost near Watson Lake in the Yukon.

Save
WASTE
BONES

— they make qlue for AIRCRAFT

...and are used for EXPLOSIVES...

GET IN TOUCH WITH YOUR LOCAL COMMITTEE

ISSUED BY PUBLIC INFORMATION, FOR NATIONAL SALVAGE OFFICE, OTTAWA
UNDER AUTHORITY OF HON. J. G. GARDINER, MINISTER OF NATIONAL WAR SERVICES

The public was constantly exhorted to save scrap of all kinds: metal, rags, paper, bones, rubber, and glass all had their place in the war effort. Government regulations even decreed that anyone buying toothpaste first had to turn in the old tube.

Meat rationing was a nuisance for both butchers and customers; when every
ounce of meat had its price in coupons and tokens, meal planning became an art.
Restaurants had meatless Tuesdays and Fridays. Alcohol was also rationed —
Ontario's low point was 12 oz a month — and bootleggers sold homemade hooch
whenever they could get enough sugar.

Money was plentiful in wartime Canada, but there were few consumer goods to
buy. Housing was also scarce, especially in urban areas where war workers or
servicemen's families occupied every liveable space. Sometimes the definition of
"liveable" was stretched pretty far, as these crowded conditions in Kingston,
Ontario, demonstrate.

This Toronto gas station bears the "signs of the times" — for war bonds, recycling, and "making it last". With gas rationed and tires almost impossible to buy, driving became a luxury — so much so that Col. Sam McLaughlin, the president of General Motors, occasionally drove a horse and buggy to work.

After the King government put PC1003 into effect in February 1944, giving workers the right to organize and join unions, labour moved quickly to build support — as in this poster erected by the Hamilton Steel Workers' Organizing Committee, which had long faced brutal union-busting tactics at Stelco.

One major beneficiary of the wartime mood was the Co-operative Commonwealth
Federation. The social democratic party soared in opinion polls and formed the
Opposition in Ontario in 1943; in 1944 it captured the government in
Saskatchewan, becoming the first socialist administration in North America.
Premier Tommy Douglas (centre) was extraordinarily popular, and for a brief
time it seemed all Canada might go "forward with the CCF". But only for a time.

Concern for the men and women overseas was never far from the minds of Canadians. Letters from home were important for military morale, even if the writer was a distant acquaintance or an unknown pen pal. Magazines and books filled in the long nervous hours and were usually passed from reader to reader until they disintegrated.

VII
THE NORMANDY CAMPAIGN

While the war raged in Africa, Sicily and Italy, the Soviet Union, and the Pacific, the bulk of the First Canadian Army was still sitting in England. The daily routine was training: a ceaseless round of exercises by platoon, company, battalion, brigade, division, corps, army, and army group — all infinitely more demanding and realistic than before Dieppe. There were courses for snipers, engineers, artillerymen, junior leaders, senior officers, and experts of every kind. A handful of qualified soldiers slipped away to join the Special Operations Executive (SOE), the British secret agents in occupied Europe. There were hell-raising leaves in London and endless nights in the pub drinking the watered wartime version of British ale. There was sex, love, and even marriage. There was everything except action — real action, against the Germans — and that was what the men wanted. They knew action could mean death, of course, but death was something that happened to someone else, not to them and their friends.

In 1944 there would be fighting enough for everyone. President Roosevelt and the American Chiefs of Staff had been pressing since 1942 for an invasion of France at the earliest possible date. So too was Stalin, whose forces were engaged in a titanic struggle with the *Wehrmacht*; if the Allies engaged the Germans in strength in France, the Nazis would be forced to draw off troops from the Eastern Front. On Stalin's order, from 1942 on Communists and their sympathizers throughout the West beat the tom-toms for a "Second Front Now", and huge rallies filled stadiums like Maple Leaf Gardens and the Montreal Forum.

For the First Canadian Army — an army that had been told by its commander, General McNaughton, to think of itself as a dagger pointing at the heart of Berlin — the calls for a second front struck a responsive chord. That was true even after Andy McNaughton left the army in December 1943 to be succeeded, a few months later, by General Harry Crerar.

Born in Hamilton, Ontario in 1888, Crerar had graduated from the Royal Military College, served in the Great War with the artillery, and risen through the ranks of the small pre-war Permanent Force. He had been sent to London at the outbreak of war, brought back to Canada to be Chief of the General Staff in 1940, and had returned to England the next year to command the 2nd Canadian Division. Then he commanded i Canadian Corps in Britain and in Italy. Crerar was an abler technician than McNaughton, and while he was not a brilliant leader in the field, he was less likely to make mistakes that could cost lives. What he was not was an inspired leader. The men of the army loved Andy McNaughton, a man who led through example. Very few loved Harry Crerar.

PLANNING FOR D-DAY

The problem of how to stage an invasion of France had been under consideration ever since the disasters of May and June 1940. Churchill and the Imperial General Staff feared the casualties that a cross-Channel assault on France could bring and looked to a strike at the alleged "soft underbelly" of Europe from the Mediterranean. By 1942 a little-known American officer, Brigadier-General Dwight Eisenhower, had produced a plan for invasion by April 1, 1943. This plan, called "Roundup", was reworked and finally accepted by the British and Americans, and the August 1942 raid on Dieppe was intended as a small dress rehearsal. The disaster of Dieppe had told the planners that it was probably impossible to seize a fortified port, and that any major assault required massive air and sea bombardment, better communications from ship to shore, and more and better landing craft of different types. The specific plan of "Roundup" was shelved. The necessity for an invasion of France remained.

The invasions of North Africa in November 1942 and Sicily in the summer of 1943 offered an opportunity to test the new amphibious doctrine that Dieppe had helped to create. The Landing Ship Tank (LST) that could carry up to twenty tanks, the Landing Craft Infantry (LCI) that carried two hundred infantry, the Landing Craft Assault (LCA) that carried almost twenty-five men, and the amphibious DUKWs that went from ship to shore and then operated on land — all these were coming off the production line and being tried in combat. While the Americans concentrated on landing ships, the British devised a number of specialized armoured vehicles inspired by the Dieppe experience — "Funnies", the troops called them. These tanks were adapted to swim, explode mines, hurl blasts of flame, and even build bridges. Everything of which human ingenuity could conceive was being readied.

Planning for the invasion was under the direction of a British officer, Lieutenant-General F.E. Morgan, Chief of Staff to the Supreme Allied Commander (Designate) or COSSAC. The new target for invasion was May 1, 1944, a date determined by the need to build enough landing craft. The ideal plan developed by COSSAC's team had envisaged five infantry divisions landing simultaneously, two more for immediate follow-up, two airborne divisions, and a further twenty divisions for build-up, but the shortage of landing craft meant that only a three-division assault seemed possible. Churchill grumbled furiously that "the destinies of two great empires seem to be tied up on some god-damned things called LSTs."

Morgan and his staff also had to determine where the landing should take place. One essential was air cover, a problem that limited the choice to the shore between Cherbourg, France and Flushing, Belgium. Suitable beaches were found only in the Pas de Calais or on the Normandy coast. The Pas de Calais was undoubtedly the best site — just twenty miles from England and with near-perfect beaches. But the Germans had been quick to realize this and their defences were very strong there. That left Normandy — specifically the Cotentin–Caen area, where the defences were comparatively light. Normandy beaches were farther from England, increasing the dangers of the crossing and the turn-around time, but on balance it seemed the better choice.

COSSAC's plan was accepted by the Combined Chiefs of Staff when they met at the Quadrant conference at Quebec City in August 1943. Also agreed to were Morgan's conditions: the *Luftwaffe* had to be shattered by a massive Allied air offensive before the invasion; the *Wehrmacht* could have no more than twelve first-class divisions in France at the chosen time and its ability to reinforce its troops there had to be limited; and some means had to be found to create an artificial port to get the invading armies' supplies ashore. With all this accepted, detailed planning for "Overlord", as the invasion of France was now to be called, went ahead. And by the end of 1943, General Dwight Eisenhower, less than two years earlier a mere brigadier-general in Washington, had been named the Supreme Allied Commander. Eisenhower had commanded the Allied forces invading North Africa, Sicily, and Italy; he was an American, and that mattered since the United States was providing the lion's share of the troops; and he had a wonderful knack for getting on with everyone and building an effective team. That was essential.

With an American in overall charge, a British officer was needed to command the armies in Normandy in the initial phase. The choice was General Bernard Montgomery, the victor of El Alamein. Montgomery was "an efficient little shit", as one British officer told an enquiring Canadian, but the important word there was "efficient". He was a victorious British general when there were few enough of those about. He had a thoroughly modern grasp of the need to inspire troops, and he ruthlessly sacked officers who failed in the field.

Monty and Ike, as the two were popularly known, immediately protested that three divisions were too few for the initial assault. The plan was reworked, more landing craft were found, and the new plan for the landing called for five divisions to land on a fifty-mile front with three airborne divisions preceding them. The First U.S. Army would land on the right, the British Second Army — incorporating the Canadians — on the left. By the evening of D-Day, the Allies intended to have eight infantry divisions and fourteen armoured regiments ashore. The new date of invasion was June 5, 1944, the day when the tides would be most favourable.

The planners had even worked out how to create the artificial harbours that would be so essential for getting supplies ashore. Immense concrete caissons would be towed from England to France and sunk into position, along with obsolete ships; the result would be a breakwater to which prefabricated piers would be attached. Cargo ships could then unload directly. Two of these "Mulberry" harbours were to be built, one for the American landing and one for the British front. The Mulberry plan was a vital secret, for the Germans had convinced themselves that the Allies had to capture a port to get ashore successfully and that, as there was nothing suitable in the Cotentin–Caen area, that area could not be the invasion site.

But if this demonstrated a rigidity of thought among the German planners, they also showed much energy and skill. The German army in France was not the strongest of the *Wehrmacht*'s forces — the real fighting, after all, was in Russia and Italy. France was more a training ground, and a resting and refitting area for units that had suffered on the Eastern Front. Even so, the Germans had 865,000 men in their Seventh Army in France, including several first-class Panzer and ss units, and these men were equipped with new weapons that were far better than anything the Allies had. The Panther and Tiger tanks could outgun and outfight the Allies' Sherman, for example, and the *Wehrmacht*'s all-purpose 88mm gun was vastly superior to any comparable British or American gun. Many of the men who made up the powerful German forces had fanatical faith in their Führer and in the Reich, and this remained unshaken, no matter what defeats their country had suffered since 1942.

The *Wehrmacht* also had a first-rate commander in France in Field Marshal Erwin Rommel. One of the most famous military men of the war, and almost as popular in Allied countries as in Germany, Rommel had been a Panzer general, a hard-driving division commander in the invasion of France in

May 1940, and a remarkably successful leader of the Afrika Korps — until he was bested by Montgomery at El Alamein in November 1942. Now he was in charge of the defence against invasion.

Rommel feared that, when the invasion came, Allied air superiority would make it impossible for reinforcements to reach the defenders on the landing beaches. The coastal divisions that manned the shore defences were not first-class troops, some units being made up of over-age or physically unfit soldiers, others of captured Soviet soldiers or conscripts from the conquered territories. If these men were to hold off an attack for any length of time, the Atlantic Wall must be reinforced by impregnable concrete blockhouses with fixed fire lanes commanding the beaches. Tens of thousands of iron "hedge-hogs" and tetrahedrons must be placed as obstacles on the shoreline and on likely sites for airborne landings, and millions of mines must be laid. The job was rushed and supplies were scarce, but Rommel's energy and shrewd assessment of the Allied possibilities made the invasion far more difficult than it might have been.

THE ALLIES LAND IN NORMANDY

While the First Canadian Army would play its role in the follow-up to the invasion, only one Canadian division was to participate in the actual D-Day assault. The formation selected was the 3rd Infantry Division, commanded by Major-General R.F.L. Keller; he would also have the 2nd Canadian Armoured Brigade under his command. Keller's division was to be directed by I British Corps in the assault phase, and from November 1943, officers from Keller's headquarters began to work with the corps headquarters. At the same time the infantry units of his division stepped up their training exercises, constantly practising amphibious assaults. The tank regiments attached to the division also had new weapons and tactics to master. The Fort Garry Horse and the 1st Hussars, regiments scheduled to land in the initial assault, had to learn how to use DD tanks — floating "duplex drive" tanks with high canvas flotation screens, and propellers to push them. All the tracked and wheeled equipment had to be waterproofed to operate in up to four feet of water.

The plan of attack for the 3rd Canadian Division called for two of its three brigades to land in the first wave on Juno Beach. The 7th Canadian Infantry Brigade, led by the Regina Rifles and the Royal Winnipeg Rifles, was to land on Mike sector; the 8th, headed by the Queen's Own Rifles and the North Shore Regiment, on Nan. In front of the landing forces would be the villages of Courseulles-sur-Mer, Bernières-sur-Mer, and St. Aubin-sur-Mer, all of which were due to be seized in the opening minutes of the invasion. To their left and

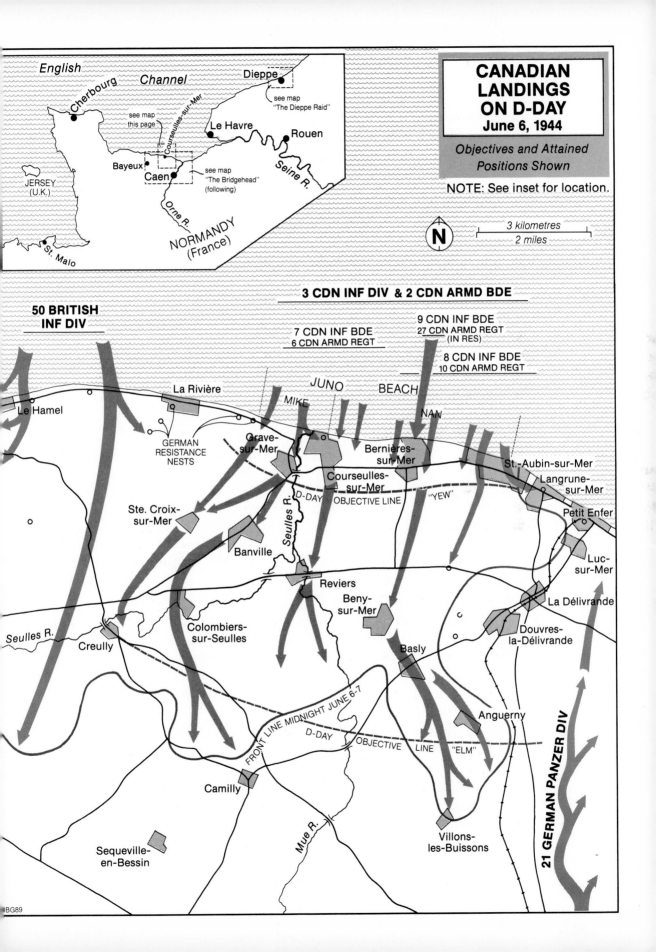

English Channel

Cherbourg

Dieppe
see map "The Dieppe Raid"

see map this page

Courseulles-sur-Mer

Le Havre

Rouen

Bayeux

Seine R.

Caen

see map "The Bridgehead" (following)

JERSEY (U.K.)

St. Malo

Orme R.

NORMANDY (France)

CANADIAN LANDINGS ON D-DAY
June 6, 1944

Objectives and Attained Positions Shown

NOTE: See inset for location.

N

3 kilometres
2 miles

3 CDN INF DIV & 2 CDN ARMD BDE

50 BRITISH INF DIV

9 CDN INF BDE
27 CDN ARMD REGT
(IN RES)

7 CDN INF BDE
6 CDN ARMD REGT

8 CDN INF BDE
10 CDN ARMD REGT

JUNO   BEACH

La Rivière

MIKE

NAN

Le Hamel

GERMAN RESISTANCE NESTS

Grave-sur-Mer

Bernières-sur-Mer

St.-Aubin-sur-Mer

Langrune-sur-Mer

Courseulles-sur-Mer

D-DAY   OBJECTIVE LINE

"YEW"

Petit Enfer

Seulles R.

Ste. Croix-sur-Mer

Luc-sur-Mer

Banville

Reviers

Beny-sur-Mer

La Délivrande

Colombiers-sur-Seulles

Douvres-la-Délivrande

Seulles R.

Creully

Basly

Anguerny

FRONT LINE MIDNIGHT JUNE 6-7

D-DAY   OBJECTIVE   LINE   "ELM"

21 GERMAN PANZER DIV

Camilly

Mue R.

Sequeville-en-Bessin

Villons-les-Buissons

BG89

right, a mile or two away, would be British divisions. Once the beachhead was consolidated, the Canadians were to move inland as far as ten miles to take and hold the high ground west of Caen. By the time this objective had been seized, the 9th Brigade and the tanks of the Sherbrooke Fusiliers would be ashore, ready to assist in beating off the expected Nazi counter-attack.

To help the invaders get ashore, the Supreme Allied Commander had brought together an overwhelming array of air and naval firepower. There were 171 squadrons of fighters and fighter-bombers to blast enemy armour, and to hit at the *Luftwaffe* if the German air force dared to take to the air. Heavy bombers would plaster the landing beaches: on Juno Beach, saturation bombing by Bomber Command of the Royal Air Force — with a very high proportion of its crews coming from the RCAF — was scheduled to begin thirty minutes before the landing. Meanwhile, destroyers and cruisers would be pounding targets ashore. Of the 7,016 ships participating in the D-Day operation, the RCN was to provide 110 of various types — destroyers, minesweepers, corvettes, and torpedo boats — including three flotillas of landing craft and the landing ships HMCS *Prince Henry* and *Prince David*, both converted armed merchant cruisers. The latter were to carry Canadian troops into action — and they would return to England with some of the first of the wounded. While the infantry and armour were going in, artillery on landing craft would add their fire to the bombardment.

Through the winter and spring the Allied air forces struck at road and rail junctions, bridges and marshalling yards, greatly restricting the *Wehrmacht*'s ability to move. To help mislead the Germans, the bombing plan took the Lancasters and B-17s all over northern France, and for every ton of bombs dropped in the Normandy region an equivalent amount was carefully targeted on the Pas de Calais.

Preceded by navy frogmen to reconnoitre beaches and clear obstacles, and by clouds of aircraft delivering the men of three airborne divisions, including the 1st Canadian Parachute Battalion, the huge Allied flotilla swept into the Baie de la Seine before dawn on June 6, 1944. Astonishingly, secrecy about the point of attack was maintained. Sailor Spud Graham took part in the D-Day invasion on HMCS *Canso*, a minesweeper. "How the Germans didn't know we were coming," he said, "I'll be Goddamned if I don't know. As far as your eye could see, there were ships. I always said that if you could jump a hundred yards at a clip you could get back to England without even wetting your feet. That's how many ships were involved."

Thorough as the planning was, there were the inevitable snafus. First, the invasion had had to be delayed one day because of poor weather. And the revised D-Day was itself a day of rain and high seas. That meant that many of the DD tanks, which had been intended to motor ashore alongside the LCAs carrying the infantry and to touch down on the beach before them, had to be landed from LSTs. A few attempted to get ashore under their own power but foundered quickly in five-foot waves. Many of the infantry, already ill from the strain of being cooped up on ship and from fear, were seasick.

The first landing craft carrying the Queen's Own Rifles hit Juno Beach at 8:12 A.M., almost half an hour late. Heavy as it was, the bombardment had not eliminated the defenders, and the queasy infantry had to run across 200 yards of open beach to the cover of the seawall under heavy fire. An 88mm gun devastated the lead platoon of A Company, and only five survivors, under command of a corporal, made it off the beach. D Company fared no better, losing half its strength in the dash for the seawall, and the riflemen who did get there had to use hand grenades to take out a nest of Germans who had survived the bombing and shelling. Rifleman Stump Gordon of Toronto had waded ashore lugging a flame-thrower that weighed almost as much as he did, somehow managing to keep the nozzle above water. "I took a shot at a pillbox, with everything whizzing around me," he remembered forty years later, "and all that came out was juice. The blasted batteries had gone."

The Regina Rifles landed on Mike sector just after 8:00 A.M.; by that time the 1st Hussars had put enough tanks on the beach to be able to provide covering fire. That was essential, as it turned out, because again the German defences were largely intact. The concrete bunkers designed to shelter machine-gun and artillery crew — they still survive virtually intact forty-five years later — were thirty-five feet across with four-foot–thick walls. The bunkers were effectively impregnable to anything but a round fired through their observation slits; some were neutralized by tanks in exactly that way. The Rifles worked their way off the beach and into Courseulles, house-clearing all the way. One of the Regina reserve companies was almost wiped out when its landing craft blew up on mines concealed by the rising tide.

The Royal Winnipeg Rifles, with an attached company from the Canadian Scottish, had as rough a time. The Scottish and two Rifles companies got ashore easily, the German gun that commanded their landing ground having been destroyed in the naval shelling. Two other companies met fierce resistance at the western edge of Courseulles, "the bombardment having failed to kill a single German", the unit war diarist noted. But the Winnipeg regiment took the beach defences, cleared mines, and established itself ashore. B Company of the Winnipeg Rifles lost almost one hundred men in a few hours.

The North Shore Regiment landed at St. Aubin. Private Joe Ryan, a signaller, had been ordered to stick close to his company commander. "He was six feet, one inch, and I am a five-foot, four-inch guy. When he stepped into the water waist-high, I thought, 'That's not so damned bad' — and jumped in — and damn near drowned." The radio he carried got drenched and did not work, and the only spare battery had been forgotten on the landing craft.

The North Shores faced a concrete bunker that had also survived the dawn shelling. Only after the bunker's hundred defenders and its anti-tank gun had caused numerous casualties and knocked out several of the Fort Garrys' tanks were the Germans eliminated. West of the town, the rest of the North Shores got into France with relative ease, though c Company had a six-hour struggle to take the hamlet of Tailleville, something accomplished with the aid of the Garrys' Shermans.

The Canadians' reserve battalions, the Canadian Scottish and Le Régiment de la Chaudière, touched down within a few minutes of the lead units. The Scottish came off the landing craft hugging bicycles that some planner had thought sure to facilitate movement inland. (They didn't.) The Chaudières suffered heavy losses from mines hidden by the tide, but still managed to take the town of Beny-sur-Mer by late afternoon, thanks to effective support from HMCS *Algonquin*, just offshore; thirteen of fifteen rounds fired landed directly atop a battery of three 88mm guns blocking the regiment's advance. By nightfall, the Canadians had pressed farther inland than any other Allied troops.

On the other D-Day beaches, the British and Americans were also getting ashore, though with difficulty. At Utah Beach on the lower end of the Cotentin peninsula the Americans landed with relative ease. But on Omaha Beach, where a golf course now amuses tourists, the U.S. 1st Infantry Division had the bloodiest landing of all, its unlucky GIs hitting a stretch controlled by effective troops operating from the high ground. The specialized British armoured vehicles, despised by the Americans, might have made a difference; instead, a total of 7,500 Americans were killed, wounded, or captured at Omaha and Utah beaches.

In the British sector things went better. On Gold Beach the 50th Division got ashore easily, and on Sword the veteran 3rd Division landed without too much difficulty but, because of fierce German resistance, failed to take its D-Day objective, the city of Caen.

Inland, the 81st and 101st U.S. Airborne divisions and the British 6th Airborne, including the 450 men of the Canadian Parachute Battalion, were scattered by heavy winds, mistakes, and evasive action by their pilots. Like many other paratroopers, Lance-Corporal Wilf De Lory of Toronto landed alone. "I'll never forget that eerie feeling of being by yourself in the middle of the night among thousands of enemy troops and not having a clue as to where the hell you were," he remembered. The Canadian battalion's task was to capture a German headquarters at Caranville, destroy a bridge over the Divette River, and hold the crossroads at Le Mesnil, atop a ridge that gave an unobstructed view of the beaches. The Canadian paratroopers accomplished their tasks. So did most of the 23,400 men in the three airborne divisions, seizing key bridges and road junctions, confusing the *Wehrmacht* high command as to the direction of the attack, and delaying German reinforcements from reaching the front. Their casualties, however, were enormous.

Canadian losses on June 6 were officially described as "light" — 340 killed, 574 wounded, and 47 captured. That was lower than the planners had feared. But to anyone who sees the row after row of graves, all dated 6 June 1944, in the Canadian military cemetery located just off the D-Day beaches at Beny-sur-Mer, "light" is not the word that comes to mind.

THE BRIDGEHEAD

By the end of D-Day, more than 130,000 soldiers had landed by sea, along with 6,000 tracked and wheeled vehicles, 600 guns, and 4,000 tons of supplies. For Eisenhower and Montgomery, for the public in the Allied countries and those nations living under Nazi tyranny, the invasion of Europe had unfolded as it should. The Allies were in France again and they were there to stay.

Their task now was to expand the bridgehead. The *Wehrmacht*'s job, of course, was to try to drive them into the sea. The first German counter-attack in strength fell upon the 3rd Canadian Division.

The North Nova Scotia Highlanders of the 9th Brigade, with the tanks of the Sherbrooke Fusiliers in support, had the task of taking the villages of Buron and Authie, on the outskirts of Caen. The Germans were in Buron, and the North Novas had to fight house to house in an effort to drive them out. At Authie, matters were worse. There the Canadian advance outstripped its artillery support and ran head on into the 12th ss Panzer Division, a crack formation made up of unblooded teenage *Hitlerjugend* led by experienced officers and non-commissioned officers, and its 25th ss Panzer-Grenadier Regiment, led by *Standartenführer* Kurt Meyer. For the first time, the Canadians encountered skilled and well-led German soldiers advancing under cover of a well-placed mortar barrage. For the first time, the Shermans faced the superior German tanks.

The result was calamitous. The Canadian battalion reeled under the assault and was ordered to pull back to Buron, itself under German attack. But disengaging proved more difficult in action than it had on exercises in England, and few managed to escape. C Company of the North Novas was wiped out, and the Sherbrooke Regiment's tanks and their green crews were unable to handle Meyer's skilled Panzer-grenadiers. Already Canadian armoured regiments were beginning to refer to their Shermans as "Ronsons", a bitter reference to the way their high-silhouetted tanks exploded into flames when hit. The Sherman's 75mm gun could not penetrate the front armour of the Panther tank, but the Panthers' high-powered gun could wipe out Allied armour at long range. The one consolation was that replacement Shermans were readily available; the Panthers were in short supply. Allied mass production, in other words, could swamp the Panzers by sheer weight of numbers. Tank crews, too, were expendable.

Many Canadians were taken prisoner in that day's fighting. That evening twenty-three of them, most from the North Novas and Fusiliers, were murdered by the men of the 12th ss Panzer Division. One sergeant of the Nova Scotia battalion observed the fate of some of his comrades: "I saw seven men from c Company…just sitting there…. Then I heard firing and saw some of the boys tipping over towards the road and a couple tipped over backwards. I could see the guards standing on the road firing at them…. After that they pushed the bodies towards the centre of the road." Many had previously been wounded; some had their hands tied behind their backs; some of the corpses were ground into pulp by tanks. Later the 12th ss would commit similar atrocities against officers and men of other Canadian units, and after the war Kurt Meyer was tried and found guilty of war crimes. His sentence of death was commuted to life imprisonment by a Canadian general who knew that Canadians, too, had killed prisoners.

The next day was much the same. At Putot and Cairon the ss Panzergrenadiers fell on the Royal Winnipeg Rifles and the Regina Rifles. The Winnipeg battalion, under enormous pressure and almost surrounded, retreated under fire. The Regina Rifles, with twenty-two Panther tanks to their front and rear, held their ground when their headquarters was overrun and were rescued by the timely arrival of Sherbrooke Fusiliers tanks. The Reginas' commanding officer, Lieutenant-Colonel Foster Matheson, actually killed a German riding a captured motorcycle through the Reginas' headquarters in Bretteville; his men knocked out six German tanks, three of them by PIAT. A counter-attack by the Canadian Scottish retook Putot that evening but again the cost was terrible. The Royal Winnipeg Rifles lost 257 men, including a number of POWs murdered by the ss. The Canadian Scottish lost 45 killed and 80 wounded.

The 3rd Canadian Division had been badly battered, but its lines remained largely intact. The 12th ss Panzer Division had also suffered heavily, losing irreplaceable tanks and absorbing heavy casualties. The result of the fighting thus far was a territorial standoff — the Canadians had not been driven into the sea — with the honours for combat success going to the Nazis.

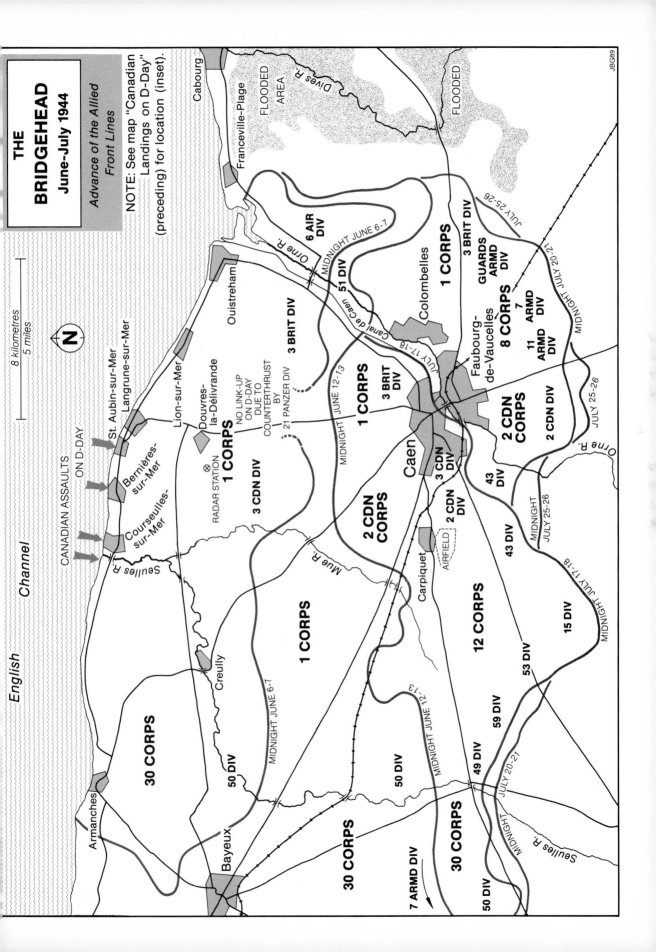

THE
BRIDGEHEAD
June-July 1944

Advance of the Allied Front Lines

NOTE: See map "Canadian Landings on D-Day" (preceding) for location (inset).

English
Channel

8 kilometres
5 miles

CANADIAN ASSAULTS ON D-DAY

Cabourg
Franceville-Plage
FLOODED AREA
Dives R.
FLOODED

St. Aubin-sur-Mer
Langrune-sur-Mer
Bernières-sur-Mer
Courseulles-sur-Mer
Lion-sur-Mer
Ouistreham
Seulles R.
Creully
Armanches
Bayeux

Douvres-la-Délivrande
RADAR STATION
NO LINK-UP ON D-DAY DUE TO COUNTERTHRUST BY 21 PANZER DIV

6 AIR DIV
MIDNIGHT JUNE 6-7
Orne R.
51 DIV
3 BRIT DIV
Canal de Caen
JULY 17-18
Colombelles
3 BRIT DIV
1 CORPS
3 BRIT DIV
GUARDS ARMD DIV
3 BRIT DIV
JULY 25-26
7 ARMD DIV
11 ARMD DIV
8 CORPS
MIDNIGHT JULY 20-21
Faubourg-de-Vaucelles
2 CDN CORPS
2 CDN DIV
Caen
3 CDN DIV
2 CDN DIV
43 DIV
43 DIV
Orne R.
MIDNIGHT JULY 25-26
MIDNIGHT JULY 17-18

1 CORPS
3 CDN DIV
MIDNIGHT JUNE 12-13
1 CORPS
2 CDN CORPS
Mue R.
Carpiquet
AIRFIELD
12 CORPS
15 DIV
53 DIV
59 DIV
49 DIV
JULY 20-21
Seulles R.
MIDNIGHT

30 CORPS
50 DIV
MIDNIGHT JUNE 6-7
1 CORPS
50 DIV
MIDNIGHT JUNE 12-13
30 CORPS
30 CORPS
50 DIV
7 ARMD DIV

JBG89

N

The Canadians had another crack at the ss on June 12. A combined British-Canadian force took the town of Rots in a confused mêlée. There was less success at Le Mesnil–Patry, one of the objectives taken by the Canadian Parachute Battalion on D-Day but subsequently abandoned. The Queen's Own Rifles were to take the town, supported by tanks of the 1st Hussars, but inexperience left D Company hanging onto the outside of the tanks when the ss opened fire. The riflemen were decimated, a few reaching the farmhouses of Le Mesnil on sheer courage; the Hussars lost nineteen tanks of B Squadron to the enemy's tanks and antitank guns and brought only two Shermans back to the Canadian lines. Le Mesnil was a demoralizing disaster.

At this point, fortunately, the Canadians were pulled out of action for two weeks. That was just as well, for the 3rd Canadian Division had suffered 1,017 fatalities and 1,814 wounded in six days of fighting. Some 70 per cent of those casualties had been suffered by infantrymen, a rate as high as or higher than that suffered in the trench fighting of the Great War.

In a few days in Normandy, the Canadians had learned much about war, much that all their years of training had failed to teach them. They knew now about the fighting skills of the Germans. They realized that digging in was not just a tiring chore but a life-saver. They understood the requirement for co-ordination between infantry, armour, and artillery, and the commanders at all levels had begun to understand the necessity of prompt and accurate information. As Matthew Halton of the CBC reported to Canada on June 20, the Canadians "were new to battle. They'd never heard the screaming shrapnel before. They hadn't been machine-gunned or sniped at. They hadn't had bombs thrown in their faces. They hadn't been overrun in their slit trenches by tanks. But they have now...."

Lieutenant-Colonel James Roberts, who commanded an armoured reconnaissance regiment in Normandy, noted later that every soldier in his first action asked himself, "How will I behave under fire? Will I act in a cowardly or frightened way?" Roberts' own experience made it "crystal clear that each soldier, no matter what his rank, is deeply influenced by the presence of his comrades and knows in his heart that he must behave in a calm and courageous manner in order to retain the respect of his fellow soldiers."

But war, as an officer of the Fort Garrys said, "was 85 per cent boredom and 15 per cent sheer terror." Some soldiers could not bear the strain, and their courage snapped. There was no shame in that, or at least there ought not to have been. A man would fight well for a long period, but then some incident or near miss would finish his ability to carry on. Battle exhaustion — or shell shock, as it was popularly known — was a reality, and some 700 Canadians were diagnosed as suffering from it in July 1944. The next month, almost twice as many were designated as "neuropsychiatric casualties" — suffering from acute fear reactions and acute and chronic anxiety.

As in the Great War, many senior officers simply failed to understand the stresses the front-line soldier operated under and the reality of battle exhaustion. They tended to see the problem as cowardice. But psychiatrists intervened, as they had not in 1914–18, to insist on a medical, not a disciplinary, response. There was no cure: soldiers admitted to rest centres rarely returned to front-line service. Treated or untreated, battle exhaustion took its toll on regiments. One report by the Canadian Scottish of the 3rd Division, dated July 28, 1944, noted that the regiment had lost 569 casualties since D-Day, leaving only 336 of those who had landed on the beaches. Of 421 disabled by that date, 117 had been evacuated as battle exhaustion cases. Another 60 men had been sent to corps rest camp or pulled out of the line because their officers and medical officers thought they needed a rest. The Scottish was a good regiment, well trained and with an admirable fighting record, but there were experiences that flesh and blood could not tolerate for too long.

Evidently, war was a learning process. Soldiers had to learn how to fight, but also how to master their fear — and the process of learning to overcome fear could only take place in action. Now that the 3rd Canadian Division and the 2nd Armoured Brigade had seen battle no one had any doubts that they would go on to give an even better account of themselves.

FROM CAEN TO "SPRING"

After six days the areas held by the Allies had been expanded to form a continuous deep bridgehead along the Normandy coast, and they had almost a third of a million men in France, along with 54,000 vehicles. The Mulberry harbours were nearing completion, but even without them more than 100,000 tons of supplies had been put ashore. The air forces were in operation on French soil, too — on June 10 RCAF squadrons No. 441, 442, and 443 began flying sorties from rough air strips just inland, "the first Allied squadrons to operate from French soil since the evacuation from Dunkirk," they boasted. Spitfires, Mustangs, and Typhoons were in the air continuously in daylight hours, shooting up everything that moved behind the German lines. The Typhoons, in particular, chewed up Nazi Panzers, spreading terror among the German troops. But just a week after D-Day, Hitler had launched the v-1 flying bombs at London, diverting Allied fighter resources that might have been used at the front.

The v-1s notwithstanding, the *Wehrmacht*'s strategy for the defence of the French coast had clearly failed. Rommel had had to deal with the Führer, who persisted in believing that the Normandy landings were just a feint, intended to divert attention from the Pas de Calais where the "real" invasion would soon occur. Panzer divisions continued to be held in reserve, long past the point of good sense. On the other hand, so overwhelming was Allied air superiority that Hitler's stubbornness probably saved his tanks for later battles.

Montgomery had a strategy too, though it was imperfectly understood by the Americans and was perhaps not entirely clear to Montgomery himself. The plan was to have the British and Canadians press hard to Caen, tying down the bulk of the German armour. That would allow the Americans to break out of the *bocage*, the Normandy hedgerows, in a giant wheeling movement to the south and east. The problem with the scheme was that it put the Canadian and British divisions in the hot seat, facing the best enemy divisions and the bulk of the Panthers.

While the Americans gathered strength and supplies for the breakout, the Canadians were moving on Carpiquet. The little town on the outskirts of Caen had an airfield that was, intelligence reported, defended by 150 of the teenage soldiers of the 12th ss. General Keller had learned that maximum force was necessary against the ss, and he sent out four battalions of infantry, the Fort Garry Horse, and all the artillery his division could muster.

It was not enough. Moving across ripening fields of wheat, the North Shore Regiment and Le Régiment de la Chaudière encountered heavy fire. The North Shores had forty-six killed in their worst day of the Normandy battle, leaving the fields strewn with "the pale upturned faces of the dead", as the regimental padre wrote. The Royal Winnipeg Rifles fared even worse, for their assault on the hangars and bunkers of the airfield lacked even the cover provided by waist-high grain. The riflemen tried twice to drive the ss out of the airfield, but failed; the Winnipegs who got farthest had to drive off ss counter-attacks to hold their hard-won ground. A company of Chaudières was overrun by the Nazis that night; some of the French Canadians were captured, bound, shot, and burned by their captors.

If Carpiquet could not be taken, Caen would be. The assault was preceded by a massive attack by RAF Bomber Command that destroyed much of the centre of the medieval city. Unfortunately, few Germans died in the raid, the enemy having sensibly removed almost all its men from the built-up areas; four hundred civilians were less lucky. Others sheltering in the great St. Etienne cathedral survived, though the old church was damaged, as was the centuries-old château on the hill in the centre of town. From the army's point of view, the raid was a total failure. All the bombers had done was to fill the street with rubble, impeding the advance and providing good defensive positions for the enemy.

3rd Canadian Division Assault Troops, Tom Wood. The secrecy of the D-Day invasion was closely guarded. Not until the landing craft had put to sea did the attacking infantry get their marked battle maps. Some were already too seasick to grasp the information. (CWM10618)

LSTs and LCTs — Normandy Assault, Tom Wood. The LCT (Landing Craft Tank) was a short-range craft, like a barge with a bow ramp, developed for assault landings. LCTs were carried across the English Channel in LSTs (Landing Ships Tank) and off-loaded near shore. Note the balloons to discourage the *Luftwaffe* attacks. (CWM10588)

Stormont Dundas and Glengarry Highlanders, Orville N. Fisher. Caen was the hub of the Nazi defences in Normandy, and Allied bombers hit the city a devastating blow on July 7. Unfortunately the *Wehrmacht* had expected this and had pulled its troops back; French civilians were killed by the thousands, however, and the ruins delayed the advance of infantry units like the "SDGS". (CWM12618)

The Deploy, Alex Colville. This extraordinarily striking watercolour by an artist who now stands in the foremost rank of Canadian painters depicts the invasion of the south of France in August 1944. French and American troops landed in the luxurious surroundings of the Riviera and then headed north and east towards Germany. (CWM10188)

Sergeant P.J. Ford, Charles Comfort. This splendid drawing of a weary-eyed sergeant from Esquimalt evocatively captures the strain of war. The Princess Patricia's Canadian Light Infantry had a proud tradition dating back to the Great War, and the unit continues to the present. (CWM12282)

Maintenance on 3.7 Guns, George Pepper. Equipment suffered as much wear and tear as men did, and sometimes was harder to replace; it was up to maintenance crews to keep it functioning. One pilot wrote after the war, "I knew that every time I flew an aircraft it had been examined and cared for to the best of human ability and I never flew a machine...that malfunctioned because of sloppy maintenance." (cwm13727)

Carrier Convoy after Dark, Bruno Bobak. The difficulties of moving armoured vehicles over unfamiliar terrain in blackout conditions can be imagined. The Bren carriers are empty here but were capable of carrying up to six infantrymen. One man would stand up front and peer ahead to guide the driver, all the time keeping a wary eye on the fluorescent patch on the carrier immediately ahead. (CWM11912)

Grave of a Canadian Trooper, Alex Colville. Canadian dead were ordinarily buried near where they fell, but the location and details were carefully noted. After the fighting ceased, the dead were reclaimed and collected together, and permanent headstones were erected. The Commonwealth War Graves Commission to this day maintains the cemeteries where Canada's sons rest. (CWM 12164)

The assault on Caen saw the 3rd Division return to some of the towns it had seen only a month before. On July 8, the Highland Light Infantry took Buron after a day-long struggle that cost it 262 men and its commanding officer. The North Novas took Authie, and the 9th Brigade captured the Abbey of Ardenne, Kurt Meyer's headquarters. The next day, the Canadians cautiously pushed their way into the city itself, astonished to be cheered as liberators by the survivors of the RAF bombing. Halton of the CBC reported the liberation to Canada:

Amid their thousands of dead and wounded men, women and children, most of them the victims of our bombing and shelling, amid worse wreckage than I've seen in any war or campaign, amid fire and smoke and bursting shells and diving enemy aircraft, several thousand people of Caen came out of the ancient abbey church where they'd been taking shelter, to watch the flag of France broken from a masthead, and to sing the *Marseillaise* with strained and broken voices and with tears running down their cheeks....

It had taken thirty-three days to reach Caen — a city that was to have been secured by the end of D-Day.

On July 18, as the American advance was stalled at St. Lô, Montgomery launched Operation "Goodwood": three British divisions set off southward from Caen towards Bourguébus Ridge, a height of land that dominated the way south along Route Nationale 158. Again, heavy bombers were supposed to clear the way; again, the enemy remained well entrenched. From their positions overlooking the plain, antitank gunners of one of Germany's crack divisions, the SS *Liebstandarte Adolf Hitler*, calmly destroyed the Shermans of the Guards Armoured Division, one of the best formations in the British army.

Now it was the Canadians' turn. Guy Simonds' II Canadian Corps, with the 3rd Division and with General Charles Foulkes' newly arrived 2nd Canadian Division, had come into operation on July 11. Operation "Atlantic", beginning on July 18, was its baptism of fire.

The two Canadian divisions had to clear Caen's south-eastern suburbs. The 3rd Division faced hand-to-hand fighting in the ruins of a steelworks at Colombelles against a *Luftwaffe* division, and at Faubourg de Vaucelles and Giberville as well. With difficulty and at heavy cost, the objectives were largely taken, and by nightfall units of the division had crossed the Orne River and reached the city's outer suburbs. The 2nd Division had an easier day, battalions clearing Louvigny, bridging the Orne, and, the next day, taking Ifs and Fleury-sur-Orne.

On July 20, however, the 2nd Division's objective was Verrières Ridge, a 250-

foot hill that dominated the road south from Caen. Verrières, like Bourgué-bus, was defended by the *Leibstandarte Adolf Hitler*. The Queen's Own Cameron Highlanders of Winnipeg on the right captured St. André-sur-Orne and held it against heavy counter-attack. On the left, Les Fusiliers Mont-Royal managed to seize Beauvoir and Troteval farms. But in the centre there was disaster. The South Saskatchewan Regiment, advancing in a rainstorm that grounded the vital Typhoons, ran smack into SS Panzers and lost more than two hundred men, including its CO. As the survivors fled with the SS in pursuit, they passed through two companies of the Essex Scottish, and panic proved contagious.

Fortunately, the two rear companies of the Scottish held and beat back the Germans. Not for long, however. The next morning the Germans attacked under cover of heavy rain, overrunning the Windsor regiment's remnants and two companies of Les Fusiliers Mont-Royal. Only the timely arrival of the Black Watch saved the 6th Brigade from complete destruction. If there was a lesson in this day's fighting, it was that a green Canadian division was no match for experienced German units. German training was better, German leadership more experienced, and the difference was simply too great. "Atlantic", Simonds' first battle in Normandy, had been a costly failure. Almost 2,000 men had been killed, wounded, or captured.

The Germans lost Field Marshal Rommel at this point. On July 17 a Typhoon had strafed a staff car near Vimoutiers, grievously wounding the *Wehrmacht* commander, and he had been replaced by Field Marshal Gunther von Kluge. On July 20 plotters in the *Wehrmacht*, convinced that Hitler was leading Germany to total destruction, attempted to kill the Führer at his headquarters in East Prussia. The dictator, who was bending over a heavy table at the moment a bomb secreted in a briefcase exploded, was deafened and shaken but not seriously hurt. His vengeance was terrible. More than 4,000 genuine and alleged opponents of the regime — army officers and civilians both — were tortured and killed. Senior officers were strangled on slaughterhouse meat-hooks while film cameras recorded their agony for Hitler's later entertainment. Rommel, Germany's most famous general, was implicated in the plot; too illustrious for exposure, he was allowed a soldier's death at his own hand.

Simonds' corps moved forward again on July 24 in Operation "Spring", another attack on Verrières. "Spring" was intended to keep the Panzers pinned around Caen and to allow the American breakout to proceed, despite delays, on July 25. There were complications in getting the operation under way, in part because the Germans made skilful use of mining tunnels south of Caen to harass the Canadians by popping up in the rear and on the flanks. But at 3:30 A.M. the Canadians moved off, under a new tactical device from

Simonds' fertile brain: "artificial moonlight", produced by bouncing search-lights off the clouds. The drawback was that the light sometimes silhouetted the attackers, making them easy targets.

That happened to the North Nova Scotia Highlanders of the 3rd Division, who struggled forward in something that soon approached chaos. Tanks of the Fort Garry Horse coming forward to assist the North Novas were shot up as well. Barely a hundred survivors made their way back to the lines. The 2nd Division had it harder still. The Royal Regiment of Canada failed to take Roc-quancourt, the concentrated fire of thirty German tanks proving too much to overcome. Then the Black Watch moved on Verrières with 325 men. The Montreal regiment surged up the slope in open order only to be slaughtered in two "killing grounds" the Germans had prepared at the summit. About 15 of them survived unscathed. And the Germans were not yet finished: an ss attack fell on the Royal Hamilton Light Infantry and its tough, determined commander, Lieutenant-Colonel John Rockingham. Rocky's Rileys (the nick-name came from the regiment's initials, RHLI) used everything they had to drive off the Panzers. When three of their supporting 17-pounder antitank guns were knocked out, they continued to fight using cumbersome PIATS, and pitching grenades. The unit held but had 200 casualties. The Black Watch lost 307. It was one of the bloodiest days of the war for the Canadians.

THE CAULDRON

Operation "Spring" had achieved one of its purposes by helping to tie down the Germans — with eleven Panzer divisions around Caen — and by leaving the armour in front of the Americans — three Panzer divisions — weaker than it might otherwise have been. On July 25, Operation "Cobra", the American breakout from the *bocage*, began at last, as General George Patton's newly formed Third U.S. Army fought its first battles. In Sicily, Patton had demon-strated that he was an aggressive and flamboyant leader and a bit of a bully. But he was a superb tank commander and he pushed the Americans forward with great speed. By July 28 the GIs were in Coutances; by the 30th they had reached the Atlantic coast at Avranches.

What would the Germans do now? Good military sense suggested they should withdraw into a defensive position behind the Seine. But good mili-tary sense was in scarce supply at Hitler's headquarters, and after the failure of the July 20 assassination attempt few generals were inclined to argue with the Führer. The result was that Hitler decided on Operation "Lüttich": the Germans would gather their Panzer divisions and before the end of the first week of August they would strike at the American army — which the Führer believed would surely crumble under attack — at Mortain and Avranches. The plan was madness, as von Kluge instantly realized. "An attack, if not immediately successful," he told the High Command, "will lay open the whole attacking force to be cut off in the west." Moreover, although Hitler refused to admit it, the Panzer divisions to be employed in the attack had been battered severely by the British and Canadians and savaged from the air. Most could muster only a few battleworthy tanks.

The plan had other failings. For one thing, the Allies knew about it, thanks to Ultra — the top secret decoding effort based at Bletchley Park in England. General Omar Bradley changed his First U.S. Army's dispositions to suit. Also, the plan pressed the German armies into a potential trap. If the British and Canadians could push south to the road junction at Falaise, the Germans might be caught in a giant pocket and eliminated. Bradley, perhaps the least bloodthirsty of Allied commanders, was exultant: "This is an opportunity that comes to a commander not more than once in a century. We are about to destroy an entire hostile army."

At this stage the First Canadian Army under General Crerar became operational. Crerar had Simonds' II Canadian Corps under his command, and the weary 3rd Division, which had been in action almost without a break since D-Day, was replaced by the newly arrived, but very green, 4th Canadian Armoured Division and its thirty-three–year–old commander, General George Kitching. Crerar's army also included I British Corps and the 1st Polish Armoured Division. The Poles — tough, silent men, far from their occupied homeland — had their own scores to settle with the Nazis.

Simonds was now aiming for a breakout to take Falaise. His plan, named "Totalize", called for his men to break through the German antitank screen that had turned "Goodwood" and "Atlantic" into costly fiascos. To do this, he planned to use darkness and heavy RAF bombing. To solve the problem of transporting the infantry against the entrenched Germans, Simonds decided to take the guns out of the "Priest" self-propelled artillery that had come ashore on D-Day and turn the vehicles into Armoured Personnel Carriers. The result was the Kangaroo — the first APC, and a brilliant solution by the one tactical thinker the Canadian army had yet produced. The carriers were soon formed into a regiment commanded by Gordon Churchill, later a senior minister in John Diefenbaker's government.

"Totalize" called for regimental-sized columns to roll forward, each consisting of tanks, specialized armoured vehicles, and a battalion of infantry aboard their Kangaroos. To find their way in this wholly new kind of night attack, the vehicle drivers would follow radio beams, searchlights, and tracer fire. "We did not expect that any of these devices would be adequate,"

Simonds later explained, "but we hoped that a combination of them all would enable direction to be kept." As the armoured columns rolled forward, following units would mop up the bypassed enemy, who by then would have been shattered by the aerial bombing. And once the lead divisions had broken the German line, three divisions would exploit the breakthrough.

At 11:30 P.M. on August 7, "Totalize" was ready to roll, just hours after "Lüttich" had launched most of the Panzer divisions westward. Inevitably, the Canadian assault became confused, despite the direction-finding aids. Each of the four columns got lost and casualties were severe, but by midday on August 7 most units had taken their objectives. The villages around Caen that had proved so costly in July did so again, but Rocquancourt, May-sur-Orne, and Fontenay finally fell. Verrières Ridge was also taken at last. But the second phase of the attack slowed as the battlefield degenerated into chaos, with the dust from thousands of tanks and vehicles filling the air and with too few roads to move thousands of men. Worse, a raid by 678 USAAF aircraft dropped many of its bombs short of the Germans and atop Canadian and Polish units. Three hundred Canadian and Polish soldiers were killed or wounded, including General Keller of the 3rd Division. Two companies of the North Shore Regiment were wiped out. Few Canadians ever again trusted the bombers.

Now an old enemy arrived on the scene: Kurt Meyer's 12th SS. While heading for "Lüttich", Meyer's unit had been diverted to deal with the threat posed by "Totalize". Riding his legendary motorcycle, Meyer himself rallied the fleeing Germans, posted the fearsome 88mm guns, and sent for Tiger tanks. The already stumbling advance bogged down further; "Totalize" was in trouble.

It would get worse. On August 9 the British Columbia Regiment's tanks set off in the darkness, with the infantry of the Algonquin Regiment aboard, to take the high ground south-west of Quesnay Wood that dominated the Caen–Falaise road. The armoured commander, Lieutenant-Colonel D.G. Worthington, radioed headquarters that he had arrived on his objective; in fact he was four miles away, in an open field and almost directly under the guns of Meyer's Panzers. The two Canadian units fought a hopeless day-long battle, losing 240 killed, wounded, and captured, and forty tanks. Worthington himself had led the struggle but died in a mortar bomb explosion.

Meyer also demolished the Queen's Own Rifles and the North Shore Regiment, as they tried to clear Quesnay Wood and reach the Laison River. The Hitler Youth allowed the Canadians to emerge from the woods, then hit them with everything they had. Another 165 Canadians fell victim to the 12th SS. So did Operation "Totalize", called off by Simonds on August 11.

It was clear that II Canadian Corps had to make another major attack.

Operation "Lüttich" had lasted little more than one day before it was shattered by American air attacks and stubborn defence. While the generals pleaded with Hitler to be allowed to withdraw, the roads to the east and safety were already filling with long columns of *Wehrmacht* and ss vehicles and horse-drawn carts. The shrinking pocket of fleeing Germans had to be closed at its nearest point, near Falaise. The Canadians, as Simonds later wrote, were "to break the pivot on which the German withdrawal to the Seine must hinge."

Simonds' new plan to reach the crucial road junction at Falaise was called "Tractable". This called for two huge blocks of armour, one provided by the 4th Armoured Division, the other by the 3rd Canadian Division and the 2nd Armoured Brigade, to move off in daylight at full speed under cover of smoke. The infantry would again move in the Kangaroos. RAF bombing would precede the advance and cover the flanks. Every available gun and fighter-bomber would be used in support, though in the interests of surprise there was to be no preliminary bombardment. The plan was crude — there were no written orders, to preserve secrecy — but it might have been able to roll over the stubborn but weakened German defences had an officer carrying a marked map not got lost and been captured. The Germans were ready, after all.

The armoured columns started forward just before noon on August 14. Very quickly disaster came from the air, when RAF bombers dropped their payloads not on the Germans in Quesnay Wood but on Canadians and Poles. This time 400 were killed, wounded, or missing. Air Marshal Sir Arthur Coningham, commanding the RAF's 2nd Tactical Air Force, was behind the lines in a Staghound armoured car, almost directly under the bombers. "You know," he told General Simonds as he brushed the dust out of his hair, "I never did believe in using heavy bombers for close support." Almost no one did after that second disaster, though Simonds, the creator of the plan, maintained that without the bombing "our casualties would have been a great deal higher."

The German defenders did their utmost to stop "Tractable" by pumping shells at the armoured boxes; one fatality was Brigadier E. L. Booth of the 4th Armoured Brigade. The Laison River also proved a more formidable obstacle than expected, with tanks bogging down on the steep banks and in the gluey mud of the river bottom. But the river was soon crossed. To everyone's surprise, Germans began surrendering; not Meyer's ss, but men from two *Wehrmacht* divisions just arrived in France from Norwegian occupation duty. The Normandy battlefield was vastly different from the coffee houses of Oslo and Bergen. Meyer's division — with only fifteen tanks left — staged a night attack on the 1st Hussars, and his teenagers, fast turning into old men under the strain of the fighting, held off repeated efforts to take Versainville.

It was now more urgent than ever to take Falaise. Patton's Third U.S. Army had reached Argentan in the south, the designated inter-army boundary. There he stopped, lest his men blunder into the Canadians. Patton asked Eisenhower if he could move on to Falaise — to "drive the British into the sea", as he put it with his usual delicacy; but the Supreme Allied Commander ordered Patton to set off for Paris with the bulk of his armour, leaving just enough at Argentan to protect the bottom of the Cauldron, as the Germans now called the gap.

Cauldron it was, too. The ixth and xixth Tactical Air Commands of the USAAF, with their Thunderbolts and Mustangs, joined the British and Canadian pilots of the 2nd Tactical Air Force in their Spitfires and Typhoons as they flew thousands of strafing and bombing sorties over the retreating Germans. The roads were clogged with tanks, trucks, horses, and men, while smoke from burning supplies and trucks hung over the whole area. Pilots could smell the burning and rotting flesh even as they flew at three hundred miles an hour. "Lüttich" had turned Normandy into a charnel house for the ss and the *Wehrmacht*.

By August 16, Simonds' divisions were ready to move once more to close the eighteen-mile gap between them and the Americans and to encircle the retreating enemy armies. The 2nd Canadian Division headed for Falaise while General Stanislaw Maczek's Polish Armoured and Kitching's 4th Canadian Armoured set forth to close the Nazi escape route. Now in command of the German forces was Field Marshal Walter Model, successor to Field Marshal von Kluge, who had killed himself rather than face the Führer's wrath at the loss of the armies in France. Model was tougher; he recalled the 2nd ss Panzer Corps, which had reached safety, to smash at the Canadians and Poles, but he needed time to extricate his men from the Cauldron.

Simonds did not propose to allow Model much of that. On the 17th, the ruins of Falaise finally fell. On the 18th two American and one Free French division at last began fighting northward from Argentan towards Chambois. The 4th Armoured took Trun and set up a defence line to hold off the retreating enemy, now advancing towards them. The Poles moved east of the Canadian division to head off Model's counter-attack, most of the division taking position on a wooded hill their commander dubbed Maczuga, or "mace".

South from Trun on August 18 came a squadron of the South Alberta Regiment led by thirty-two–year–old Major David Currie, along with a company of the Argyll and Sutherland Highlanders under Lieutenant (Acting Major) Ivan Martin. Their objective was St. Lambert-sur-Dives, through which passed the last road open to the enemy. By the afternoon of August 20 two additional companies of infantry had joined Currie's little group to face waves of Germans. Currie's antitank weapons had destroyed trucks and Panthers but they proved ineffective against the largest German tank, the Tiger. The Canadian called for artillery support from the big 5.5-inch medium guns, and the heavy shells did the trick.

But the day's carnage was terrible. All Currie's officers were killed or wounded, and Currie, forced to be everywhere at once, directed the fire of his few remaining tanks and antitank guns, and knocked out a Tiger by himself. The citation for his Victoria Cross quoted one of Currie's NCOs: "We knew at one stage that it was going to be a fight to the finish, but he was so cool about it, it was impossible for us to get excited." His command had destroyed seven tanks, twelve of the deadly 88mm guns, and forty vehicles, and had killed, wounded, or captured an incredible 2,900 Germans. General Simonds recalled being unable to use a road in the area because it was piled high with German dead.

At Maczuga, the Poles were in a desperate struggle. Their tanks wreaked havoc on the Germans, as did artillery fire from the 4th Medium Regiment of the Royal Canadian Artillery; its batteries were directed onto target by their liaison officer with the Poles, Captain Pierre Sévigny, later a Cabinet minister. But the Poles had received no fresh supplies of food, ammunition, or gasoline, and their casualties were heavy under the unrelenting German attack. "Tonight," the senior survivor told his officers, "tonight we die." The survivors — the Poles lost 135 officers and 2,192 men — were relieved at noon the next day, August 21, by the Shermans of the Canadian Grenadier Guards. With Poland still in German hands, the Polish division was of course unable to fill its ranks with reinforcements. The only solution was to comb the ranks of German POWs for Poles, and to draft all found into the division!

With the Falaise Gap closed, the fighting moved rapidly eastward. The battle had been an unquestioned Allied victory, though the Canadian difficulty in closing the pocket around Model's troops had allowed many to escape. A number of senior Canadian commanders, General Kitching among them, were replaced by September. Still, the German army had lost half its men in Normandy and most of their equipment. Since D-Day, 300,000 Germans had been killed or captured, and there were 200,000 more isolated in fortified French ports on the Atlantic, certain to be taken whenever the Allies chose to assault them. Moreover, German losses in equipment were staggering: 2,200 tanks had been destroyed, countless trucks, innumerable guns. General Leclerc, commanding de Gaulle's French forces that were now leading the drive for Paris, commented that it all seemed like the spring of 1940 in reverse: "complete disorder on the enemy side." It was true, though the Germans had a capacity to reorganize and rearm that the French army in 1940 had lacked.

BACK TO DIEPPE: ON TO ANTWERP

The war was not yet won. The problem for the Allies, with their armies still driving forward, was supply. As they crossed the Seine, Eisenhower's mechanized divisions rapidly outran their logistical support. Modern armies devour vast quantities of ammunition, gasoline, and a host of supplies from bridging equipment to boot laces. The ports in Allied hands had only limited capacity, and truck convoys and improvised airlifts could not get enough fuel and ammunition to the armoured divisions now rolling forward at speed. "Inevitably we will be checked," Eisenhower admitted ruefully.

The Germans, of course, realized this and determined to defend the towns they still held on the English Channel. While the British, French, and Americans freed Paris and moved into Belgium, the First Canadian Army had the task of capturing a succession of defended and fortified ports.

For Montgomery, Allied strategy now depended on a single critical choice. If supplies were short, it was a mistake to keep all the armies moving forward; instead, a single powerful thrust should be directed at Germany. Get bridgeheads over the Rhine as soon as possible, then drive twenty divisions across the North German plain at Berlin. The result might be victory in 1944 — vital to Britain, which was out of men as well as money. Naturally, Monty claimed command of this mailed fist; the Americans would play the secondary role.

Whether his strategy was militarily correct or not, it was politically unacceptable. The American public would simply not tolerate seeing U.S. troops in a subsidiary role, and General Eisenhower and his Anglo-American staff, none too impressed with Montgomery's command of the Normandy battlefront, fully realized this. Eisenhower, a tough man when he had to be, rejected Montgomery's plan.

The task of the First Canadian Army would be the same no matter whether Ike or Monty prevailed. The Canadians had the extreme left of the Allied line and the task of opening the French ports. Their coastal advance also meant that they were forced to bridge the rivers at their mouths, the widest points. The Canadians faced a fierce fight in crossing the Seine but then the army moved quickly to liberate Rouen. By September 1, the 2nd Division was back at Dieppe, that port of bitter memories; happily, this time the defenders had gone. The 2nd Division paraded to honour its dead of 1942. Crerar attended the ceremony and was ticked off by Montgomery for missing a field marshal's conference; the unrepentant general insisted that a Canadian ceremony took precedence.

The same day, the 3rd Division took Le Tréport. But neither port had the capacity to supply more than a small portion of the Allies' needs. Antwerp, the great inland Belgian port on the Scheldt River, could, and the British captured the city, with its twenty-eight miles of docks largely intact, on September 4. The Germans were by this time, as Guy Simonds noted after the war, in "a state bordering panic...officers were deserting, commandeering cars and making for Germany, not from cowardice but in the belief it was all over...." Simonds added that his men had found a German 88mm gun in perfect working order, with ammunition stacked beside it. "When I saw that gun, I knew that we would win. It was the first time I had ever seen a German gun position abandoned without a fight." At that point, the banks of the Scheldt could have been readily cleared, freeing the port for use; unaccountably, the too-cautious British failed to move, and the opportunity was lost.

Frantic to restore a front in France and the Low Countries, on September 4 Hitler declared that Boulogne, Calais, Dunkirk, and Walcheren Island in the Scheldt estuary were fortresses to be held to the last. Canadians would pay bitterly in blood for the British slowness and for Hitler's decree.

The Canadians had to cross the wide River Somme first, and then take Boulogne in Operation "Wellhit", a task Simonds gave to the 3rd Division. Heavy bombers (called in by Simonds, who went over General Crerar's head to Bomber Command) and artillery softened the defences, but the Germans held out for six days in their strongly fortified hilltop positions. On September 23 the *Wehrmacht* finally surrendered, 9,500 prisoners going into the bag. Canadian casualties were 634. The 3rd Division then assaulted Calais on September 25. Action continued until October 1, when 7,500 Germans gave up. Donald Pearce, a lieutenant in the infantry, was not amused by the German commander after the surrender:

> [He] was content enough about the defeat; it was an objective fact, no tears shed over it at all. But he was burningly interested in knowing the details of the Allied tactics: "Now why did you come in from the precise direction you did, when we were sure that you would come in from over here? What an interesting piece of tactics.... Had you come in just here, where we also expected you, do you suppose you could have succeeded? We had a warm reception prepared for you, if you had come in here...." What he was interested in was the tactical lessons.... This is not exactly stupidity, I suppose; but then, what is it, if not what the divisional commander called it — "Damned nonsense"?

The Canadians were experienced combat soldiers now, but evidently there still remained differences between a professional army and one composed largely of citizen soldiers. The Canadians simply wanted to get the whole dirty job over with so that they could go home. It would take eight more months, and thousands more dead, to complete the task.

The invasion of France on June 6, 1944, was an extraordinary military feat. Simply massing the landing craft for the assault was an organizational triumph, as this array of laden and camouflaged Landing Craft Tanks (LCTs) at Southampton on June 4 suggests. Every port across the south of England saw a similar scene.

The Canadian army contribution to the D-Day assault was provided by the 3rd Division — some of its men are seen here on a Landing Craft Infantry (LCI) — and the 2nd Armoured Brigade. The LCI carried more than 150 soldiers and could drop them right on the beach.

Organized and effective as they were, the invasion planners nonetheless had some
curious ideas. "Give the infantry bicycles so they can move inland quickly," some
colonel must have decided, and as a result at least one 3rd Division infantry
battalion dutifully waded ashore carrying two-wheelers. The bikes were scrapped
within hours.

The Nazi defences on the Normandy coast were based on enormous concrete bunkers, almost all of which survive to this day. The bunkers were formidable obstacles but the *Wehrmacht* soldiers manning them were not Hitler's best troops. Here, a lance-corporal dispatch rider and a private guard prisoners in front of a captured bunker, while wounded infantry are helped to an aid station.

The Germans, calculating that the Allies had to capture a major port, did not expect the invasion to come in Normandy; they had not reckoned on the Mulberry, a brilliant combination of floating concrete caissons and ships that could be sunk to form a breakwater and pierheads. The Americans and the British each had a Mulberry, though the U.S. one soon was disabled by storms.

Caen was supposed to be captured on D-Day, but skilful defence kept the city in
Nazi hands for a month, and fighting continued on the outskirts after that. On July
18 these men of the 8th Infantry Brigade waited by the side of the road at nearby
Ranville. Note the battledress, far too heavy for July weather, the fixed bayonets
and entrenching tools, and the air of tension.

To clear the way for Operation "Totalize" — the Canadian advance to Falaise — more than a thousand bombers blasted the German lines on Verrières Ridge at midnight, August 7. Although the effect appears apocalyptic, Nazi resistance remained fierce, and the resulting clouds of dust and smoke made the night advance all the more confusing.

The key Canadian position was at St. Lambert-sur-Dives, where a squadron of the South Alberta Regiment and B company of the Argyll and Sutherland Highlanders fought savagely for several days, wreaking fearful destruction on the Germans and taking 2,900 prisoners.

General Simonds' men struggled to close the Falaise gap against desperate
opposition from ss and *Wehrmacht* troops; the town of Falaise was taken on
August 17, and the gap was closed two days later.

When the *Wehrmacht* withdrew, they left mines and booby-traps behind. These three Royal Canadian Engineers are using a magnetic detector to seek out metal mines (the Germans soon developed wooden mines instead).

The sappers' tedious, painstaking work is in sharp contrast to the romantic image of war — as in the saturnine portrait of a Canadian sniper below.

As the Canadians advanced eastwards, the wide mouth of the River Seine posed a major barrier. Engineers had to operate ferries until the bridges destroyed by the enemy could be rebuilt.

Once the Seine was crossed, Dieppe — with all its bitter memories — was next. This time the Germans retreated as the 2nd Division arrived, and rejoicing Dieppois welcomed the Canadians with wine and flowers. The division staged a massive parade on September 3 to commemorate the débâcle two years before.

Three French civilians recognize their country's debt to Canada by laying flowers on the grave of a sergeant of the army's Film and Photo Unit at Fleury-sur-Orne. Individual units often buried their comrades where they fell, carefully keeping records of locations.

VIII
VICTORY

With France now all but cleared of the Nazis, the outcome of the war was no longer in doubt, though the Germans showed remarkable recuperative powers. v-1 and, soon, v-2 missiles rained down on London, beginning a terrible new era in warfare. Jet fighters, much faster and more manoeuvrable than propeller-driven aircraft, began to come off the German production lines. Despite Allied bombing, tank production in the Reich was at its peak, and Panzer units were being rebuilt. There were even units to equip; seventy divisions were being manned and armed in the West, a process that saw sixteen-year-olds inducted, training units cannibalized, and the middle-aged and infirm put into uniform. Neither the *Wehrmacht* nor the ss was as formidable as it had been a year or two before; but Hitler's legions had not yet been battered into submission.

THE BATTLE FOR THE SCHELDT

Though the First Canadian Army had barely reached Belgian soil, Montgomery's forces plunged forward into The Netherlands. The field marshal's plan was to launch a combined ground and airborne invasion code-named "Market Garden" on September 17, 1944, to secure crossings over the River Maas and the two main branches of the Rhine. Paratroopers seized several bridges and established a bridgehead at Arnhem, but then lost it again in a vicious fight. The failure of "Market Garden" was a serious loss, for the approaches to the great Belgian port of Antwerp were still held by the Germans, though the city itself was in Allied hands. Until the approaches were cleared, Allied armies would not be able to get the supplies they needed by the shortest and most direct route. Responsibility for clearing the approaches fell to the First Canadian Army, under the acting command of General Guy Simonds while Harry Crerar recovered from a serious attack of dysentery.

Antwerp lay on the Scheldt River, fifty miles from the sea. To the north of the river's estuary was the peninsula of South Beveland, and the strongly defended Walcheren Island. All this land was low-lying, as was the south shore of the estuary, where the reclaimed land of the polders was below sea level and the water was held back by fifteen-foot–high dikes topped by roads. The dikes and two large canals would serve as solid defensive positions for the Germans.

Simonds' plan for the Scheldt battle was straightforward. The 2nd Canadian Division was to attack north of the estuary while the 3rd took the south. Tough, ruthless when necessary, Simonds was just forty-one years old in October 1944. He was one of Montgomery's favourites, almost the only Canadian general for whose military skills the field marshal had any regard. And Simonds, like his hero, had no qualms about firing battalion or brigade commanders who could not or would not drive their men to achieve the impossible.

Certainly the Scheldt battlefield verged on the impossible. The ground was sodden and the mud thigh-deep as the under-strength infantry units of the 2nd Division's 4th and 5th brigades headed north towards the narrow isthmus to South Beveland. The soldiers from the Royal Hamilton Light Infantry, the Black Watch, and the Calgary Highlanders started out on October 6 with the object of capturing the farm town of Woensdrecht, which controlled the German land route from Beveland.

The Germans were ready for them. Their guns, mounted on the reverse slope of the only high ground in the area, commanded the flat, muddy approaches to Woensdrecht, and they had breached the dikes and flooded the polders. The Royal Regiment of Canada tried and failed to take the causeway isthmus, suffering heavy losses in the process — the casualties inevitably falling heaviest on platoon commanders and junior leaders, who had to get the attacks moving. The Black Watch also failed, two days of fighting costing the Montreal unit eighty-one casualties for not a yard. The Calgary Highlanders were next, in an epic struggle against entrenched German paratroopers that lasted from October 7 to October 10. On October 13 — "Black Friday" — the Black Watch launched itself in a daylight attack over 1,200 yards of beet fields. The result was tragic. Every one of the unit's company commanders was killed or wounded. One of them, still functioning despite his wounds, reported that he had only four men left out of the ninety who had begun the attack. For the second time in four months, the Black Watch was wiped out as a unit.

Not until October 16, when the Royal Hamilton Light Infantry launched a heavily supported night attack, was the assault renewed. Jumping off at 3:30

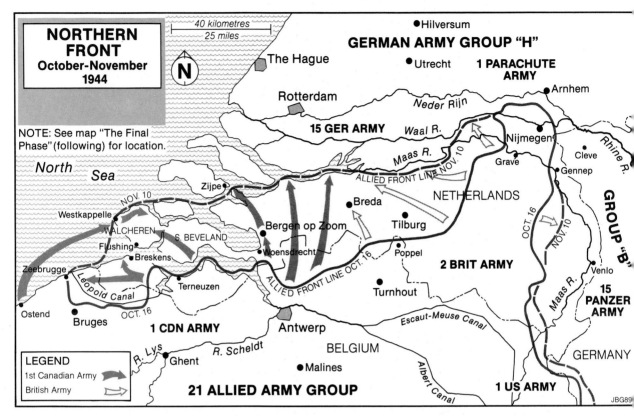

A.M. with the fire from 168 guns leading the way, the RHLI was initially successful, but the paratroopers soon counter-attacked, overrunning one company and sending its survivors fleeing to the rear. The Germans were driven off only when Major Joe Pigott, another RHLI company commander, called down a massive artillery barrage on his own positions. The 4,000 shells knocked out the German tanks and killed or wounded most of the paras. Pigott won the DSO for his actions that day. But as the RHLI's commanding officer, Lieutenant-Colonel Denis Whitaker, later noted, his battalion's estimated strength after that night and morning's fighting was only 6 officers and 157 men, barely a fifth of normal. Finally, on October 24, the job of cutting the isthmus was completed by units of the 5th and 6th brigades.

Again the cost was high. The Fusiliers Mont-Royal — under Major Jimmy Dextraze, a future Chief of the Defence Staff — suffered grievously in an attack on Nederheide, half a mile east of Woensdrecht. The FMRs also had to bear the indignity of being bombarded with leaflets: "French Canadians, Soldiers of the Regt. of Mont Royal.... You are in a country where there is nothing but rivers and canals. The English were clever enough to send you to the most difficult battlefield. You are *not* obliged to fight. Lay down your arms, helmet and belt, desert, stick your hands up, put up the white flag and you are saved." The

Wehrmacht propagandists were right about one thing—the Scheldt *was* the most difficult battlefield.

Once Beveland had been isolated, the rest of the north shore was cleared quickly, though only after hard fighting. The 4th Brigade led the assault and pressed on for forty-eight hours, until battalions of the 6th Brigade took the lead. Assisted by a seaborne assault across the West Scheldt by British troops, the 6th Brigade crossed the Beveland Canal on October 27–28. Beveland was soon cleared of the enemy, and now only Walcheren Island remained.

Walcheren was joined to Beveland by a causeway 1,200 yards long and 40 yards wide — just wide enough for a road and a railway. The Germans commanded this uninviting route with machine-gun fire, and the unlucky Black Watch, again stuck with an impossible task, suffered heavily in the first attempt to cross. An assault by the Calgary Highlanders pushed across the causeway but was then driven back by German flame-throwers. George Teasdale of the Calgarys remembered the Germans "firing shells from the other end, bouncing them off the road, and they were ricocheting back and forth all over the place.… I think I got close to the other side.…" On November 2 Le Régiment de Maisonneuve managed to cross the narrow strip of land and establish a few platoons tenuously on Walcheren. Only then, after a prodigal waste of lives and courage, did staff officers recognize that the bridgehead would be a hopeless base for new attacks. At this point the Canadians were relieved by British troops under command of the First Canadian Army. Walcheren was finally cleared on November 8, after Simonds came up with a brilliant plan for a massive artillery and air bombardment to breach the dikes and flood much of the island, thus creating new beaches for amphibious assault by British commandos, army units, and the 4th Special Service Brigade — again under the First Canadian Army's command.

South of the estuary, the 3rd Canadian Division was just as heavily engaged, as it struggled to eliminate a pocket of German troops based at Breskens. The main obstacle, the Leopold Canal, was crossed only with the assistance of massed flame-throwers. The Germans continued their stubborn resistance but were eventually subdued when an amphibious assault launched with the aid of "Buffaloes" — a new troop-carrier that could carry thirty men across almost any water obstacle — completely surprised them. The historian of the North Shore Regiment recalled that the campaign was "a misery they had not known before. It was like Indian warfare, small sections taking desperate chances, probing, feeling, trying to outguess the enemy"—and all this in muddy fields where the cold and wet seeped right into the bones.

Great ingenuity was required to operate in such conditions. For example, Le Régiment de la Chaudière improvised a bridge across the Uitwaterings

Canal by driving a Bren-gun carrier into the water and piling earth, planks, and steel beams on top of the submerged vehicle. "It worked perfectly," 8th Brigade commander Brigadier James Roberts recalled, "and, next morning, the Queen's Own Rifles passed over it and through the Chaudières...." By November 3, the south bank was secure.

The Battle of the Scheldt had cost 6,367 Canadian casualties, a terribly high price for five weeks' fighting that could have been avoided. But once the German-laid mines had been cleared from the river, the port of Antwerp was opened and the supplies necessary for the final push into Germany could readily reach the front. Field Marshal Montgomery congratulated Simonds for the First Canadian Army's success: the operations had been "conducted under the most appalling conditions of ground—and water—and the advantage in these respects favoured the enemy. But in spite of great difficulties you slowly and relentlessly wore down the enemy resistance, drove him back, and captured great numbers of prisoners." More than 41,000 had been taken. Monty added that "It has been a fine performance, and one that could have been carried out only by first class troops."

THE CONSCRIPTION CRISIS

After the Scheldt battle, the First Canadian Army entered a three-month period of rest, recuperation, and light action. That was fortunate for soldiers weary from five months' unrelenting warfare and a long march from the Normandy beaches to the Dutch polders. But there were few long leaves for the men. "We knew why leaves were so scarce," Major Ben Dunkelman of the Queen's Own Rifles wrote. "Thanks to Prime Minister Mackenzie King's handling of the Conscription Issue at home...." In Italy, Brigadier Bill Murphy was even more bitter. "I personally will never cast another Liberal vote as long as King has anything to do with the party." Of all the armies, he told his family, "only that of Canada has no provisions for home leave"—and the soldiers were convinced that the reason was "that there are no men to replace them—except the Zombie army"—the derisively named home defence conscripts. "And to preserve [the Zombies'] precious skins the volunteers just have to take it." The prime minister's handling of the manpower issue was now to be tested in the greatest domestic crisis of the war.

The issue was reinforcements. The defence minister, Colonel J. Layton Ralston, had gone to Italy and north-west Europe in September 1944 to see for himself the condition of the army and to check out disturbing rumours about reinforcement shortages. To his shock, Ralston had discovered after characterically painstaking enquiry that the truth was even worse than the rumours.

There was such a shortage of infantry reinforcements that some poorly trained soldiers had been sent to the front, along with men recently recovered from wounds. That hurt morale and fighting efficiency, which in turn led to further casualties. Ralston returned to Canada determined to press the issue of conscription, determined to force Mackenzie King to honour the pledge he had made in 1942: "not necessarily conscription, but conscription if necessary". Now, Ralston insisted, conscription was demonstrably necessary to provide at least 15,000 infantry reinforcements to keep the battalions up to strength. And those men, he argued, could only be found among the 60,000 NRMA trained soldiers in Canada.

Not so, Mackenzie King replied. What he had meant by "necessary" was *necessary to win the war*. Who could doubt, with the Russians pressing west and the Allies east, that Germany would soon be compelled to give up the fight? Why tear the country apart so late in the war? As the struggle in the Cabinet intensified, suddenly it all came clear to him: the ministers opposing him on conscription were almost the same as those who had opposed the great program of social welfare that had been gradually put in place since the beginning of 1944. The push for conscription, he decided, was part of a conspiracy of reactionaries.

At this point King's thoughts turned to General McNaughton, the much-beloved soldier who had taken the 1st Canadian Division overseas in 1939 and built it up into an army. McNaughton had been recalled in late 1943 because British officers doubted his abilities, and Ralston, no admirer, had gone along with the move. The general and the defence minister had little love for each other. More to the point, McNaughton thought conscription the wrong way to recruit an army. He remained enormously popular with the troops and the public, sought by all three parties and often proposed as a first Canadian-born governor general.

On November 1, 1944 came one of the climactic Cabinet meetings in Canadian history. The conscription issue was once more rehashed at length. Then, King said, "I thought we ought to, if possible, reach a conclusion without further delay." He wanted McNaughton to be defence minister:

> the people of Canada would say that McNaughton was the right man for the task, and since Ralston had clearly said that he himself did not believe we could get the men without conscription, while McNaughton believed we could, and that he, Ralston, would have to tender his resignation...that I thought if Ralston felt in that way he should make it possible for us to bring McNaughton into the Cabinet at once—the man who was prepared to see this situation through. I said that in regard to a resignation...he had

tendered his resignation to me some two years ago and had never withdrawn it....

The axe had fallen, wielded by the brutal master of politics. But it was a gamble. Would Ralston's friends resign with him? King sat quietly while Ralston said his farewells, shook hands around the table, and left. No one departed the council chamber with him.

The news of Ralston's sacking put the conscription crisis on the front pages in screaming headlines. To King's horror, and to McNaughton's distress, the publicity created a firestorm of reaction against the once-popular general. Audiences booed and jeered when he tried to rally the country behind the no-conscription policy. Worse yet, the NRMA soldiers resisted the new appeals that their officers made to them to volunteer for overseas service. The Zombies had heard those arguments many times before and, as one put it, "If Mackenzie King wants me to go overseas, he'll have to send me. I'm damned if I'll volunteer to help out this government."

Thus, by the third week of November the reinforcement crisis remained much as it had under Ralston. The shortage of trained infantry remained, the conscriptionist ministers were again getting restive, and King faced yet another crisis. How could he get out of it this time?

The answer came on November 22, when McNaughton telephoned. "The Headquarters staff here," King recorded the general as saying, "had all advised him that the voluntary system would not get the men....it was the most serious advice that could be tendered...." At once, King said, "there came to mind the statement that I had made to Parliament in June [1942] about the action the government would necessarily take if we were agreed that the time had come when conscription was necessary." Now conscription *was* necessary — not to win the war, but to save the government — and King prepared to reverse the course he had held so steadfastly.

But how could the prime minister justify the switch to himself—and to Louis St. Laurent, the Minister of Justice since late 1941 and the key Quebec minister? That was no problem for a mind so agile. The advice of the generals, he rationalized, constituted nothing less than a revolt, "the surrender of the civil government to the military", a "palace revolution". Better to yield to conscription than to see democracy destroyed. Tough and clear-minded as he always was, St. Laurent nonetheless went along with this fiction. Air minister Power would not, however, and promptly resigned to keep faith with his promises to Quebec.

The crisis was effectively over. King told the Cabinet of his *volte-face*, and the ministers passed an order-in-council sending up to 16,000 NRMA soldiers overseas. Across the country, reverberations rattled a few windows. Quebec newspapers and politicians railed against the government, while many English Canadians called for King's head for all the delays. But King survived a vote of confidence in Parliament, likely helped by the fact that both a conscriptionist, Ralston, and an anti-conscriptionist, Power, had left his government. After all, what better illustrated the essential moderation of his policy?

At Terrace in British Columbia — inland from Prince Rupert — a brigade of NRMA men mounted guns on the single rail line and announced that they were on strike. Senior officers, who had been attending a conference in Vancouver, returned and quietly restored order. Despite a large number of desertions, 12,908 NRMA men went overseas before the end of the war, and 2,463 were posted to units of the First Canadian Army. As it happened, the predictions of "wastage" that had provoked the reinforcements crisis had been incorrect. The three-month hiatus between the Battle of the Scheldt and the army's return to action prevented thousands of casualties. The transfer of I Canadian Corps from Italy to north-west Europe in February 1944 also provided a respite. Further conscription measures therefore proved unneeded, and it could be argued that the whole crisis had been unnecessary—but no one, in November 1944, could foresee that.

INTO GERMANY

If the First Canadian Army was in a static period, the war nevertheless went on. In December 1944 the Germans suddenly struck at the First U.S. Army in enormous force through the heavily forested and lightly manned Ardennes. Hitler's aim was to reach Antwerp, trapping huge armies and creating a second Dunkirk. The First Canadian Army was not directly involved in this titanic struggle; had the *Wehrmacht* made it to Antwerp, the Canadians too would have been caught in the trap, but General Eisenhower quickly moved his armies to counter the threat. Although units of the Yanks dissolved in scenes of great chaos, others held on, especially at the critical road junction of Bastogne, and the line was soon restored. The Ardennes attack may have been Hitler's last offensive gasp, but it demonstrated that the *Wehrmacht* remained a formidable foe even with its back to the wall.

A wily foe, too. On Christmas Eve, as Ben Dunkelman remembered, the Germans sang carols and fired tracers into the air, "as good as any display of fireworks". The Canadians opposite them in the line relaxed, left their slit trenches, and watched. "At this point, without warning, the enemy let loose a tremendous barrage of fire at our positions."

On New Year's Day, RCAF squadrons were among the targets for the *Luft-*

waffe's counterpart to the Battle of the Bulge. Eight hundred planes, including a captured Spitfire, tried to catch the Allied flyers with New Year's Eve hangovers. Scores of Allied aircraft were wrecked and burned — but so were *Luftwaffe* planes when the Allies responded. RCAF squadrons had some of their best days, and — unlike the Germans — they could make good their losses.

By February 1945 the Canadians were back in action. With General Crerar again in command, the First Canadian Army participated in massive operations to destroy the remaining Nazi armies west of the Rhine. Under Crerar were thirteen divisions, including nine British divisions and units of Belgians, Dutch, Poles, and Americans. It was the largest force ever commanded in operations by a Canadian officer. The plan was for Crerar's army to strike south-east to clear the land between the Maas and Rhine rivers.

The Canadians faced three lines of German defensive works: a strong line of outposts; the Siegfried Line, or West Wall, running through the wooded area of the Reichswald; and the fortified Hochwald area, again heavily forested and protecting the Rhine crossings at Wesel. The plan to break these lines was code-named "Veritable".

"Veritable" began on February 8 with a massive air and artillery bombardment. "I don't know what effect [the bombardment] had on the enemy," one Canadian remembered, "but, by God, [it] frightened me." Then came the tanks and, behind them, the Canadian infantry, cracking the outpost line — held by a scratch German division — with fewer casualties than expected. But in the Reichswald forests the going was slower, the resistance stronger, as the *Wehrmacht* fought stubbornly and with cunning on German soil. Donald Hough, a photo interpreter with the Royal Canadian Engineers, remembered the way the Germans used dummy artillery to draw fire and mislead the attackers—one battery was "heavily camouflaged and had a flash simulator in it which sent off flashes for two rounds ranging and ten rounds gunfire."

The Germans, who were desperate to delay the advance while they rushed in reinforcements of high quality parachute and Panzer troops, had flooded the low-lying ground, creating the familiar quagmire that Canadian soldiers had been obliged to deal with in the Scheldt fighting. When the 3rd Canadian Division faced a weak Grenadier Regiment, they reported that the floods were the "greatest enemy", and one officer remembered that he had had to help two short men through the deep spots, holding their battledress collars so their chins stayed out of the freezing water. Even so, by February 10 the 9th Canadian Infantry Brigade had broken through the Siegfried Line defences and fulfilled the promise of the popular 1939 song "to hang out the washing on the Siegfried Line". Hough recalled that the troops put up a sign and "on a line suspended on poles hung the proverbial washing." In fierce fighting, the Reichswald was cleared by February 13.

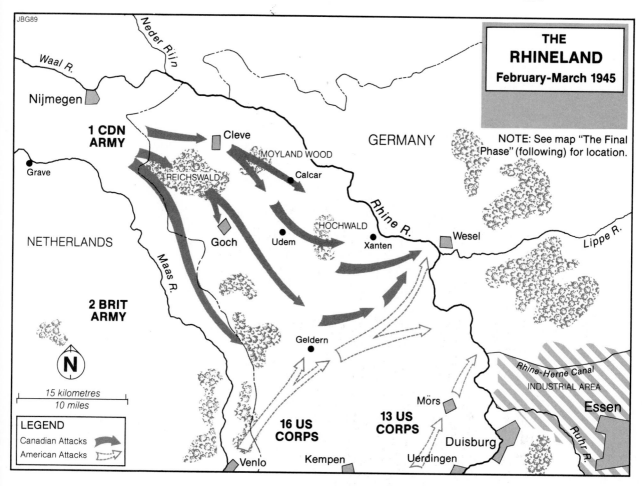

Then strong pockets of resistance had to be eliminated in Moyland Wood and along the Goch–Calcar road, a task entrusted to units of II Canadian Corps. Infantry of the Royal Winnipeg Rifles, the 1st Canadian Scottish, the Royal Hamilton Light Infantry (Rileys), the Royal Regiment, and the Essex Scottish did the job. The Canadian Scottish suffered especially heavy losses against German paratroopers; they had 140 casualties on February 18–19, including 53 taken prisoner after a counter-attack. The Winnipeg Rifles lost even more, but finally crushed enemy resistance in Moyland Wood on the 21st.

The Hochwald was next. Situated on a ridge in front of the ancient town of Xanten, the forest was to be the object of Operation "Blockbuster" on February 26. Although German paratroop units launched an attack on the jumping-off point of the 2nd Division just hours before the planned start of "Blockbuster", the enemy was driven back by a company of Rileys and tanks of the Fort Garry Horse. As a result, "Blockbuster" started on schedule at 3:45 A.M., the troops moving in Kangaroos or aboard tanks and finding their way with the aid of artificial moonlight. The Cameron Highlanders of the 6th Brigade, assigned a critical objective, almost faltered when their commanding officer was killed. Major D.M. Rodgers, one of the Winnipeg regiment's company commanders, took over, personally cleared three houses of snipers, and ensured that the assault took the ground as planned. The major won the DSO for his gallantry.

On the 3rd Division's front, the Queen's Own Rifles had a difficult time attacking Mooshof, where they were forced to cross an open slope studded with pockets of paratroopers. The German tactics were very effective, as Major Dunkelman explained:

No rigid defence: under attack, they hold on as long as possible in their excellently concealed slit trenches, then withdraw to prepared positions a little further back. Instantly, previously ranged mortar and artillery fire is poured on the positions they've just vacated—even if a few of their own men are still there. The shelling is coordinated with infantry assaults to retake the ground they've lost. Superb tactics.

Twice the QOR's leading platoon was driven back by German fire, and a Nazi counter-attack left the platoon with only five unwounded survivors. Sergeant Aubrey Cosens took command, ran twenty-five yards in the open to a tank of the 1st Hussars that had finally arrived to lend support, and—sitting exposed in front of the turret—directed fire against the German position. Then he broke up another counter-attack by plunging the tank directly into the midst of the Germans. Next Cosens organized a counter-attack by his men and directed the tank to ram one of the farm buildings that had been turned into a fortified German position. He then cleared the building and two others, winning the awe of his riflemen. Cosens had killed at least twenty Germans, and captured as many more. But the sergeant was not invincible, and as he went to report to his company commander he was cut down by a German sniper. The Victoria Cross was posthumously awarded to Sergeant Cosens.

On the last day of February, the Canadians attacked the Hochwald proper, losing scores of men to enemy mines and fire before finally clearing it on March 4. Xanten fell on the 8th, and on March 10 resistance ceased west of the Rhine. Canadian casualties in operations "Veritable" and "Blockbuster" numbered 5,304. The Germans had lost untold numbers of dead and more than 22,000 prisoners.

I Canadian Corps, fresh from the Italian front, now joined Crerar's First Canadian Army. The new arrivals were astonished at the endless air cover, the profusion of armour, and the flow of supplies that the north-west European front received. For the first time all major Canadian units were under one command. The expanded First Canadian Army crossed the Rhine on March 23 in Operation "Plunder". The troops were ferried across the great river in Buffaloes under cover of a massive artillery barrage, and the resistance was comparatively light, the Germans clearly having consumed their last effective resources west of the Rhine. "It begins to look as if the Hun has lost all his fight and confidence," the Irish Regiment's padre wrote home. "The general picture certainly indicates the fall of all organized resistance. What is making them continue?"

By the beginning of April, the Canadian army was driving rapidly northwards. Its task was to clear the north-eastern Netherlands, the German coast east to the Elbe, and the western Netherlands. II Canadian Corps handled the first two tasks, while I Canadian Corps undertook the latter.

The fighting was never easy—even *in extremis* the German soldier remained the best fighting man in the world—but the advances were rapid. II Corps cleared Deventer, Zwolle, Groningen, Emden, Wilhelmshaven, and Oldenburg. Some units found and enjoyed the spoils of war. Trooper Bill McDowell of the 8th Reconnaissance Regiment wrote home that "we took a lot of boats off a canal, and they were full of wine, candy and food." His unit "sure did a lot of wine drinking and had a good time as we could get anything we wanted with the candy."

I Corps captured Arnhem and Appeldoorn — where, Farley Mowat wrote, "the only shots fired were those fired into the air by the [Hastings and Prince Edward Regiment] C.O.'s pistol as he sought to clear a path through the civilian throngs." The Canadians were preparing to assault the German defences around Utrecht when the Nazi *Reichskommissar* in The Netherlands offered to permit food to be brought in to feed the starving Dutch—the official daily ration in April of that "hunger winter" amounted to 320 calories—if the Canadians stopped their advance. Field Marshal Montgomery agreed, and a *de facto* truce went into effect on April 28. One soldier of the Saskatoon Light Infantry remembered that first night: "It was too quiet. You were so used to sleeping with shells landing all about you," Bob Stier recalled, "that when it became quiet that night, nobody could fall asleep." Food was carried into this heavily populated area of Holland by truck convoys, or dropped from the air. A pilot officer in Bomber Command, Colin Friesen, recollected that "Thank you, Canadians!" had been painted on the rooftops — but he also recalled that, in accordance with the truce, the aircraft had to keep to routes and heights agreed to by the Germans. "I remember watching the German ack-ack guns and I can recall them following our progress…. And then the Dutch people would appear everywhere in the vicinity of the drop…everywhere waving banners and caps—and I'm sure of it, you felt you could hear them cheering." You could, too.

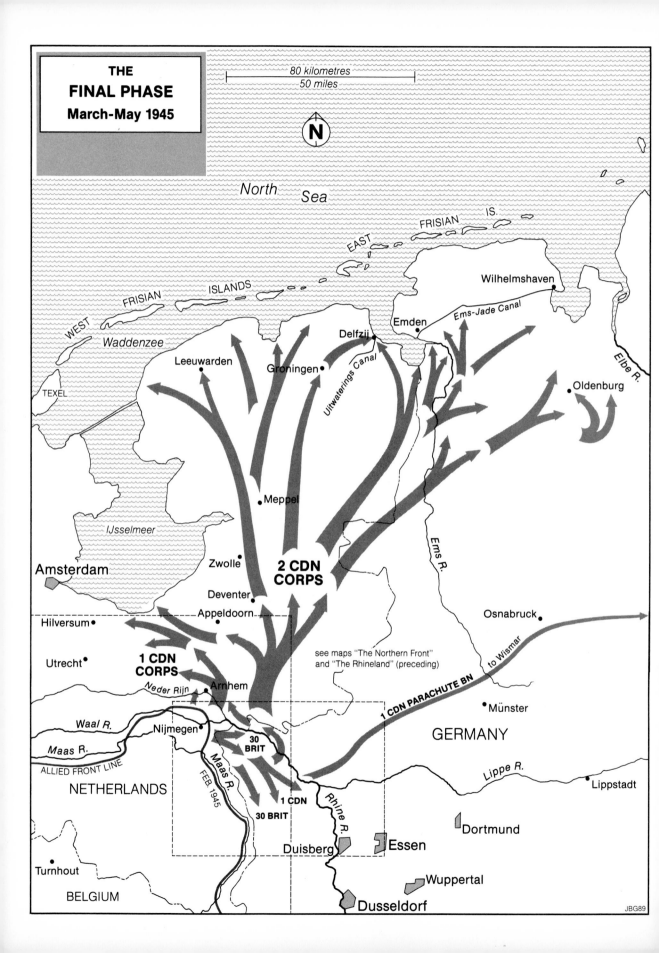

THE
FINAL PHASE
March-May 1945

80 kilometres
50 miles

N

North   Sea

FRISIAN   IS.

EAST

Wilhelmshaven

Emden   *Ems-Jade Canal*

FRISIAN

ISLANDS

Delfzij

Elbe R.

WEST

Waddenzee

Leeuwarden

Groningen

Uitwaterings Canal

Oldenburg

TEXEL

Ems R.

Meppel

IJsselmeer

2 CDN
CORPS

Amsterdam

Zwolle

Osnabruck

Deventer

Hilversum   Appeldoorn

see maps "The Northern Front"
and "The Rhineland" (preceding)

Utrecht

1 CDN
CORPS

to Wismar

1 CDN PARACHUTE BN

Arnhem

Münster

Neder Rijn

GERMANY

Waal R.

Nijmegen

30
BRIT

Maas R.

Lippe R.

Maas R.
FEB. 1945

ALLIED FRONT LINE

Lippstadt

NETHERLANDS

1 CDN

Rhine R.

30 BRIT

Turnhout

Duisberg

Essen

Dortmund

BELGIUM

Wuppertal

Dusseldorf

JBG89

End of a War

By the end of April, the war in Europe truly seemed to be drawing to a close. On April 25, American and Soviet soldiers, happy but already a little wary of each other, had met at Torgau, cutting the remnants of the Third Reich in two. The Russian armies were crushing everything in their path. Soviet tanks and grenadiers were already inching their way through the rubble of Berlin against fanatical resistance from old men and young boys. The American, British, and Canadian armies were moving eastwards with speed, now rounding up prisoners by the tens of thousands as German will at last began to collapse. The Soviets were so feared, their desire for revenge against the Nazis who had slaughtered millions in the Soviet Union so obvious, that the main aim of German soldiers—and civilians—was to end up on the Allied side of the final armistice line.

The Germans had reason to be afraid. By now, the Allies had liberated concentration camps in Eastern Europe and on German soil. For years there had been rumours of horrible atrocities, but most Canadians had tended to discount them as propaganda. Now the truth was there for everyone to see. The pitiful survivors, dressed in their striped rags, were literally skin and bones. General Georges Vanier, the Canadian ambassador in Paris, reported after seeing the camp at Buchenwald that he could actually see "how [their] knee and ankle joints held together." In death camps such as Auschwitz, the "showers" that had produced not water but Zyklon-B gas, the ovens used to dispose of millions of corpses, stood as mute testimony to the Nazis all-too-successful attempts to eliminate the Jews, gypsies, and other *Untermenschen* of Europe. Outraged Allied commanders rounded up local townsfolk and marched them through the camps. In future, they believed, no one would ever be able to deny that such atrocities had occurred. Soviet commanders unleashed their soldiers on the population, and the rape of both young and old became a daily occurrence.

There was sporadic fighting and still more death. As late as May 4, an officer and the padre of the Canadian Grenadier Guards left their lines to try to assist German wounded. Both were killed. They were almost the last Canadians killed in action in the European theatre, as General Crerar called off all operations the moment he learned that surrender negotiations were in progress. The war *was* drawing to a close.

The Führer of the Third Reich, the man responsible for the great war that had devastated the continent and caused misery around the world, was now living a mole-like existence in his deep bunker in the centre of Berlin. On April 29, Adolf Hitler married his mistress, Eva Braun, and the next day the Nazi leader and his bride committed suicide. While most of the Führer's personal staff took part in a wild orgy, others in the entourage killed themselves and their children. Hitler's body was taken to the surface and burned with the aid of gasoline.

A few days later, on May 2, the German armies in Italy surrendered. In Germany, however, Grand Admiral Karl Dönitz — Hitler's choice as successor — delayed the surrender as long as possible to permit more troops and civilians to reach the Allied lines. Surrender negotiations in north-west Europe began at last on May 4, to conclude only in the early morning hours of May 7. Effective at 8:00 A.M. May 7, the war in Europe was over.

At the front, the reaction was not one of jubilation. "I think we were all a bit numb," Major-General Harry Foster of the 1st Canadian Division recalled. "Six and a half years is a long time for any man to be thinking about just trying to stay alive.... I think everyone was just too bloody tired to get excited." Lieutenant John Bennett, who was with his artillery unit near the German naval base at Emden, remembered "a tremendous feeling of relief. They issued us two rations of rum that morning." And a navy man explained, "The stress level we had maintained for so long was replaced by a feeling that can only be described as subdued and a little sad."

Robert Rintoul, a corporal in the Royal Canadian Dragoons, had more profound feelings of relief. Just before the surrender, his squadron had been pinned down by German artillery fire, and he and his comrades at first refused to believe the good news. "Ah, that's all bunk, propaganda," was their initial reaction; the war was supposed to be over "but the Germans were still using shells."

Farther away from the front, the joy was unconfined. John Gray, an army intelligence officer, helped liberate a Dutch city after Nazi surrender. His jeep passed a house full of German soldiers "waving and yelling excitedly, as joyously as the liberated Dutch."

This we weren't quite in a mood for yet, and we hurried by with only a perfunctory acknowledgement of this forgive-and-forget gesture. It wasn't just a rough hockey game we had all been playing, and even if these men had not committed the mindless bestialities of the Nazis...they could not expect us to stop thinking them loathsome just because pieces of paper had been signed saying the shooting would stop.

A Dutch teenager in The Hague remembered the arrival of the liberating troops:

...I saw a tank in the distance, with one soldier's head above it, and the blood drained out of my body, and I thought: *Here comes liberation.* And as the tank came nearer, I had no breath left, and the soldier stood up, and he was like a saint. There was a big hush over all the people, and it was suddenly broken by a big scream, as if it was out of the earth. And the people climbed on the tank, and took the soldier out, and they were crying. And we were running with the tanks and the jeeps all the way into the city.

Such moments almost made up for the war's suffering.

The celebrations in Paris were, well, French. Barney Oldfield, a soldier on leave, was decorated with kisses by pretty *jeunes filles*. "We knocked on a house door and were invited in to celebrate with a family." Another soldier, Charlie Cunningham, was in Paris on a three-day pass on May 8. "I think I kissed and hugged half the women in Paris that day. All ages. And I don't think I had two drinks out of the same bottle all day." In London, celebrants mobbed Piccadilly Circus, while more solemn crowds gathered in front of Buckingham Palace waiting for Churchill and the king.

At home in Canada, the celebration got out of hand. Not in Toronto, where thousands danced in the streets and three Mosquito bombers dropped tickertape. Not in Ottawa, where enthusiasm was likely dulled by Mackenzie King's address of thanksgiving. Not in Vancouver, where people remembered that the war with Japan had still to be won. But in Halifax it was different.

Halifax had nearly doubled in size during the war, with some 60,000 servicemen added to the Nova Scotia capital's peacetime population of 65,000. Many of the newcomers, in addition to chafing under military discipline, hated the town, disliked the locals, and bitterly resented the antiquated liquor laws. The resentment boiled over when VE-Day came and businesses, restaurants, and stores – including liquor stores — shut down for the holiday. Despite plenty of notice, service commanders had done nothing to plan for the VE-Day mood. Nor had civil authorities. Milling, frustrated sailors and some soldiers and airmen, joined by civilians, sacked Keith's Brewery and attacked liquor stores, "liberating" 65,000 quarts of booze. One participant remembered coming across a sergeant "who had a full case of Canadian Club. He had already emptied one bottle and was selling the others at fifty cents each." Certainly there was alcohol enough to fuel rioting and the looting of more than five hundred businesses, including restaurants and taverns. While some celebrated the coming of peace by coupling on Citadel Hill, other women were raped, three rioters died, and two hundred more were arrested. The mayor blamed the navy, and declared, "It will be a long time before the people of Halifax forget the great crime." The navy took the lesson to heart. When VJ-Day came in September, things were different, as Chief Engine Room Artificer Walt Farrell recalled. "They had a real party. There was no rough stuff. They had orchestras and everything [at the base]. Had a real good time. Everybody had all the booze they could drink.... There wasn't a window broken in Halifax...."

POLITICS AT HOME

The silencing of the guns in Europe meant that domestic politics picked up steam. Mackenzie King had already announced that a federal election was to take place on June 11, not at all coincidentally the same day that a provincial election was scheduled for Ontario. But Premier George Drew, a fierce opponent of the federal Liberals, moved his election up one week to June 4. A Tory victory in Ontario would help John Bracken's federal Progressive Conservatives.

At the beginning of the federal campaign few expected a Liberal win. The memories of the conscription crisis the previous November were still strong, and the general feeling was that there had been too much death and suffering, too long a period of high taxes, too much Mackenzie King. Or so everyone thought.

But who were the voters to cast their ballots for? In Quebec, no federal politician stood high in the public estimation. In English Canada the CCF had clearly peaked at least a year before and though M.J. Coldwell, the party leader, was admired, a business-backed propaganda campaign depicted his party as "national socialists, eager to nationalize everything that moved". After all the wartime regimentation, that did not sit well with many. The Tories, expecting to be swept to power on a wave of anti-government sentiment, vowed to use conscripts in the war against Japan, and continually harked back to such Liberal failures as the wartime reinforcements crisis. Bracken was uninspiring as a speaker, and his promises roused little enthusiasm at a time when most people were worrying about the impact of peace on the economy. Did the end of the war mean another economic collapse like that of the Great Depression?

Mackenzie King's campaign was pitched to deal with this widespread fear. Liberal posters promised "a New Social Order", a CCF future without socialism. King talked little about the war, urging one London, Ontario audience to "Remember, it is with the future, not with the past, that you should be concerned." His government had implemented social welfare; "We have already placed on the statutes of Canada, law after law to deal with the situations that will have to be met through the coming years." One measure was family allowances, the centrepiece of the King campaign; every month, said one piece of Liberal election literature, family allowances would pour $132,981 into Cochrane, Ontario, and $153,891 into Welland. Such numbers, replicated across the land, translated into jobs and sales for merchants. Social welfare was a guarantee that, even if the economy slipped, no one would starve.

The result of the balloting on June 11 was unaffected by George Drew's Ontario triumph a week before. The King Liberals won 41 per cent of the popular vote and 127 seats while the Tories took only 28.5 per cent and 67 seats. The CCF drew 14.7 per cent of public support and won 28 seats. In the armed forces' vote, the Liberals won 35 per cent of the total, the CCF 32 per cent, and the Tories, despite their eagerness for conscription, only 26 per cent. That was perhaps the most astonishing result of the voting. J. Douglas Harvey, a young RCAF bomber pilot, remembered a large crowd of officers and airmen booing the prime minister in England:

> "Who is this guy?" Many didn't know but we were booing lustily. Finally a ground crew flight sergeant enlightened me.
> "It's Mackenzie King," he said.
> "Who's he?" I asked.
> A look of disdain came over the flight sergeant's face. "Our prime minister, you asshole."
> I really hadn't known, nor had half the crowd in that hangar. Yet we all booed vigorously. It took several years before I fully understood how much the Canadian serviceman detested the man and his weak-kneed war policies.

Still, there could be little doubt that Quebec, as one writer noted, "saved our King". Quebeckers gave King more than 50 per cent of their votes and 53 seats. Presumably the French-speaking electorate had remembered that King had, after all, fought against conscription, a memory undoubtedly sharpened by the way the Conservatives kept harping on the reinforcement question.

Mackenzie King was duly grateful to the nation. As he wrote in his diary, "The relief of mind that I experienced is indescribable.... almost as if I had had a bath after a dusty and dirty journey, with the storm of lies, misrepresentations, insinuations...which I have had to pass during the past few weeks.... I felt a real vindication in the verdict of the people...."

Whatever the reason, Mackenzie King had won once more. The great magician of Canadian politics had conjured victory out of certain defeat. Perhaps he won because Canada's war effort had been so impressive in military, economic, and industrial terms. Whatever their political allegiance, Canadians had to recognize that the main job — the job that *had* to be done — had been done well.

THE ATOMIC AGE BEGINS

By May 1945, the Japanese Empire had shrunk to a small portion of its vast extent at the floodtide of victory in 1942. Then Tokyo had threatened Australia and India; now, aside from remnants of once-great armies struggling against the inevitable in Burma and garrisons on a few Pacific atolls, only the home islands remained. Japan's wooden cities were being torched in massive American bombing raids, and the once-mighty Imperial Japanese Navy had virtually all been sunk. But the Japanese soldier remained a daunting foe, and no one expected an easy or unopposed invasion of the home islands.

Canada was to participate in that invasion with army, navy, and air contingents. In September 1944, the Cabinet War Committee had decided that "as a basis for planning, but without any commitment", the Canadian army would provide one division and ancillary troops to operate with the Americans. Up to 30,000 battle-experienced troops, to be found from men serving in the European theatre, would make up the force. And, as the prime minister told Parliament on April 4, 1945, the force would be chosen "from those who elect to serve in the Pacific theatre". No conscription, in other words. Moreover, each volunteer was entitled to thirty days' home leave before posting to the Pacific.

In the RCN, with the cruiser HMCS *Uganda* already in the Pacific and HMCS *Ontario* under orders, the volunteers-only rule caused serious problems. Officers and ratings serving in Europe or Canada who volunteered for the Pacific were posted immediately to the cruiser *Ontario*. But those sailors already on the *Uganda* also had the right to decide if they wished to volunteer for Pacific service. *Uganda* had been engaged in operations off Okinawa and Japan; despite appeals by its officers, the majority of the ship's crew decided not to volunteer, and the cruiser embarrassingly had to return to Canada on July 27, 1945. In Canada, Petty Officer Earle Johnson remembered, with delight unaltered after forty years, that he had volunteered for the Pacific to get the thirty days' leave. "But…we beat them out — we got the leave, but didn't have to go to Japan," because the war ended before his ship was ready. "We were sent home instead!"

The army division for the Pacific war, the 6th Canadian, was organized on

American lines with regiments instead of brigades. In command was Major-General Bert Hoffmeister, who had been a successful armoured division commander in Italy and north-west Europe. His men were to concentrate at training camps across Canada, then move to Kentucky for further exercises.

The plans were in hand, and 24,000 officers and men had been posted to the Canadian Army Pacific Force, when the war against Japan came to its sudden conclusion in August. The atomic bombing of Hiroshima on the 6th and of Nagasaki on the 9th forced Japan to sue for peace and ended the Pacific war on August 14. Only a few realized that the A-bomb had changed warfare for ever. Even fewer had known that much of the wartime research into the secrets of the atom had been carried out in Canada, largely by British and French scientists, under the aegis of the National Research Council, and that Canadian uranium had been a vital resource. With the end of wartime secrecy, the government was quick to make its part known. Curiously, Ottawa kept silent until the 1980s about code-breaking work run by the National Research Council's "Examination Unit". The unit had cracked some Japanese army codes, as well as eavesdropping on German ship traffic — and on the Vichy French legation that had stayed in Ottawa until November 1942.

The survivors of the Hong Kong force and a few additional Canadians were among the thousands of prisoners of war held by Japan. All had suffered unspeakable treatment in their prisons, with beatings a regular occurrence and starvation the norm. After the surrender, remembered John Stroud, one of those captured when Hong Kong fell on Christmas Day, 1941, American aircraft flew over the POW camp at Niigata and dropped "everything we needed". Included were large pails of ketchup, one of which hit a tree and exploded, showering Stroud with red. "I thought, 'I've survived all this and now I've been wounded.'"

Without any logistical support in the Pacific, the Canadian government had to rely on the British and American forces in its efforts to help Canadian POWs. Leading the effort to rescue the 1,085 Canadians held in Japan was Brigadier Richard S. Malone, attached to General MacArthur's staff. In a CBC broadcast to Canada, Malone said, "It was hard for the prisoners to believe that they were now free. Some of them had just about given up hope in their prisons." Malone then quoted a prayer written by a Canadian officer after he had been locked up in Hong Kong for three years and was "beginning to wonder if we were really coming."

You know Lord how one has to strive at Sanshepow to
   keep alive.
And how there isn't much to eat —

Some rice and greens at Argyle Street.
It's not much, God, when dinner comes,
To find it's boiled chrysanthemums....
So what I really want to say is if we soon don't get
    away,
From Sanshepow and Argyle Street,
Then please Lord could we have some meat —
A luscious fragrant heaped up plateful.
And also Lord we would be grateful
If you would grant a living boon and send some Red
    Cross parcels soon.

A GRATEFUL NATION

Canada was fully intending to grant a "living boon" to all its veterans.
Nowhere were bitter memories of the Great War more pronounced. Ian
Mackenzie, King's Minister of National Health and Pensions, had made a
career as an advocate for his fellow veterans. He could remember the old
complaints about pensions, settlement, and the "soldiers' bonus". Everything that had been sought by the men who returned in 1919 was included in
the new "Veterans' Charter". But first a scheme had to be developed to bring
them from Europe. The army worked out a complicated point system to
determine priority for repatriation. Soldiers received two points for each
month of service in Canada, three for each month overseas, and a 20 per cent
bonus if they were married. Points were deducted for periods of non-
performance of military duty, such as time spent in detention for infractions
against military law. A high score got you home faster, though top priority was
given to those who volunteered for the Pacific war. As General Harry Crerar
told his men, shipping space was in terribly short supply, and Canadians were
competing for that space with their Allies. That was why the battalions and
regiments that had fought together through Italy, France, and the Low Countries could not go home as units.

Once the men and women got home, each received thirty days' leave. Dis-
charge then followed; at the peak of demobilization, in the winter of 1945–46,
3,000 men and women were being returned to "civvy street" each day. Thanks
to the efforts at reconstruction planning that had got under way at the very
beginning of the war, and to the Department of Veterans Affairs (DVA), created
in 1944, each veteran received $100 to buy civilian clothing and a war service
gratuity of $7.50 for each thirty days' service, plus an additional 25 cents for
each day overseas. In addition, veterans drew one week's pay for each six

months' service outside Canada. In all, these gratuities went to just under one million men and women and amounted to an average of $488 each. Since compulsory savings had been deducted from men overseas, to deter overspending and British resentment, most veterans had a tidy nest egg.

In addition to that benefit, the government paid unemployment insurance premiums for more than half a million ex-service personnel. It passed the Veterans' Land Act to help settle 33,000 on the land as farmers and assisted thousands more in purchasing land. It offered loans to those who wanted to set themselves up in business. The DVA oversaw a vast training program that sent tens of thousands to vocational programs and helped rehabilitate the wounded and injured. Those who declined further education or vocational training or did not seek assistance settling on the land received instead a "re-establishment credit". This did not come in the form of cash; instead it could be used for the acquisition, repair, or modernization of a home; purchase of furniture; or to help start a business. (NRMA men who had not gone "active" did not receive this credit.) And there was a generous scheme of pensions for widows and dependants and for those whose lives had been permanently altered by physical or mental wounds. Canada wanted to be generous. By most contemporary standards, and certainly in comparison with 1919, a rich array of benefits awaited the veterans. It was no more than they deserved.

Tens of thousands of qualified veterans went to university to enrol or to finish degrees interrupted by the war. The universities, small, understaffed, and underequipped, had to prepare for this flood of veterans. At the University of British Columbia, President N.A.M. MacKenzie solved the housing and classroom needs of his campus by moving in 370 army huts from bases all across the province. Other universities followed suit, and veterans who had hoped that they had seen the last of H-huts now found themselves living and attending class in them. Toronto opened a new engineering school in abandoned war factories in the suburb of Ajax. Ottawa's Carleton University was virtually created by veterans.

Improvisation was the order of the day, but thousands of vets — most of whom had learned to discipline themselves and to organize their time in the service — became lawyers, doctors, engineers, and teachers as quickly as they could. Some universities speeded up their programs: UBC helped by giving veterans a year's worth of classes in four months.

However many grants and programs there were for the men and women who came home, the transition to peace was harrowing to many. Some Canadian soldiers had been overseas since December 1939 without once returning home, longer, they joked, than any soldiers since Alexander the Great's. Servicemen had worked in trades where killing was necessary, where cruelty often outweighed compassion. Now they were to return to a society where, thank goodness, the war's devastation had never touched down, where different mores prevailed, and where few who had not seen service overseas could understand the horror that air crew, infantrymen, or survivors of the U-boat war had come through.

Worse still, the veterans had not seen their wives or watched their children grow up. The strain that such prolonged separation placed on families and marriages was inevitable and immense. As Brigadier James Roberts wrote in a memoir, "I had left Canada in November 1941 and written regularly" to his wife once a week. "Like other Canadians, I had known several women in England during our three years of training there, but it had never even remotely crossed my mind that I would not return to Canada and resume my life with Helen." But Roberts fell in love with a woman he met in The Netherlands, and when he returned to Toronto, it was to a difficult situation.

> I found Helen waiting for me at the Union Station and I was very glad to see her again, after an absence of nearly four years. We took a taxi to her apartment, made coffee, and settled down to talk about our personal affairs. As to the war years, they never seemed to have happened; she did not seem to be interested, and I found little to talk about with her except the important question of what we were going to do.... I told her openly that I had fallen in love and that I wanted a divorce....

That happened to many veterans. Many others found that their wives had made other arrangements while they were overseas.

Still other soldiers, sailors, and airmen faced the problem of integrating British, French, Dutch, or Italian war brides into their families at home. Many had exaggerated the extent of "Daddy's ranch in Toronto", as one "Herbie" cartoon teased. The brides themselves had to adjust to a new culture, and while they were generally greeted with kindness and warmth, there were hostile moments.

Harder still was the effort faced by those who had lost a husband or father overseas. Private Elmer Johnson of the Loyal Edmonton Regiment died on the Senio River in Italy just days before I Canadian Corps pulled out of the line to rejoin the First Canadian Army in north-west Europe. Years later his son, who had been just three years old in 1945, wrote of what it meant to grow up without a father:

> I can't remember how I felt when told of his death, not knowing the meaning of the word. But as I grew in consciousness, his absence became a fact

of my life — like being a boy and not a girl, or living with people who were my family and not somebody else's. I came to realize I would never see him, but it wasn't something I could rationally get my mind around.

Because everybody else I knew had a father, I felt set apart, like one of the strange people hidden in backrooms or attics. It also meant I didn't have an obvious and recognizable identity: I didn't belong to Dr. X or Shift Boss Y. However, I did have a privileged spiritual link. While my classmates uttered abstractions during the daily rote muttering of the Lord's Prayer, I had a picture in my mind of "Our Father, who art in Heaven".…

The return to normalcy was hard indeed; the astonishing thing is that so many veterans managed so successfully to pick up the pieces of their lives and to begin to earn a peacetime living.

As the First Canadian Army advanced on the left flank of the Allies, mud, water, and cold combined to make conditions miserable. Here, a column of Sherman tanks moves slowly through North Beveland, alongside a flooded field carefully planted with stakes by the *Wehrmacht* to prevent glider landings.

Men of the 3rd Canadian Infantry Division, who cleared the enemy from the
muddy devastation of the Breskens pocket, came to be known as "water rats".
Veterans of the earlier war would have recognized the scene — and envied the
array of vehicles supporting the infantry.

The Dutch liked the Canadians, and their gratitude and hospitality to their liberators remain warm to this day; the Canadians reciprocated. These men of the Fort Garry Horse seem quite at home as they work on a broken tank tread.

By April 1945, the Germans were beaten. But however battered the *Wehrmacht* was, its soldiers continued to resist stoutly. Here, men of the South Saskatchewan Regiment are pinned down under fire in a farmyard.

The South Saskatchewans carry out mopping-up operations along Holland's Oranje Canal.

As the Canadians moved into Germany, the men were ordered not to fraternize with the enemy. Other posters, more practical, warned of VD.

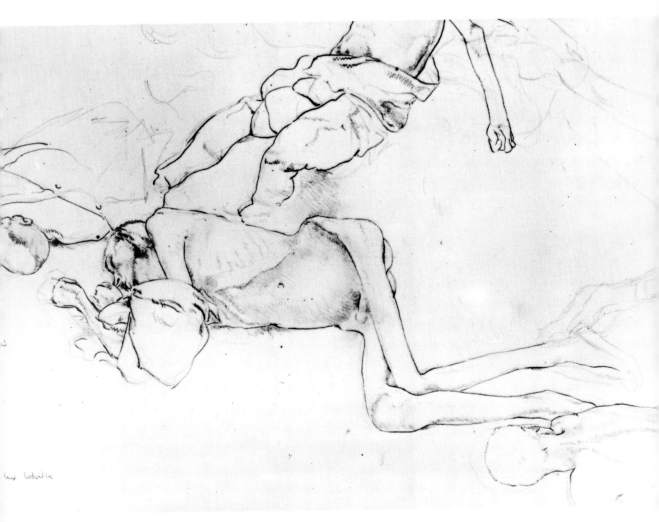

As concentration camps were liberated and word spread of the Nazi atrocities, fraternizing became a less attractive prospect, at least for a time. War artist Alex Colville sketched *Bodies in a Grave, Belsen Germany* on May 1, 1945.

The Germans had been driven back into the shrunken Reich, but the war would not end until the Western Allies linked up with the Soviets. Hitler's dream of conquest had turned into nightmare. Top, house-to-house battles complete the destruction of a German town; above, German POWs wash up in a stream.

VE-Day — May 8, 1945 — saw joyful celebrations across most of Canada, like these revellers at King and Bay streets in Toronto.

In Halifax VE-Day was a different story: the ill-timed closing of bars, restaurants, and liquor stores provoked rioting, violence, and vandalism, and shops were looted and demolished. One sailor and his girlfriend slept off their alcoholic stupor on a bed in a furniture-store window.

The task of bringing the boys home was complicated. Shipping space was limited, and a complex points system determined who went when. Here, the ss *Pasteur* docks in Halifax in June 1945.

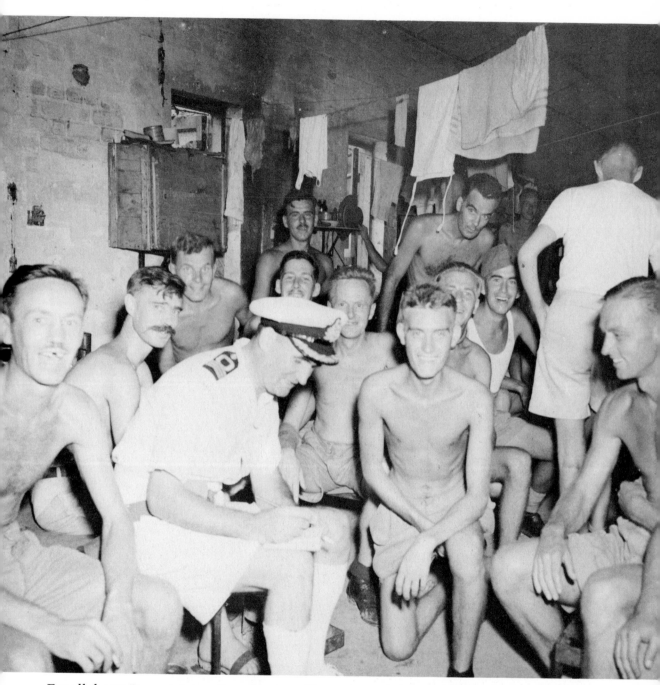

For all the VE-Day rejoicing, Canada was still at war until August 15, when Japan surrendered following the atomic bombing of Hiroshima and Nagasaki. The Japanese surrender meant freedom for the Canadians captured at Hong Kong on Christmas Day, 1941. The survivors were in appalling condition, brutalized, starving, and sick. Here, an officer from HMCS *Prince Robert* begins the inevitable paperwork before repatriation.

The Ontario Regiment finally comes home to Oshawa on November 29, 1945 —
after endless delays and two frustrating false starts. Many of the troopers had
been away for over four years.

In spring 1945, Mackenzie King had attended the San Francisco conference where the UN charter was drawn up. No wonder he looks so pleased with himself; through shrewdness and fancy footwork he had kept his party in power, led his country's phenomenal war effort, and won Canada international clout that would have been unimaginable six years earlier. Behind King are three of Canada's senior diplomats: (from left) Hume Wrong, Charles Ritchie, and Norman Robertson.

"Back to Civvy Street" was the goal of nearly every serviceman, and the armed services and the Department of Veterans Affairs tried to smooth the way. Rehabilitation courses began in Europe, while troops were waiting for transport; once they were home, counselling was offered on all kinds of personal and professional problems, and a variety of re-establishment grants and programs was available.

In the wake of repatriated soldiers, sailors, and airmen came more than 47,000 war brides, among them these apprehensive mothers arriving in February 1946. Here, too, the government tried to help, providing free sea and rail passage, as well as food allowances and medical attention. These young families faced some difficult adjustments, but the majority settled in and began a new life.

But all the rehabilitation in the world could not undo war's destruction. For some
— like this RCAF veteran disabled in an explosion — the loss was permanent.

The Canadian War Cemetery at Calais.

IX
A NATION FORGED IN FIRE

The Canada to which the veterans returned in 1945 and 1946 seemed like God's country. Compared to the devastation that was Germany, Japan, and Italy, compared to the ruination and privation that hung over Europe and Asia, Canada really was blessed. The nation had escaped the destruction that war had brought to most of the rest of the world. In fact, war had brought unparalleled prosperity to a country that in 1939 had been trapped in the Great Depression. A new Canada had emerged, forged in the fires of war.

For the men and women who returned from overseas there were the veterans' benefits, there were jobs, there was care for the wounded and pensions for the maimed in body and mind. The country made what amends it could for the dislocation of all these lives.

For those who did not return, the nation maintains military cemeteries scattered across Britain, France, Belgium, The Netherlands, Germany, Italy, Hong Kong, and a dozen other locations where Canadians fought and died. The beautiful grounds, lovingly tended—the stark headstones with their simple messages from parents, wives, or children — cannot fail to bring tears to the eyes of all who visit their quiet precincts.

We should weep for the dead of the Second World War. Some Canadian soldiers, sailors, and airmen died while performing acts of high courage. But the Aubrey Cosens and Andy Mynarskis were always few in number. Many died while simply trying to carry out the orders they had been given. Take that hill, bomb that factory, guard that convoy — such objectives, multiplied by ten thousand instances, were the war for most servicemen who came under fire. Countless other men and women trained for war but spent their time in the multitude of essential, unglamorous jobs that make every modern military machine operate.

Some of those who died or were wounded were victims of bungles, incompetent planning, and inadequate equipment. Seamen suffered horrible deaths because the Canadian navy was forced to use inferior equipment. Soldiers killed or captured on Hong Kong's steep hills had found themselves there because planners in London underestimated the Japanese and because their counterparts in Ottawa occasionally suffered spasms of misguided imperial loyalty. Those who bombed Germany in underpowered and underarmed aircraft suffered from the government's sins of omission and commission. We try to forget these mistakes today, papering over the guilty memories with assurances that all who died were brave, that all showed great courage under fire, that the defeats and the disasters, recorded with a care that suggests a kind of pride, were almost things of beauty. They weren't. The dead of the Second World War deserve to be remembered with more clarity than that provided by history glorified with romance.

Many have also forgotten other, equally important facts about that war. All these young Canadians (and we should not forget that the great majority were in their late teens and early twenties) fought for some important goals. Words like "freedom" and "democracy" tend to make Canadians blush and scrape their toes in the dirt in embarrassment. But the war against fascism was about freedom and democracy. There is too much naivety afoot these days, a feeling that no war can be a just war, that no cause can be worth dying for. The horrors of the Vietnam War and the ominous shadow of the nuclear arms race have made most Canadians unable to realize that once it was different.

The Second World War was a just war. The war against the unspeakable evil of Hitler's Germany, the savage buffoonery of Mussolini's Italy, and the sinister militarism of Tojo's Japan had to be fought, and had to be won. If the Axis had triumphed, the outcome could only have been unspeakable tyranny and institutionalized horror. The Second World War, Canadians should always remember, was fought to determine whether the world was to be slave or free. Those young Canadians, along with their comrades from the United States, Britain, and the other Allied nations, fought and won the most important battle of the modern era.

Many of those who served only dimly realized the importance of the struggle in which they fought. Not all were politically sophisticated, and the war's bloody horror — to say nothing of the obscene jockeying of politicians and generals for national or personal advantage — often made it nearly impossible to realize that noble ends were sought. Nor were they easier to see after victory left half of Europe under a Soviet tyranny as odious as Hitler's. But those ends were there and, at root, the men and women in uniform or at home in the factories and on the farms knew it.

Gerard Adriaenssens was with the Belgian Resistance when the Canadian army liberated his family farm near Knokke in October 1944. Thirty years later he started an annual march on November 1 to commemorate the liberation. When he was asked why, Adriaenssens said that a platoon of men had bedded down in his barn for one night in that hard October, and that their demeanour had remained fixed in his mind:

> They were not Rambo soldiers, as one now imagines, but rather quiet, simple boys with a dull look in their eyes, who mourned their comrades who fell that day. They sat there quietly and knew that it might be their turn to offer their lives the next day so that we here in Europe might live in freedom, friendship and peace.
>
> That is what we must tell the youth: the sacrifice these young Canadian soldiers freely gave for us.... they will always be remembered.

They should always be remembered — and not just by Europeans.

The death and destruction unleashed by the Second World War was unparalleled. Those men and women who gave their lives might have written great books, discovered cures for disease, or, more likely, simply have lived out their days in peace in their native land. They lost the chance for a full life because of forces beyond their control, beyond their country's control — forces most of them comprehended only dimly.

Canada and Canadians have had freedom and the fruits of victory since 1945. It is true that we have had precious little peace in that time — the victors moved into the Cold War before the ruins of Germany and Japan had ceased smouldering. But freedom has remained — and had we not fought, freedom would have been lost.

Was it worth it? Was it worth the death, the maiming, the unending pain? That is a terrible question if posed by someone who lost a son, a husband, or a father at Ortona, on HMCS *St. Croix*, or in a Lancaster over the Ruhr. Even so, there can be only one answer. Was it worth it? Oh, yes.

APPENDIX A

1st Canadian Infantry Division

4th Reconnaissance Regiment (Princess Louise Dragoon Guards)

1st Infantry Brigade
  The Royal Canadian Regiment
  The Hastings and Prince Edward Regiment
  48th Highlanders of Canada
2nd Infantry Brigade
  Princess Patricia's Canadian Light Infantry
  Seaforth Highlanders of Canada
  Loyal Edmonton Regiment
3rd Infantry Brigade
  Royal 22e Régiment
  Carleton and York Regiment
  West Nova Scotia Regiment

Saskatoon Light Infantry (MG)

1st Field Regiment RCHA
2nd Field Regiment
3rd Field Regiment
1st Anti-Tank Regiment
2nd Light Anti-Aircraft Regiment

2nd Canadian Infantry Division

8th Reconnaissance Regiment (14th Canadian Hussars)

4th Infantry Brigade
  Royal Regiment of Canada
  Royal Hamilton Light Infantry
  Essex Scottish Regiment
5th Infantry Brigade
  The Black Watch (Royal Highland Regiment) of Canada
  Le Régiment de Maisonneuve
  The Calgary Highlanders
6th Infantry Brigade
  Fusiliers Mont-Royal
  Queen's Own Cameron Highlanders
  South Saskatchewan Regiment
  Toronto Scottish Regiment (MG)

*The authors regret that space limitations require the omission of some Arms and
  Services of First Canadian Army.

4th Field Regiment
5th Field Regiment
6th Field Regiment
2nd Anti-Tank Regiment
3rd Light Anti-Aircraft Regiment

3rd Canadian Infantry Division

7th Reconnaissance Regiment (17th Duke of York's Royal Canadian Hussars)

7th Infantry Brigade
  Royal Winnipeg Rifles
  Regina Rifle Regiment
  1st Bn, Canadian Scottish Regiment
8th Infantry Brigade
  Queen's Own Rifles of Canada
  Le Régiment de la Chaudière
  North Shore (New Brunswick) Regiment
9th Infantry Brigade
  Highland Light Infantry of Canada
  Stormont, Dundas and Glengarry Highlanders
  North Nova Scotia Highlanders

Cameron Highlanders of Ottawa (MG)

12th Field Regiment
13th Field Regiment
14th Field Regiment
3rd Anti-Tank Regiment
4th Light Anti-Aircraft Regiment

4th Canadian Armoured Division

29th Reconnaissance Regiment (South Alberta Regiment)

4th Armoured Brigade
  21st Armoured Regiment (Governor General's Foot Guards)
  22nd Armoured Regiment (Canadian Grenadier Guards)
  28th Armoured Regiment (British Columbia Regiment)
10th Infantry Brigade
  Lincoln and Welland Regiment
  Algonquin Regiment
  Argyll and Sutherland Highlanders of Canada (Princess Louise's)
  Lake Superior Regiment (Motor)

15th Field Regiment
23rd Field Regiment (Self-Propelled)
5th Anti-Tank Regiment
4th Light Anti-Aircraft Regiment

5th Canadian Armoured Division

3rd Armoured Reconnaissance Regiment (Governor General's Horse Guards)

5th Armoured Brigade
 2nd Armoured Regiment (Lord Strathcona's Horse) (Royal Canadians)
 5th Armoured Regiment (8th Princess Louise's New Brunswick Hussars)
 9th Armoured Regiment (British Columbia Dragoons)
11th Infantry Brigade
 Perth Regiment
 Cape Breton Highlanders
 Irish Regiment of Canada
 Westminster Regiment (Motor)

 17th Field Regiment
 8th Field Regiment (Self-Propelled)
 4th Anti-Tank Regiment
 5th Light Anti-Aircraft Regiment

1st Armoured Brigade

11th Armoured Regiment (Ontario Regiment)
12th Armoured Regiment (Three Rivers Regiment)
14th Armoured Regiment (Calgary Regiment)

2nd Armoured Brigade

6th Armoured Regiment (1st Hussars)
10th Armoured Regiment (Fort Garry Horse)
27th Armoured Regiment (Sherbrooke Fusiliers)

I Canadian Corps Troops

1st Armoured Car Regiment (Royal Canadian Dragoons)

7th Anti-Tank Regiment
1st Survey Regiment
1st Light Anti-Aircraft Regiment (Lanark and Renfrew Scottish Regiment)

II Canadian Corps Troops

18th Armoured Car Regiment (12th Manitoba Dragoons)

6th Anti-Tank Regiment
2nd Survey Regiment
6th Light Anti-Aircraft Regiment

First Canadian Army Troops

25th Armoured Delivery Regiment (Elgin Regiment)
1st Armoured Personnel Carrier Regiment

1st Army Group, Royal Canadian Artillery
  11th Army Field Regiment
  1st Medium Regiment
  2nd Medium Regiment
  5th Medium Regiment

2nd Army Group, Royal Canadian Artillery
  19th Army Field Regiment
  3rd Medium Regiment
  4th Medium Regiment
  7th Medium Regiment
  2nd Heavy Anti-Aircraft Regiment (Mobile)

Royal Montreal Regiment
Canadian Parachute Battalion (with 6th British Airborne Division)

APPENDIX B

PRINCIPAL SHIPS OF THE ROYAL CANADIAN NAVY
1939–1945

Class	Ship	Class	Ship
Cruiser	Ontario		Skeena
	Uganda		(sunk 25 Oct. '44)
Escort Carrier	Nabob	*Frigate*	Annan
	Puncher		Antigonish
Armed Merchant Cruiser	Prince David		Beacon Hill
	Prince Henry		Buckingham
	Prince Robert		Cap de la Madeleine
Destroyer	Algonquin		Cape Breton
	Annapolis		Capilano
	Assiniboine		Carlplace
	Athabaskan		Charlottetown
	(sunk 29 Apr. '44)		Chebogue
	Buxton		Coaticook
	Chaudière		Dunver
	Columbia		Eastview
	Fraser		Ettrick
	(sunk 25 June '40)		Fort Erie
	Gatineau		Glace Bay
	Haida		Grou
	Hamilton		Hallowell
	Huron		Inch Arran
	Iroquois		Joliette
	Kootenay		Jonquière
	Margaree		Kirkland Lake
	(sunk 23 Oct. '40)		Kokanee
	Niagara		La Hulloise
	Ottawa		Lanark
	(sunk 14 Sept. '42)		Lasalle
	Ottawa		Lauzon
	Qu'Appelle		Lévis
	Restigouche		Loch Achanalt
	Saguenay		Loch Alvie
	St. Clair		Loch Morlich
	St. Croix		Longueuil
	(sunk 20 Sept. '43)		Magog
	St. Francis		Matane
	St. Laurent		Meon
	Saskatchewan		Monnow
	Sioux		Montreal

273

Class	Ship	Class	Ship
	Nene		Barrie
	New Glasgow		Battleford
	New Waterford		Beauharnois
	Orkney		Belleville
	Outremont		Bittersweet
	Penetang		Bowmanville
	Port Colborne		Brandon
	Poundmaker		Brantford
	Prestonian		Buctouche
	Prince Rupert		Calgary
	Ribble		Camrose
	Royalmount		Chambly
	Runnymede		Charlottetown
	St. Catharines		(sunk 11 Sept. '42)
	Saint John		Chicoutimi
	St. Pierre		Chilliwack
	St. Stephen		Cobalt
	Ste. Thérèse		Cobourg
	Seacliffe		Collingwood
	Springhill		Copper Cliff
	Stettler		Dauphin
	Stone Town		Dawson
	Stormont		Drumheller
	Strathadam		Dundas
	Sussexvale		Dunvegan
	Swansea		Edmundston
	Teme		Eyebright
	Thetford Mines		Fennel
	Toronto		Fergus
	Valleyfield		Forest Hill
	(sunk 7 May '44)		Fredericton
	Victoriaville		Frontenac
	Waskesiu		Galt
	Wentworth		Giffard
Corvette	Agassiz		Guelph
	Alberni		Halifax
	(sunk 21 Aug. '44)		Hawkesbury
	Algoma		Hepatica
	Amherst		Hespeler
	Arnprior		Humberstone
	Arrowhead		Huntsville
	Arvida		Kamloops
	Asbestos		Kamsack
	Athol		Kenogami
	Baddeck		Kincardine

Class	Ship		Class	Ship

Kitchener

Lachute

La Malbaie

Leaside

Lethbridge

Lévis
(sunk 19 Sept. '41)

Lindsay

Long Branch

Louisburg
(sunk 6 Feb. '43)

Louisburg

Lunenburg

Matapedia

Mayflower

Merrittonia

Midland

Mimico

Moncton

Moose Jaw

Morden

Nanaimo

Napanee

New Westminster

Norsyd

North Bay

Oakville

Orangeville

Orillia

Owen Sound

Parry Sound

Peterborough

Petrolia

Pictou

Port Arthur

Prescott

Quesnel

Regina (sunk 9 Aug. '44)

Rimouski

Rivière du Loup

Rosthern

Sackville

St. Lambert

St. Thomas

Saskatoon

Shawinigan
(sunk 25 Nov. '44)

Shediac

Sherbrooke

Smiths Falls

Snowberry

Sorel

Spikenard
(sunk 10 Feb. '42)

Stellarton

Strathroy

Sudbury

Summerside

The Pas

Thorlock

Tillsonburg

Timmins

Trail

Trentonian
(sunk 22 Feb. '45)

Trillium

Vancouver

Ville de Québec

West York

Wetaskiwin

Weyburn
(sunk 22 Feb. '43)

Whitby

Windflower
(sunk 7 Dec. '41)

Woodstock

Minesweeper Bayfield

Bellechasse

Blairmore

Border Cities

Brockville

Burlington

Canso

Caraquet

Chedabucto
(sunk 21 Oct. '43)

Chignecto

Clayoquot
(sunk 24 Dec. '44)

Comox

Class	Ship	Class	Ship
	Coquitlam		Oshawa
	Courtenay		Outarde
	Cowichan		Portage
	Cranbrook		Port Hope
	Daerwood		Quatsino
	Digby		Quinte
	Drummondville		Red Deer
	Esquimalt		Revelstoke
	(sunk 16 Apr. '45)		Rockcliffe
	Fort Frances		Rossland
	Fort William		St. Boniface
	Fundy		St. Joseph
	Gananoque		Sarnia
	Gaspé		Sault Ste. Marie
	Georgian		Stratford
	Goderich		Swift Current
	Granby		Thunder
	Grandmère		Transcona
	Guysborough		Trois-Rivières
	(sunk 17 Mar. '45)		Truro
	Ingonish		Ungava
	Kalamalka		Vegreville
	Kapuskasing		Wallaceburg
	Kelowna		Wasaga
	Kenora		Westmount
	Kentville		Winnipeg
	Lachine	*Armed*	Ambler
	Lavallee	*Yachts*	Beaver
	Llewellyn		Caribou
	Lloyd George		Cougar
	Lockeport		Elk
	Mahone		Grizzly
	Malpeque		Husky
	Medicine Hat		Lynx
	Melville		Moose
	Middlesex		Otter
	Milltown		(sunk 26 Mar. '41)
	Minas		Raccoon
	Miramichi		(sunk 7 Sept. '42)
	Mulgrave		Reindeer
	New Liskeard		Renard
	Nipigon		Sans Peur
	Nootka (Nanoose)		Vison
	Noranda		Wolf

APPENDIX C

RCAF SQUADRONS IN THE SECOND WORLD WAR

Home War Establishment

No. 1 Fighter Squadron (renumbered 401, 1 Mar. '41)
No. 2 Army Co-operation Squadron (disbanded 16 Dec. '39)
No. 3 Bomber Squadron (disbanded 5 Sept. '39)
No. 4 Bomber Reconnaissance Squadron WAC
No. 5 Bomber Reconnaissance Squadron EAC
No. 6 Bomber Reconnaissance Squadron WAC
No. 7 General Purpose Squadron (disbanded 10 Sept. '39)
No. 8 Bomber Reconnaissance Squadron WAC
No. 9 Bomber Reconnaissance Squadron (disbanded 1 Sept. '44) WAC
No. 10 Bomber Reconnaissance Squadron EAC
No. 11 Bomber Reconnaissance Squadron WAC
No. 12 Composite Squadron
No. 13 Seaplane and Bomber Reconnaissance Training Squadron (disbanded
    9 Nov. '42) WAC
No. 14 Fighter Squadron (renumbered 442, 8 Feb. '44)
No. 110 Army Co-operation Squadron (renumbered 400, 1 Mar. '41)
No. 111 Fighter Squadron (renumbered 440, 8 Feb. '44)
No. 112 Army Co-operation Squadron (renumbered 402, 1 Mar. '41)
No. 113 Bomber Reconnaissance Squadron (disbanded 23 Aug. '44) EAC
No. 115 Bomber Reconnaissance Squadron (disbanded 23 Aug. '44) WAC
No. 116 Bomber Reconnaissance Squadron EAC
No. 117 Bomber Reconnaissance Squadron (disbanded 15 Dec. '43) EAC
No. 118 Fighter Squadron (renumbered 438, 18 Nov. '43)
No. 119 Bomber Reconnaissance Squadron (disbanded 15 Mar. '44) EAC
No. 120 Bomber Reconnaissance Squadron (disbanded 1 May '44) WAC
No. 121 Composite Squadron EAC
No. 122 Composite Squadron WAC
No. 123 Army Co-operation Squadron (renumbered 439, 1 Jan. '44)
No. 124 Ferry Squadron
No. 125 Fighter Squadron (renumbered 441, 8 Feb. '44)
No. 126 Fighter Squadron EAC
No. 127 Fighter Squadron (renumbered 443, 8 Feb. '44)
No. 128 Fighter Squadron (disbanded 15 Mar. '44) EAC
No. 129 Fighter Squadron (disbanded 30 Sept. '44) EAC
No. 130 Fighter Squadron (disbanded 15 Mar. '44) EAC
No. 132 Fighter Squadron (disbanded 30 Sept. '44) WAC

(EAC = Eastern Air Command; WAC = Western Air Command)

277

No. 133 Fighter Squadron WAC
No. 135 Fighter Squadron WAC
No. 145 Bomber Reconnaissance Squadron EAC
No. 147 Bomber Reconnaissance Squadron (disbanded 15 Mar. '45) WAC
No. 149 Bomber Reconnaissance Squadron (disbanded 15 Mar. '44) WAC
No. 160 Bomber Reconnaissance Squadron EAC
No. 161 Bomber Reconnaissance Squadron EAC
No. 162 Bomber Reconnaissance Squadron (served in Coastal Command) EAC
No. 163 Fighter Squadron (disbanded 15 Mar. '44) WAC
No. 164 Transport Squadron EAC
No. 165 Transport Squadron WAC
No. 166 Communications Squadron WAC
No. 167 Communications Squadron EAC
No. 168 Heavy Transport Squadron
No. 170 Ferry Squadron

RCAF Overseas

No. 400 Army Co-operation (later Fighter-Reconnaissance) Squadron 2 TAF
No. 401 Fighter Squadron
No. 402 Fighter Squadron 2 TAF
No. 403 Fighter Squadron 127 Wing 2 TAF
No. 404 Coastal Squadron
No. 405 Bomber Squadron (a Pathfinder squadron)
No. 406 Night Fighter/Intruder Squadron
No. 407 Coastal Squadron
No. 408 Bomber Squadron 6 Group
No. 409 Night Fighter Squadron 2 TAF
No. 410 Night Fighter Squadron
No. 411 Fighter Squadron 2 TAF
No. 412 Fighter Squadron 2 TAF
No. 413 General Reconnaissance Squadron (disbanded 23 Feb. '45)
    (served in Ceylon)
No. 414 Fighter Reconnaissance Squadron 2 TAF
No. 413 Torpedo Bomber Squadron
No. 416 Fighter Squadron 2 TAF
No. 417 Fighter Squadron (served in Middle East, Italy)
No. 418 Intruder Squadron 2 TAF
No. 419 Bomber Squadron 6 Group
No. 420 Bomber Squadron 331 Wing (served in North Africa, Italy)
No. 421 Fighter Squadron 127 Wing 2 TAF 6 Group
No. 422 Coastal Squadron
No. 423 General Reconnaissance Squadron 6 Group
No. 424 Bomber Squadron (flew North Africa, Italy) 331 Wing
No. 425 Bomber Squadron (the French-Canadian "Alouette" squadron)
No. 426 Bomber Squadron 331 Wing 6 Group

No. 427 Bomber Squadron 6 Group
No. 428 Bomber Squadron 6 Group
No. 429 Bomber Squadron 6 Group
No. 430 Fighter-Reconnaissance Squadron 2 TAF
No. 431 Bomber Squadron 6 Group
No. 432 Bomber Squadron 6 Group
No. 433 Bomber Squadron 6 Group
No. 434 Bomber Squadron 6 Group
No. 435 Transport Squadron (served in Burma)
No. 436 Transport Squadron (served in Burma)
No. 437 Transport Squadron
No. 438 Fighter Bomber Squadron 2 TAF
No. 439 Fighter-Bomber Squadron 2 TAF
No. 440 Fighter-Bomber Squadron 2 TAF
No. 441 Fighter Squadron 2 TAF
No. 442 Fighter Squadron 2 TAF
No. 443 Fighter Squadron 2 TAF
No. 664 Air Observation Post Squadron, 1st Cdn Army
No. 665 Air Observation Post Squadron, 1st Cdn Army
No. 666 Air Observation Post Squadron, 1st Cdn Army

(6 Group = 6(RCAF) Group, Bomber Command; 2 TAF = 2 Allied Tactical Air Force)

ACKNOWLEDGEMENT OF PICTURE SOURCES

The government of Canada holds the copyright for most of the paintings reproduced in this book, and has given permission for their reproduction. Every reasonable effort has been made to trace the ownership of other copyright materials. Information enabling the Publisher to rectify any reference or credit in future printings will be welcomed.

Sources of colour illustrations are acknowledged following the legends on the colour plates in question. Unless otherwise indicated, all are from the Canadian War Museum (CWM), Canadian Museum of Civilization, National Museums of Canada. Photography at the museum was done by William Kent. Sources of black-and-white illustrations are as below. For reasons of space the following abbreviations have been used:

CWM: Canadian War Museum;
CT: City of Toronto Archives;
CT/GM: City of Toronto Archives, *Globe and Mail* collection;

NAC: National Archives of Canada;
NAM: National Aviation Museum;
NFB: National Film Board;
PABC: Public Archives of British Columbia.

Page i: NAC(PA-115568); ii: NAC-(PA-153495); iii: NAM(6702); vi: NAC(C-87139); viii: NAC(PA-129054); 19: NAC: 20 (left): PABC(A-1657), (right): NAC(C-67469); 21: NAC(C-16787); 22 (top): NAC(C-24958), (bottom): NAC(NL-3890); 23 (top): NAC(C-85091), (bottom): NAC(PA-129610); 24: courtesy of Syd Charendoff and Boston Mills Press; 25 (top): CT/GM(61001), (bottom): CT/GM(61431); 26: CT/GM(65880); 27 (top): NAC(*Canada's Weekly*, 06/28/40), (bottom): NFB(XA-120); 56 (top): CT/GM(68142), (bottom): NAC(C-68669); 57 (top): CT/GM(69562), (bottom): CT/GM(67237); 58 (top): NAC(PA-170287), (bottom): NAC(PA-108300); 59 (top): NAC(C-99610), (bottom): CT/GM(66374); 60: NAC(C-49742); 61 (top): CT(SC-488), (bottom): NAC(C-46350); 62: Provincial Archives of Manitoba: Canadian Army Photo Coll. (N-10857); 63: NAC(PA-119399); 64: NAC(C-14160); 65: NAC(C-87124); 87: NAC(PA-112993); 88: NAC(PA-145502); 89: NAC(PA-116836); 90: NAC(PA-170292); 91 (top): NAC(PA-136082), (bottom): NAC(PA-139291); 92 (top): NAC(PA-142415), (bottom): NAC(O-893-406); 93 (top): NAC(PA-105924), (bottom): Public Archives of Nova Scotia: H.B. Jefferson Coll.; 94: NAC(PA-111512); 95: NAC(PA-113917); 96 (top): NAC(PA-170770), (bottom): NAC(PA-151742); 97 (top): NAC(PA-105943), (bottom): NAC(PA-170288); 119 (top): NAC(PL-2039), (bottom): CT/GM(64826); 120 (top): NAC(PA-140658), (bottom): NAC(C-60392); 121: NAM(6021); 122 (top): NAM(16250), (bottom): NAM(16654); 123: NAC(PL-3051); 124: NAC(PL-10008); 125 (top): NAC(PL-19507), (bottom): NAC(PL-28520); 126: CWM(11356); 127: CFPU-PL30780; 128 (top): NAC(PL-61240), (bottom): NAC(PL-144284); 129: NAC(PL-30121); 151: NAC(PA-130247); 152: NAC(PA-163670); 153: NAC(PA-170290); 154: NAC(PA-144103); 155 (top): NAC(PA-114482), (bottom): NAC(PA-116844); 156 (top): NAC(PA-170289), (bottom): NAC(PA-132782); 157: NAC(PA-107935); 158: NAC(PA-170291); 159: NAC(PA-116852); 160: NAC(PA-152835); 161: NAC(PA-115188); 162: NAC(PA-152839); 163 (top): NAC(PA-115031), (bottom): Reproduced under the authority of the Dept. of National Defence; 175: NAC(C-1700); 176: NAC(C-9128); 177: NAC(C-87431); 178: NAC(PA-112885); 179 (top): NAC(PA-113194), (bottom): NAC(PA-121715); 180: NAC(C-33441); 181: CT(SC-488); 182 (top): CT/GM(98887), (bottom): NAC(PA-112901); 183 (top): CT(SC-488), (bottom): CT(SC-488); 184: Saskatchewan Archives Board; 185 (top): CT(SC-488), (bottom): CT(SC-488); 211: NAC(PA-137130); 212: NAC(PA-129053); 213: NAC(PA-135963); 214: NAC(PA-136280); 215: York Univ. Archives, *Telegram* collection; 216: NAC(PA-129128); 217: NAC(PMR-82-060); 218: NAC(PA-116586); 219: NAC(PA-129135); 220 (top): NAC(PA-137307), (bottom): NAC(PA-140408); 221: NAC(PA-135958); 222: NAC(PA-131233); 223: NAC(PA-107940); 248: NAC(PA-138429); 249: NAC; 250: NAC; 251: NAC; 252: NAC(PA-113908); 253: NAC; 254: CWM(12123); 255 (top): NAC(PA-170460), (bottom): NAC; 256: CT/E.R. White collection (4636); 257: Dalhousie Univ. Archives; 258: NAC(PA-112367); 259: NAC(PA-145983); 260: CT/GM(100525); 261: NAC(C-23272); 262: NAC(C-49434); 263: CT/GM(102055); 264: NAC(C-49447); 265: Veterans Affairs Canada.

INDEX